Viz Graphic Novel

Vol. 2
Action Edition

Story and Art by
Nobuyuki Anzai

Flame of Recca

Vol. 2

Action Edition

Story and Art by
Nobuyuki Anzai

English Adaptation/Lance Caselman
Translation/Joe Yamazaki
Touch-up & Lettering/Kelle Han
Graphics & Cover Design/Sean Lee
Editor/Eric Searleman

Managing Editor/Annette Roman
Editor-in-Chief/William Flanagan
Director of Licensing and Acquisitions/Rika Inouye
VP of Sales & Marketing/Liza Coppola
Sr. VP of Editorial/Hyoe Narita
Publisher/Seiji Horibuchi

Printed in Canada

Published by VIZ, LLC
P.O. Box 77064
San Francisco, CA 94107

Action Edition
10 9 8 7 6 5 4 3 2 1
First printing, September 2003

For advertising rates or media kit, e-mail advertising@viz.com

store.viz.com

www.viz.com

ANIMERICA
ANIME & MANGA MONTHLY アニメリカ
www.animerica-mag.com

Viz Graphic Novel

FLAME OF RECCA™

Vol. 2

Story & Art by Nobuyuki Anzai

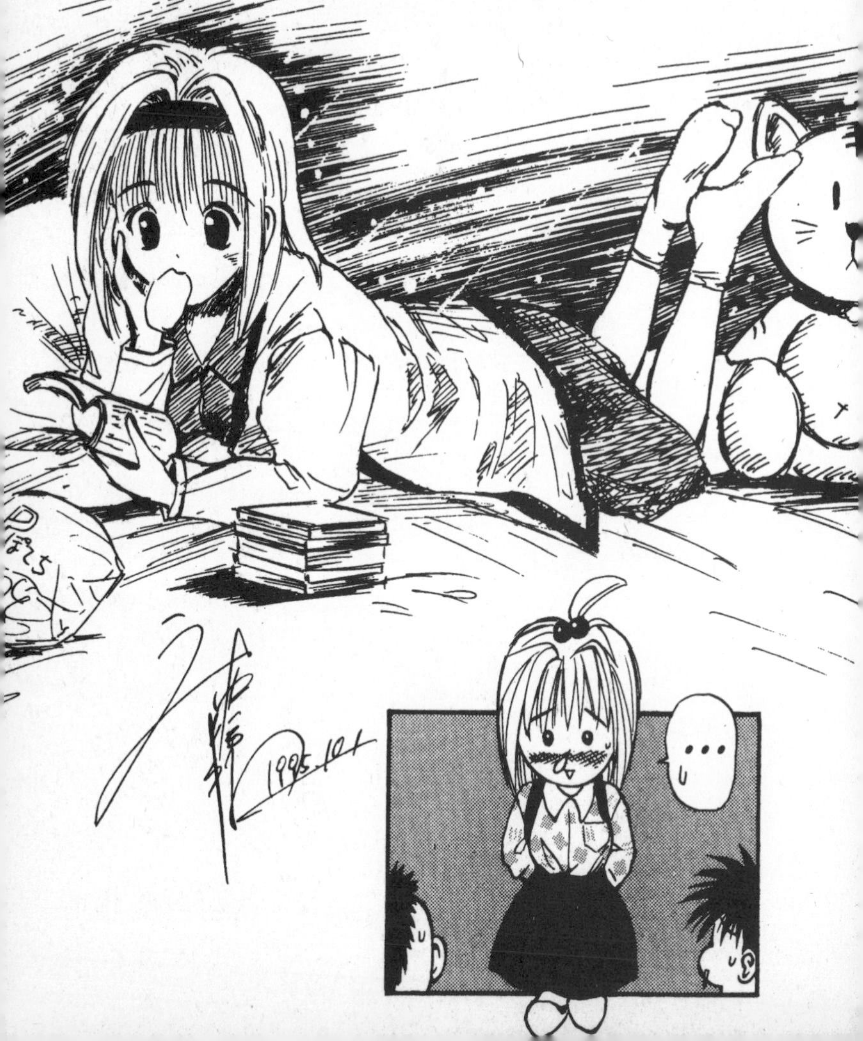

Contents

Part Ten:
YANAGI COMES OVER

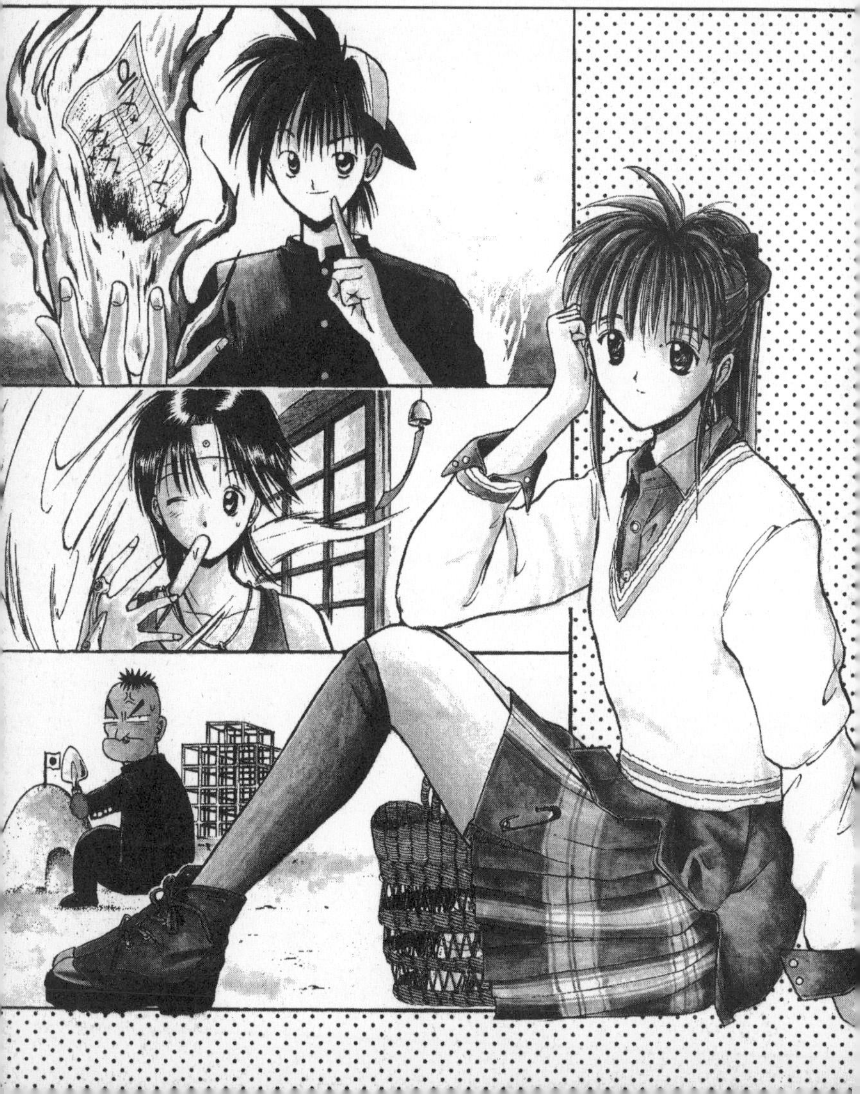

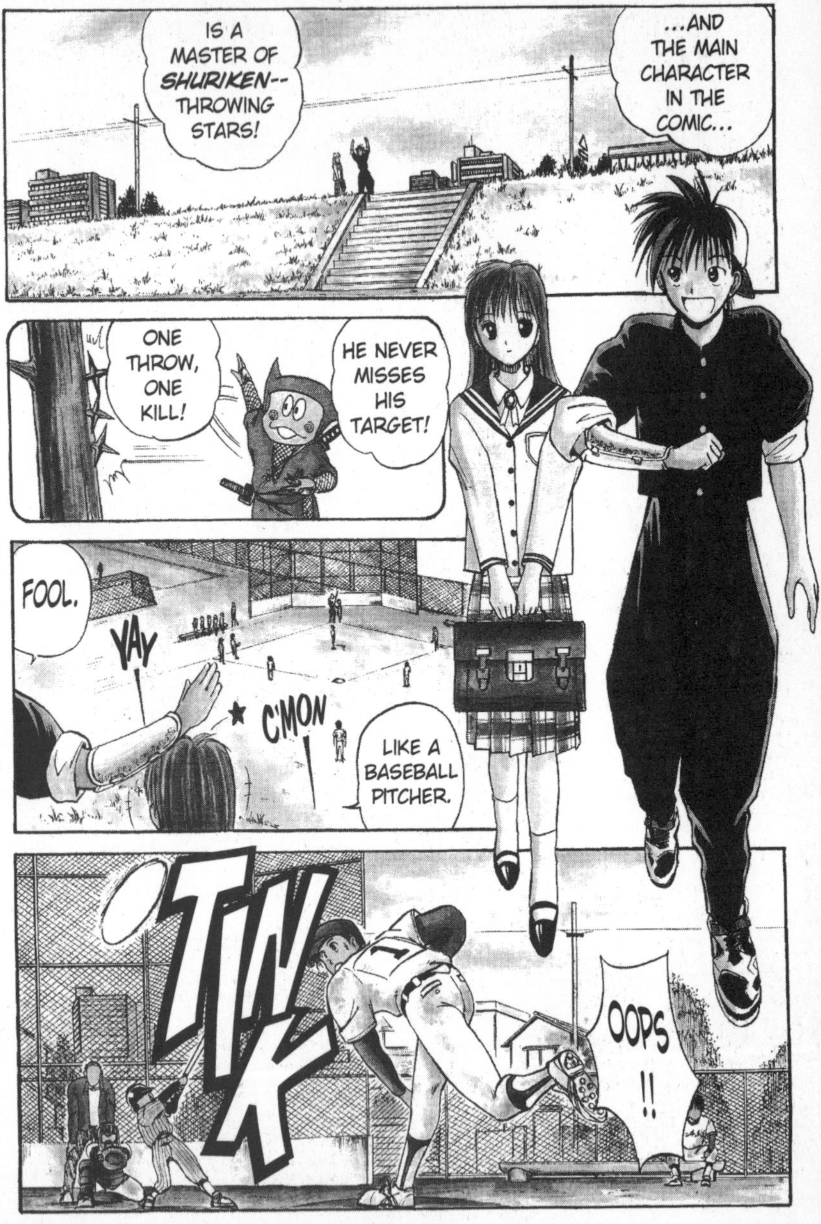
...AND THE MAIN CHARACTER IN THE COMIC...
IS A MASTER OF SHURIKEN--THROWING STARS!
HE NEVER MISSES HIS TARGET!
ONE THROW, ONE KILL!
LIKE A BASEBALL PITCHER.
C'MON
YAY
FOOL.
OOPS !!
TINK

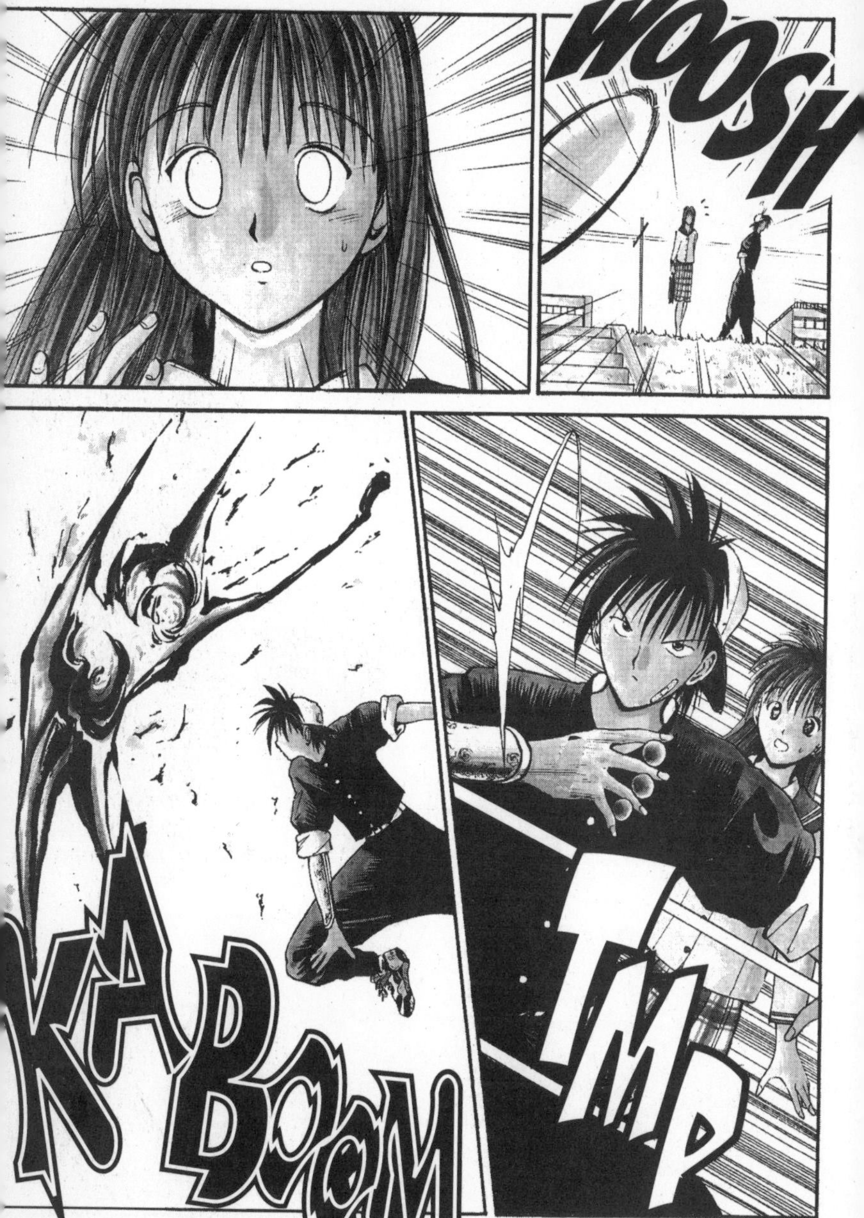
WOOSH
TMP
KA BOOM

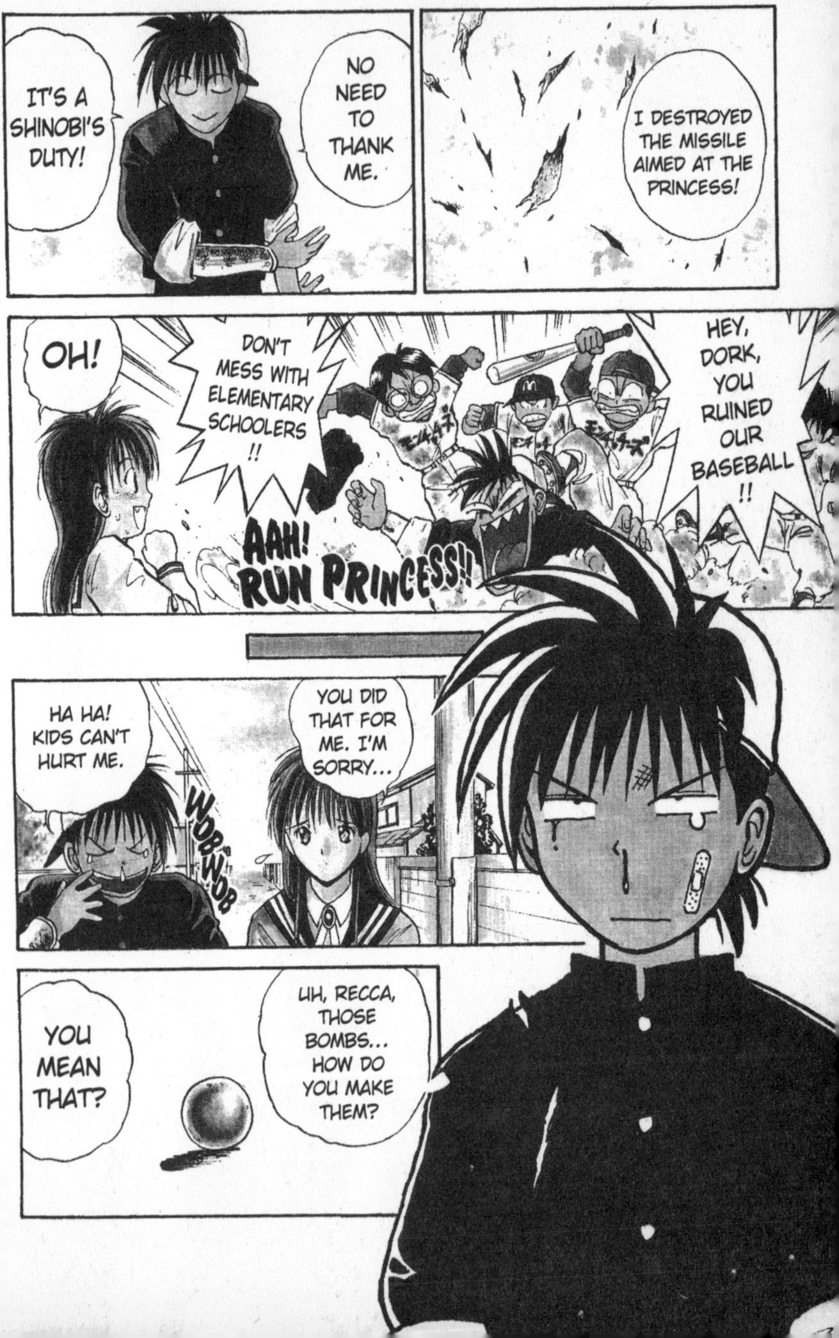

I DESTROYED THE MISSILE AIMED AT THE PRINCESS!
NO NEED TO THANK ME.
IT'S A SHINOBI'S DUTY!
HEY, DORK, YOU RUINED OUR BASEBALL!!
DON'T MESS WITH ELEMENTARY SCHOOLERS!!
AAH! RUN PRINCESS!!
OH!
YOU DID THAT FOR ME. I'M SORRY...
HA HA! KIDS CAN'T HURT ME.
WOB WOB
UH, RECCA, THOSE BOMBS... HOW DO YOU MAKE THEM?
YOU MEAN THAT?

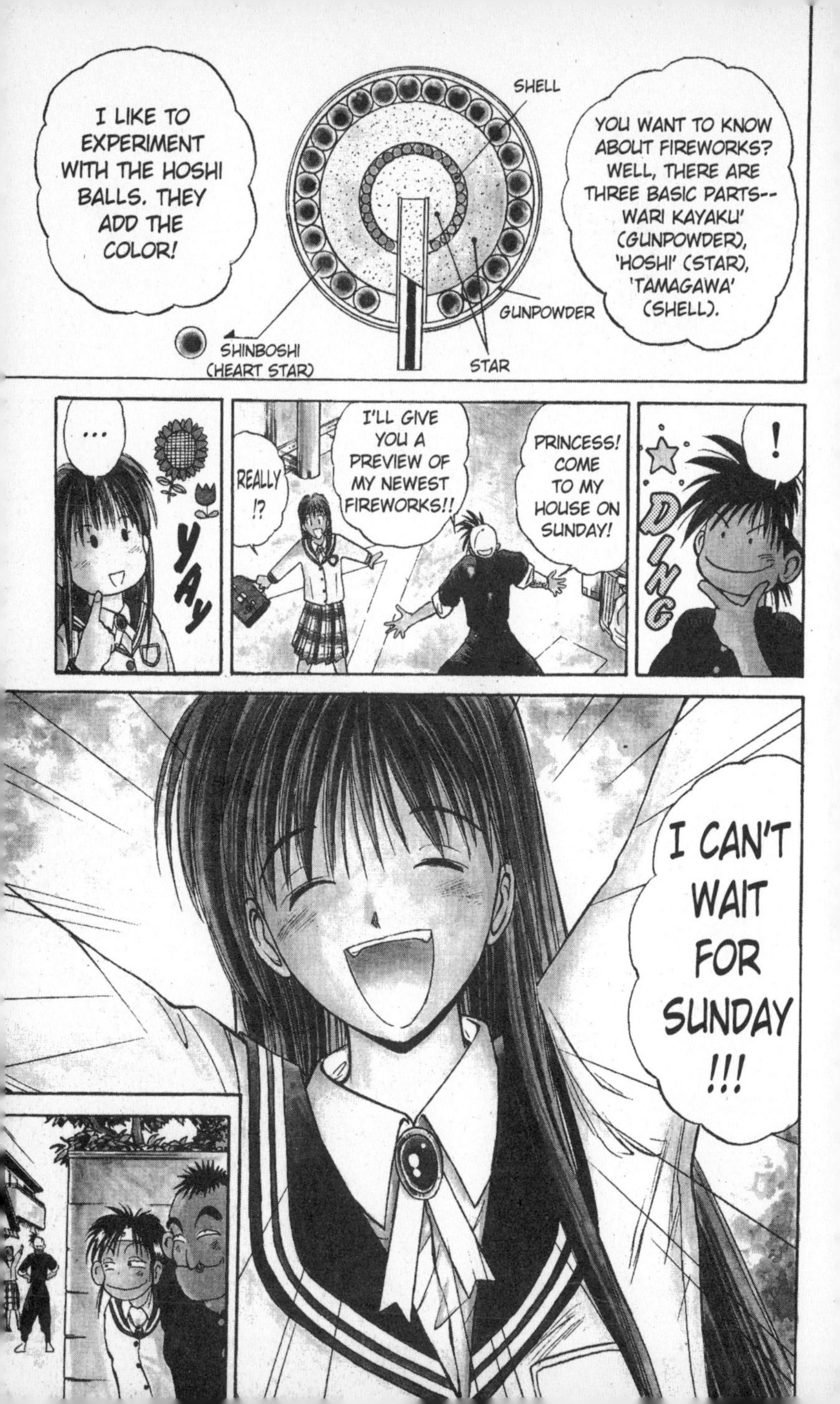
YOU WANT TO KNOW ABOUT FIREWORKS? WELL, THERE ARE THREE BASIC PARTS-- WARI KAYAKU' (GUNPOWDER), 'HOSHI' (STAR), 'TAMAGAWA' (SHELL).
SHELL
GUNPOWDER
STAR
SHINBOSHI (HEART STAR)
I LIKE TO EXPERIMENT WITH THE HOSHI BALLS. THEY ADD THE COLOR!
!
DING
PRINCESS! COME TO MY HOUSE ON SUNDAY!
I'LL GIVE YOU A PREVIEW OF MY NEWEST FIREWORKS!!
REALLY !?
...
YAY
I CAN'T WAIT FOR SUNDAY !!!

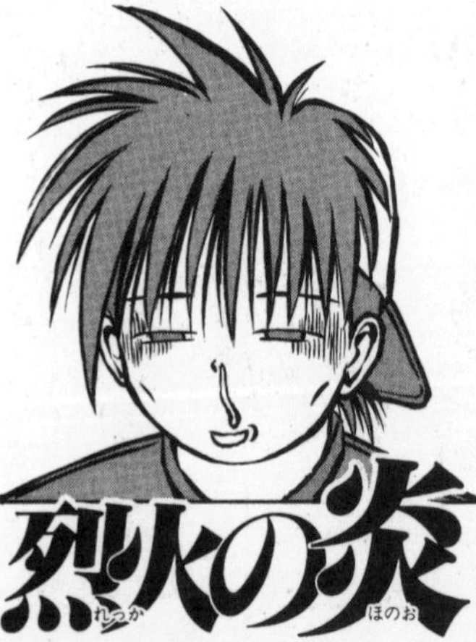

烈火の炎

れっか　ほのお

~FLAME OF RECCA~

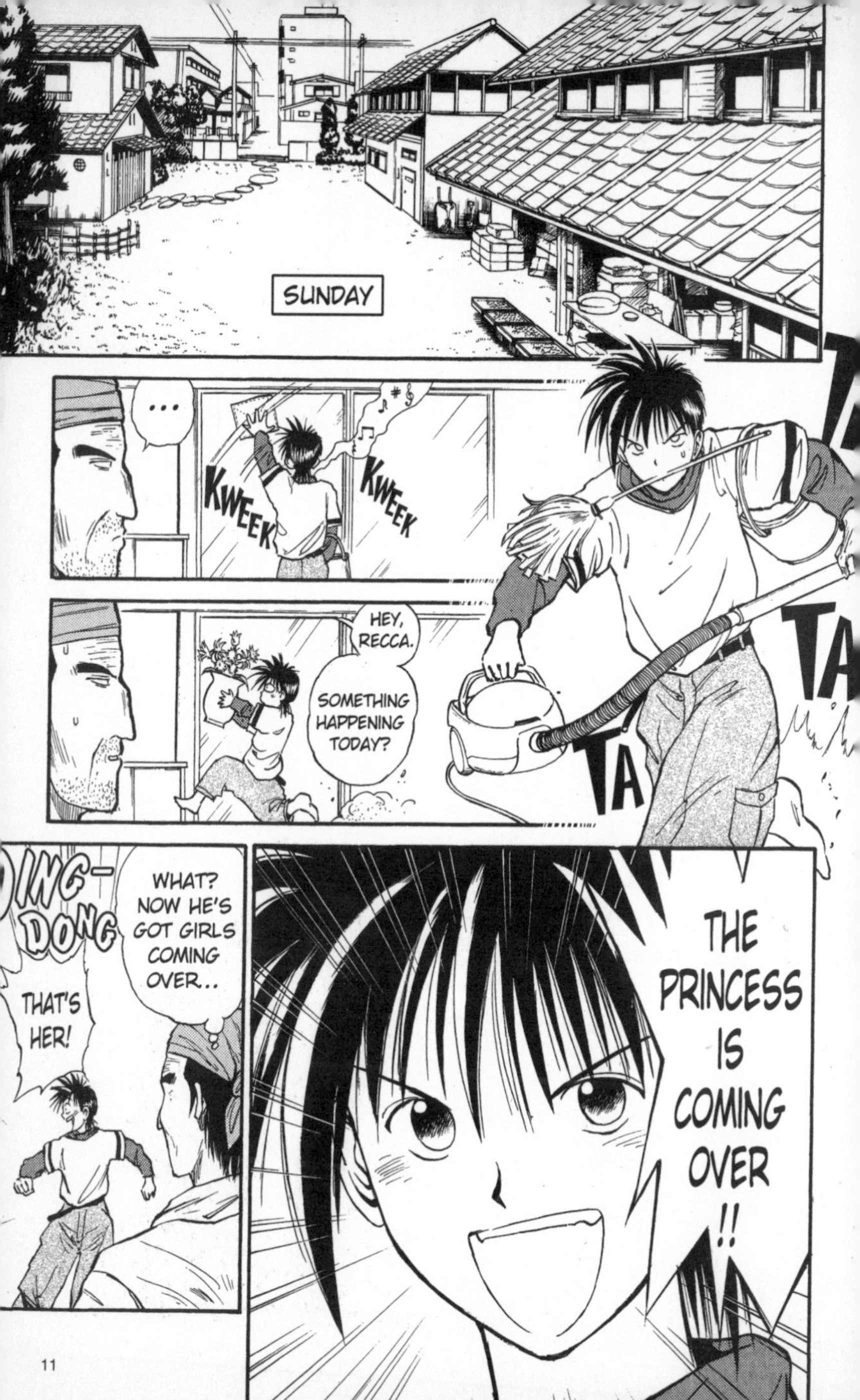
SUNDAY
...
KWEEK
KWEEK
HEY, RECCA.
SOMETHING HAPPENING TODAY?
TA
TA
TA
THE PRINCESS IS COMING OVER!!
WHAT? NOW HE'S GOT GIRLS COMING OVER...
DING-DONG
THAT'S HER!

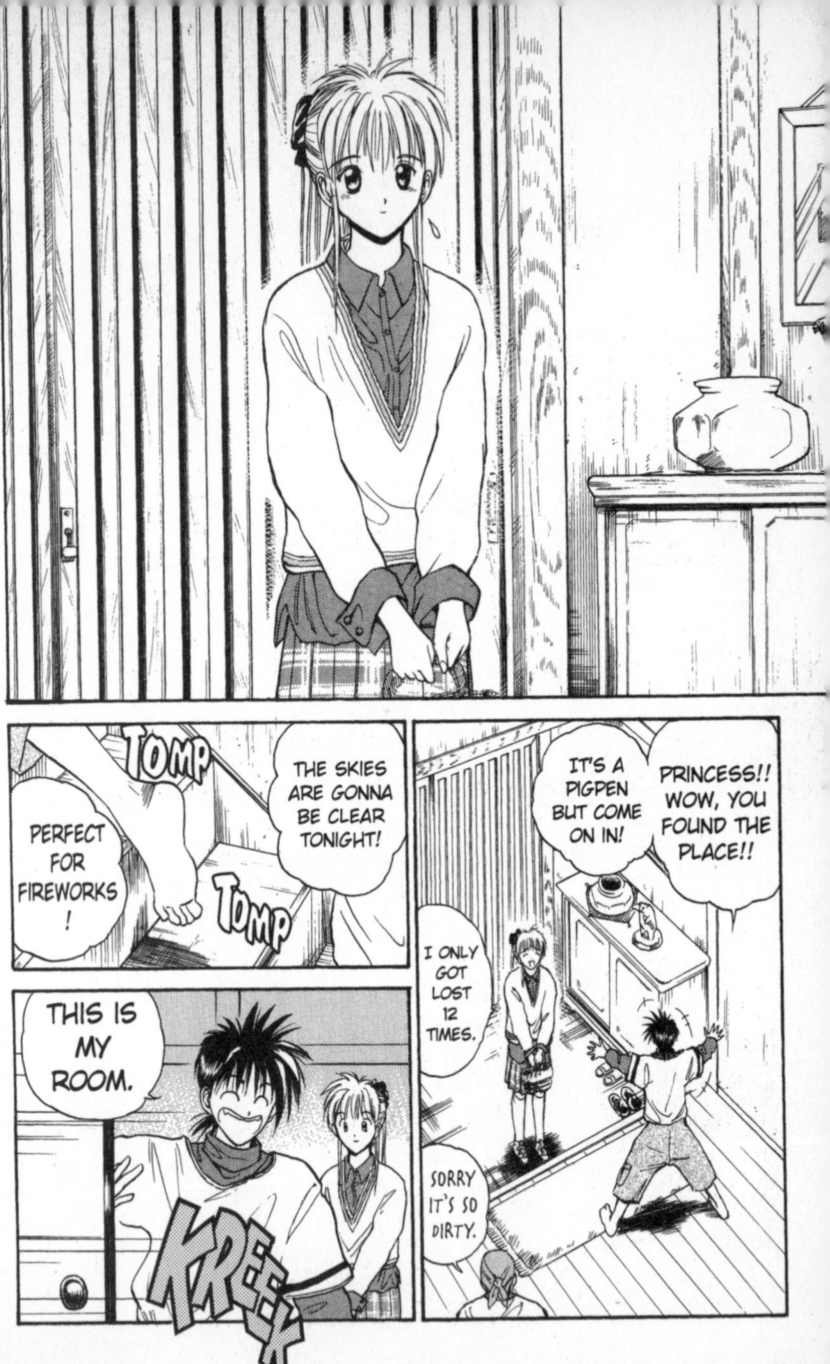
PRINCESS!! WOW, YOU FOUND THE PLACE!!
IT'S A PIGPEN BUT COME ON IN!
I ONLY GOT LOST 12 TIMES.
SORRY IT'S SO DIRTY.
THE SKIES ARE GONNA BE CLEAR TONIGHT!
TOMP
PERFECT FOR FIREWORKS!
TOMP
THIS IS MY ROOM.
KREEK

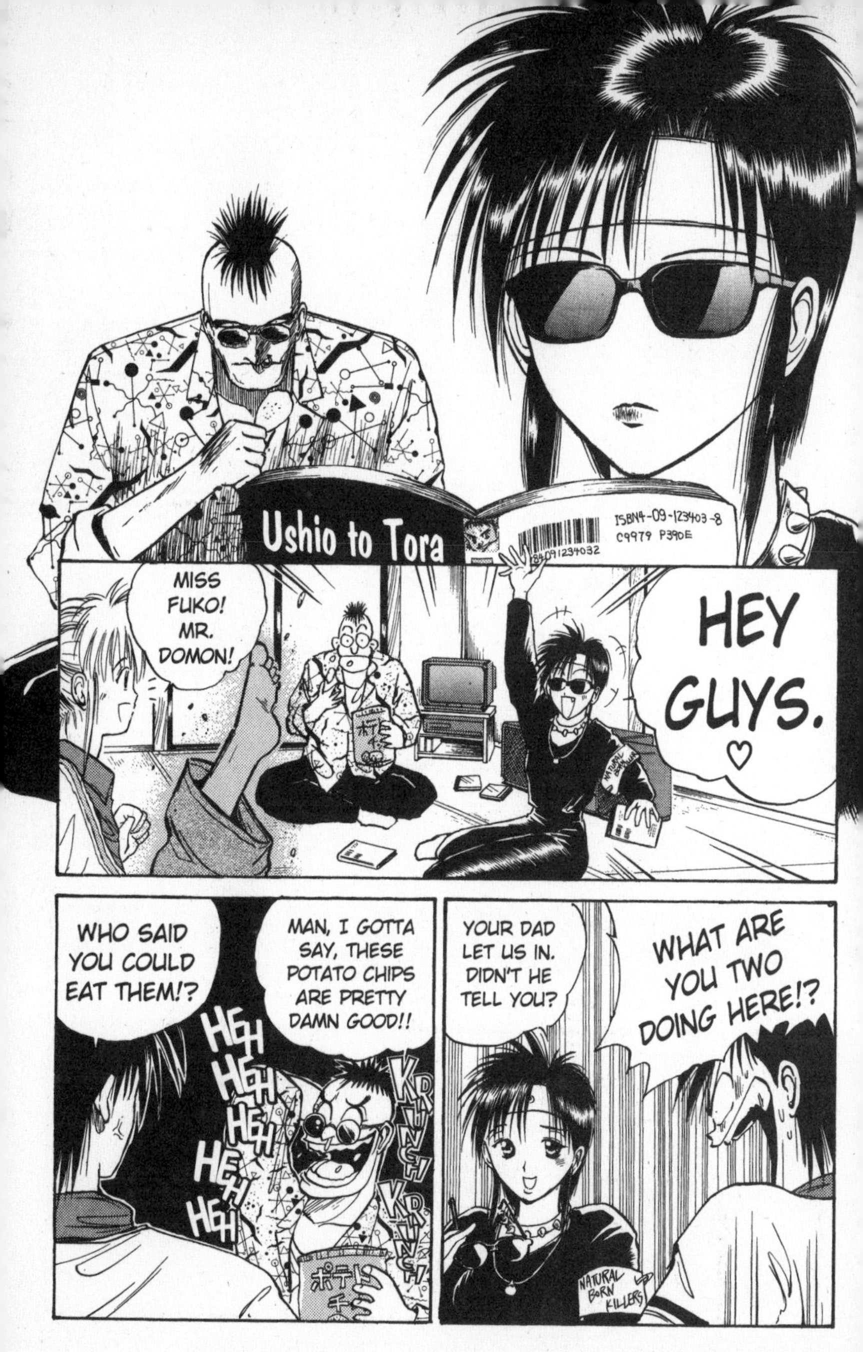
ISBN4-09-123403-8
C9979 P390E
Ushio to Tora
HEY GUYS. ♡
MISS FUKO! MR. DOMON!
WHAT ARE YOU TWO DOING HERE!?
YOUR DAD LET US IN. DIDN'T HE TELL YOU?
NATURAL BORN KILLERS
MAN, I GOTTA SAY, THESE POTATO CHIPS ARE PRETTY DAMN GOOD!!
KRUNCH KRUNCH
WHO SAID YOU COULD EAT THEM!?
HEH HEH HEH HEH HEH

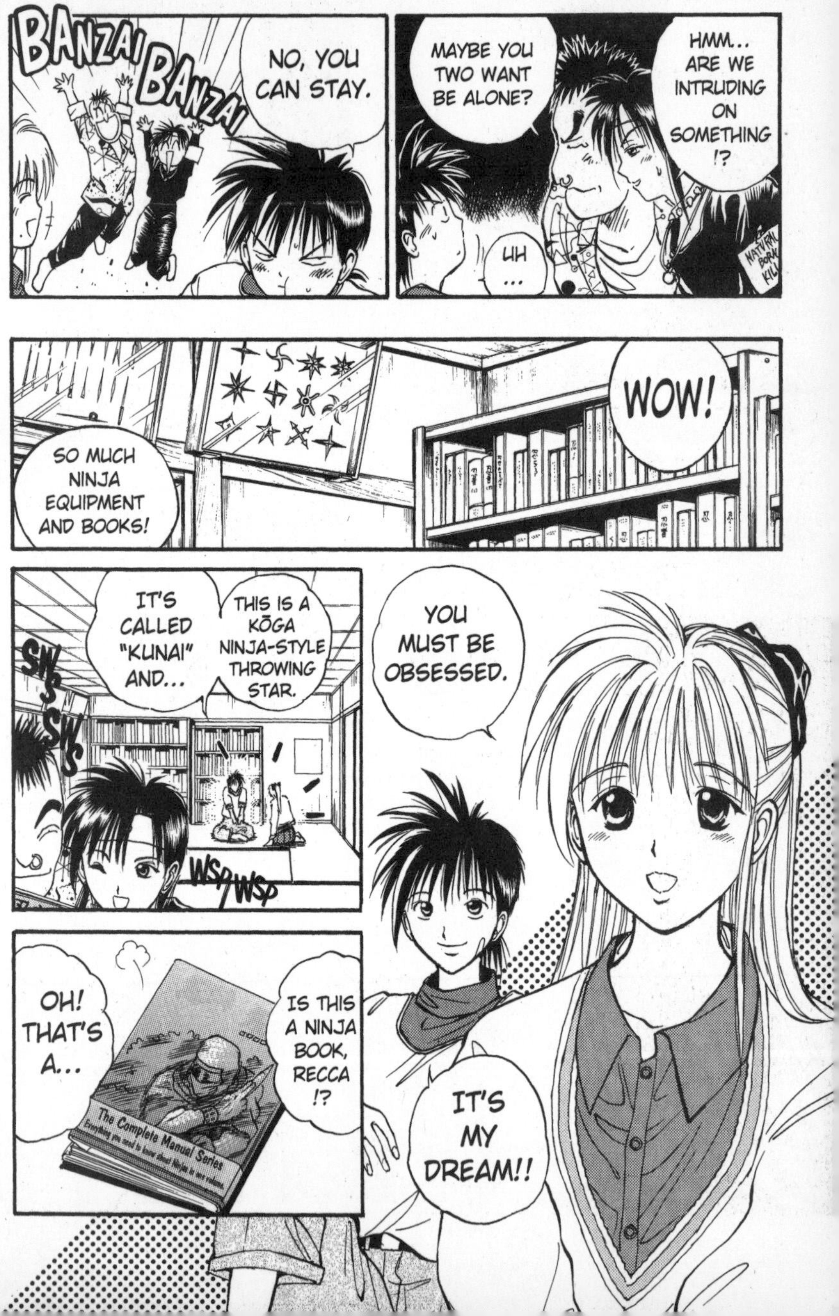
HMM... ARE WE INTRUDING ON SOMETHING !?
MAYBE YOU TWO WANT BE ALONE?
UH ...
NO, YOU CAN STAY.
BANZAI BANZAI
WOW!
SO MUCH NINJA EQUIPMENT AND BOOKS!
THIS IS A KŌGA NINJA-STYLE THROWING STAR.
IT'S CALLED "KUNAI" AND...
SWS SWS
WSP WSP
YOU MUST BE OBSESSED.
IS THIS A NINJA BOOK, RECCA !?
OH! THAT'S A...
The Complete Manual Series
IT'S MY DREAM!!

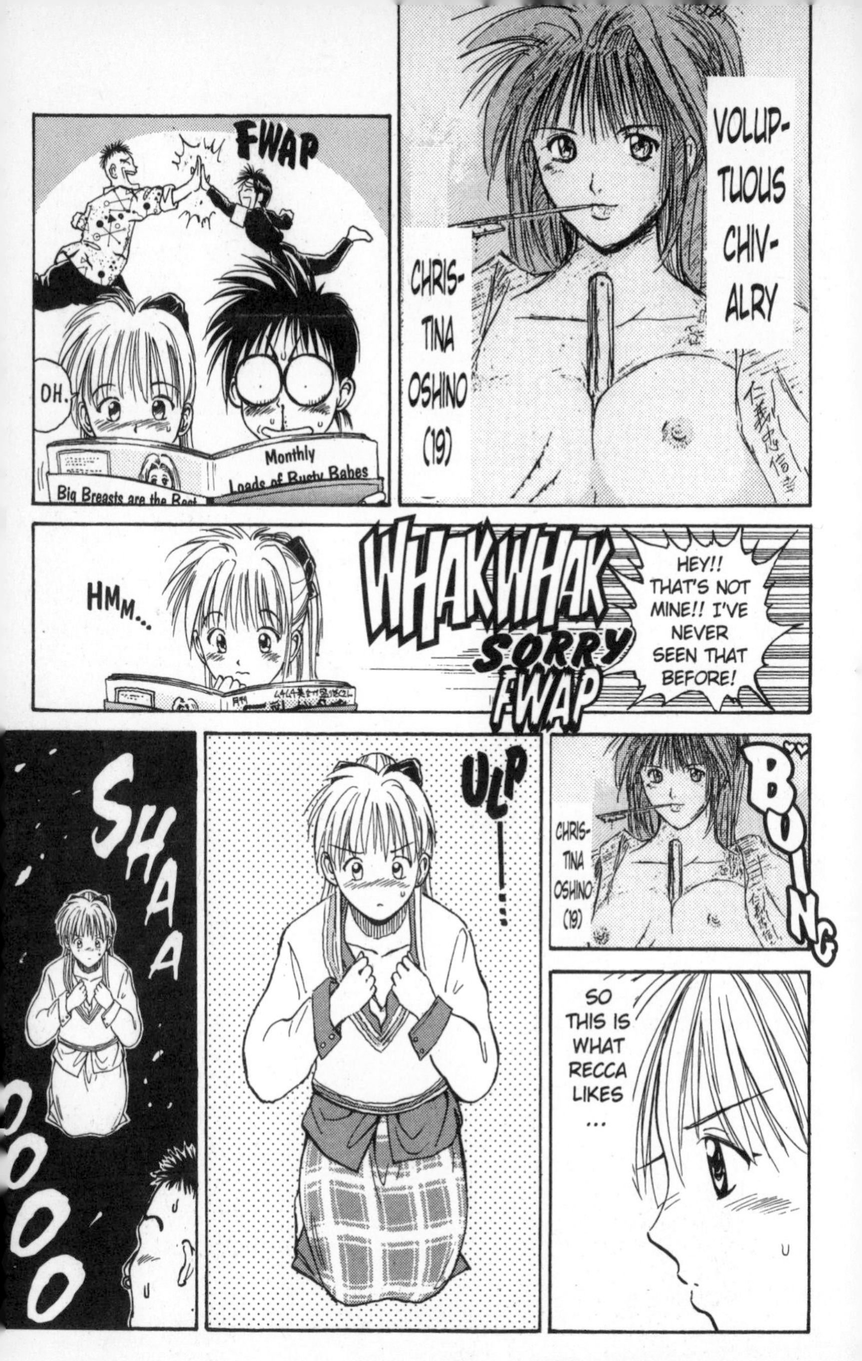

VOLUP-TUOUS CHIV-ALRY
CHRIS-TINA OSHINO (19)
FWAP
OH.
Monthly Loads of Busty Babes
Big Breasts are the Best
HEY!! THAT'S NOT MINE!! I'VE NEVER SEEN THAT BEFORE!
WHAK WHAK
SORRY
FWAP
HMM...
BOING
CHRIS-TINA OSHINO (19)
SO THIS IS WHAT RECCA LIKES ...
ULP !!
SHAAOOOO

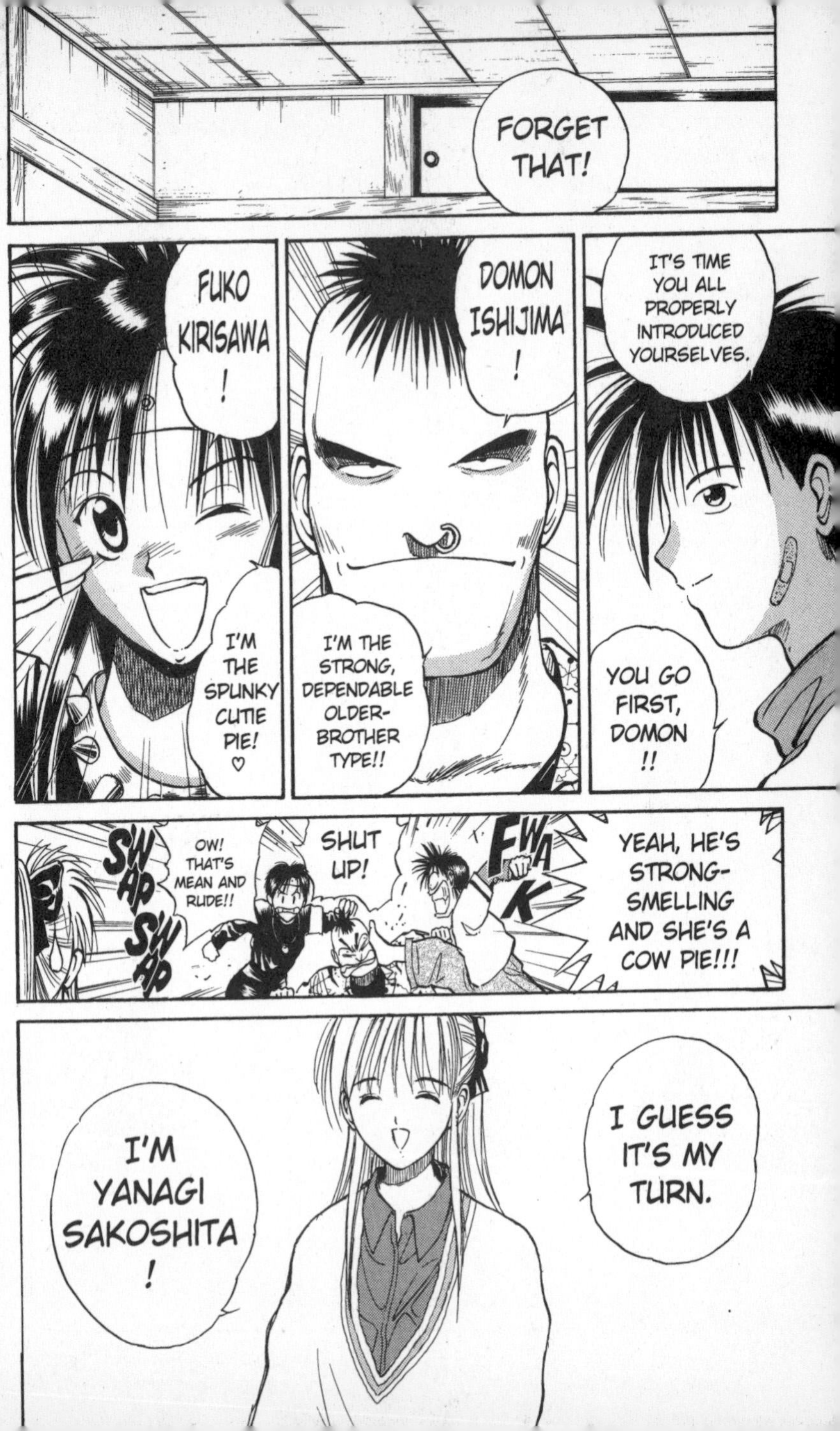
FORGET THAT!
IT'S TIME YOU ALL PROPERLY INTRODUCED YOURSELVES.
YOU GO FIRST, DOMON!!
DOMON ISHIJIMA!
I'M THE STRONG, DEPENDABLE OLDER-BROTHER TYPE!!
FUKO KIRISAWA!
I'M THE SPUNKY CUTIE PIE! ♡
YEAH, HE'S STRONG-SMELLING AND SHE'S A COW PIE!!!
FWAK
SHUT UP!
OW! THAT'S MEAN AND RUDE!!
SWAP SWAP
I GUESS IT'S MY TURN.
I'M YANAGI SAKOSHITA!

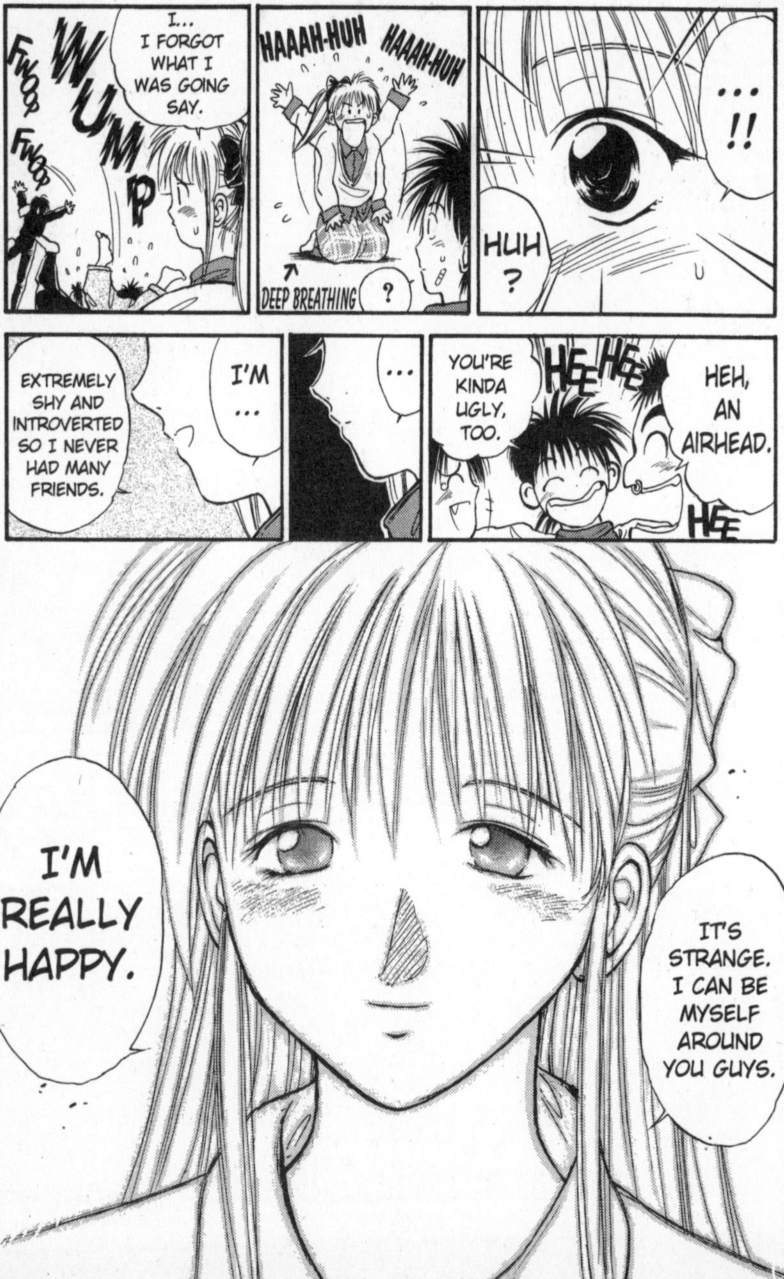

...!!
HUH?
HAAAH-HUH
HAAAH-HUH
?
DEEP BREATHING
I... I FORGOT WHAT I WAS GOING SAY.
WUMP
FWOOP
FWOOP
HEH, AN AIRHEAD.
HEE
HEE
HEE
YOU'RE KINDA UGLY, TOO.
...
I'M ...
EXTREMELY SHY AND INTROVERTED SO I NEVER HAD MANY FRIENDS.
IT'S STRANGE. I CAN BE MYSELF AROUND YOU GUYS.
I'M REALLY HAPPY.

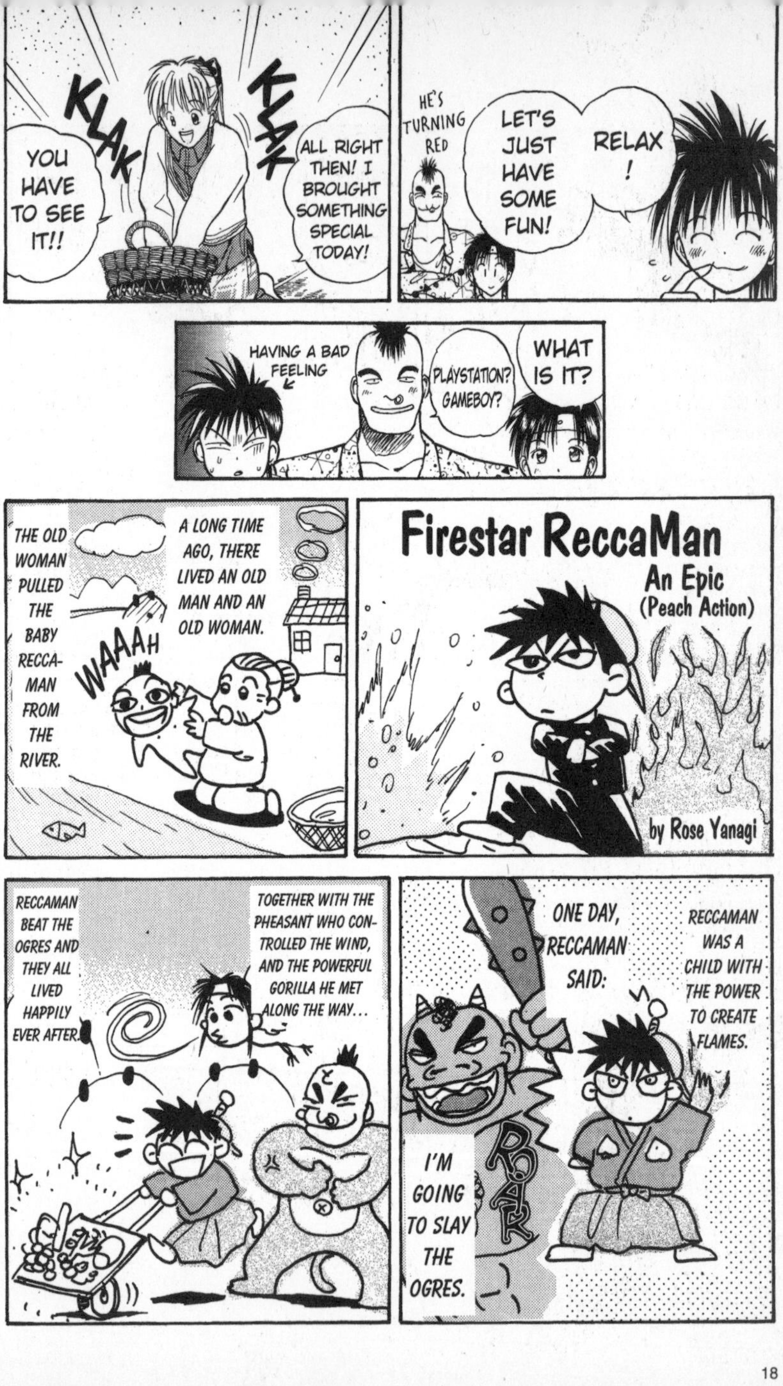
RELAX!
LET'S JUST HAVE SOME FUN!
HE'S TURNING RED
ALL RIGHT THEN! I BROUGHT SOMETHING SPECIAL TODAY!
KLAK
KLAK
YOU HAVE TO SEE IT!!
WHAT IS IT?
PLAYSTATION? GAMEBOY?
HAVING A BAD FEELING
Firestar ReccaMan
An Epic
(Peach Action)
by Rose Yanagi
A LONG TIME AGO, THERE LIVED AN OLD MAN AND AN OLD WOMAN.
THE OLD WOMAN PULLED THE BABY RECCA-MAN FROM THE RIVER.
WAAAAH
RECCAMAN WAS A CHILD WITH THE POWER TO CREATE FLAMES.
ONE DAY, RECCAMAN SAID:
I'M GOING TO SLAY THE OGRES.
ROAR
TOGETHER WITH THE PHEASANT WHO CON-TROLLED THE WIND, AND THE POWERFUL GORILLA HE MET ALONG THE WAY...
RECCAMAN BEAT THE OGRES AND THEY ALL LIVED HAPPILY EVER AFTER.

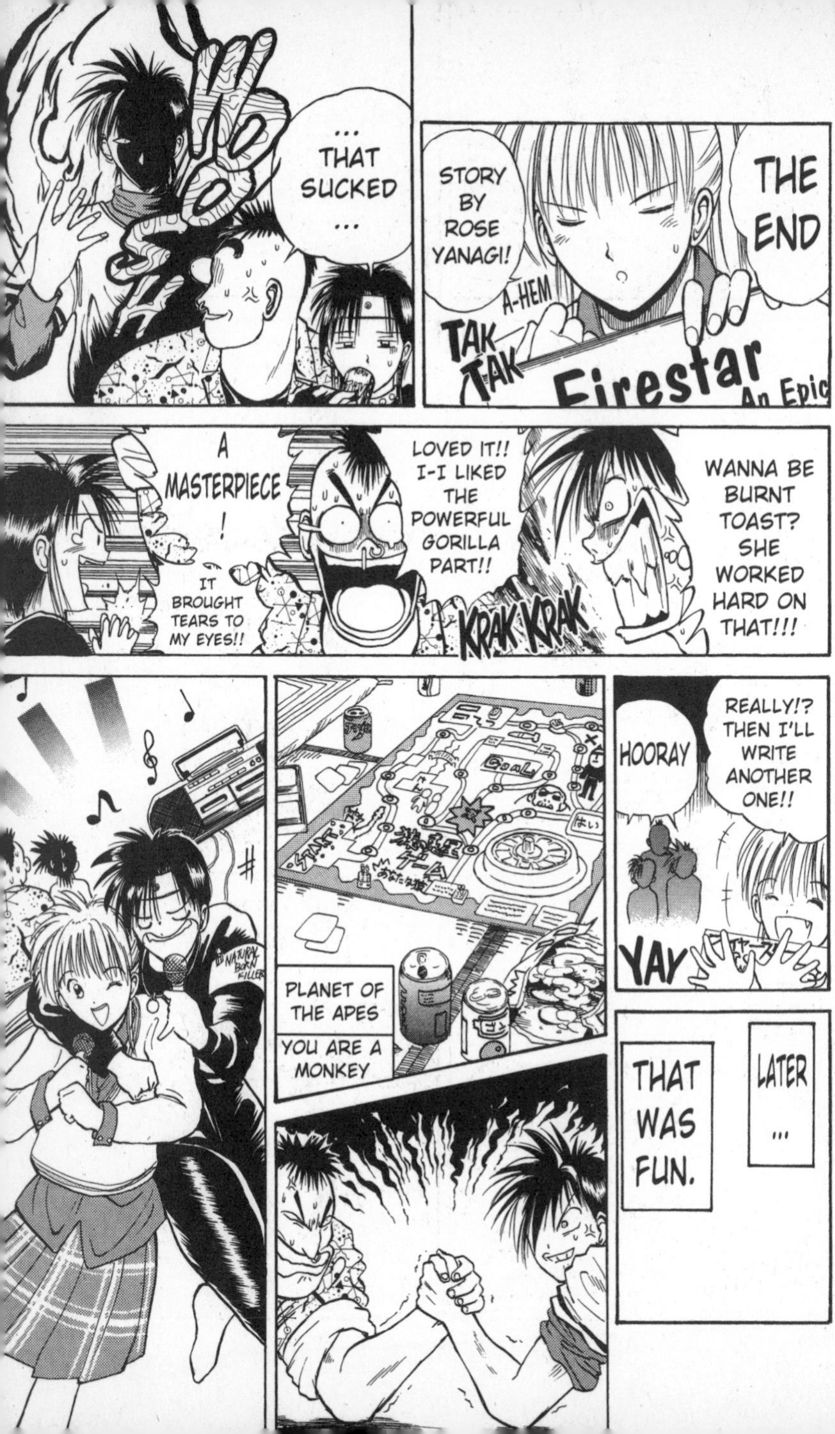
THE END
STORY BY ROSE YANAGI!
A-HEM
TAK TAK
Firestar
An Epic
... THAT SUCKED ...
WANNA BE BURNT TOAST? SHE WORKED HARD ON THAT!!!
KRAK KRAK
LOVED IT!! I-I LIKED THE POWERFUL GORILLA PART!!
A MASTERPIECE!
IT BROUGHT TEARS TO MY EYES!!
REALLY!? THEN I'LL WRITE ANOTHER ONE!!
HOORAY
YAY
LATER ...
THAT WAS FUN.
START
GOAL
PLANET OF THE APES
YOU ARE A MONKEY
NATURAL BORN KILLER

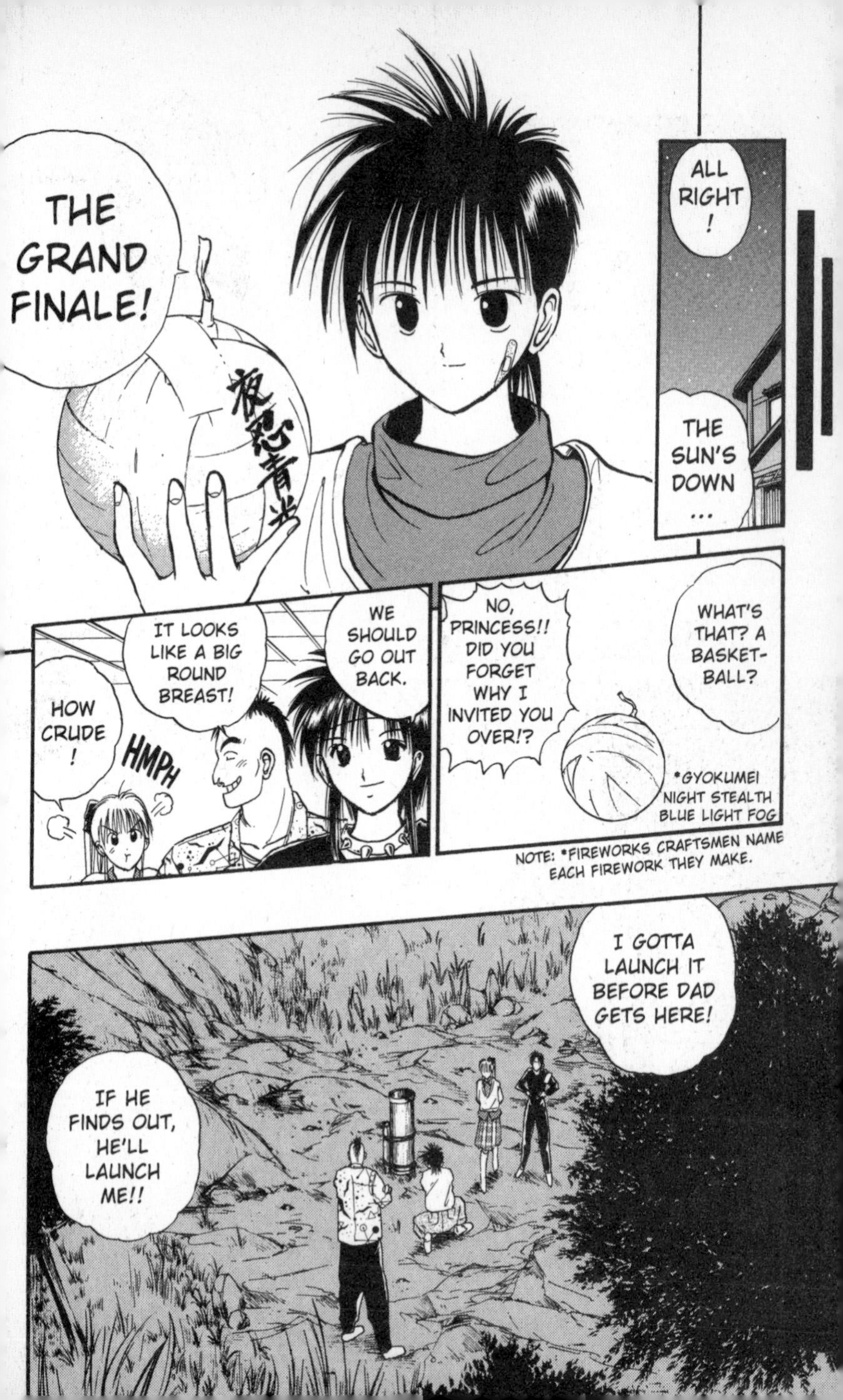
ALL RIGHT!
THE SUN'S DOWN ...
THE GRAND FINALE!
夜忍青光
WHAT'S THAT? A BASKET-BALL?
NO, PRINCESS!! DID YOU FORGET WHY I INVITED YOU OVER!?
*GYOKUMEI NIGHT STEALTH BLUE LIGHT FOG
WE SHOULD GO OUT BACK.
IT LOOKS LIKE A BIG ROUND BREAST!
HMPH
HOW CRUDE!
NOTE: *FIREWORKS CRAFTSMEN NAME EACH FIREWORK THEY MAKE.
I GOTTA LAUNCH IT BEFORE DAD GETS HERE!
IF HE FINDS OUT, HE'LL LAUNCH ME!!

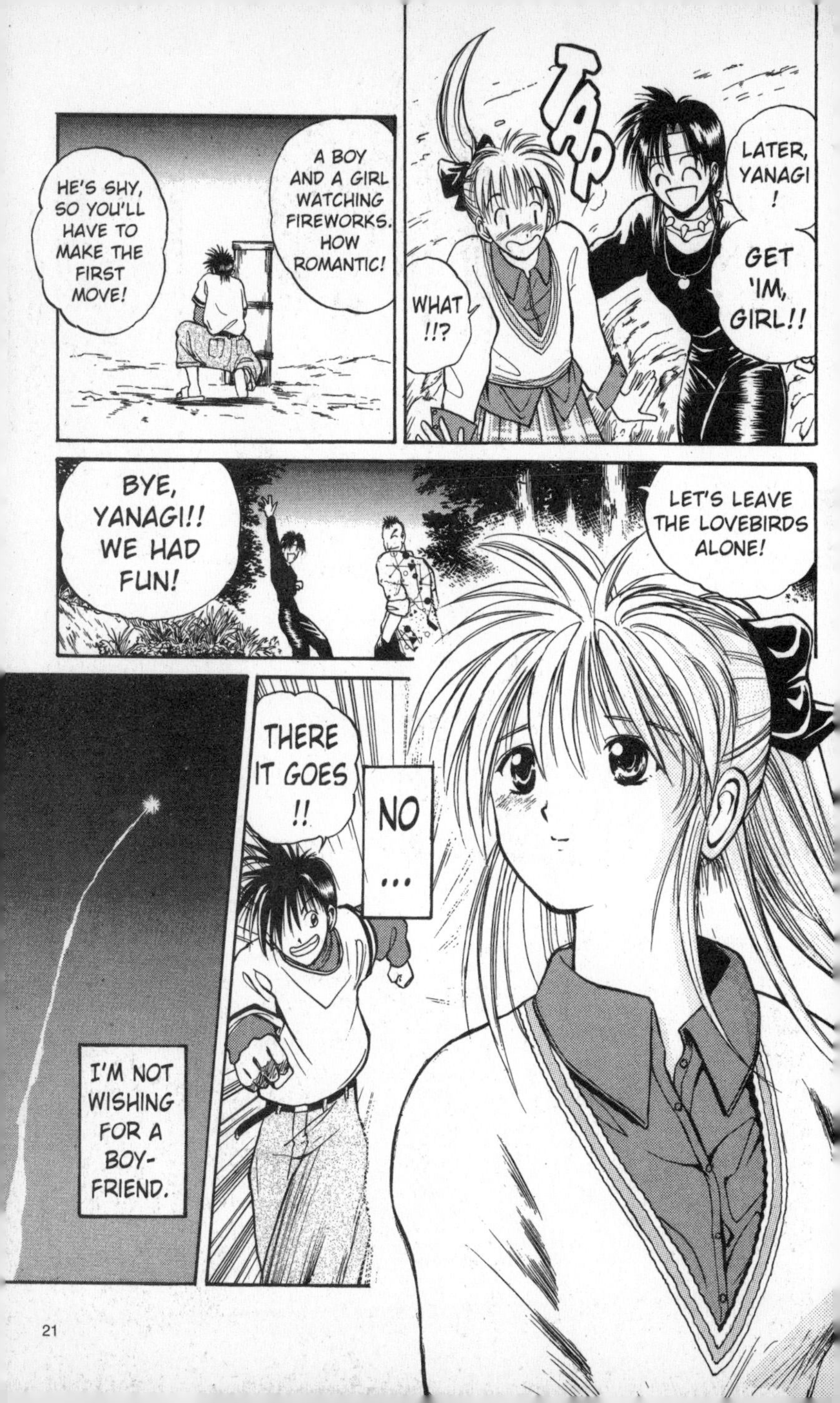
LATER, YANAGI!
GET 'IM, GIRL!!
TAP
WHAT!!?
A BOY AND A GIRL WATCHING FIREWORKS. HOW ROMANTIC!
HE'S SHY, SO YOU'LL HAVE TO MAKE THE FIRST MOVE!
LET'S LEAVE THE LOVEBIRDS ALONE!
BYE, YANAGI!! WE HAD FUN!
THERE IT GOES!!
NO...
I'M NOT WISHING FOR A BOY-FRIEND.

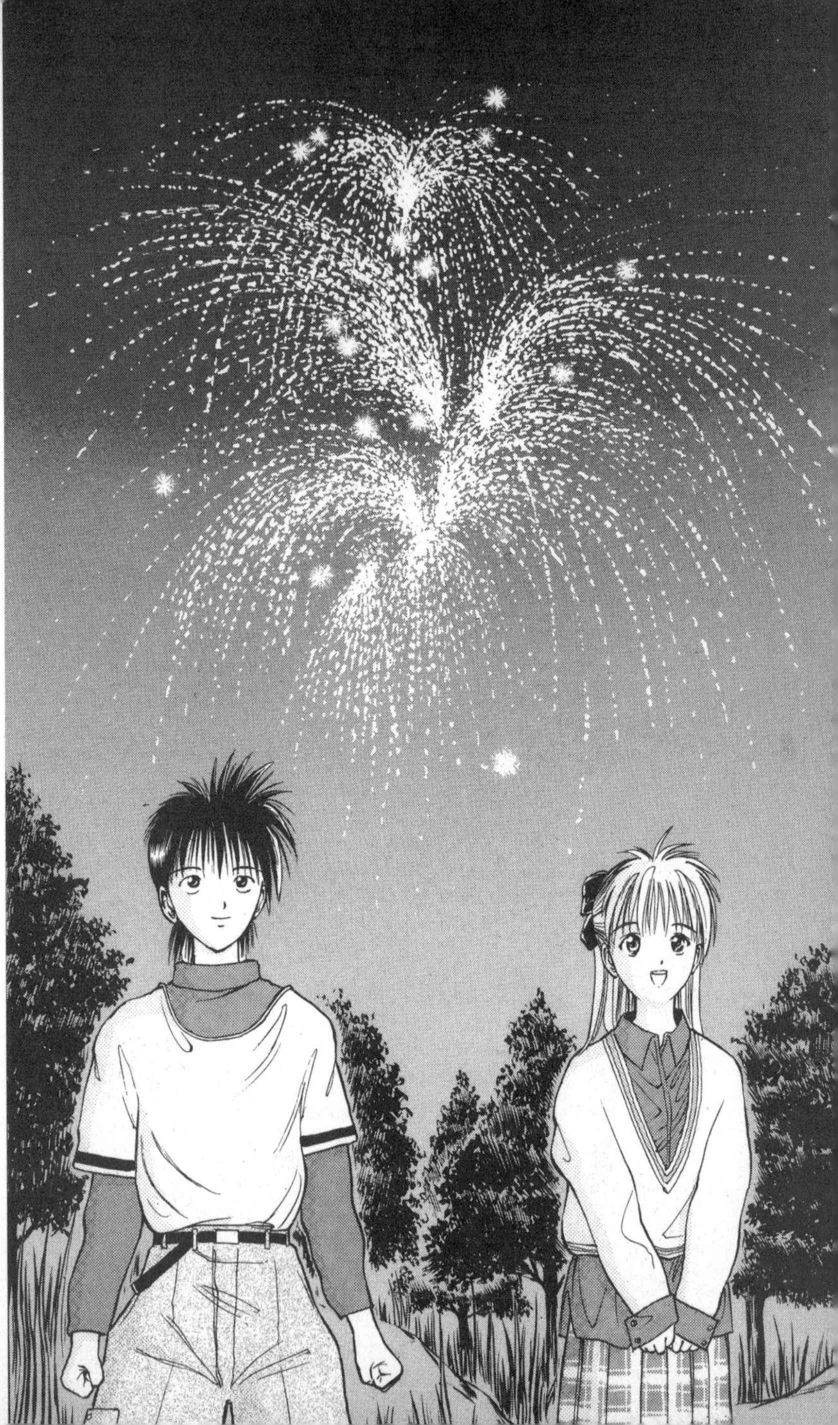

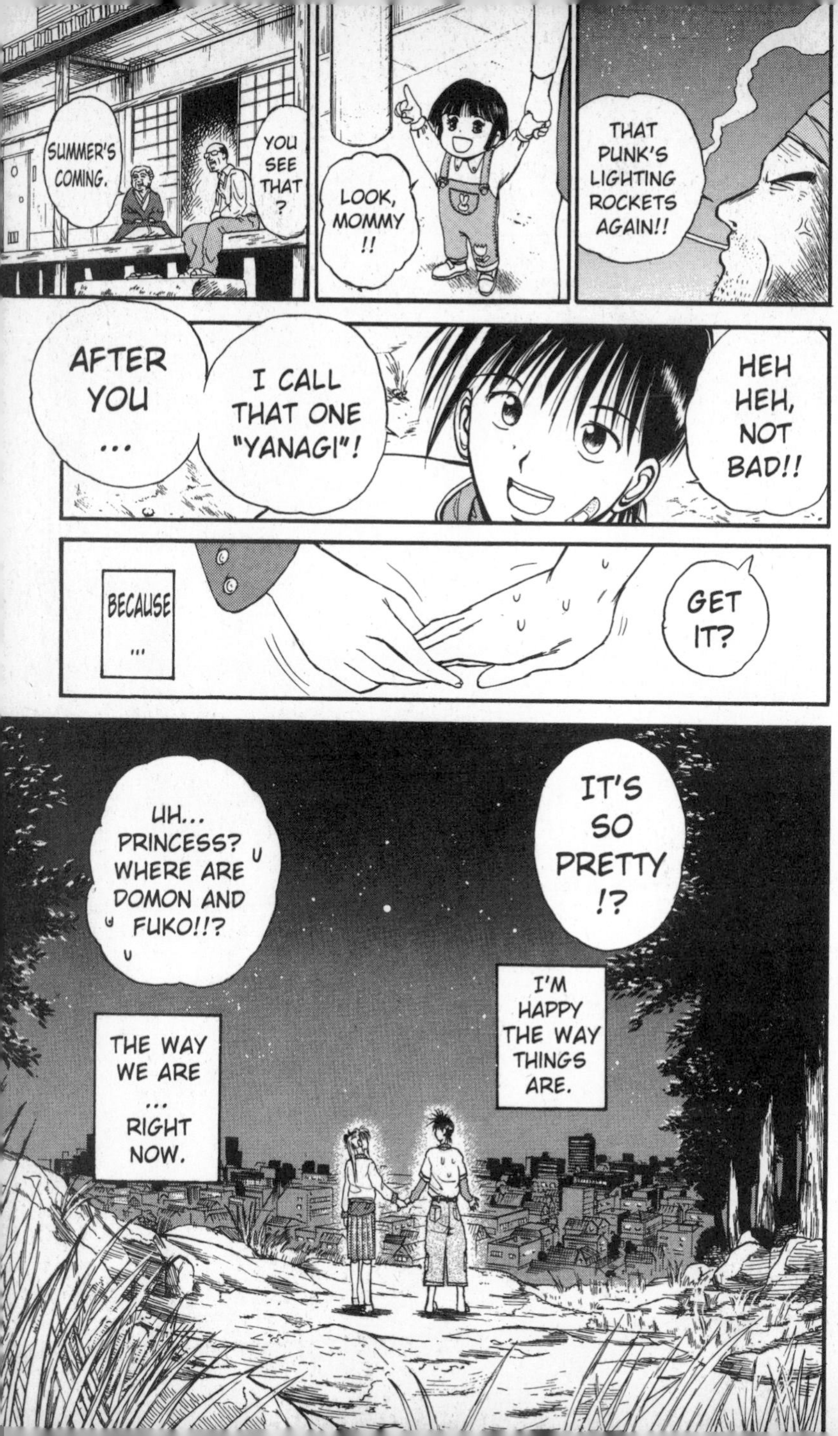

THAT PUNK'S LIGHTING ROCKETS AGAIN!!
LOOK, MOMMY !!
YOU SEE THAT ?
SUMMER'S COMING.
HEH HEH, NOT BAD!!
I CALL THAT ONE "YANAGI"!
AFTER YOU ...
GET IT?
BECAUSE ...
IT'S SO PRETTY !?
UH... PRINCESS? WHERE ARE DOMON AND FUKO!!?
I'M HAPPY THE WAY THINGS ARE.
THE WAY WE ARE ... RIGHT NOW.

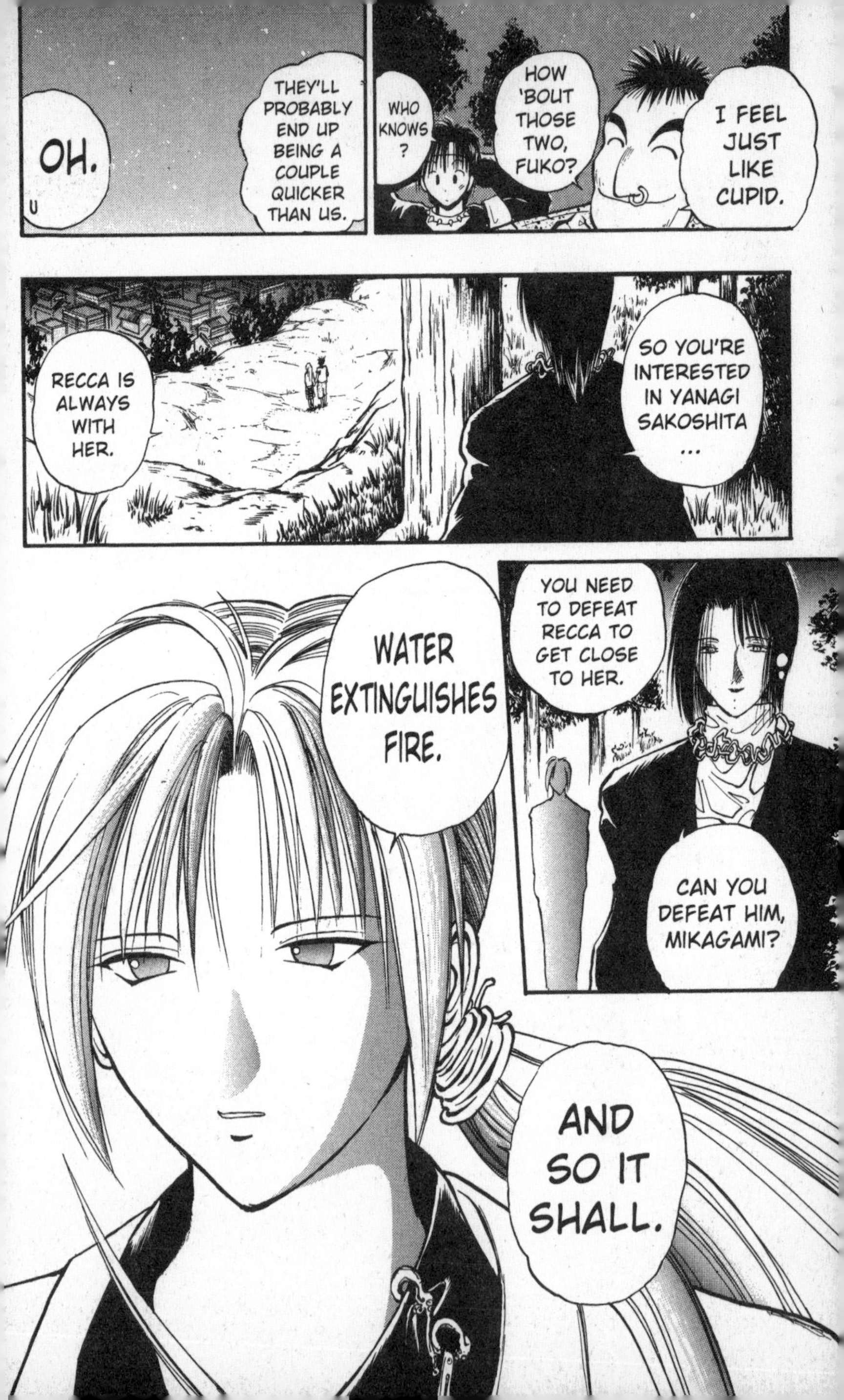
I FEEL JUST LIKE CUPID.
HOW 'BOUT THOSE TWO, FUKO?
WHO KNOWS?
THEY'LL PROBABLY END UP BEING A COUPLE QUICKER THAN US.
OH.
SO YOU'RE INTERESTED IN YANAGI SAKOSHITA...
RECCA IS ALWAYS WITH HER.
YOU NEED TO DEFEAT RECCA TO GET CLOSE TO HER.
CAN YOU DEFEAT HIM, MIKAGAMI?
WATER EXTINGUISHES FIRE.
AND SO IT SHALL.

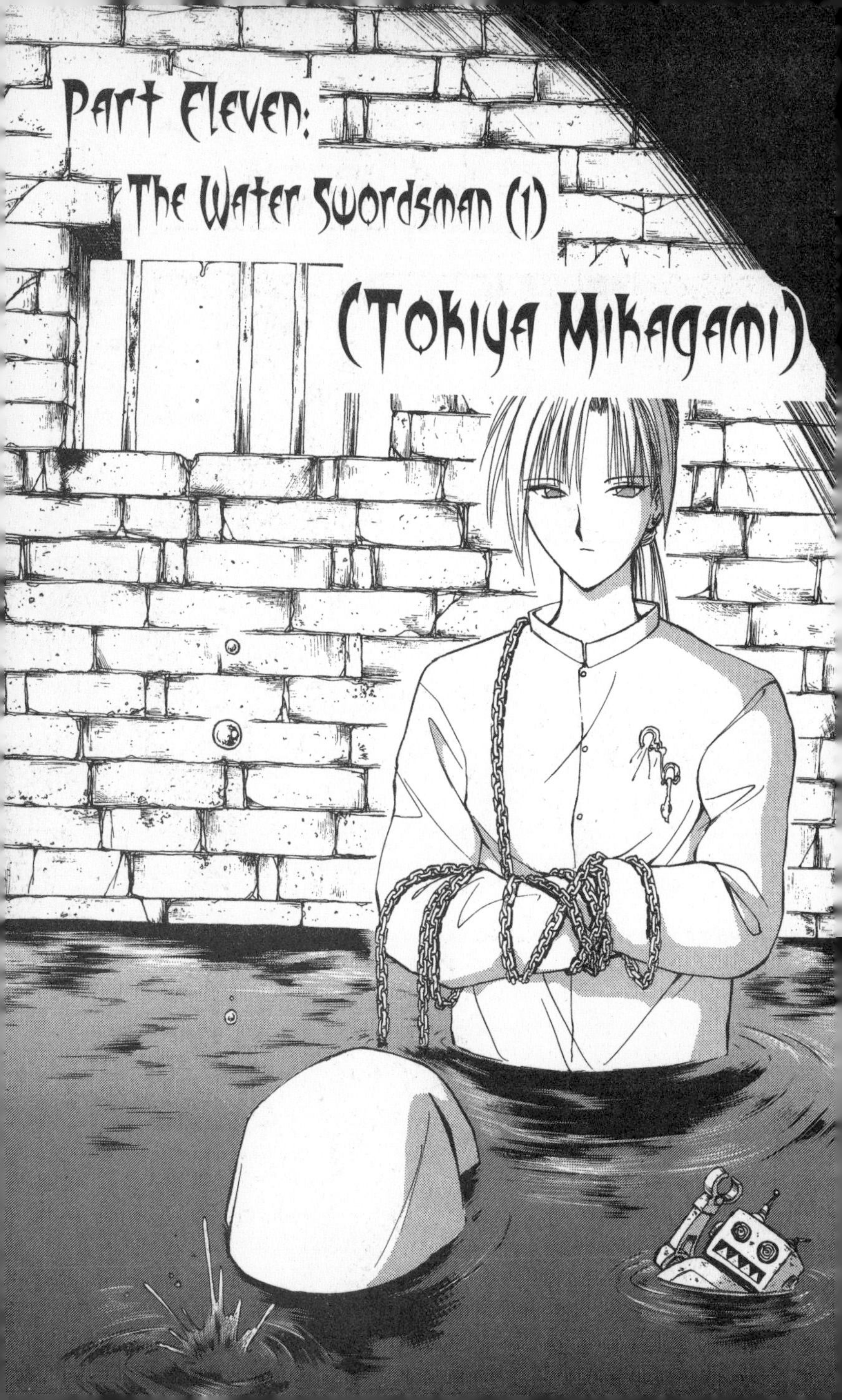
Part Eleven:
The Water Swordsman (1)
(Tokiya Mikagami)

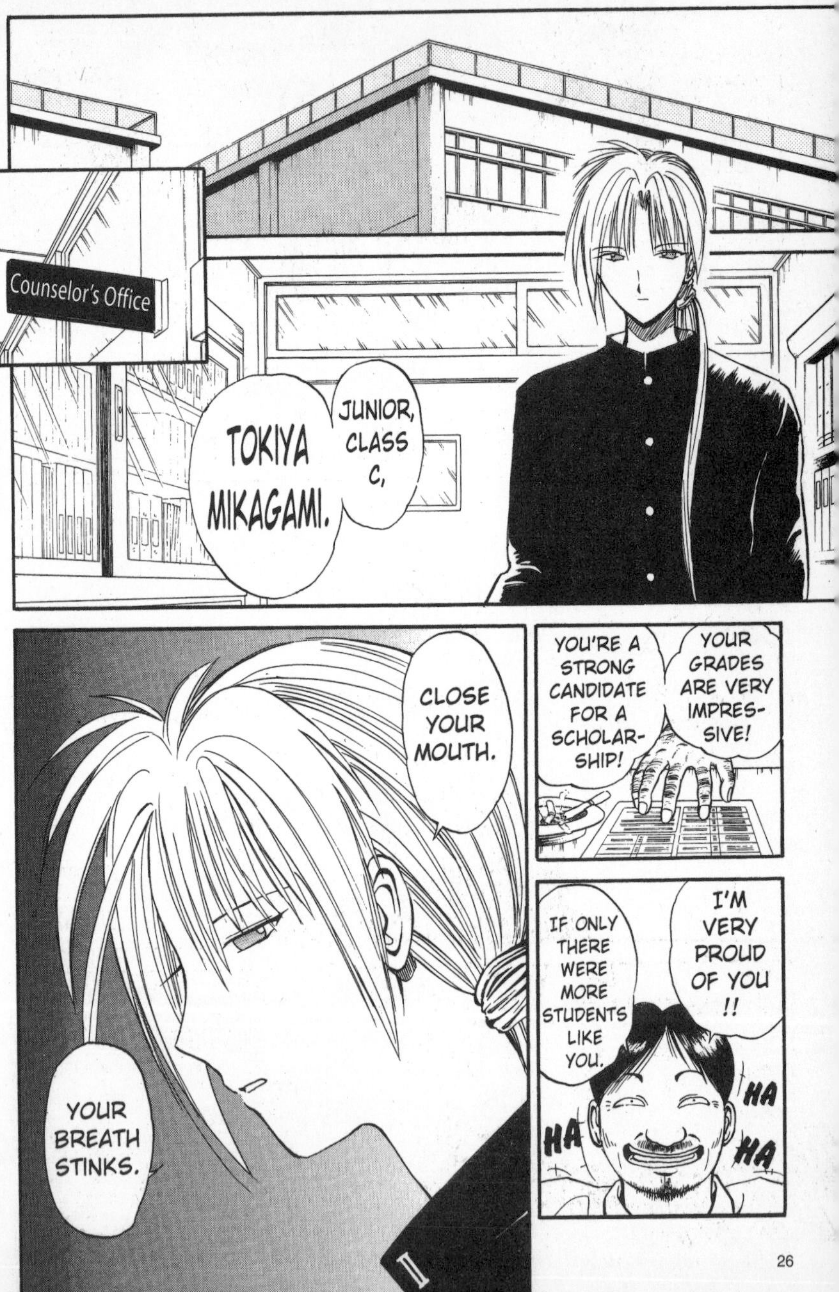
Counselor's Office
JUNIOR, CLASS C,
TOKIYA MIKAGAMI.
YOUR GRADES ARE VERY IMPRES-SIVE!
YOU'RE A STRONG CANDIDATE FOR A SCHOLAR-SHIP!
I'M VERY PROUD OF YOU !!
IF ONLY THERE WERE MORE STUDENTS LIKE YOU.
HA
HA
HA
HA
CLOSE YOUR MOUTH.
YOUR BREATH STINKS.

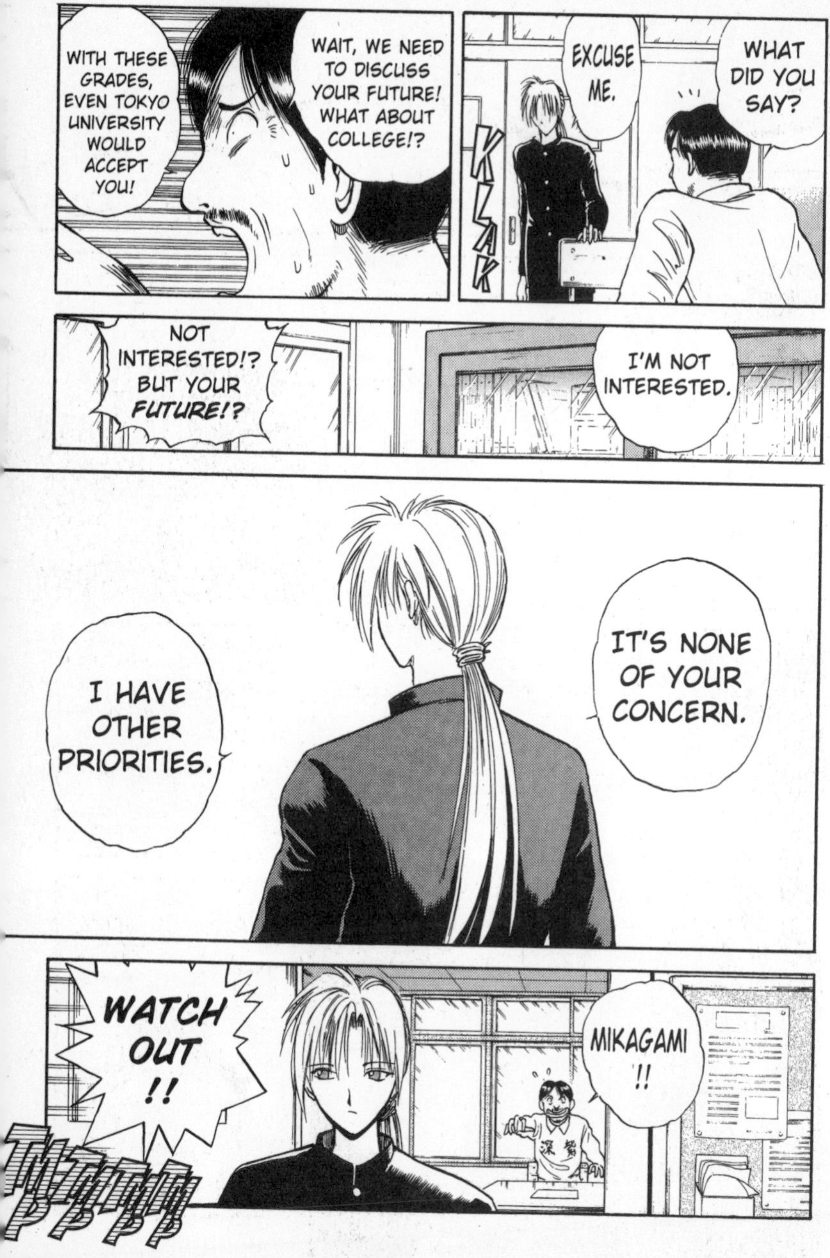

WITH THESE GRADES, EVEN TOKYO UNIVERSITY WOULD ACCEPT YOU!
WAIT, WE NEED TO DISCUSS YOUR FUTURE! WHAT ABOUT COLLEGE!?
KLAK
EXCUSE ME.
WHAT DID YOU SAY?
NOT INTERESTED!? BUT YOUR FUTURE!?
I'M NOT INTERESTED.
I HAVE OTHER PRIORITIES.
IT'S NONE OF YOUR CONCERN.
WATCH OUT !!
MIKAGAMI !!

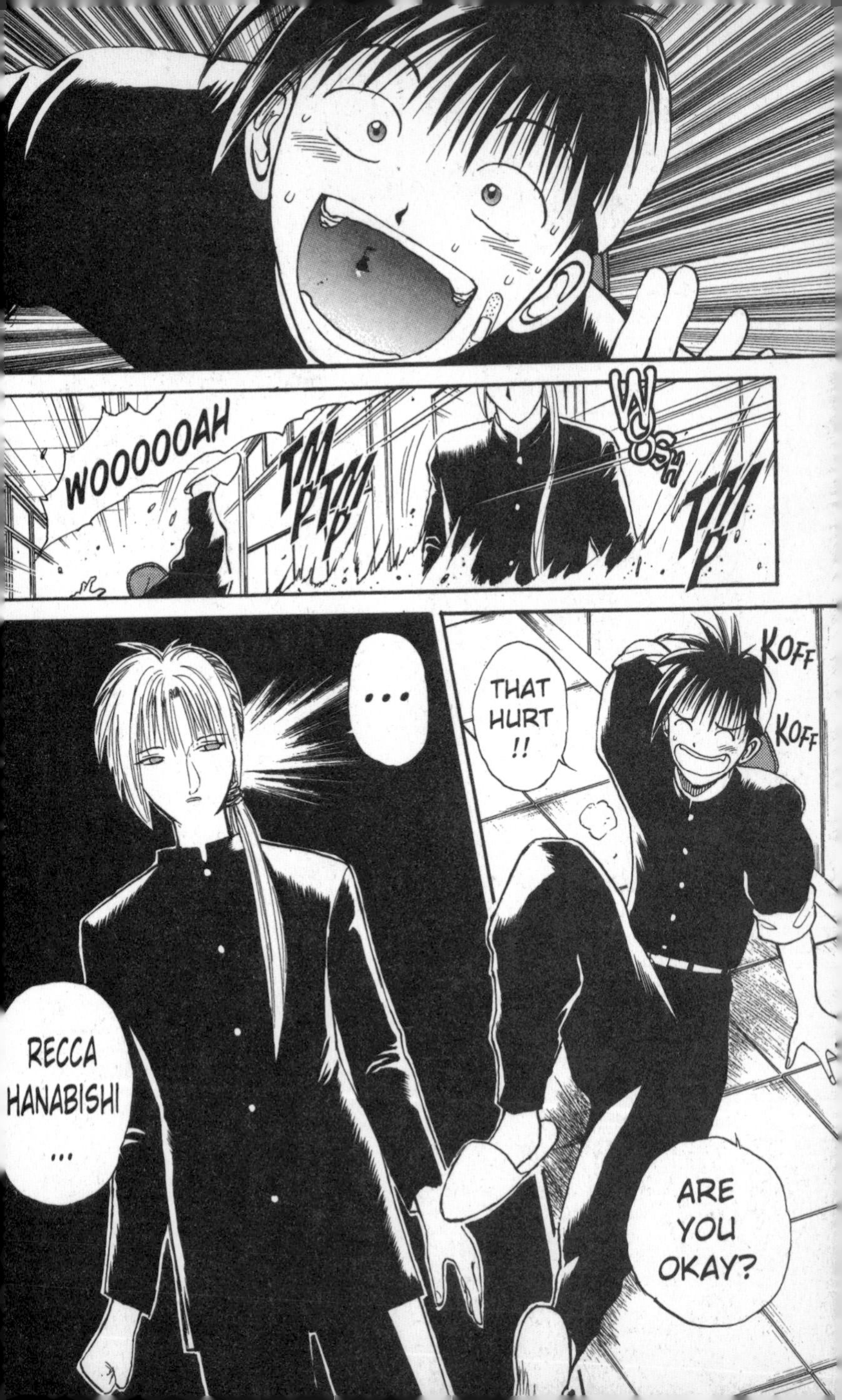
WOOSH
TMP
TMP-TMP
WOOOOOAH
KOFF
KOFF
THAT HURT !!
...
ARE YOU OKAY?
RECCA HANABISHI ...

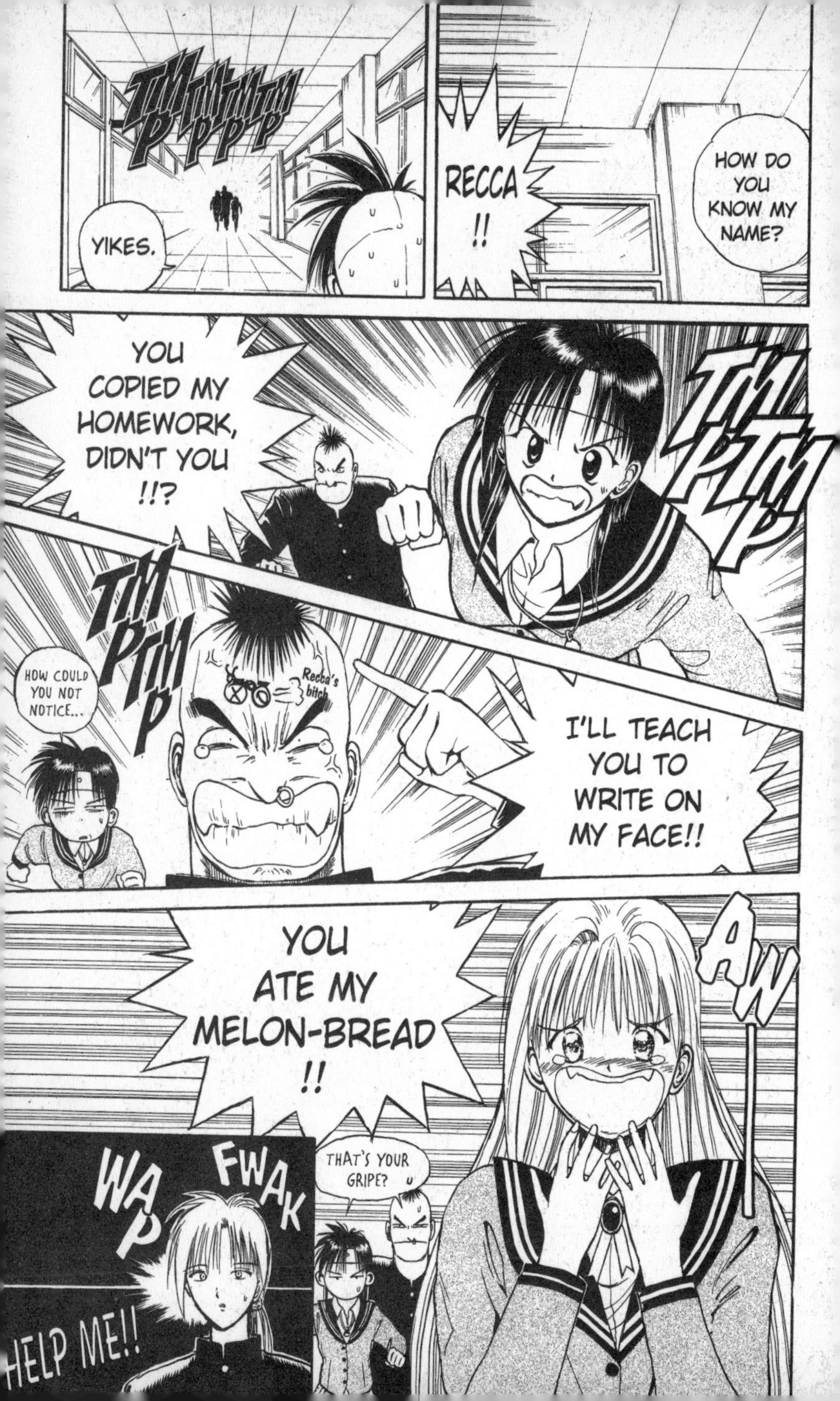
HOW DO YOU KNOW MY NAME?
RECCA !!
TMTMTMTMTM PPPPP
YIKES.
TMPTMP
YOU COPIED MY HOMEWORK, DIDN'T YOU !!?
TMPTMP
Recca's bitch
I'LL TEACH YOU TO WRITE ON MY FACE!!
HOW COULD YOU NOT NOTICE...
AW
YOU ATE MY MELON-BREAD !!
THAT'S YOUR GRIPE?
FWAK
WAP
HELP ME!!

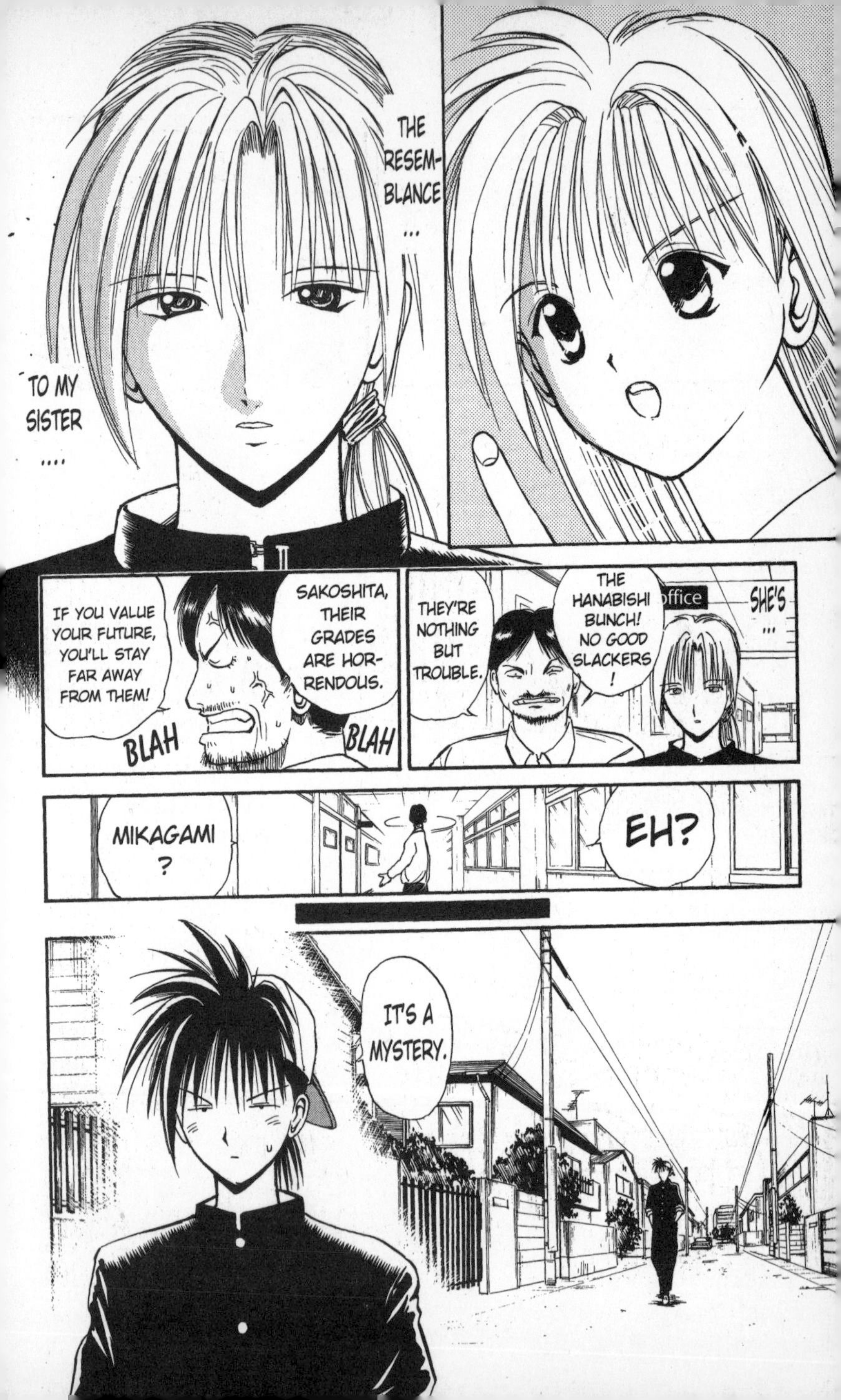
THE RESEMBLANCE ...
TO MY SISTER ....
SHE'S ...
office
THE HANABISHI BUNCH! NO GOOD SLACKERS!
THEY'RE NOTHING BUT TROUBLE.
SAKOSHITA, THEIR GRADES ARE HORRENDOUS.
BLAH
IF YOU VALUE YOUR FUTURE, YOU'LL STAY FAR AWAY FROM THEM!
BLAH
EH?
MIKAGAMI ?
IT'S A MYSTERY.

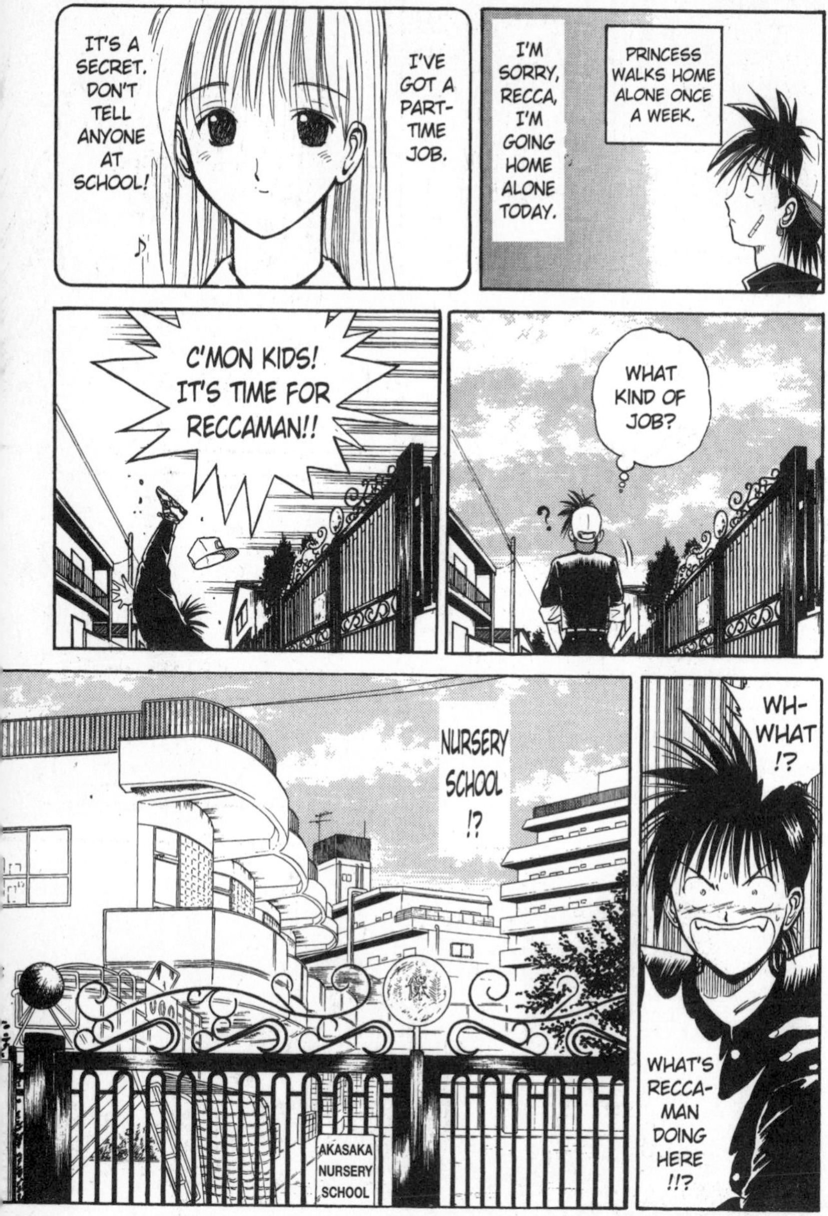

PRINCESS WALKS HOME ALONE ONCE A WEEK.
I'M SORRY, RECCA, I'M GOING HOME ALONE TODAY.
I'VE GOT A PART-TIME JOB.
IT'S A SECRET. DON'T TELL ANYONE AT SCHOOL!
WHAT KIND OF JOB?
C'MON KIDS! IT'S TIME FOR RECCAMAN!!
WH-WHAT !?
WHAT'S RECCA-MAN DOING HERE !!?
NURSERY SCHOOL !?
AKASAKA NURSERY SCHOOL

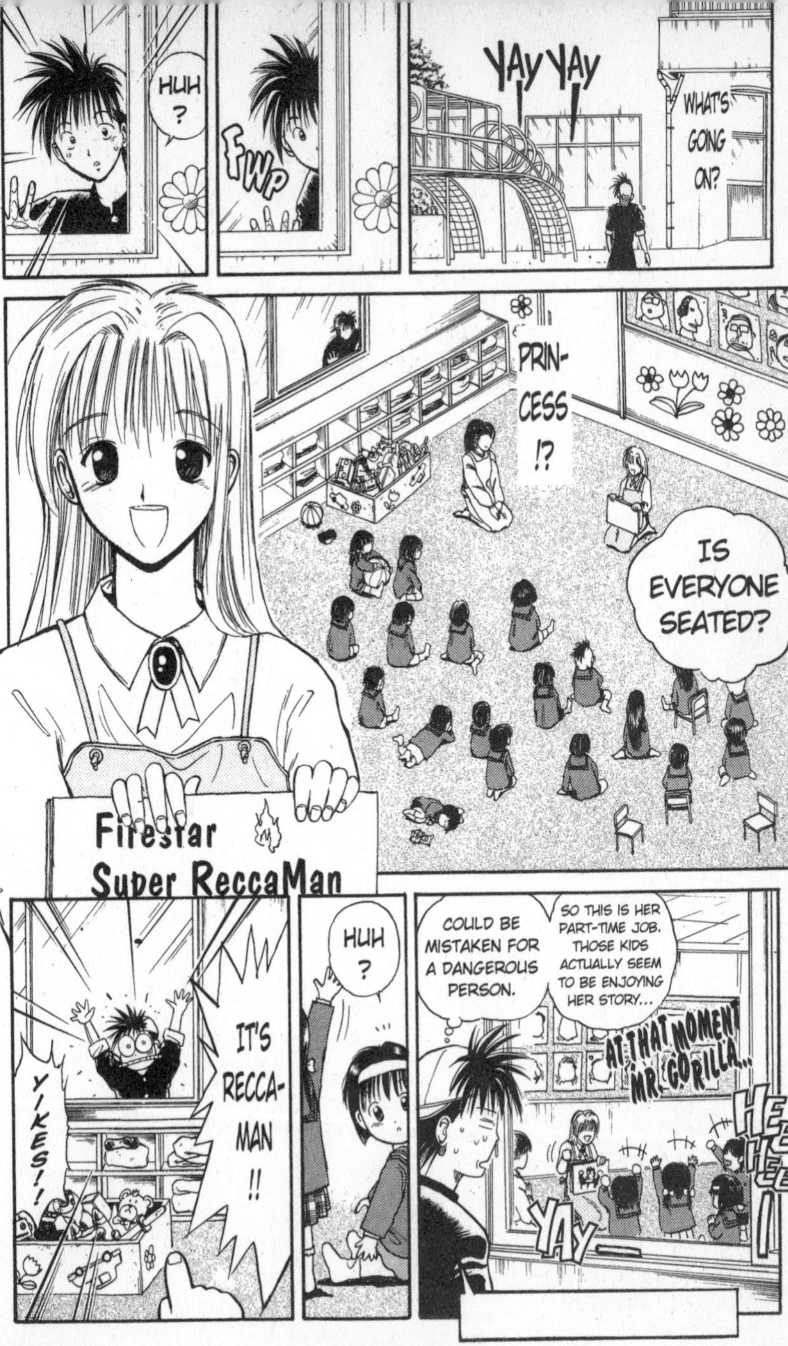

HUH?
FWP
YAY YAY!
WHAT'S GOING ON?
PRINCESS!?
IS EVERYONE SEATED?
Firestar Super ReccaMan
YIKES!!
IT'S RECCA-MAN!!
HUH?
COULD BE MISTAKEN FOR A DANGEROUS PERSON.
SO THIS IS HER PART-TIME JOB. THOSE KIDS ACTUALLY SEEM TO BE ENJOYING HER STORY...
AT THAT MOMENT MR. GORILLA...
HEE HEE!
YAY

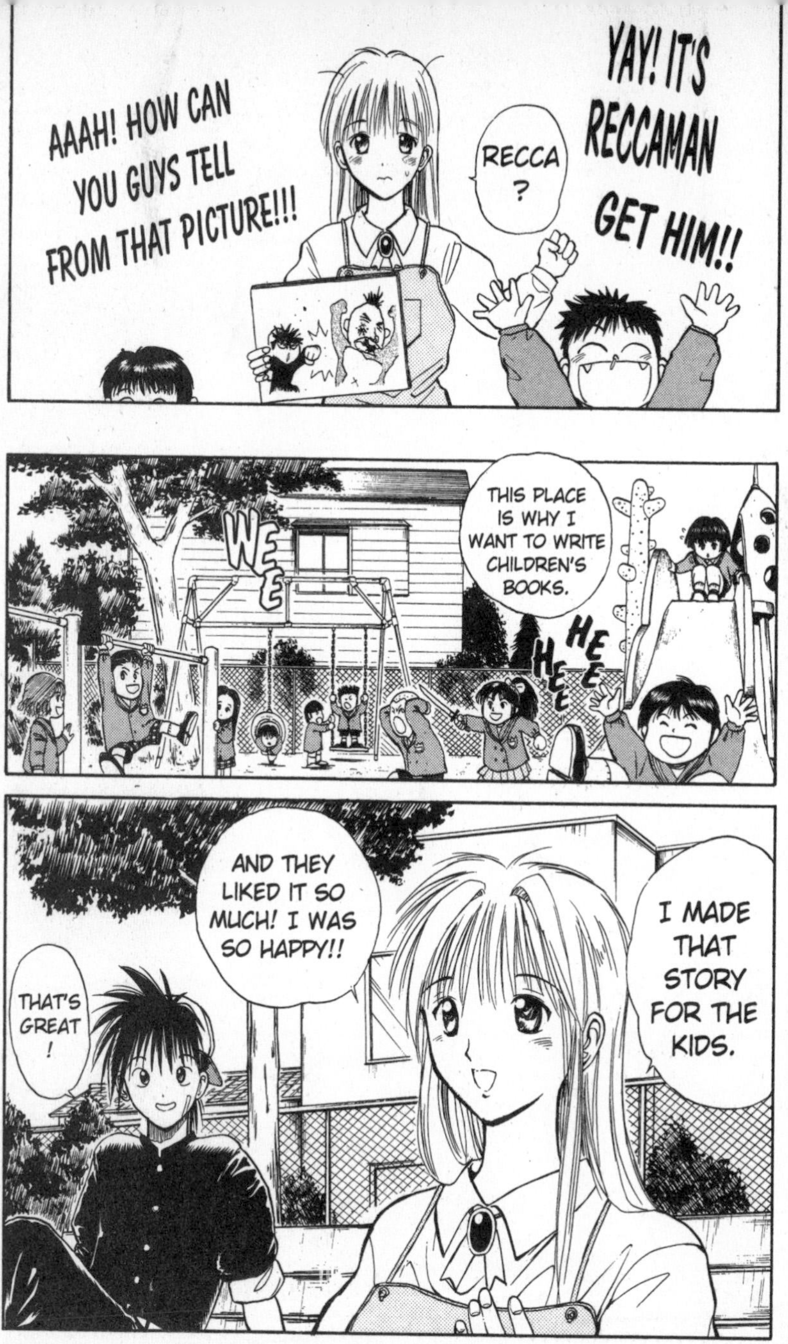

YAY! IT'S RECCAMAN GET HIM!!
RECCA ?
AAAH! HOW CAN YOU GUYS TELL FROM THAT PICTURE!!!!
THIS PLACE IS WHY I WANT TO WRITE CHILDREN'S BOOKS.
HEE HEE
WEE
I MADE THAT STORY FOR THE KIDS.
AND THEY LIKED IT SO MUCH! I WAS SO HAPPY!!
THAT'S GREAT !

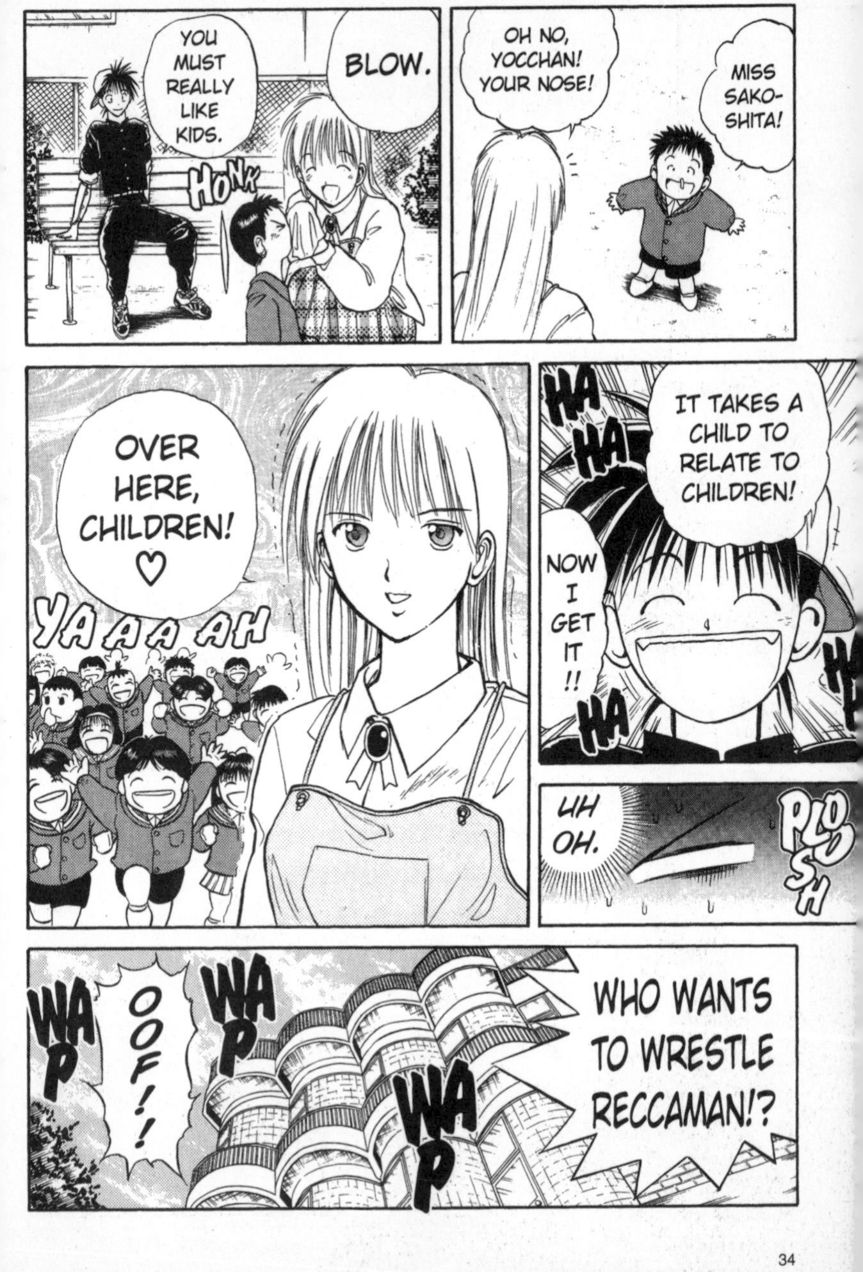
MISS SAKO-SHITA!
OH NO, YOCCHAN! YOUR NOSE!
BLOW.
HONK
YOU MUST REALLY LIKE KIDS.
HA HA
IT TAKES A CHILD TO RELATE TO CHILDREN!
NOW I GET IT!!
HA
UH OH.
PLOSH
OVER HERE, CHILDREN! ♡
YAAAAH
WHO WANTS TO WRESTLE RECCAMAN!?
WAP
WAP
OOF!!
WAP

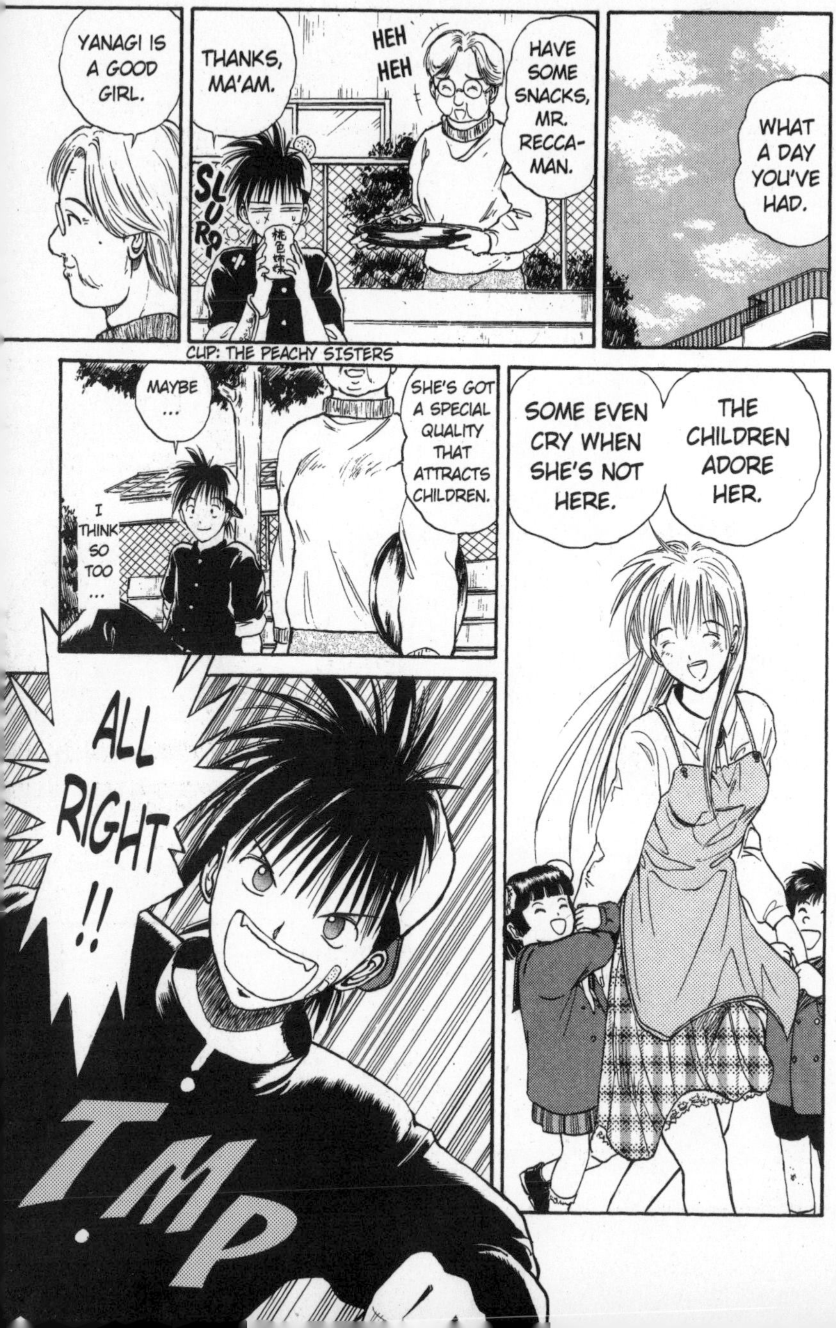
WHAT A DAY YOU'VE HAD.
HAVE SOME SNACKS, MR. RECCA-MAN.
HEH HEH
THANKS, MA'AM.
SLURP
YANAGI IS A GOOD GIRL.
CUP: THE PEACHY SISTERS
THE CHILDREN ADORE HER.
SOME EVEN CRY WHEN SHE'S NOT HERE.
SHE'S GOT A SPECIAL QUALITY THAT ATTRACTS CHILDREN.
MAYBE ...
I THINK SO TOO ...
ALL RIGHT !!
T.M.P.

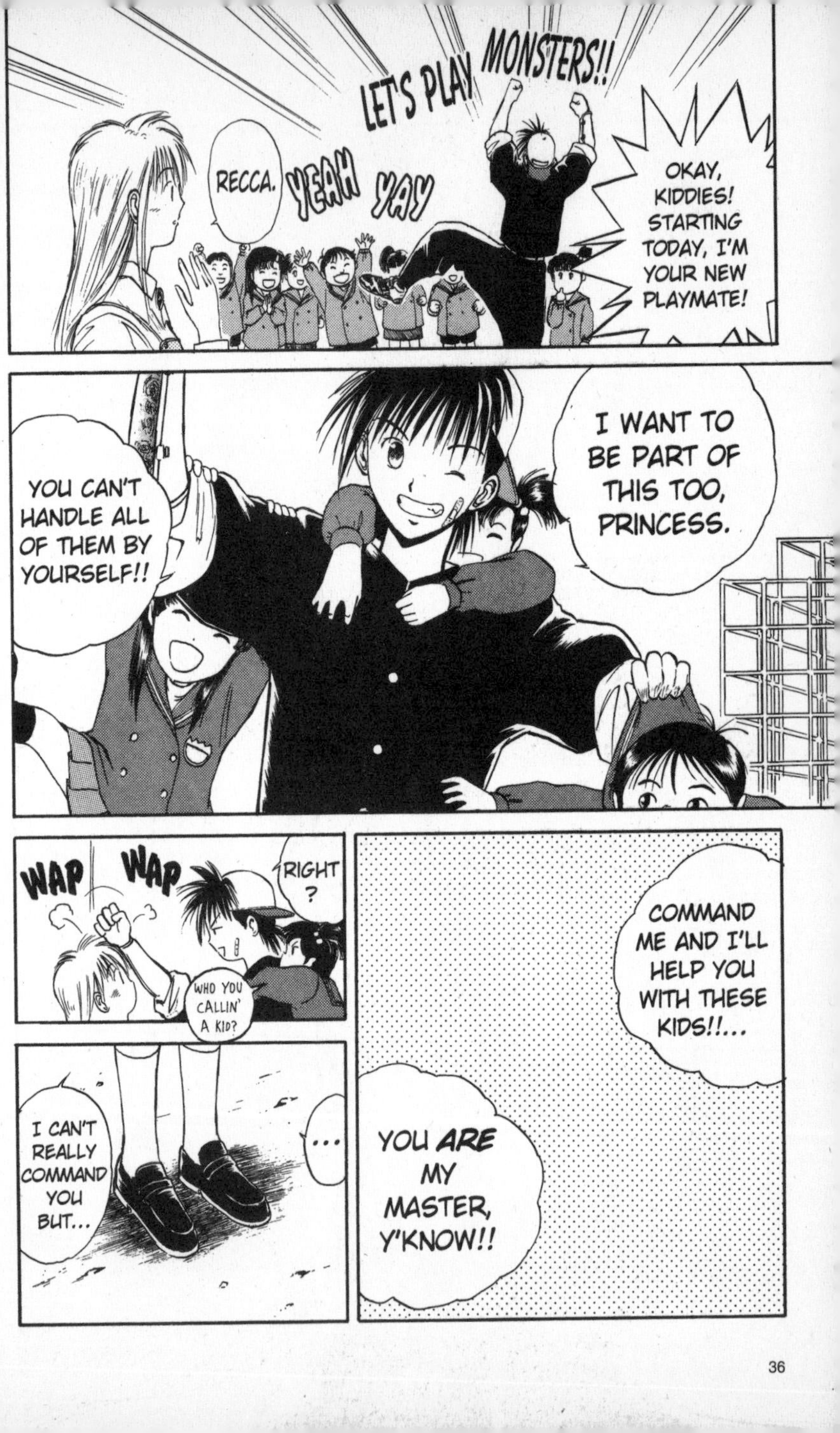
OKAY, KIDDIES! STARTING TODAY, I'M YOUR NEW PLAYMATE!
LET'S PLAY MONSTERS!!
YEAH
YAY
RECCA.
I WANT TO BE PART OF THIS TOO, PRINCESS.
YOU CAN'T HANDLE ALL OF THEM BY YOURSELF!!
RIGHT?
WAP
WAP
WHO YOU CALLIN' A KID?
COMMAND ME AND I'LL HELP YOU WITH THESE KIDS!!...
...
I CAN'T REALLY COMMAND YOU BUT...
YOU *ARE* MY MASTER, Y'KNOW!!

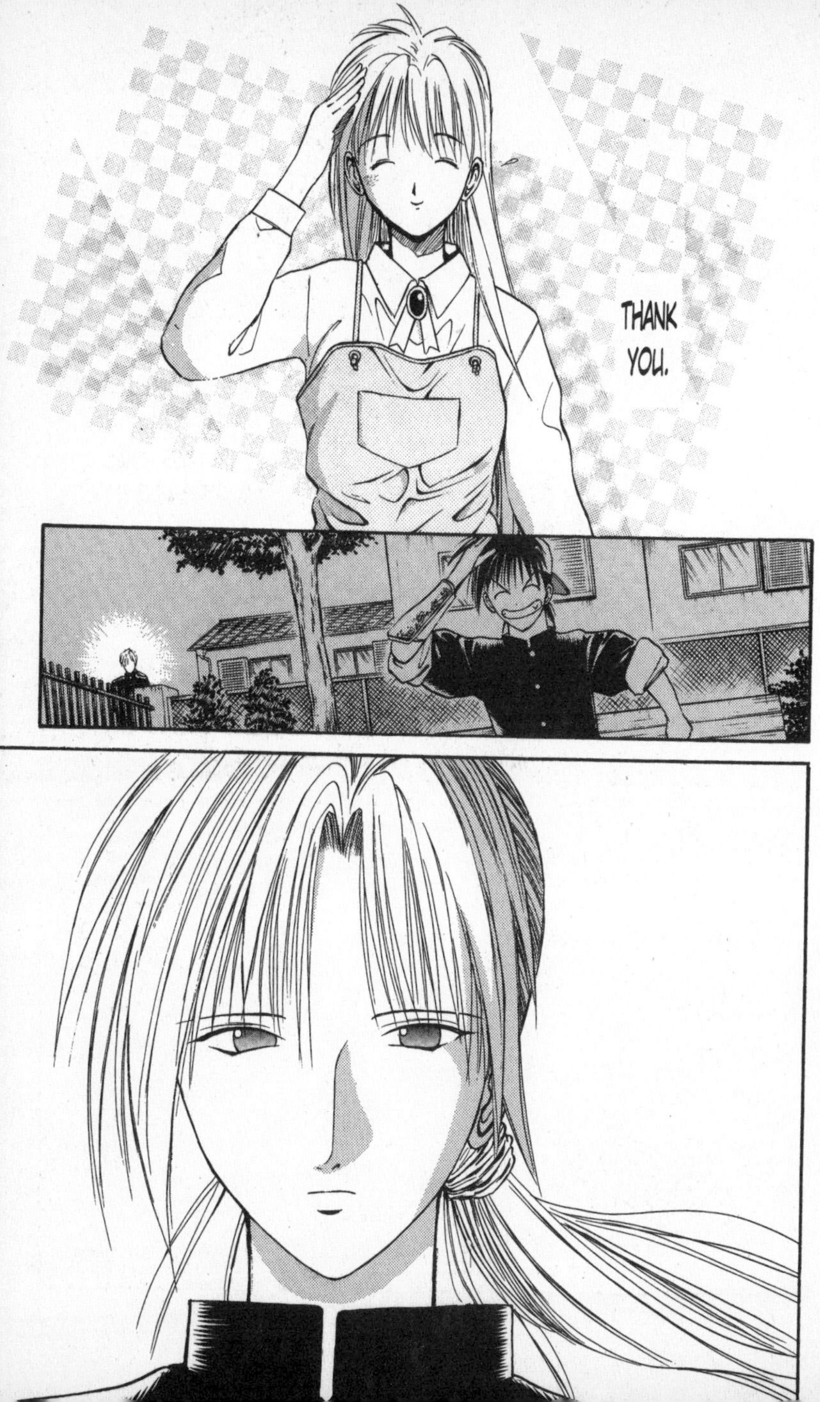
THANK YOU.

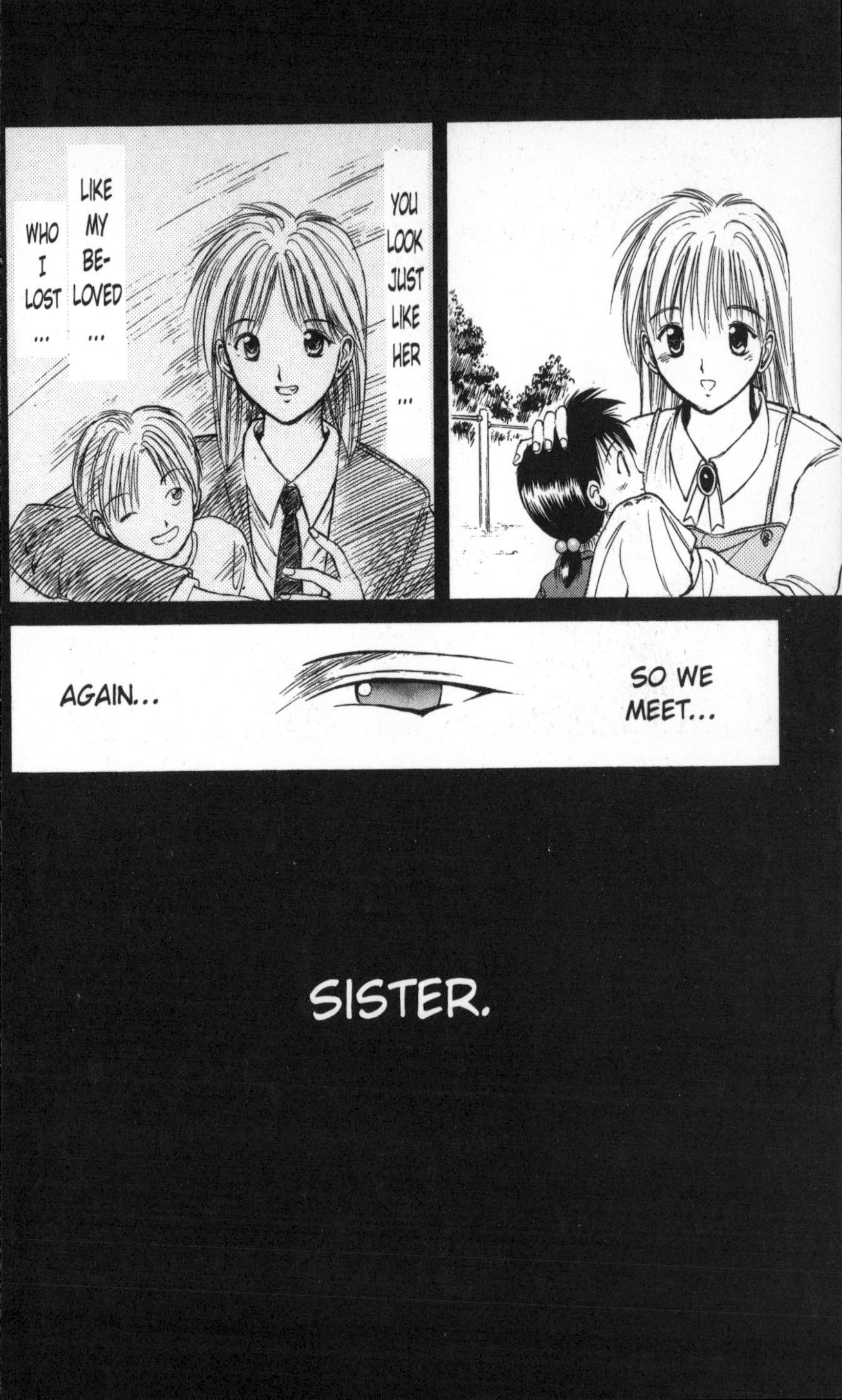
YOU LOOK JUST LIKE HER...
LIKE MY BE-LOVED...
WHO I LOST...
SO WE MEET...
AGAIN...
SISTER.

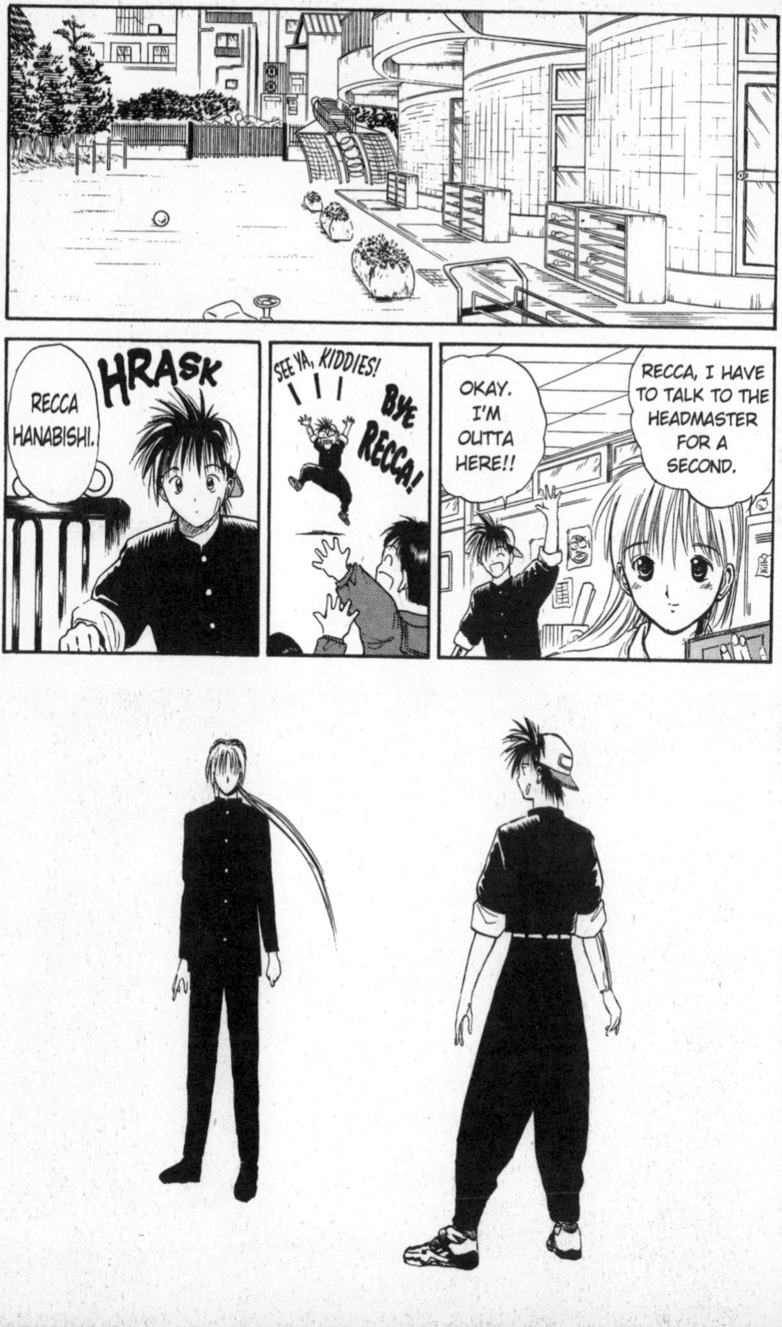

HRASK
RECCA HANABISHI.
SEE YA, KIDDIES!
BYE RECCA!
RECCA, I HAVE TO TALK TO THE HEADMASTER FOR A SECOND.
OKAY. I'M OUTTA HERE!!

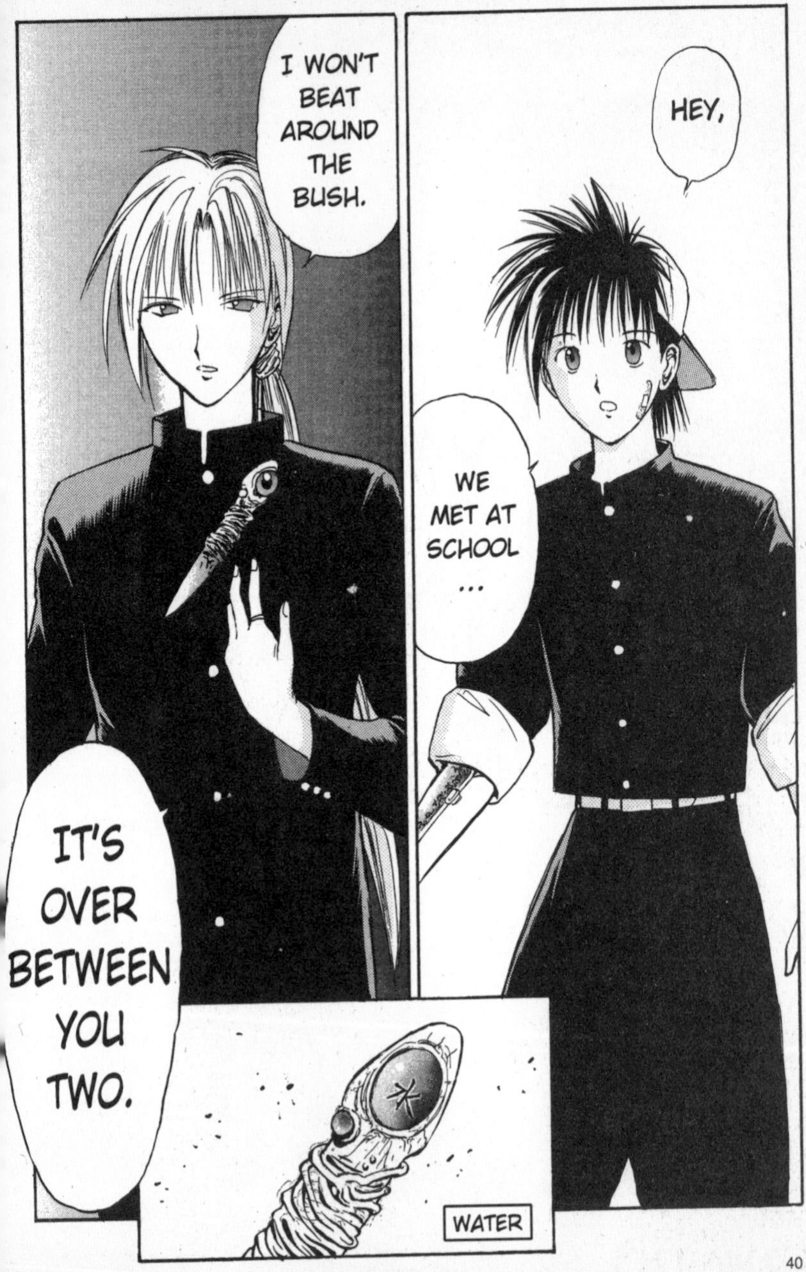
HEY,
WE MET AT SCHOOL ...
I WON'T BEAT AROUND THE BUSH.
IT'S OVER BETWEEN YOU TWO.
WATER

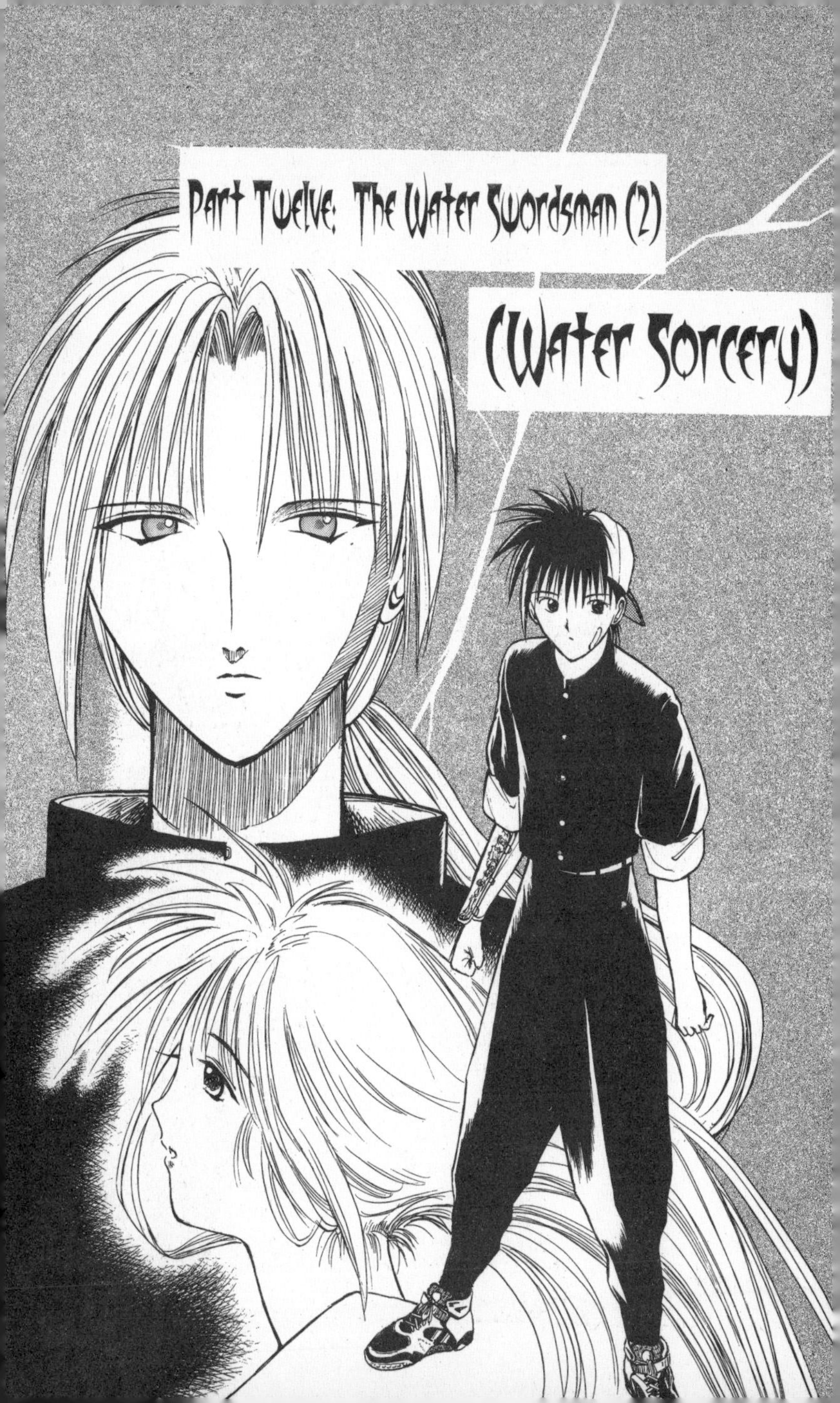
Part Twelve: The Water Swordsman (2)
(Water Sorcery)

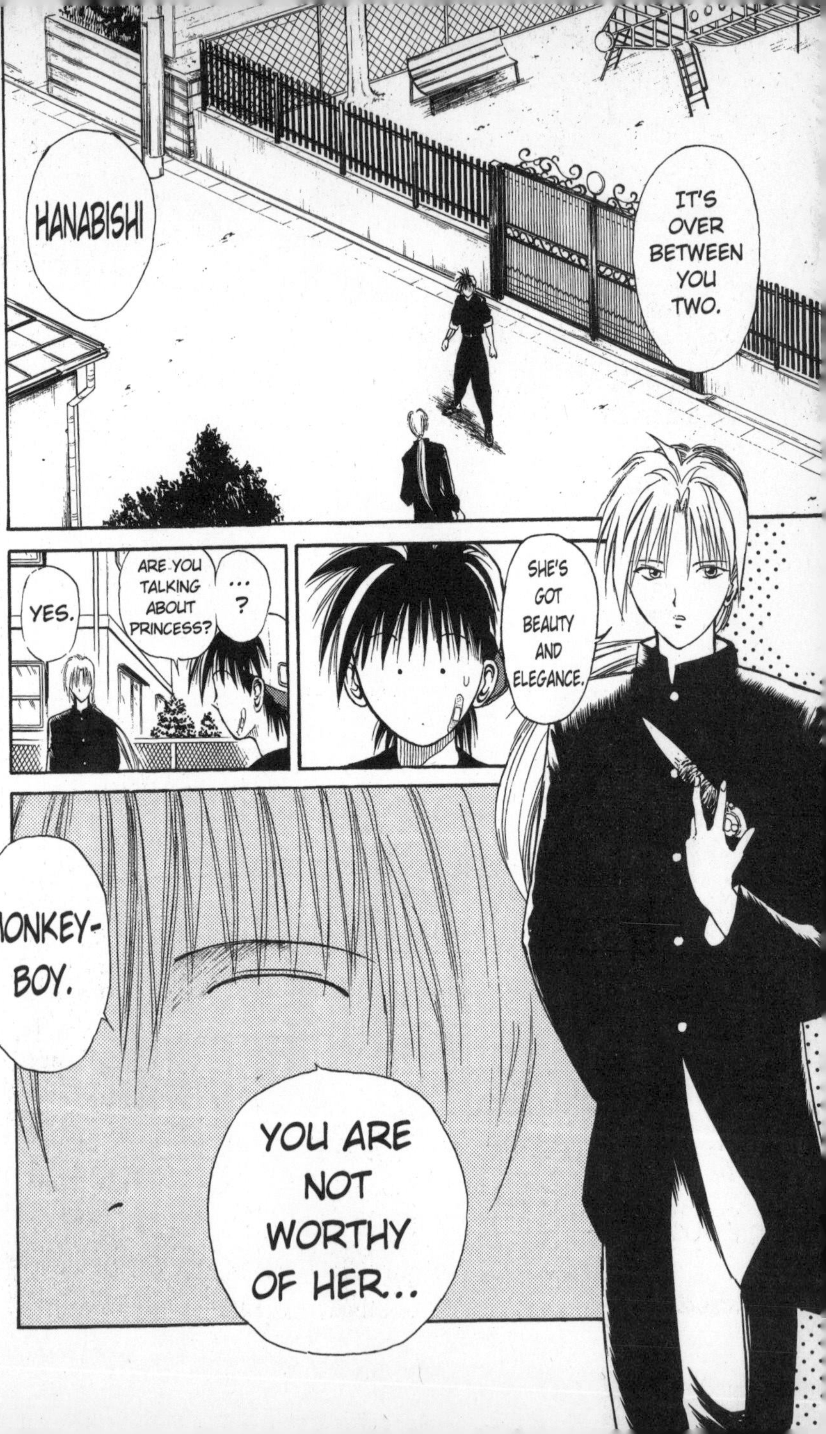
IT'S OVER BETWEEN YOU TWO.
HANABISHI
SHE'S GOT BEAUTY AND ELEGANCE.
...?
ARE YOU TALKING ABOUT PRINCESS?
YES.
YOU ARE NOT WORTHY OF HER..
MONKEY-BOY.

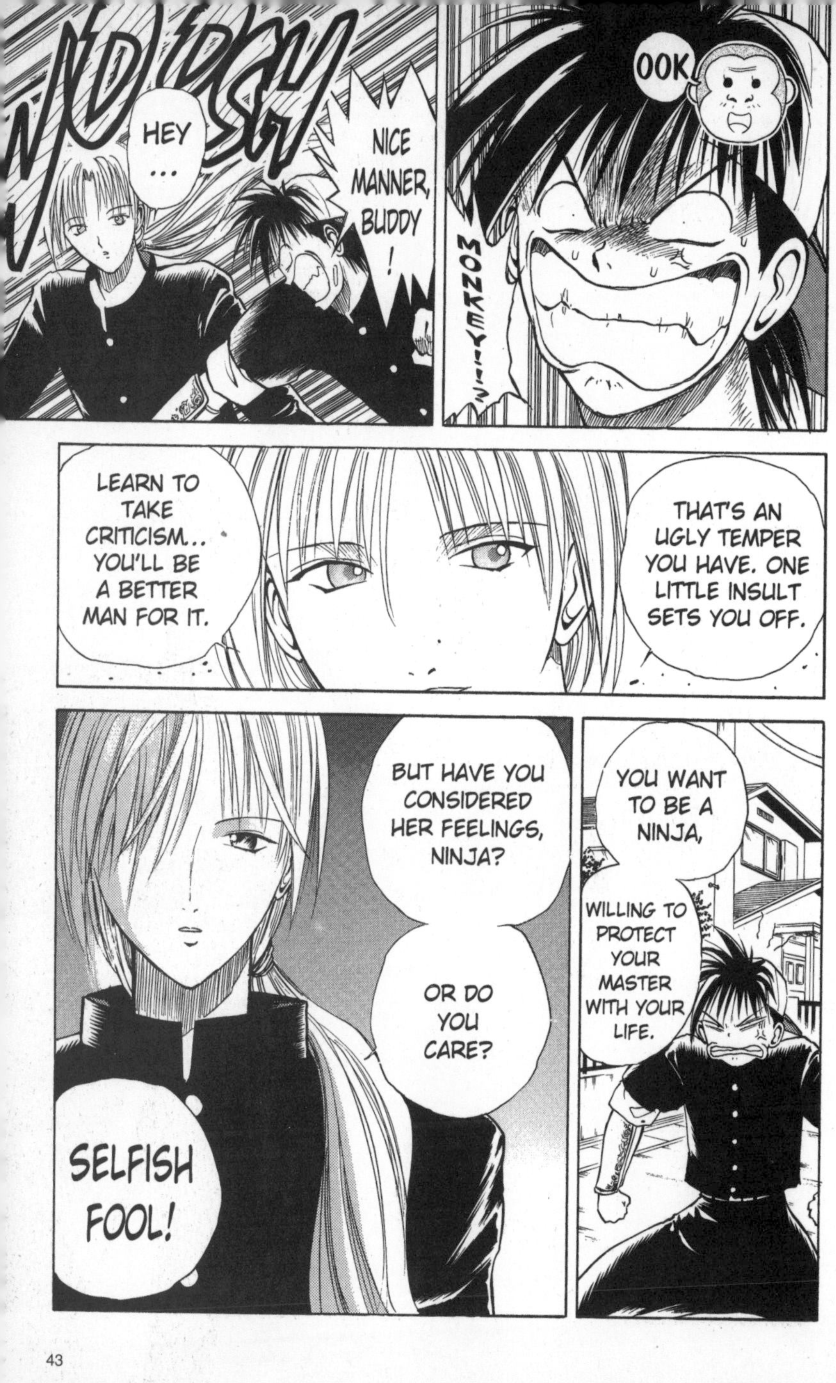
OOK
MONKEY!!!?
NICE MANNER, BUDDY!
HEY...
THAT'S AN UGLY TEMPER YOU HAVE. ONE LITTLE INSULT SETS YOU OFF.
LEARN TO TAKE CRITICISM... YOU'LL BE A BETTER MAN FOR IT.
YOU WANT TO BE A NINJA,
WILLING TO PROTECT YOUR MASTER WITH YOUR LIFE.
BUT HAVE YOU CONSIDERED HER FEELINGS, NINJA?
OR DO YOU CARE?
SELFISH FOOL!

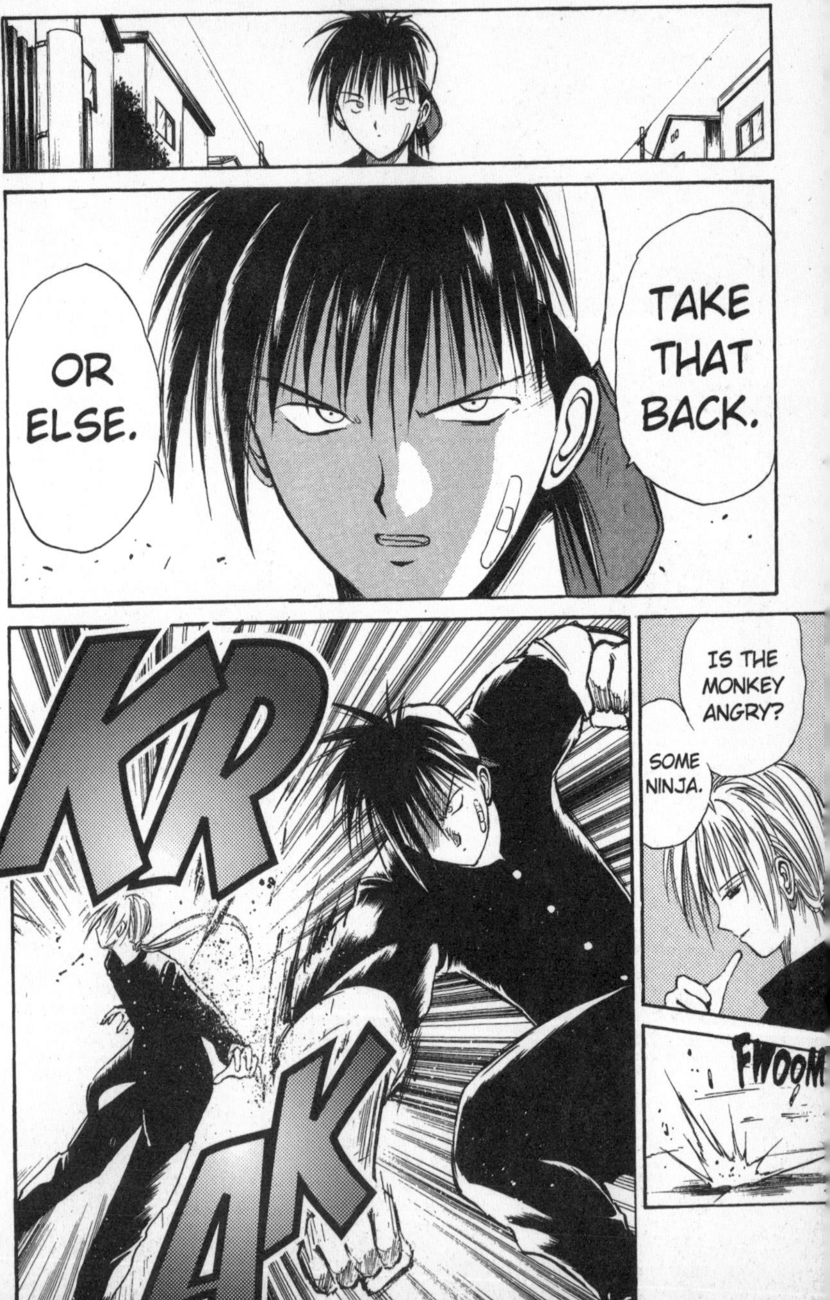
TAKE THAT BACK.
OR ELSE.
IS THE MONKEY ANGRY?
SOME NINJA.
FWOOM
KRAK

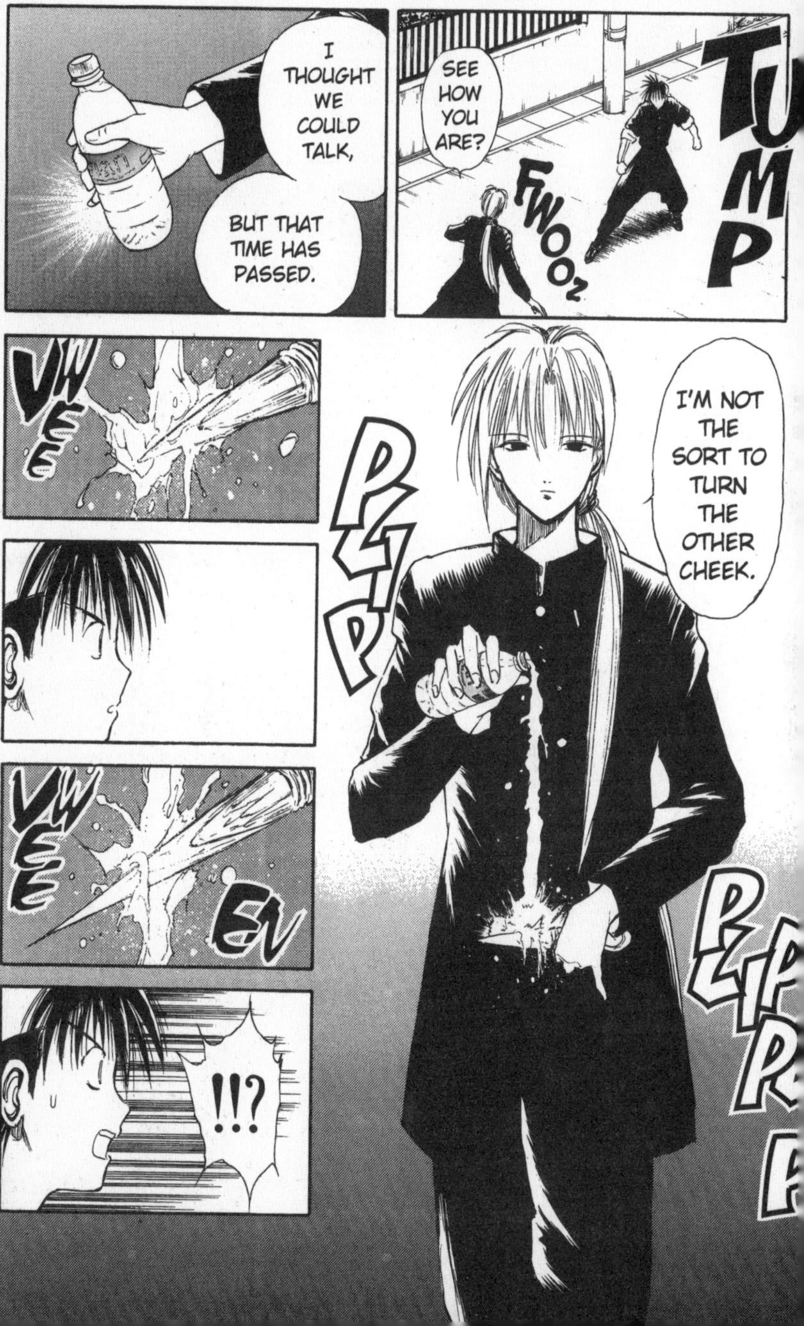
SEE HOW YOU ARE?
FWOOZ
TUMP
I THOUGHT WE COULD TALK,
BUT THAT TIME HAS PASSED.
I'M NOT THE SORT TO TURN THE OTHER CHEEK.
PLIP
VWEE
VWEE
EN
!!?

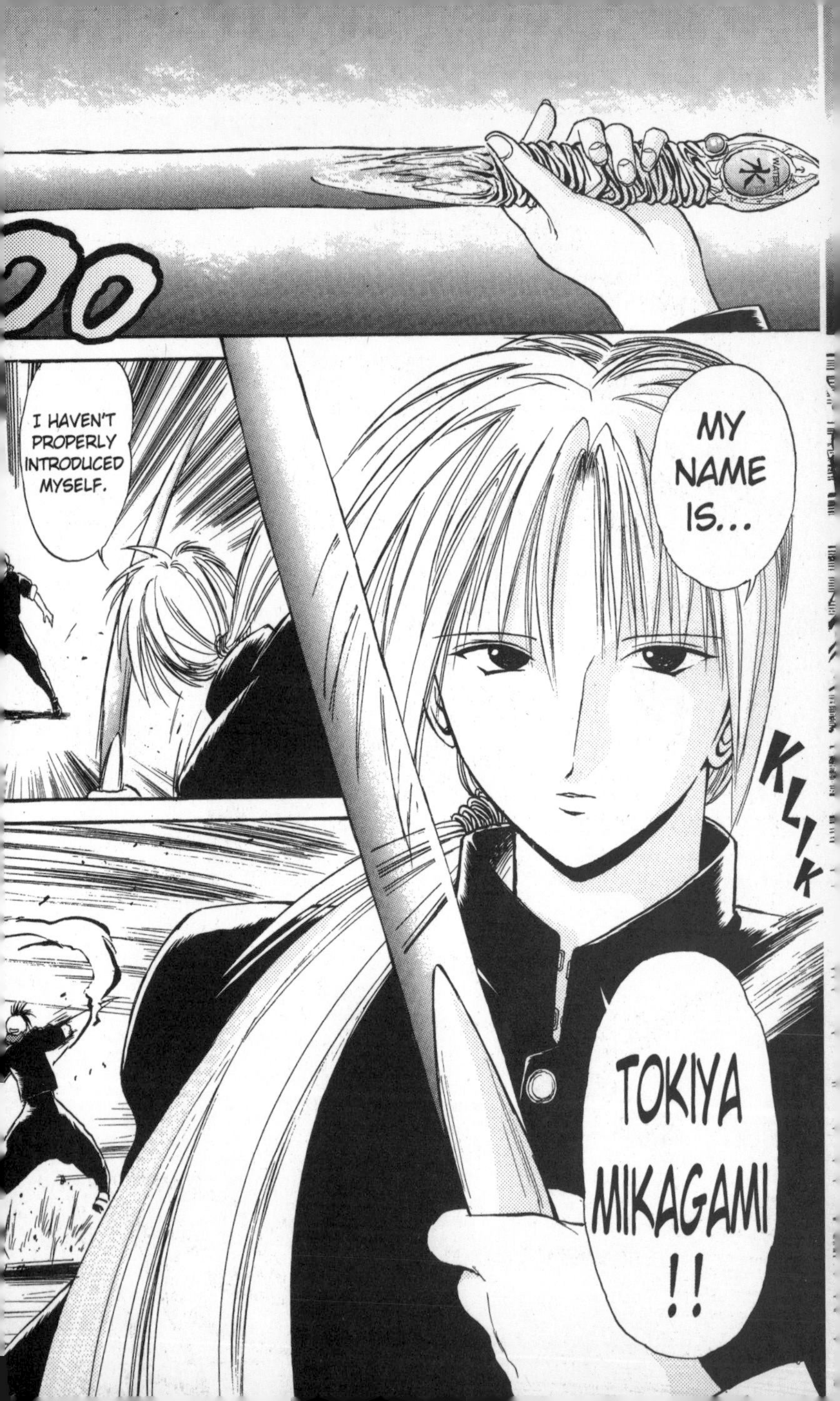

WATER
水
MY NAME IS...
I HAVEN'T PROPERLY INTRODUCED MYSELF.
KLIK
TOKIYA MIKAGAMI !!

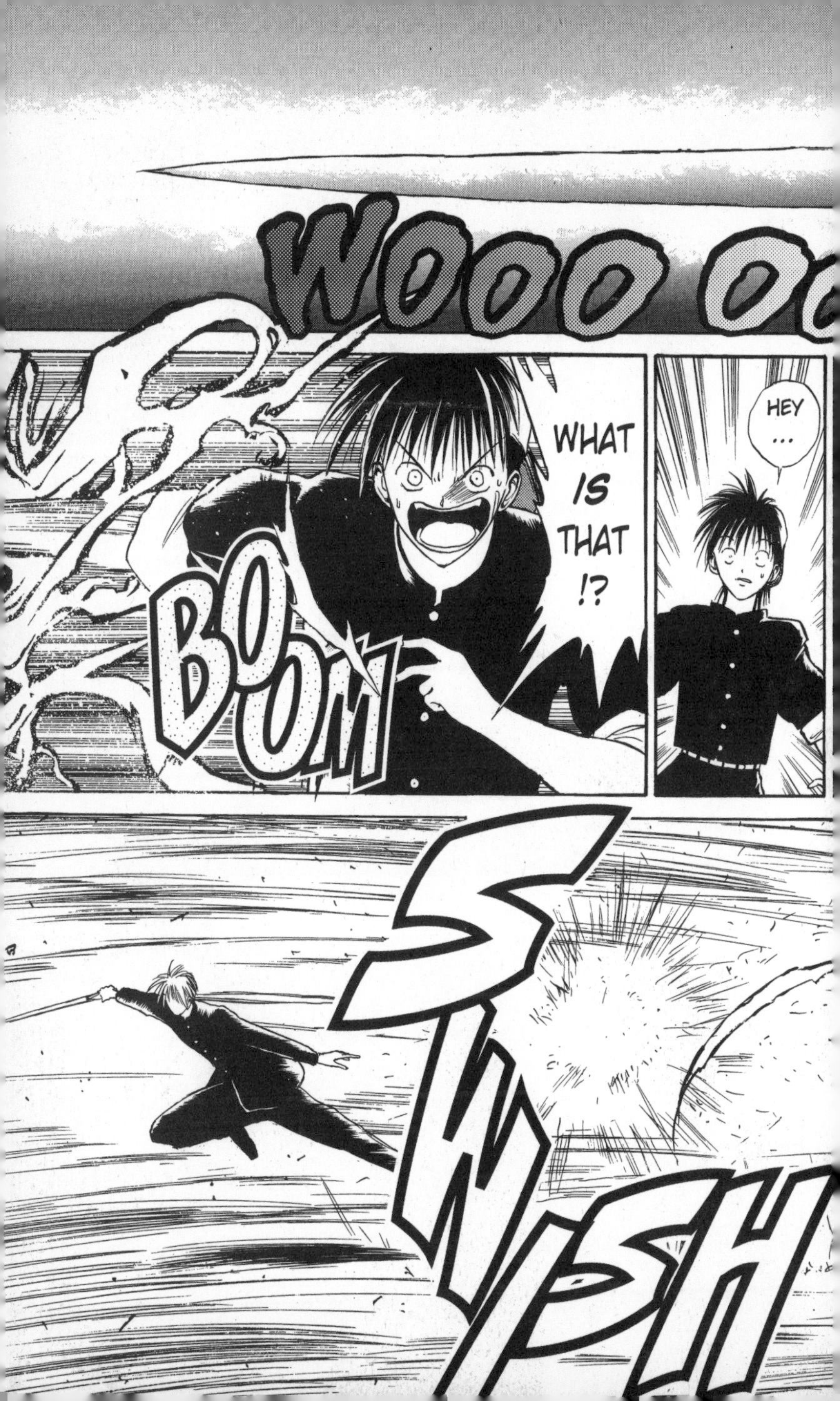
WOOO O
HEY ...
WHAT IS THAT !?
BOOM
SWISH

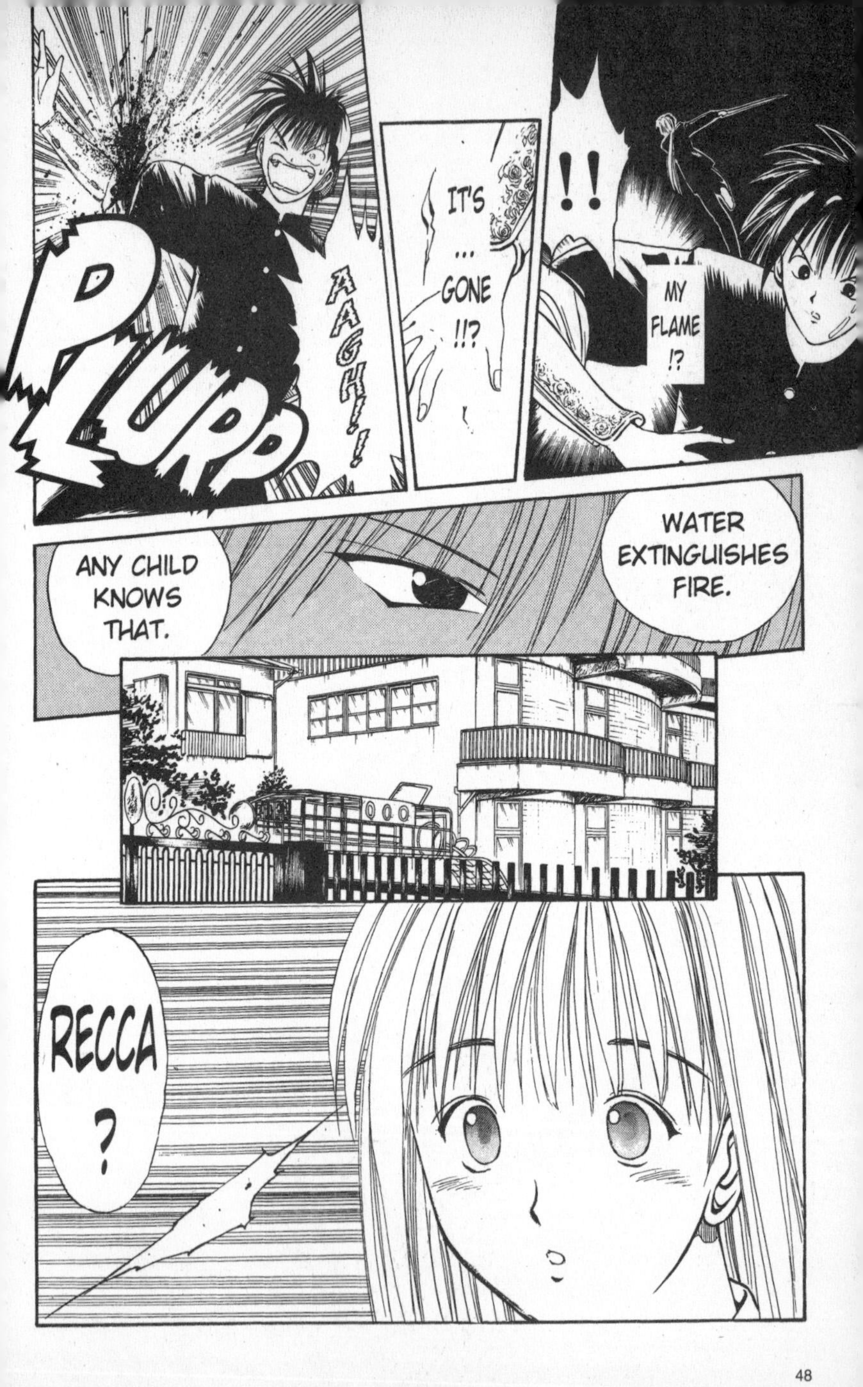
!!
MY FLAME !?
IT'S ... GONE !!?
PLURP
AAGH!!
WATER EXTINGUISHES FIRE.
ANY CHILD KNOWS THAT.
RECCA ?

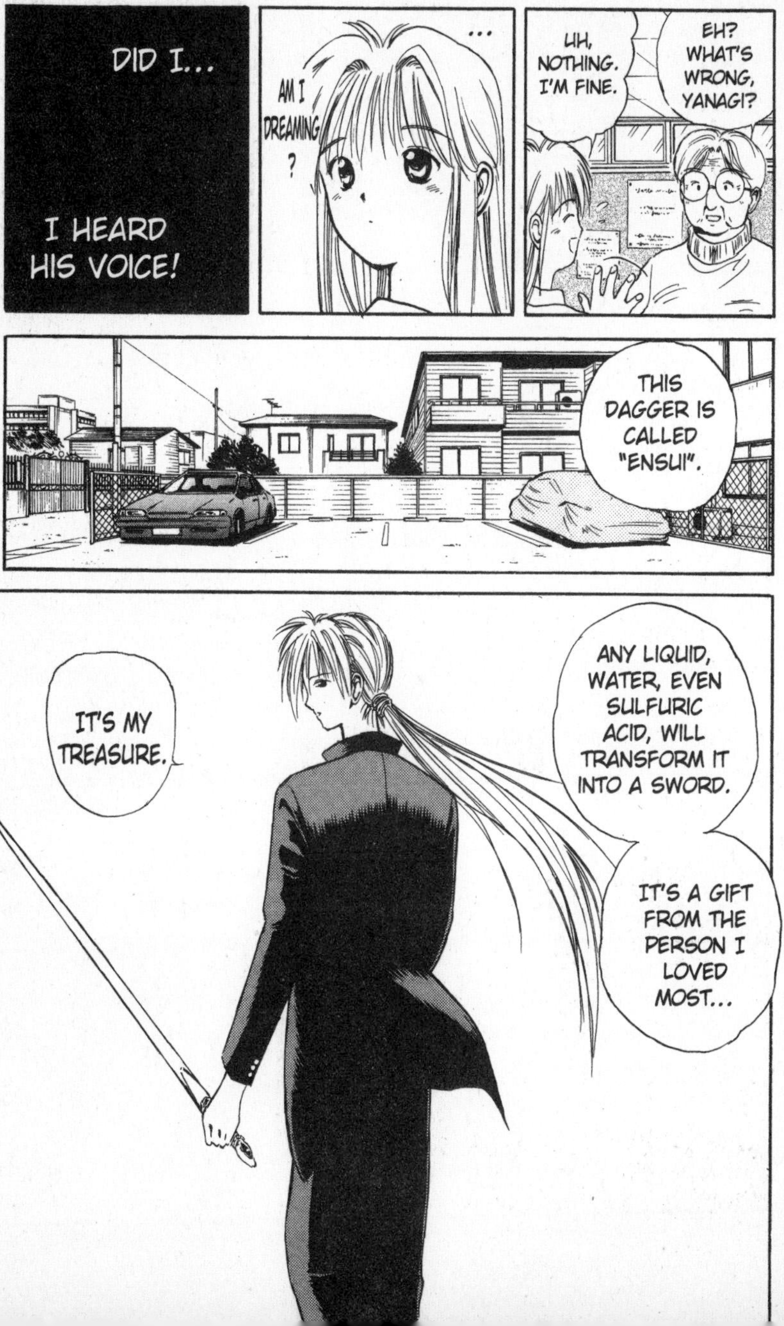
DID I...
I HEARD HIS VOICE!
...
AM I DREAMING?
EH? WHAT'S WRONG, YANAGI?
UH, NOTHING. I'M FINE.
THIS DAGGER IS CALLED "ENSUI".
ANY LIQUID, WATER, EVEN SULFURIC ACID, WILL TRANSFORM IT INTO A SWORD.
IT'S A GIFT FROM THE PERSON I LOVED MOST...
IT'S MY TREASURE.

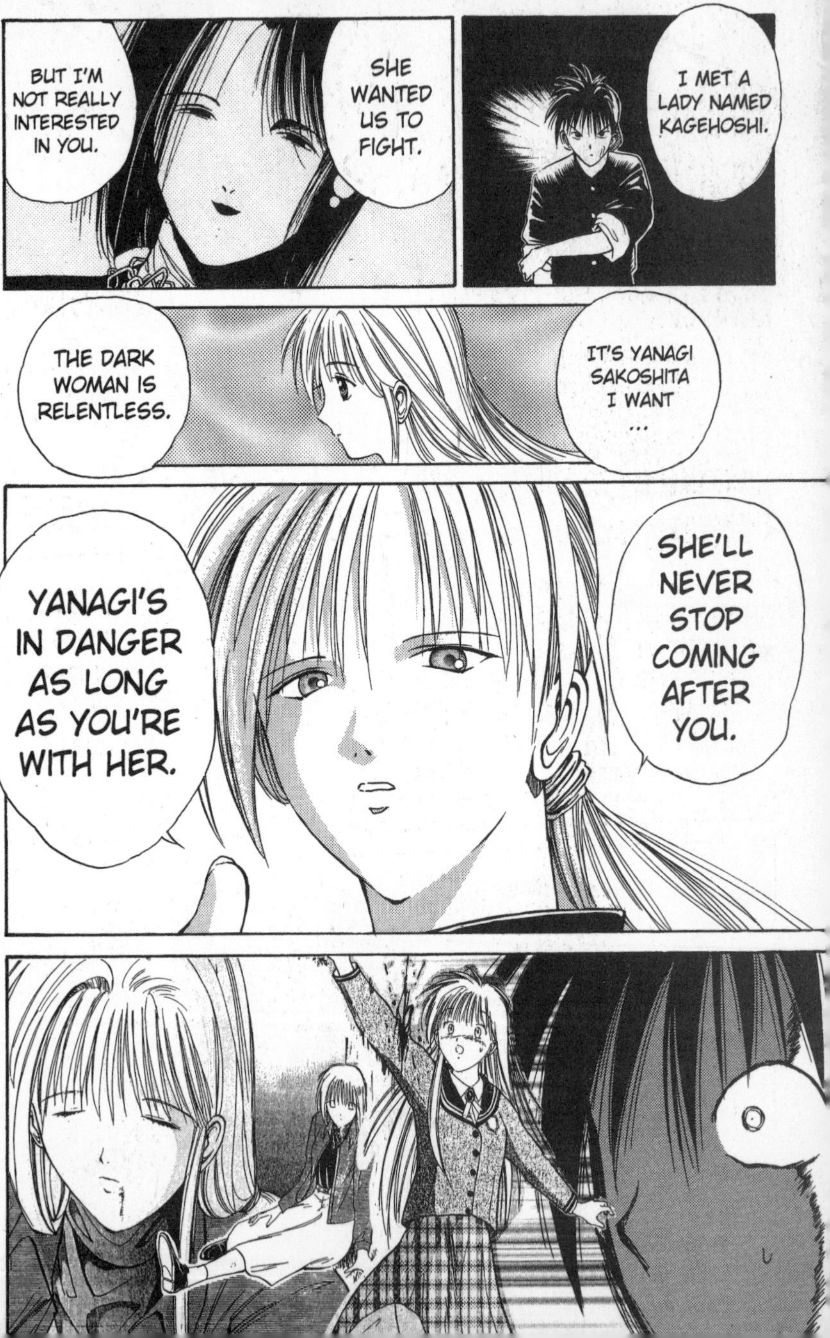
I MET A LADY NAMED KAGEHOSHI.
SHE WANTED US TO FIGHT.
BUT I'M NOT REALLY INTERESTED IN YOU.
IT'S YANAGI SAKOSHITA I WANT ...
THE DARK WOMAN IS RELENTLESS.
SHE'LL NEVER STOP COMING AFTER YOU.
YANAGI'S IN DANGER AS LONG AS YOU'RE WITH HER.

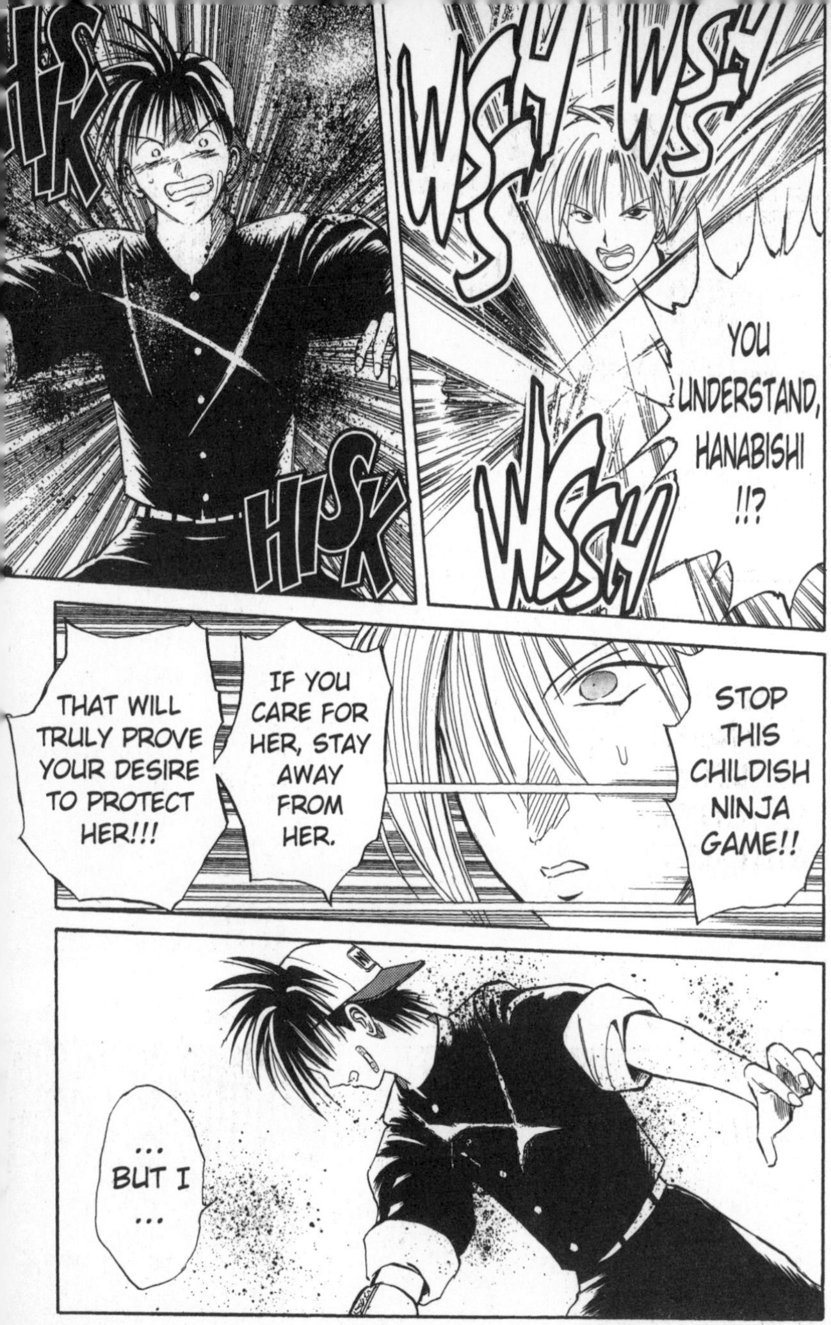
WSH WSH
WSH
YOU UNDERSTAND, HANABISHI !!?
HISK
HISK
STOP THIS CHILDISH NINJA GAME!!
IF YOU CARE FOR HER, STAY AWAY FROM HER.
THAT WILL TRULY PROVE YOUR DESIRE TO PROTECT HER!!!
... BUT I ...

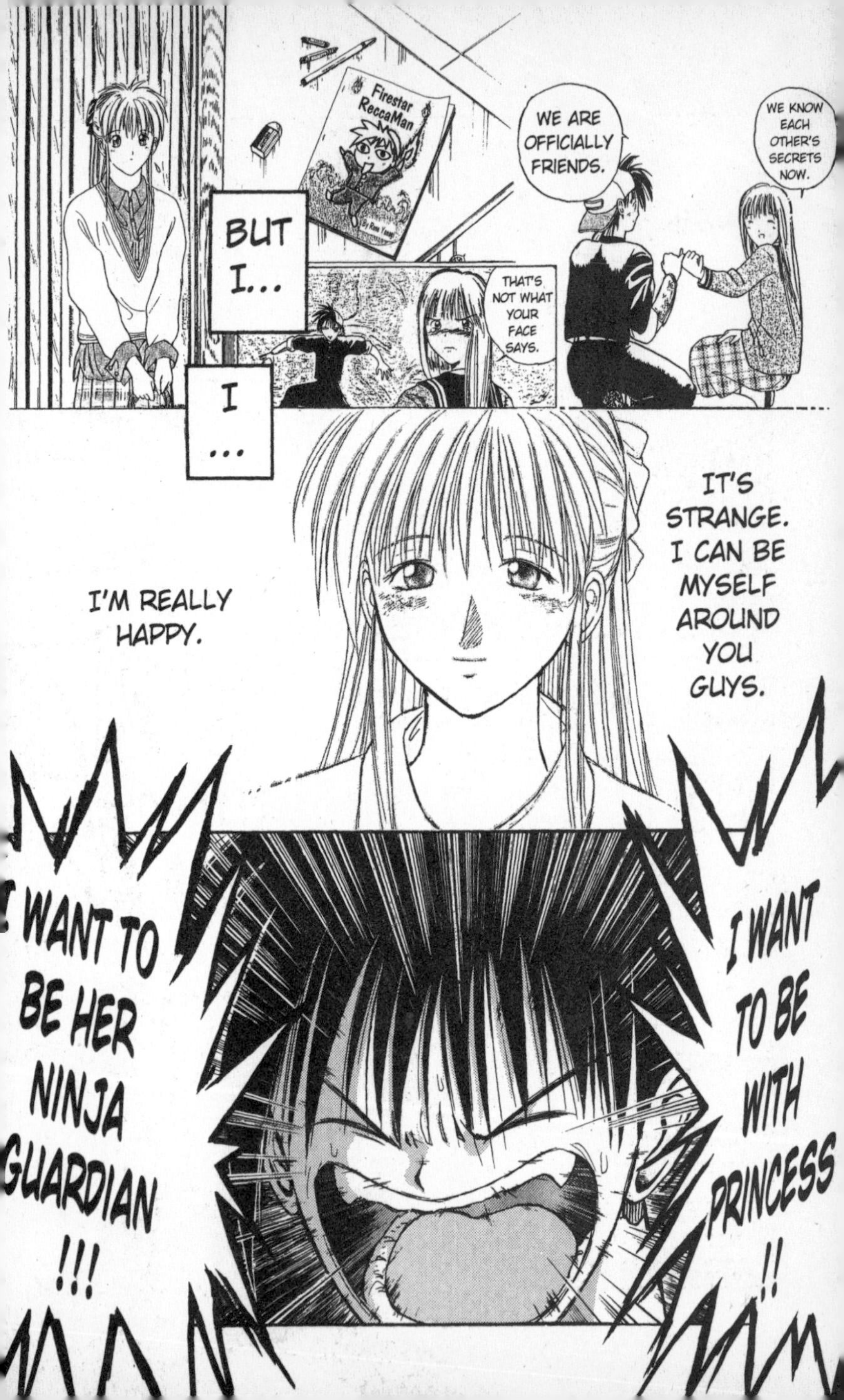
Firestar ReccaMan
WE KNOW EACH OTHER'S SECRETS NOW.
WE ARE OFFICIALLY FRIENDS.
THAT'S NOT WHAT YOUR FACE SAYS.
BUT I...
I ...
IT'S STRANGE. I CAN BE MYSELF AROUND YOU GUYS.
I'M REALLY HAPPY.
I WANT TO BE WITH PRINCESS!!
I WANT TO BE HER NINJA GUARDIAN!!!

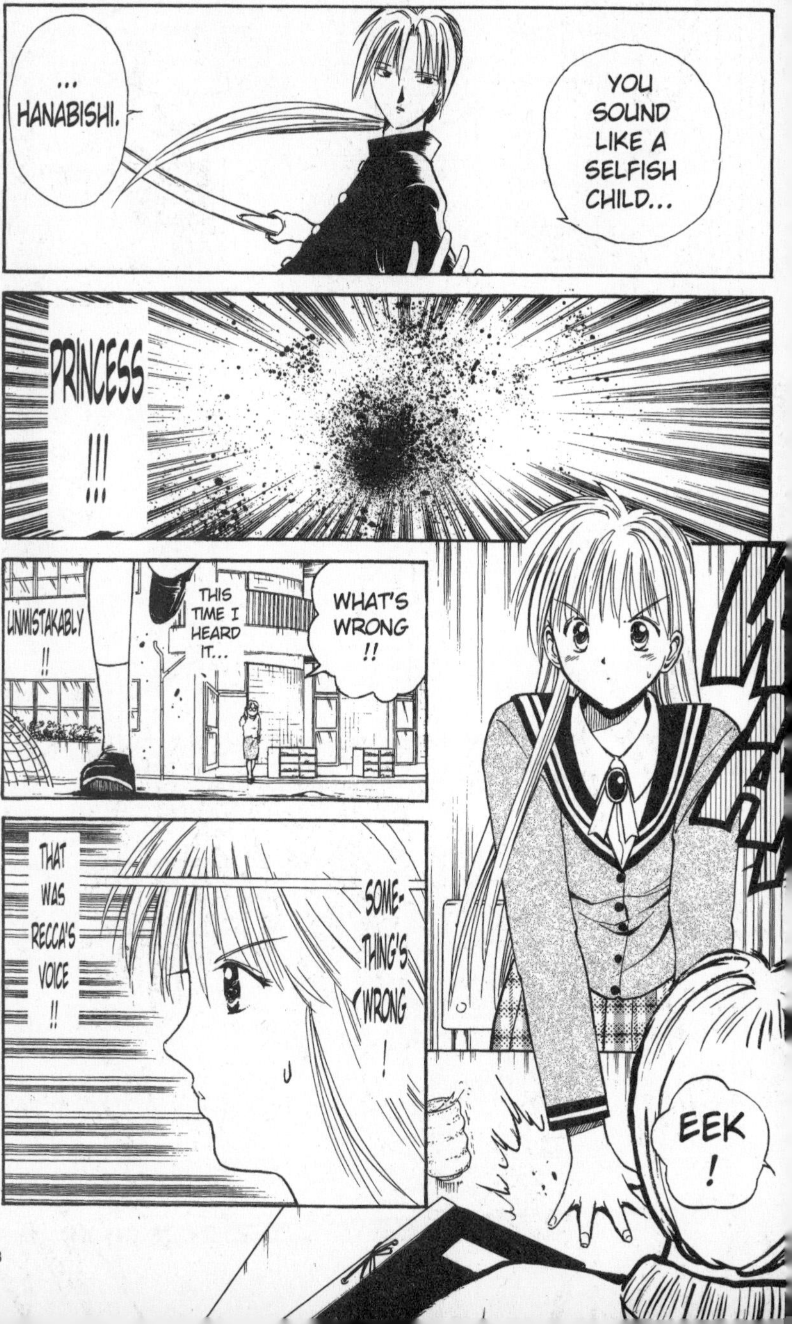
YOU SOUND LIKE A SELFISH CHILD...
... HANABISHI.
PRINCESS !!!
WHAT'S WRONG !!
THIS TIME I HEARD IT...
UNMISTAKABLY !!
EEK !
SOME-THING'S WRONG !
THAT WAS RECCA'S VOICE !!

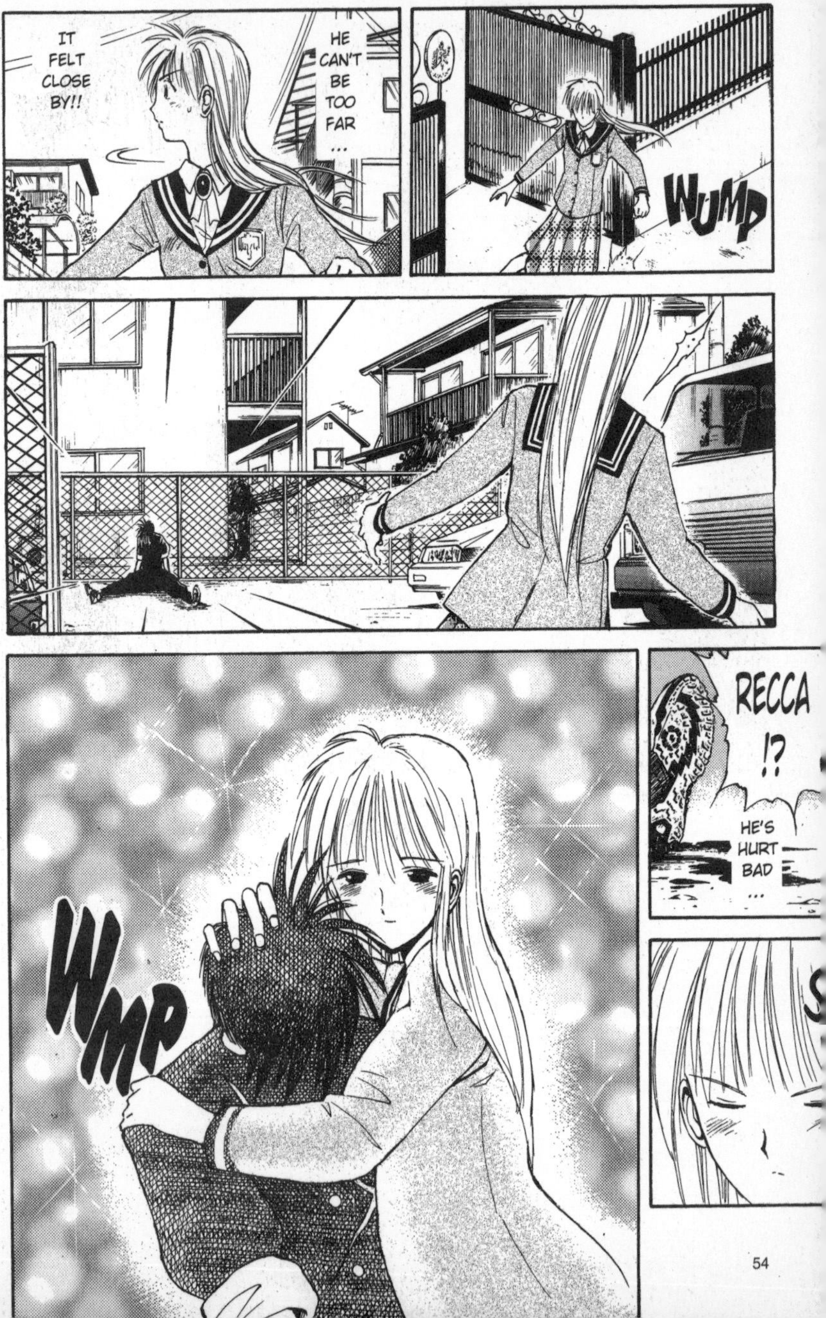

IT FELT CLOSE BY!!
HE CAN'T BE TOO FAR ...
WUMP
RECCA !?
HE'S HURT BAD ...
WMP

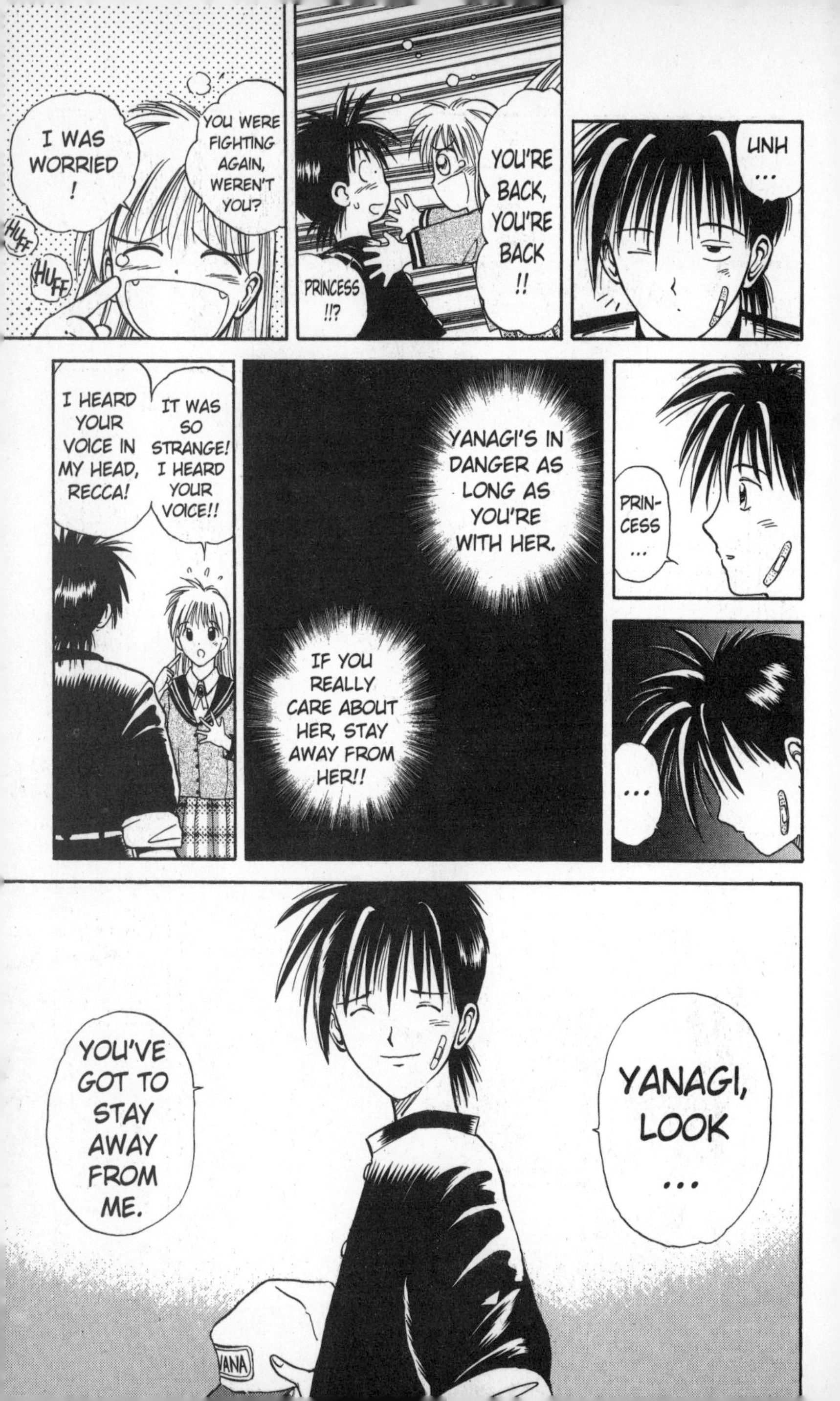
UNH ...
YOU'RE BACK, YOU'RE BACK !!
PRINCESS !!?
YOU WERE FIGHTING AGAIN, WEREN'T YOU?
I WAS WORRIED !
HUFF
HUFF
PRIN-CESS ...
...
YANAGI'S IN DANGER AS LONG AS YOU'RE WITH HER.
IF YOU REALLY CARE ABOUT HER, STAY AWAY FROM HER!!
IT WAS SO STRANGE! I HEARD YOUR VOICE!!
I HEARD YOUR VOICE IN MY HEAD, RECCA!
YANAGI, LOOK ...
YOU'VE GOT TO STAY AWAY FROM ME.

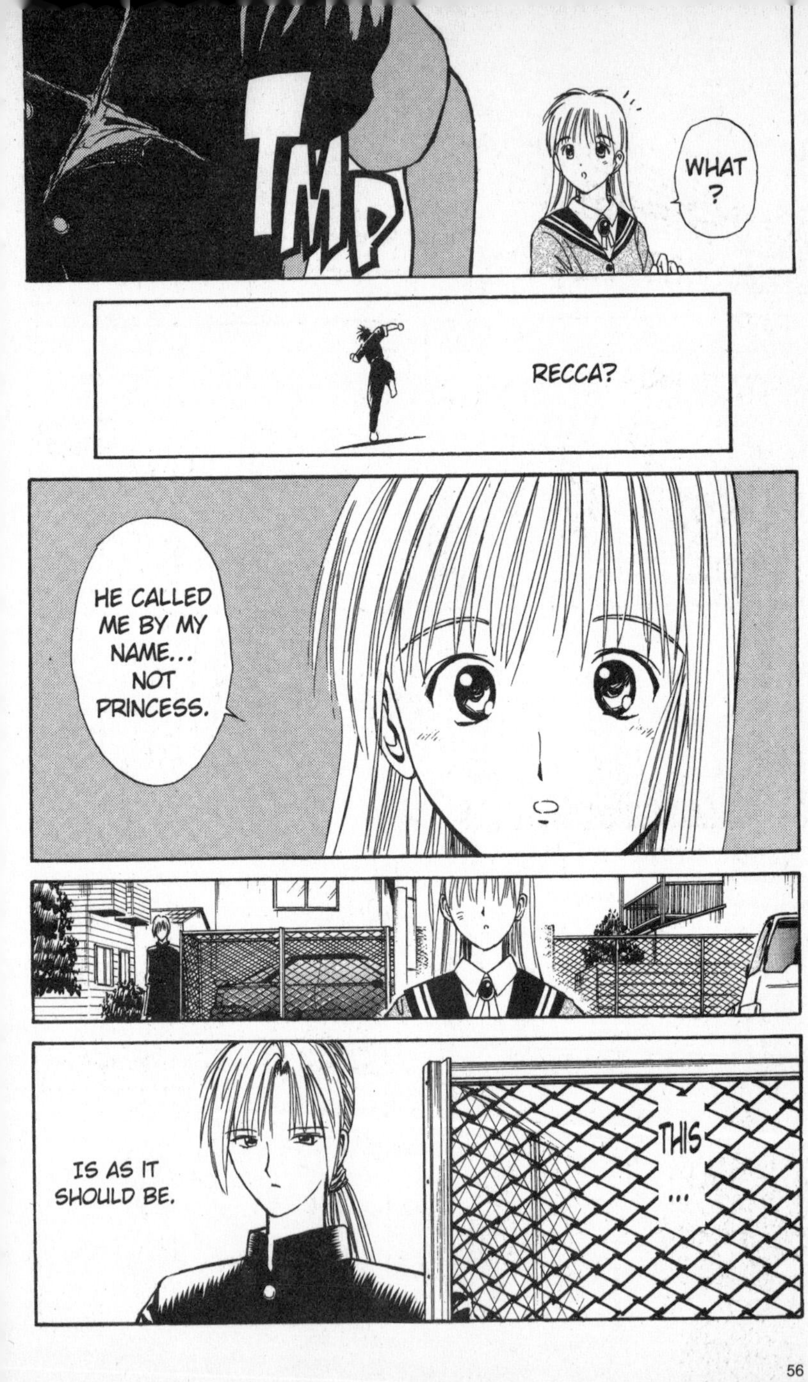
TMP
WHAT ?
RECCA?
HE CALLED ME BY MY NAME... NOT PRINCESS.
THIS ...
IS AS IT SHOULD BE.

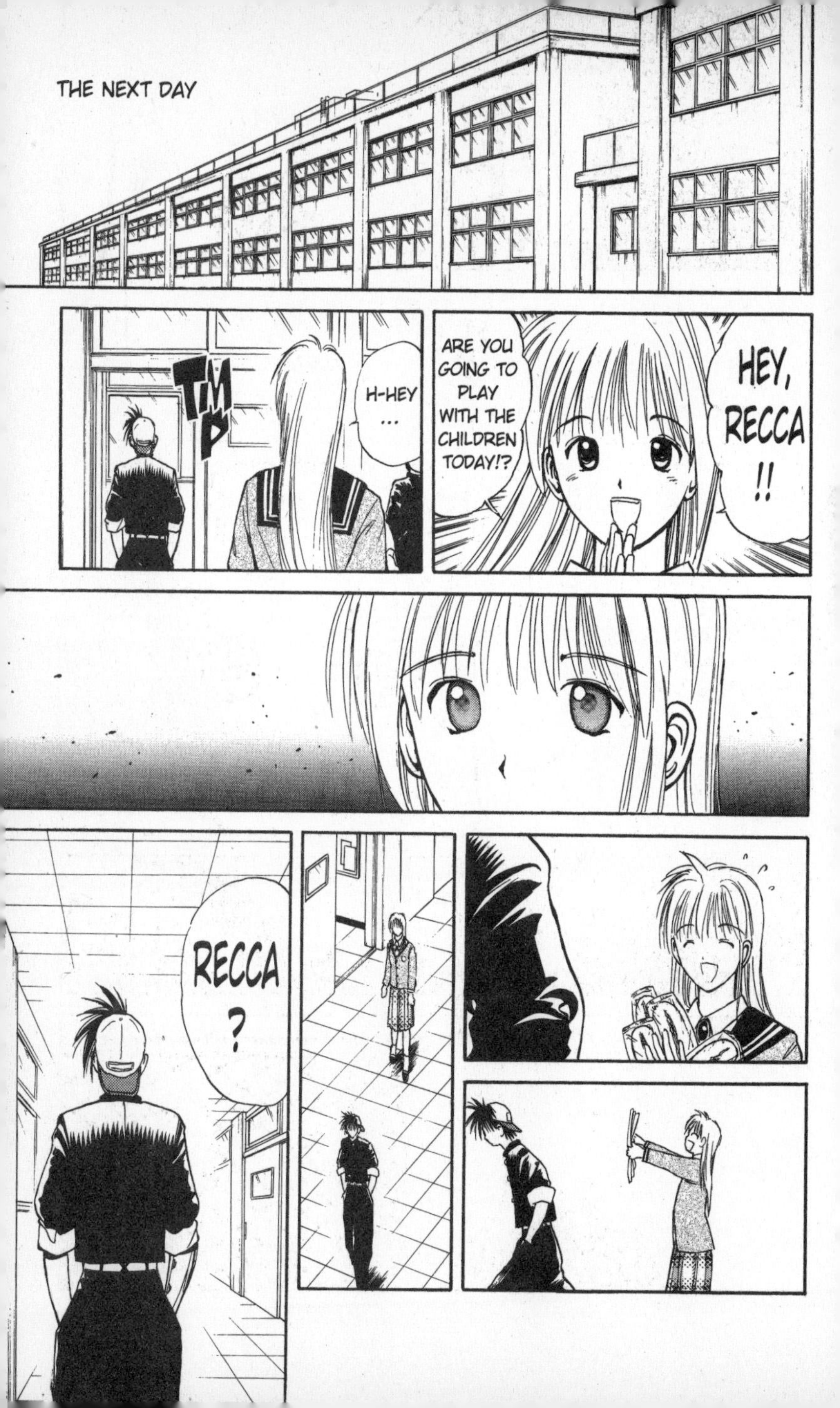
THE NEXT DAY
HEY, RECCA !!
ARE YOU GOING TO PLAY WITH THE CHILDREN TODAY!?
H-HEY ...
TMP
RECCA ?

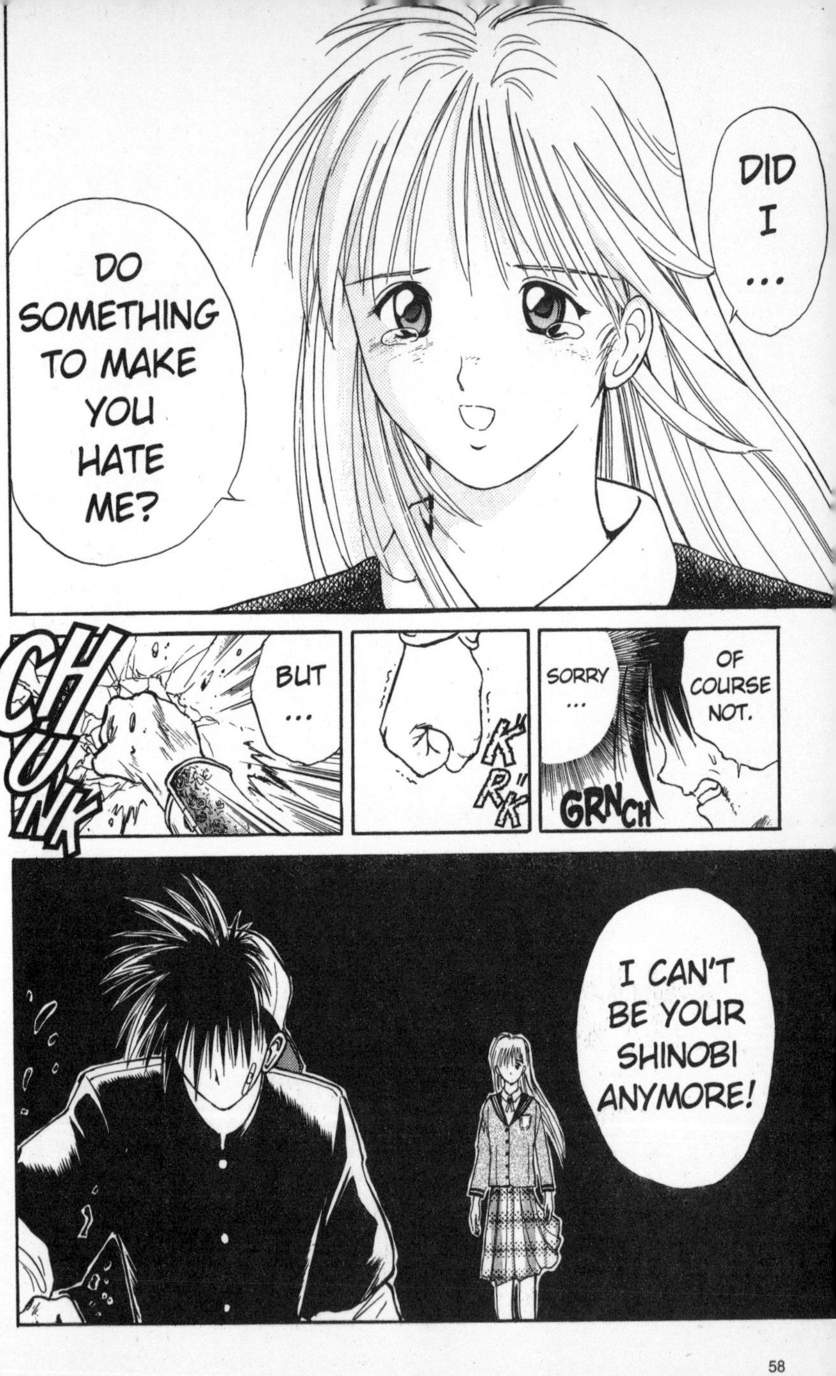
DID I ...
DO SOMETHING TO MAKE YOU HATE ME?
OF COURSE NOT.
SORRY ...
GRNCH
K'R'K
BUT ...
CHUNK
I CAN'T BE YOUR SHINOBI ANYMORE!

烈火の炎

~FLAME OF RECCA~

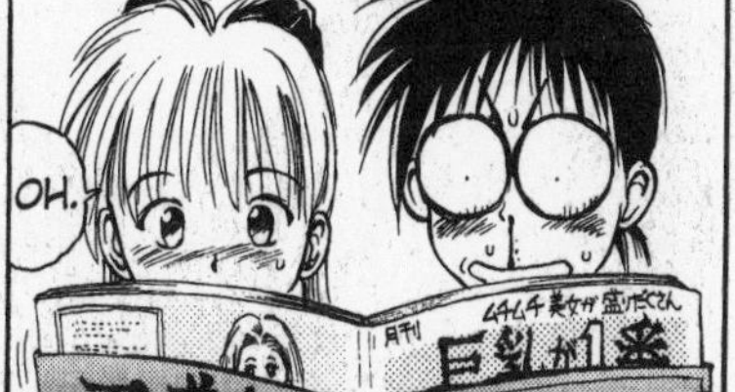
OH.
ムチムチ美女が盛りだくさん
月刊

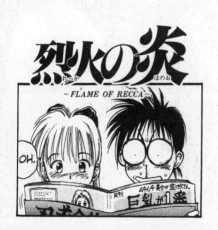

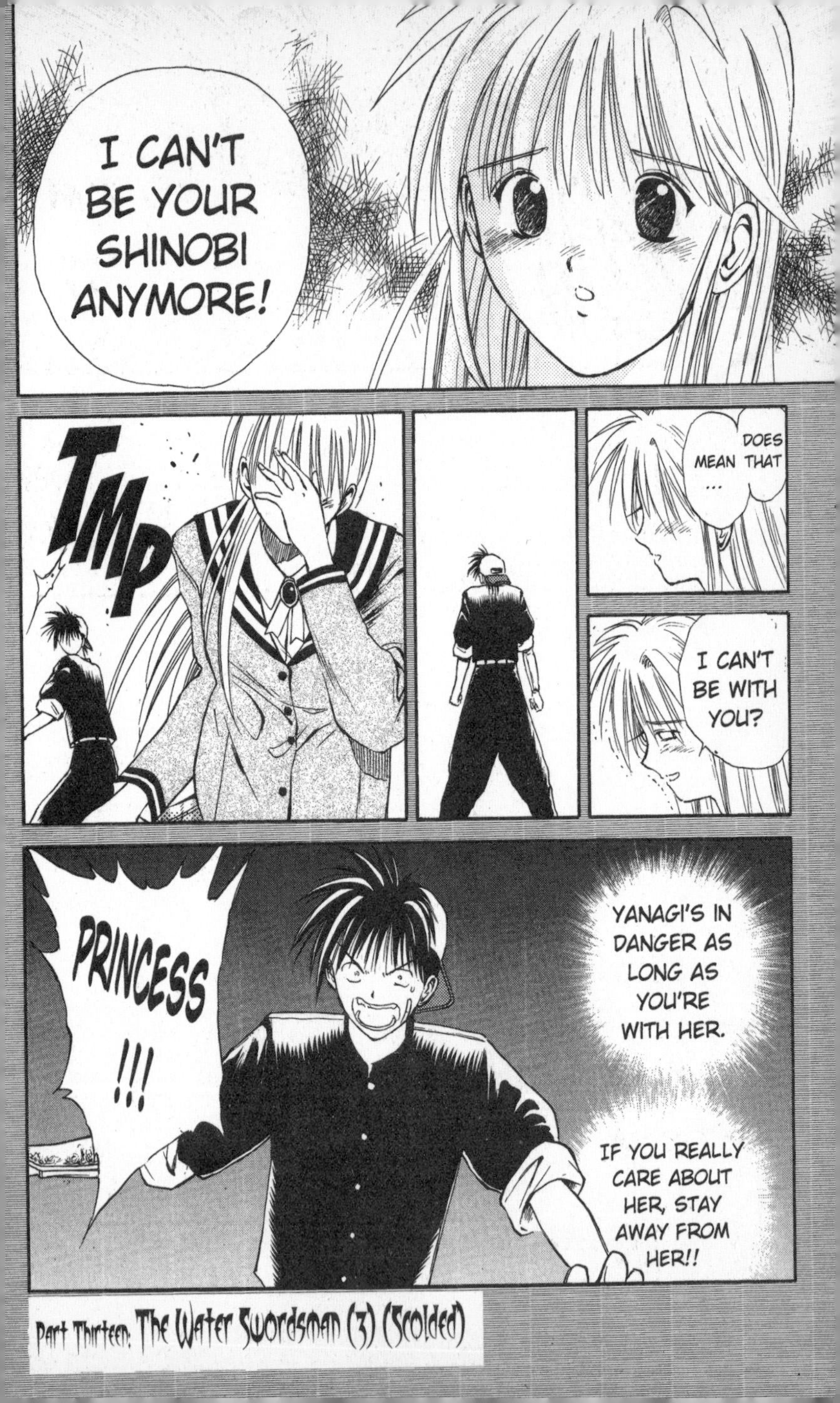
I CAN'T BE YOUR SHINOBI ANYMORE!
DOES MEAN THAT ...
I CAN'T BE WITH YOU?
TMP
YANAGI'S IN DANGER AS LONG AS YOU'RE WITH HER.
IF YOU REALLY CARE ABOUT HER, STAY AWAY FROM HER!!
PRINCESS !!!

Part Thirteen: The Water Swordsman (3) (Scolded)

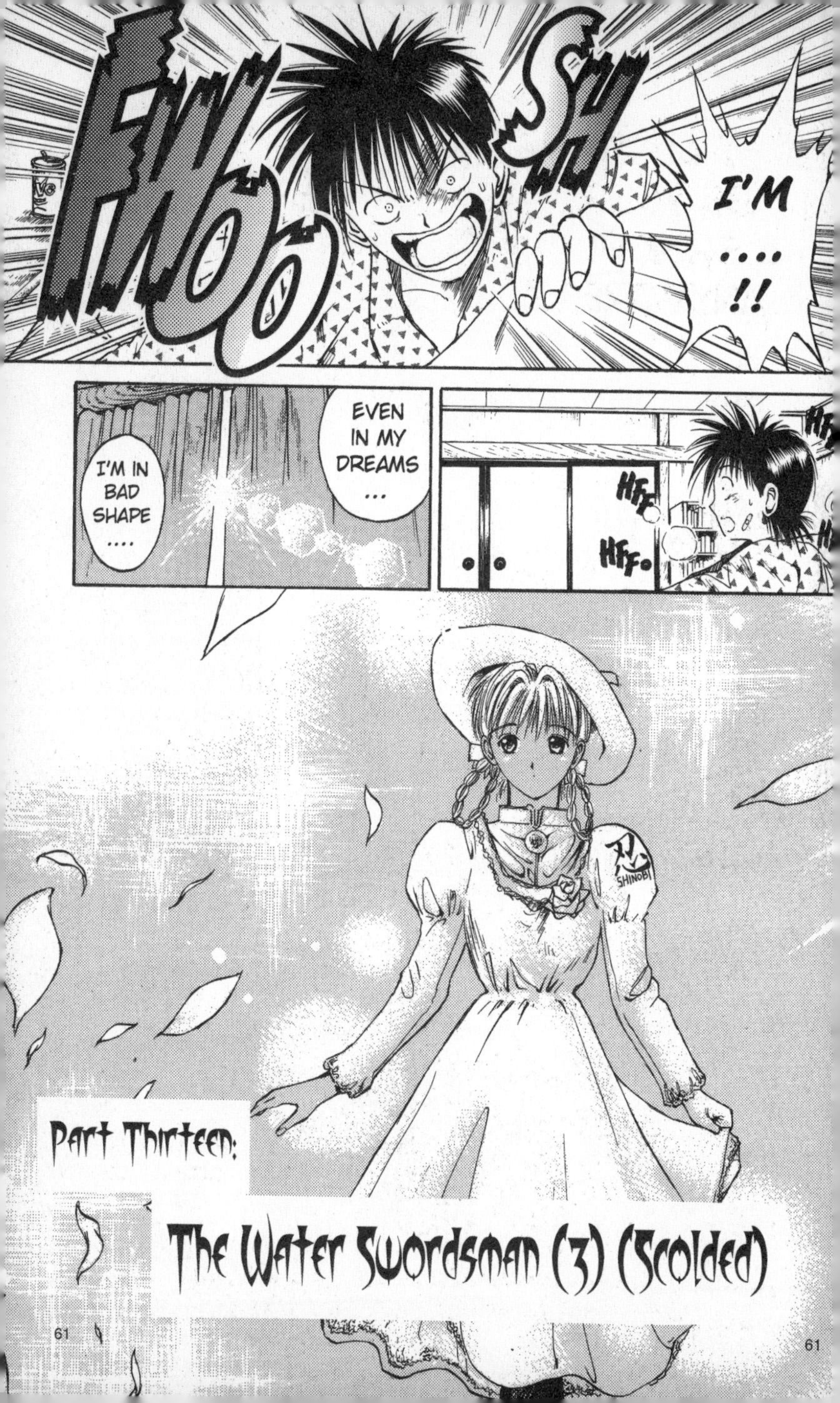
FWOOSH
I'M .... !!
HFF HFF
EVEN IN MY DREAMS ...
I'M IN BAD SHAPE ....
SHINOBI
Part Thirteen:
The Water Swordsman (3) (Scolded)

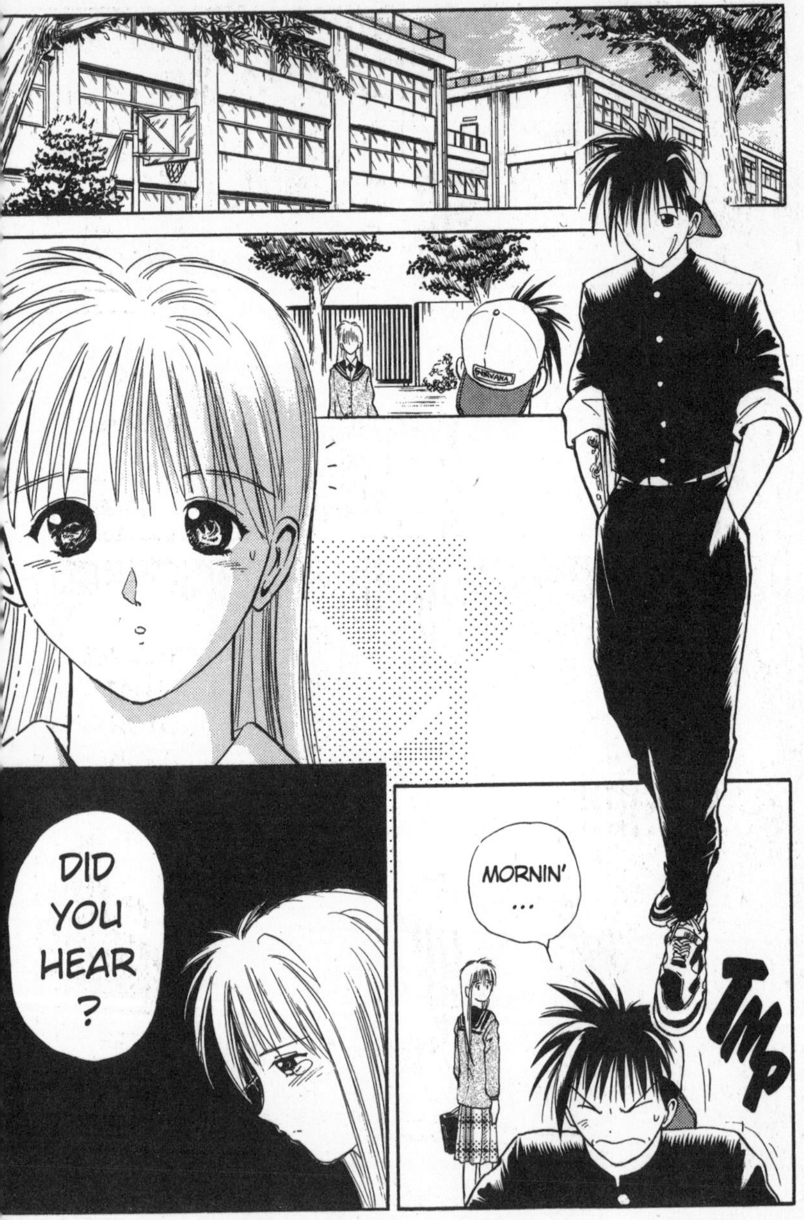
MORNIN' ...
TMP
DID YOU HEAR ?

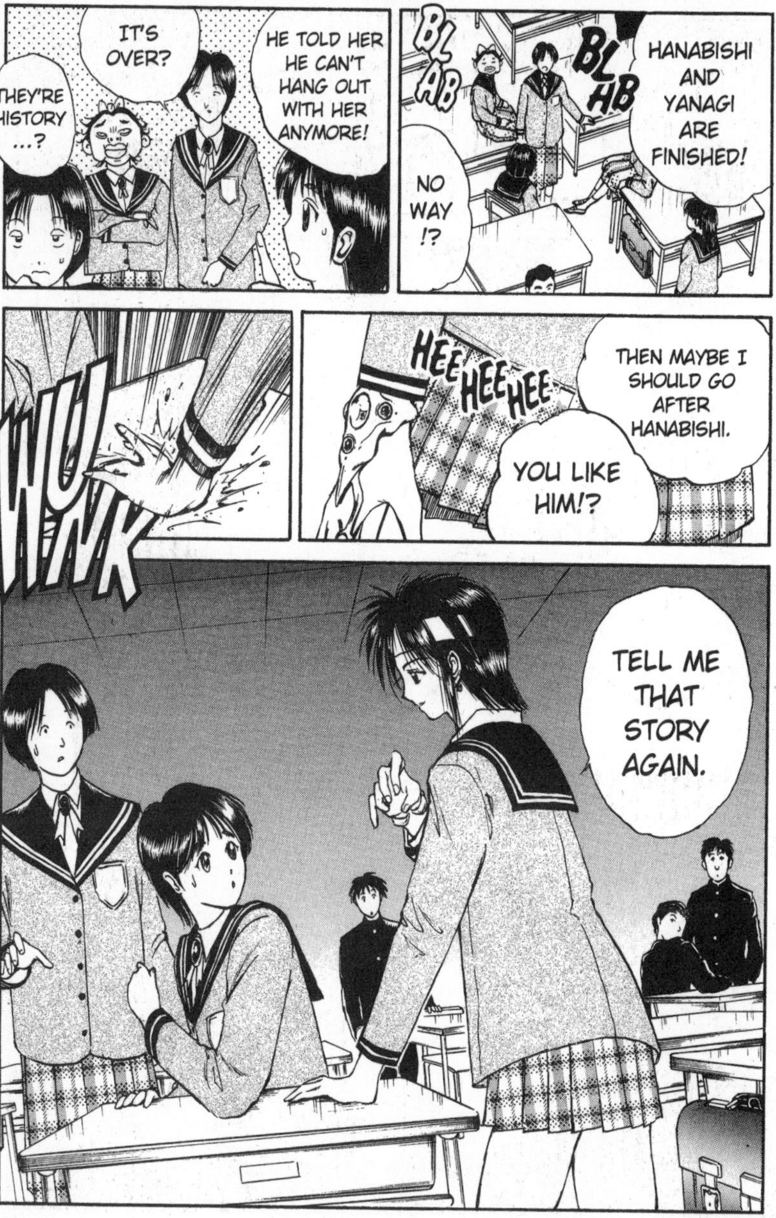

IT'S OVER?
THEY'RE HISTORY ...?
HE TOLD HER HE CAN'T HANG OUT WITH HER ANYMORE!
BLAB BLAB
HANABISHI AND YANAGI ARE FINISHED!
NO WAY !?
WHUNK
HEE HEE HEE
THEN MAYBE I SHOULD GO AFTER HANABISHI.
YOU LIKE HIM!?
TELL ME THAT STORY AGAIN.

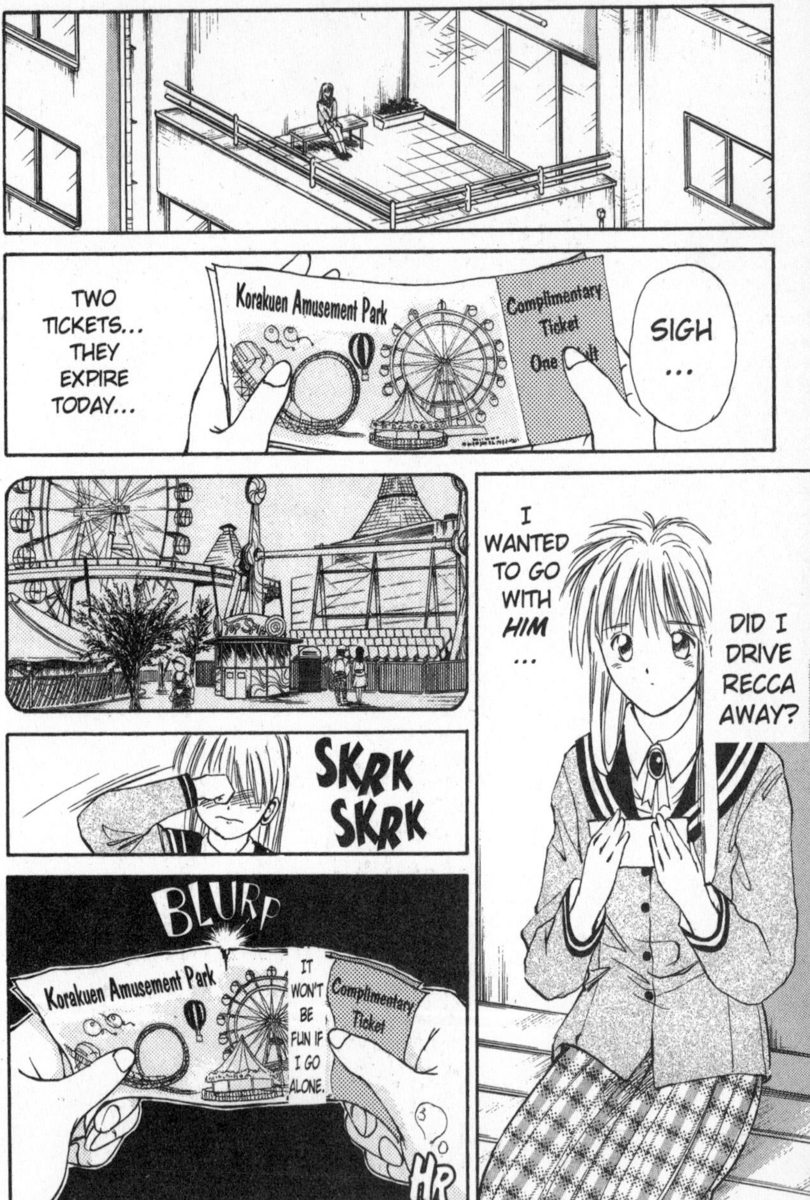

TWO TICKETS… THEY EXPIRE TODAY…
Korakuen Amusement Park
Complimentary Ticket One
SIGH…
I WANTED TO GO WITH *HIM*…
DID I DRIVE RECCA AWAY?
SKRK SKRK
BLURP
Korakuen Amusement Park
IT WON'T BE FUN IF I GO ALONE.
Complimentary Ticket
HRSSK

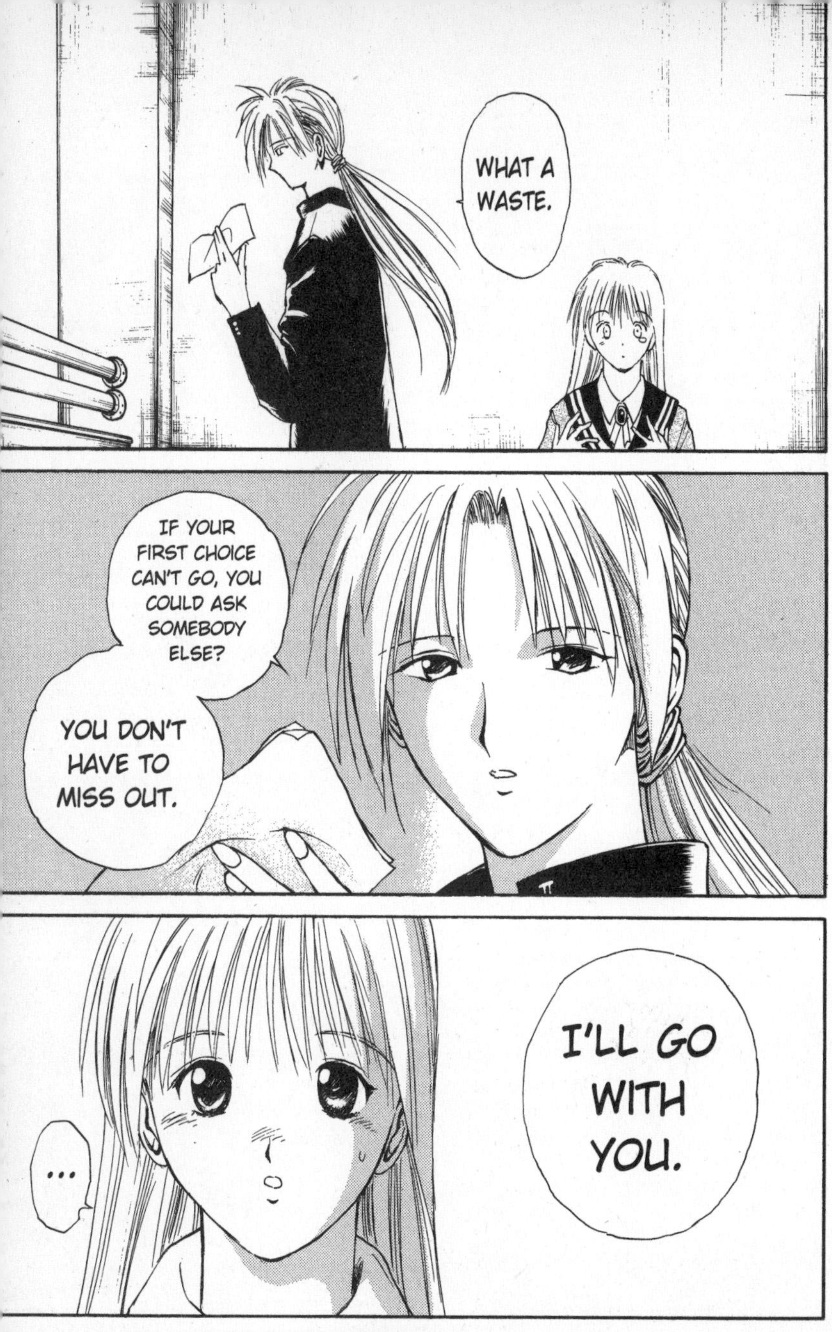
WHAT A WASTE.
IF YOUR FIRST CHOICE CAN'T GO, YOU COULD ASK SOMEBODY ELSE?
YOU DON'T HAVE TO MISS OUT.
I'LL GO WITH YOU.
...

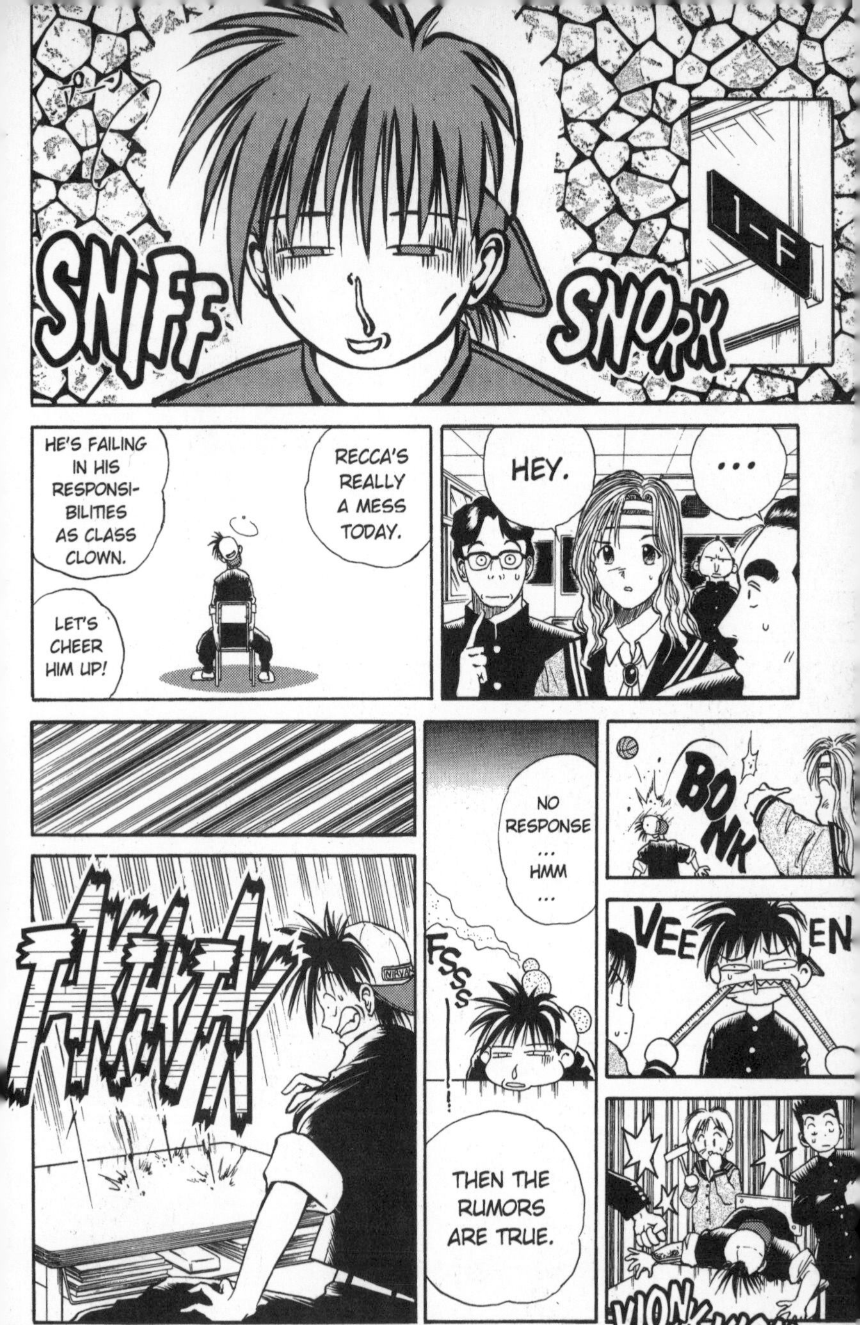

SNORK
SNIFF
1-F
...
HEY.
RECCA'S REALLY A MESS TODAY.
HE'S FAILING IN HIS RESPONSI-BILITIES AS CLASS CLOWN.
LET'S CHEER HIM UP!
BONK
VEE
EN
KLONK KLONK
NO RESPONSE ... HMM ...
FSSS
THEN THE RUMORS ARE TRUE.
THWAK

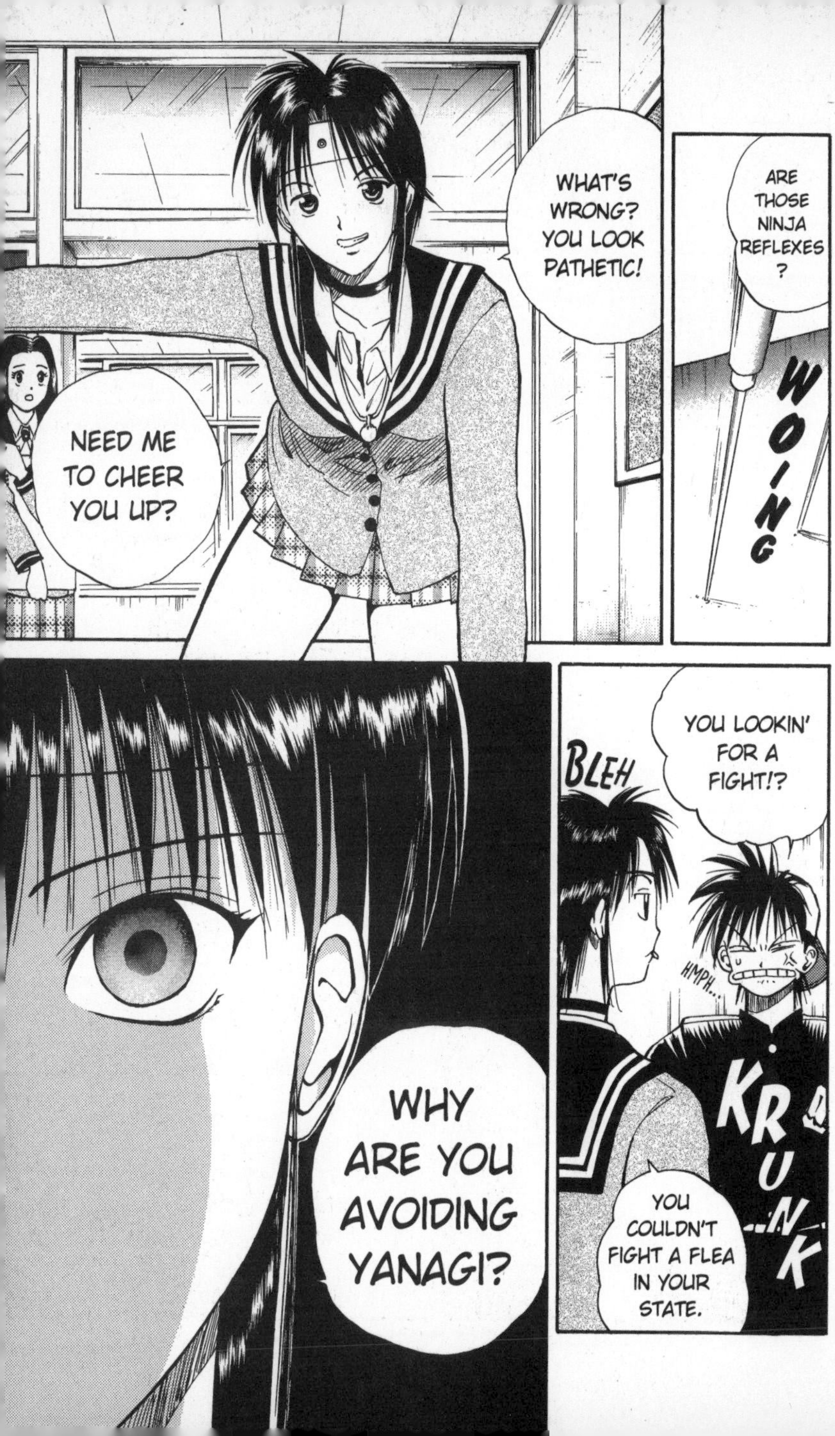
ARE THOSE NINJA REFLEXES?
WOING
WHAT'S WRONG? YOU LOOK PATHETIC!
NEED ME TO CHEER YOU UP?
BLEH
YOU LOOKIN' FOR A FIGHT!?
HMPH...
KRUNK
YOU COULDN'T FIGHT A FLEA IN YOUR STATE.
WHY ARE YOU AVOIDING YANAGI?

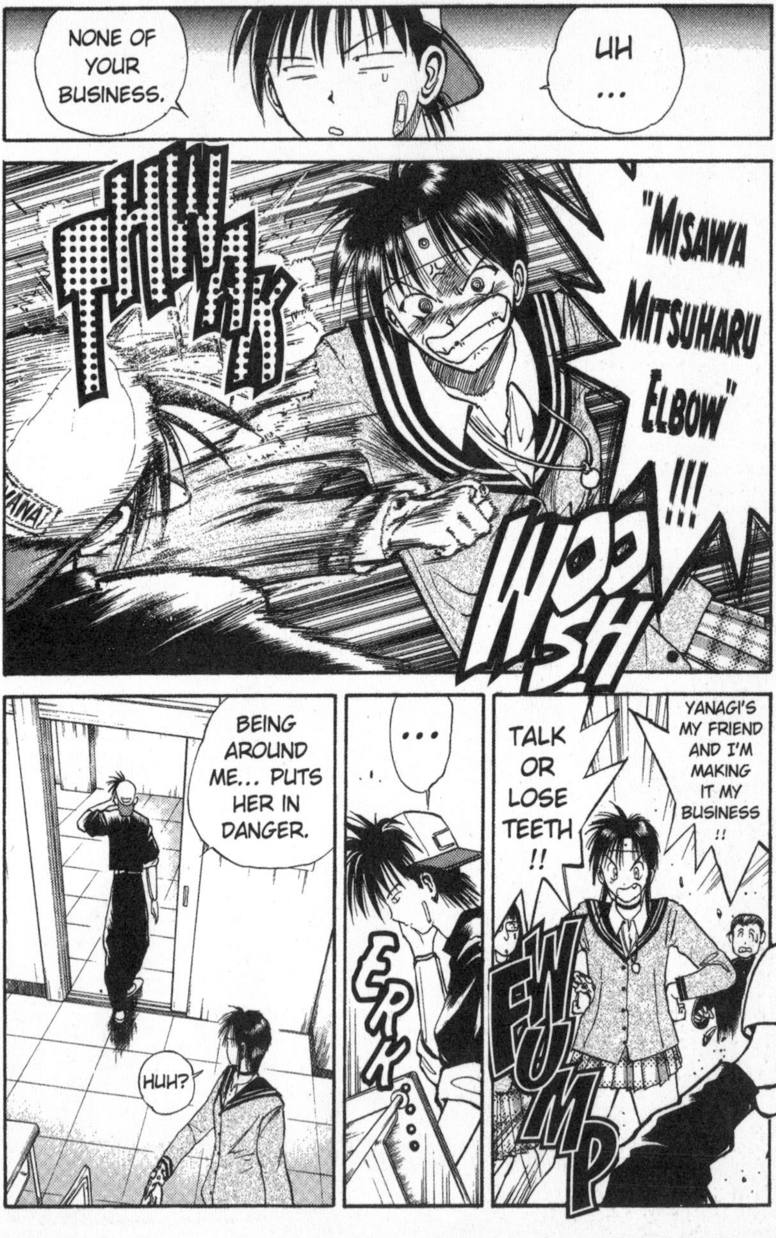
UH ...
NONE OF YOUR BUSINESS.
"MISAWA MITSUHARU ELBOW" !!!
THWAK
WOOSH
YANAGI'S MY FRIEND AND I'M MAKING IT MY BUSINESS !!
TALK OR LOSE TEETH !!
FWUMP
...
ERK
BEING AROUND ME... PUTS HER IN DANGER.
HUH?

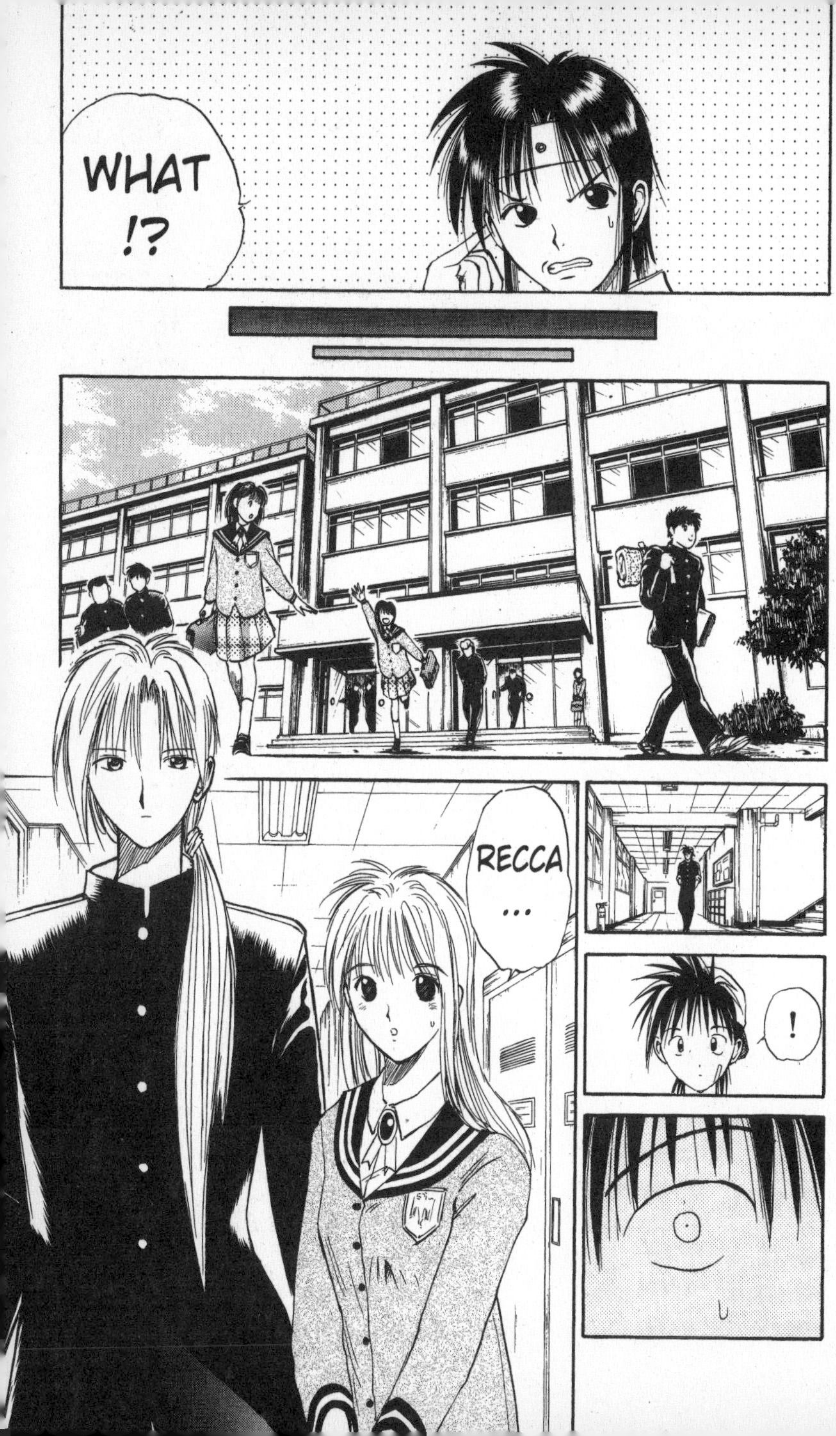
WHAT !?
RECCA ...
!

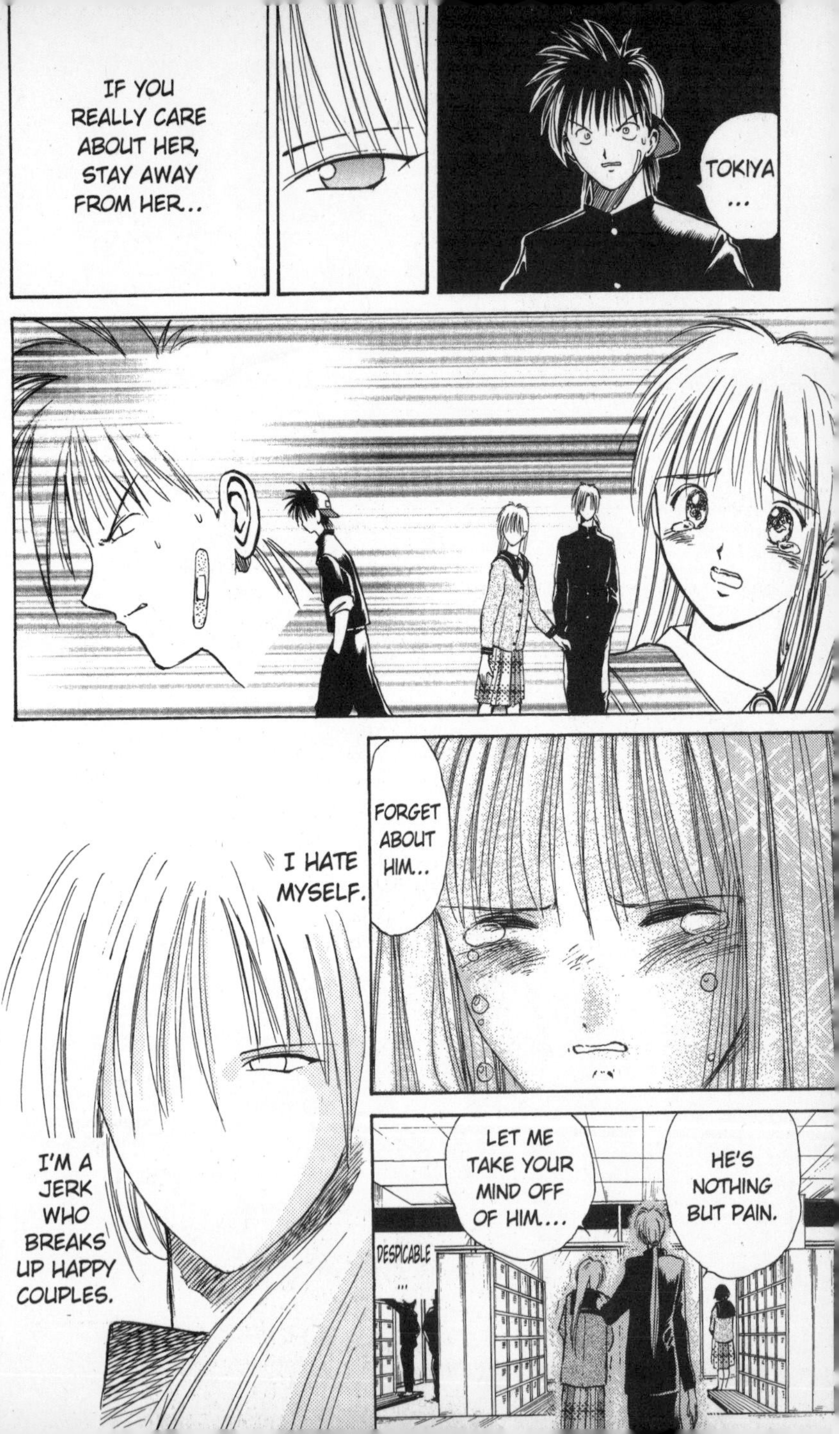
TOKIYA ...
IF YOU REALLY CARE ABOUT HER, STAY AWAY FROM HER..
FORGET ABOUT HIM..
I HATE MYSELF.
HE'S NOTHING BUT PAIN.
LET ME TAKE YOUR MIND OFF OF HIM...
DESPICABLE ...
I'M A JERK WHO BREAKS UP HAPPY COUPLES.

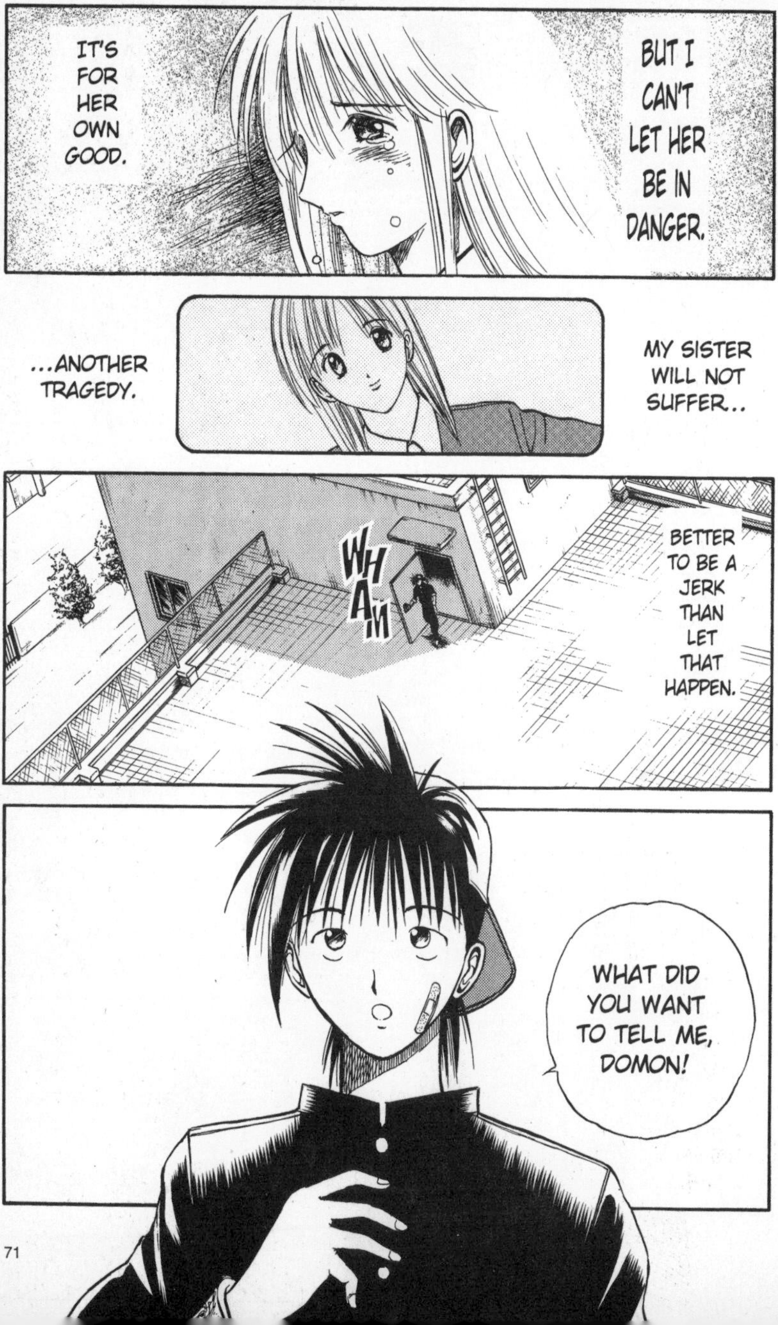
BUT I CAN'T LET HER BE IN DANGER.
IT'S FOR HER OWN GOOD.
MY SISTER WILL NOT SUFFER...
...ANOTHER TRAGEDY.
BETTER TO BE A JERK THAN LET THAT HAPPEN.
WHAM
WHAT DID YOU WANT TO TELL ME, DOMON!

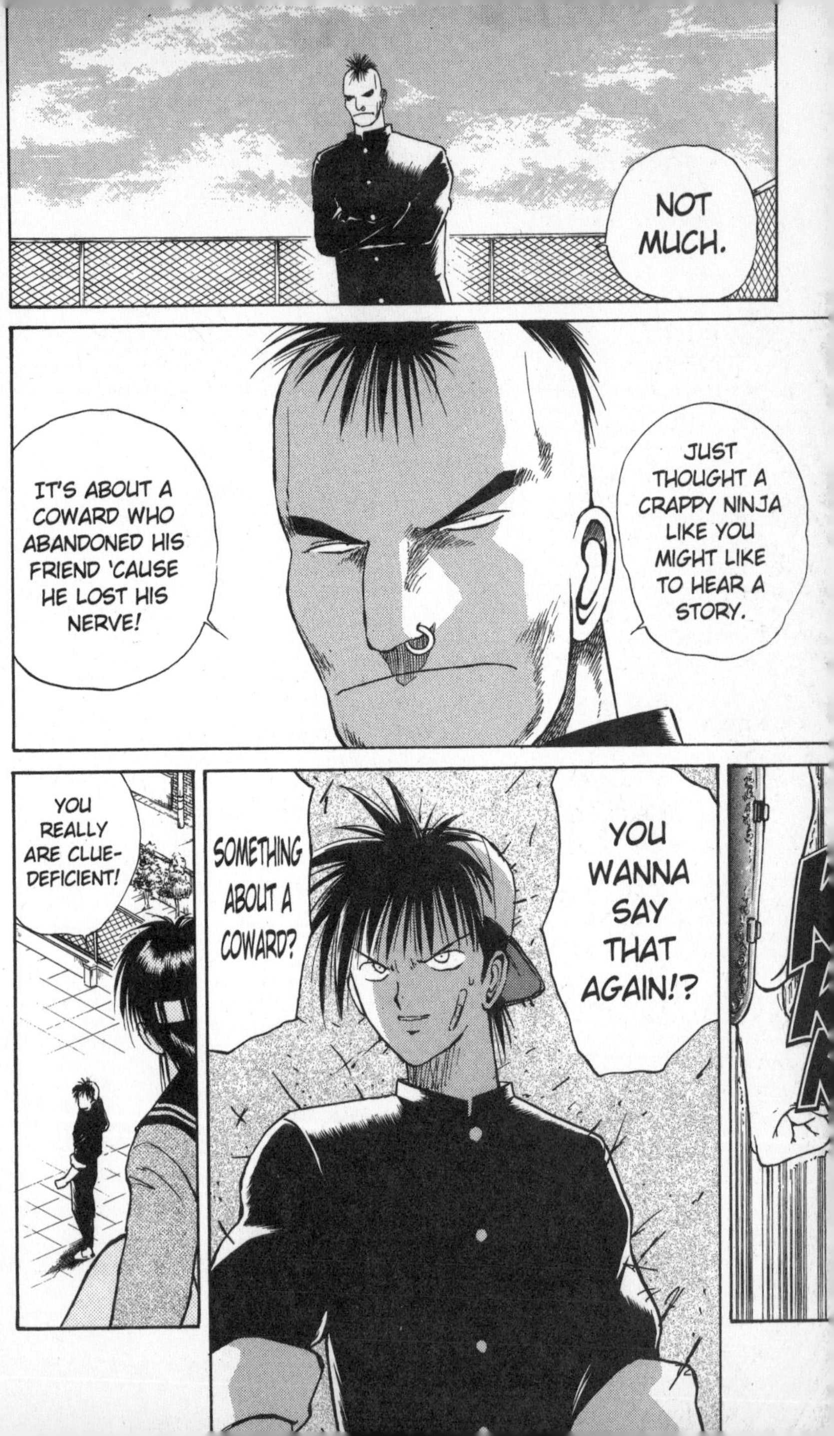
NOT MUCH.
JUST THOUGHT A CRAPPY NINJA LIKE YOU MIGHT LIKE TO HEAR A STORY.
IT'S ABOUT A COWARD WHO ABANDONED HIS FRIEND 'CAUSE HE LOST HIS NERVE!
YOU WANNA SAY THAT AGAIN!?
SOMETHING ABOUT A COWARD?
YOU REALLY ARE CLUE-DEFICIENT!

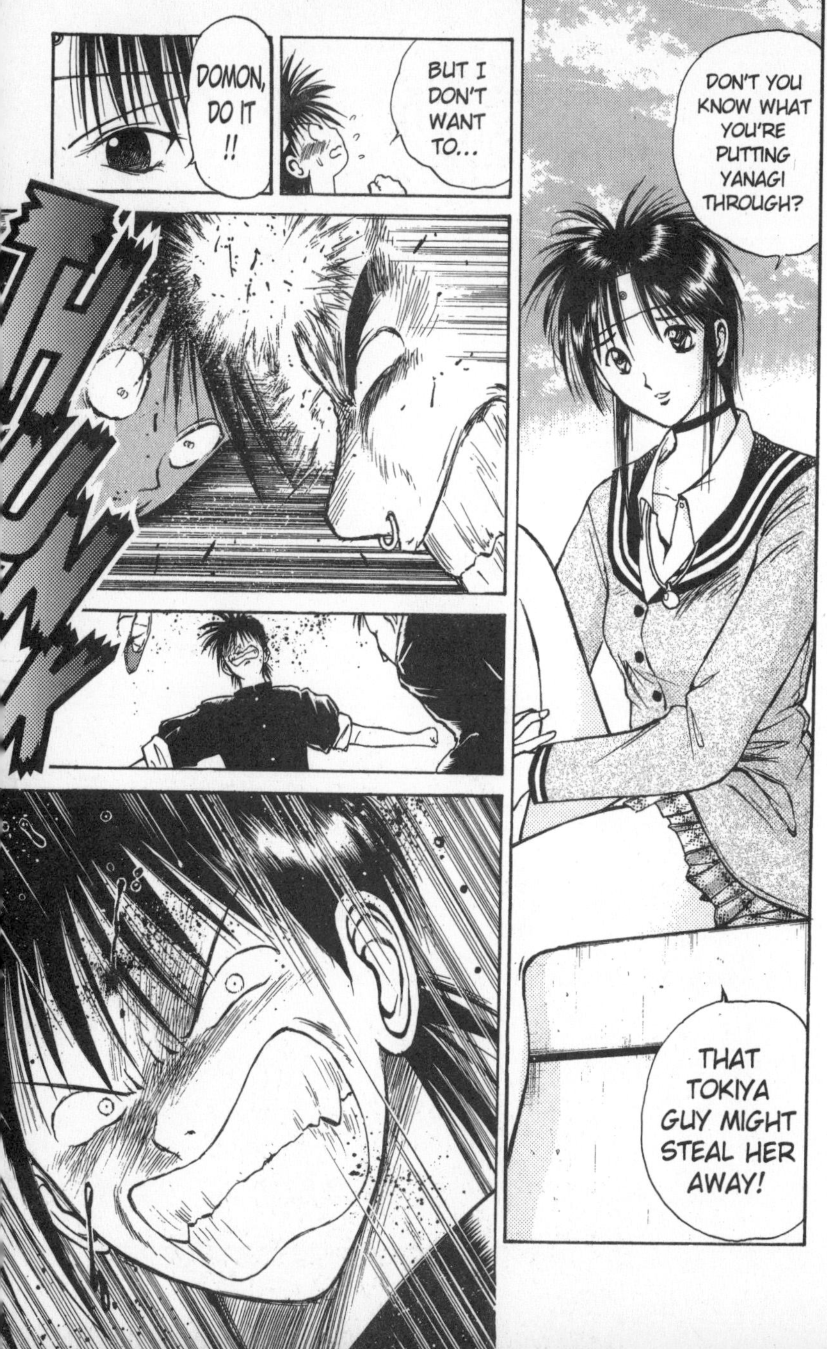
DON'T YOU KNOW WHAT YOU'RE PUTTING YANAGI THROUGH?
THAT TOKIYA GUY MIGHT STEAL HER AWAY!
BUT I DON'T WANT TO...
DOMON, DO IT !!

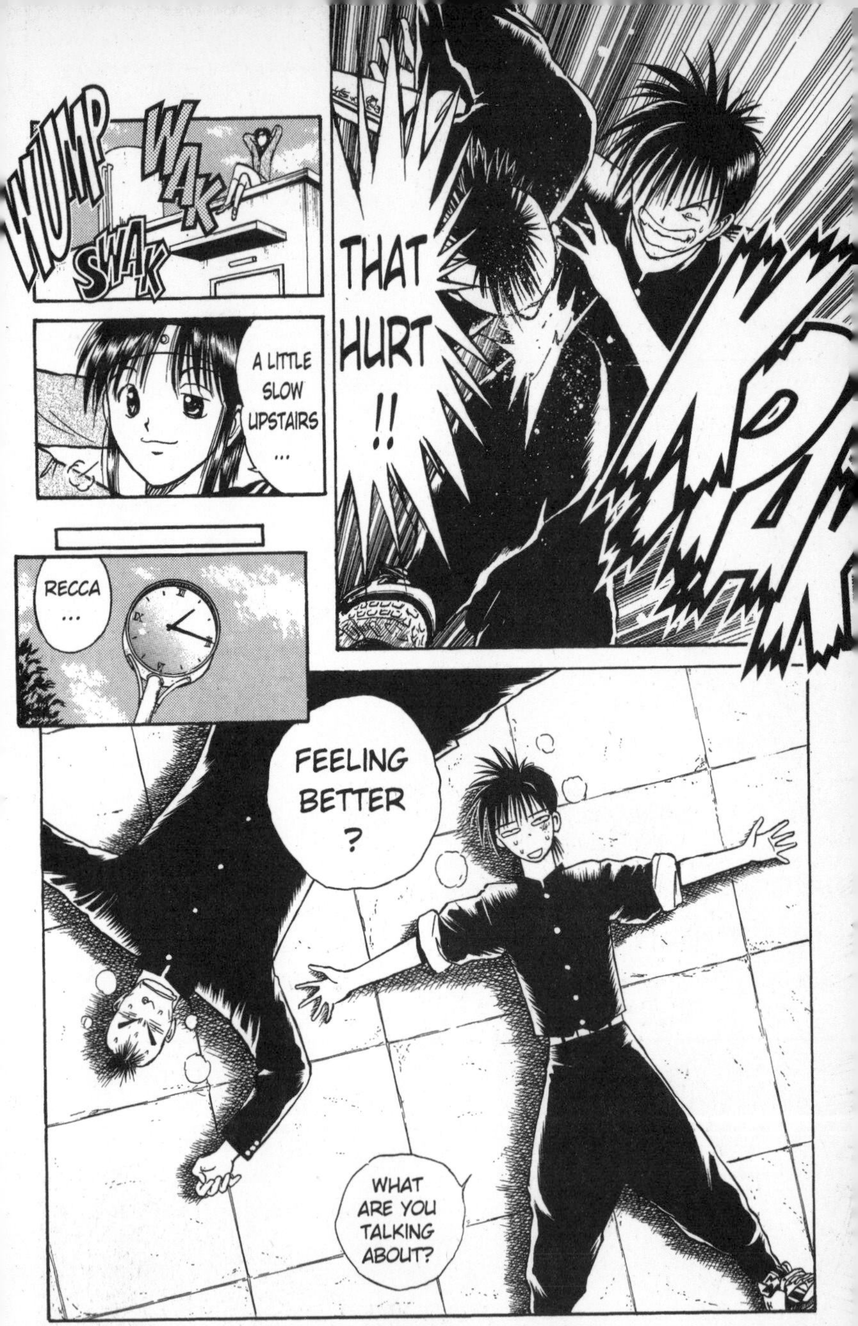
THAT HURT!!
WUMP
WAK
SWAK
A LITTLE SLOW UPSTAIRS...
RECCA...
FEELING BETTER?
WHAT ARE YOU TALKING ABOUT?

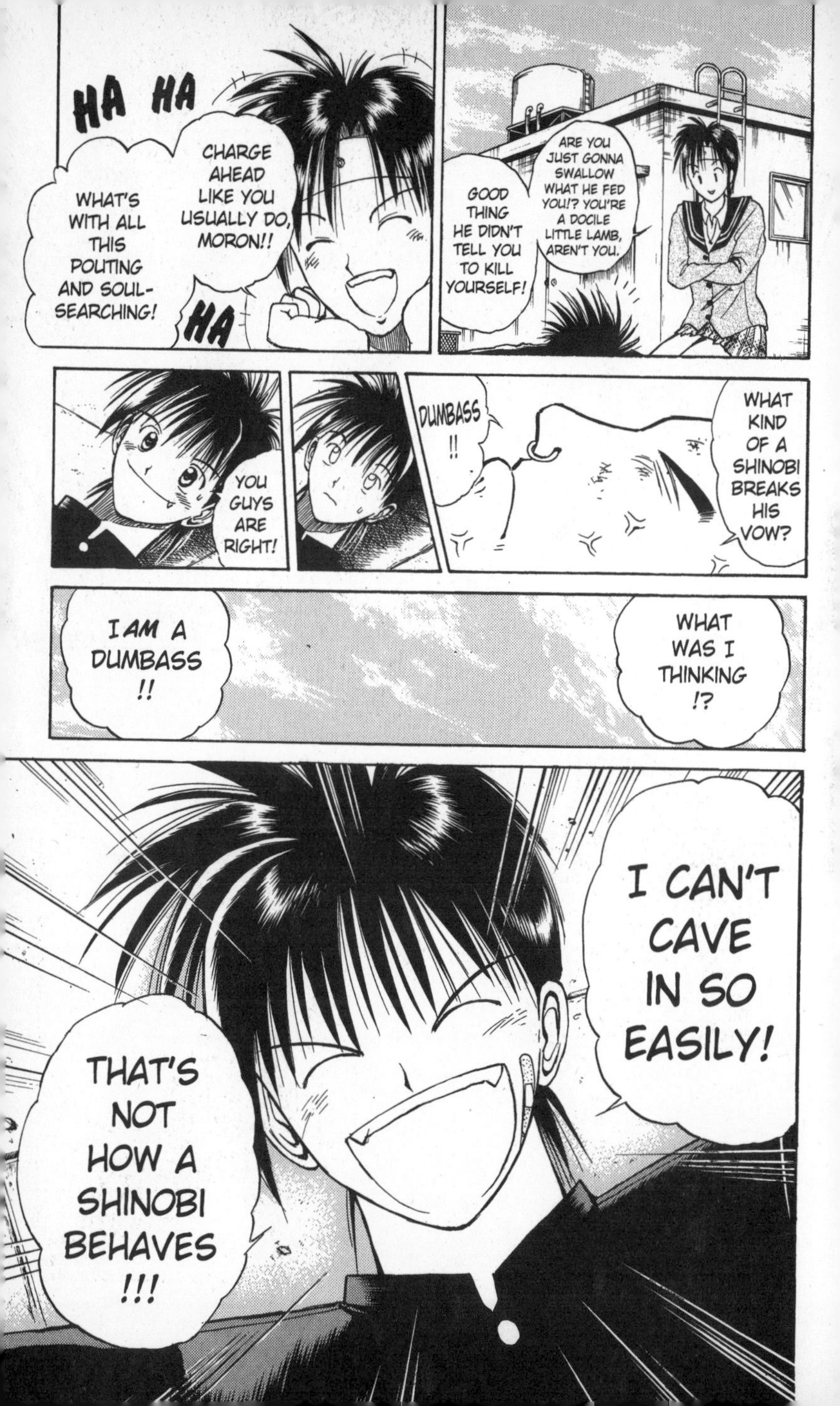
ARE YOU JUST GONNA SWALLOW WHAT HE FED YOU!? YOU'RE A DOCILE LITTLE LAMB, AREN'T YOU.
GOOD THING HE DIDN'T TELL YOU TO KILL YOURSELF!
CHARGE AHEAD LIKE YOU USUALLY DO, MORON!!
WHAT'S WITH ALL THIS POUTING AND SOUL-SEARCHING!
HA HA
HA
WHAT KIND OF A SHINOBI BREAKS HIS VOW?
DUMBASS !!
YOU GUYS ARE RIGHT!
WHAT WAS I THINKING !?
I AM A DUMBASS !!
I CAN'T CAVE IN SO EASILY!
THAT'S NOT HOW A SHINOBI BEHAVES !!!

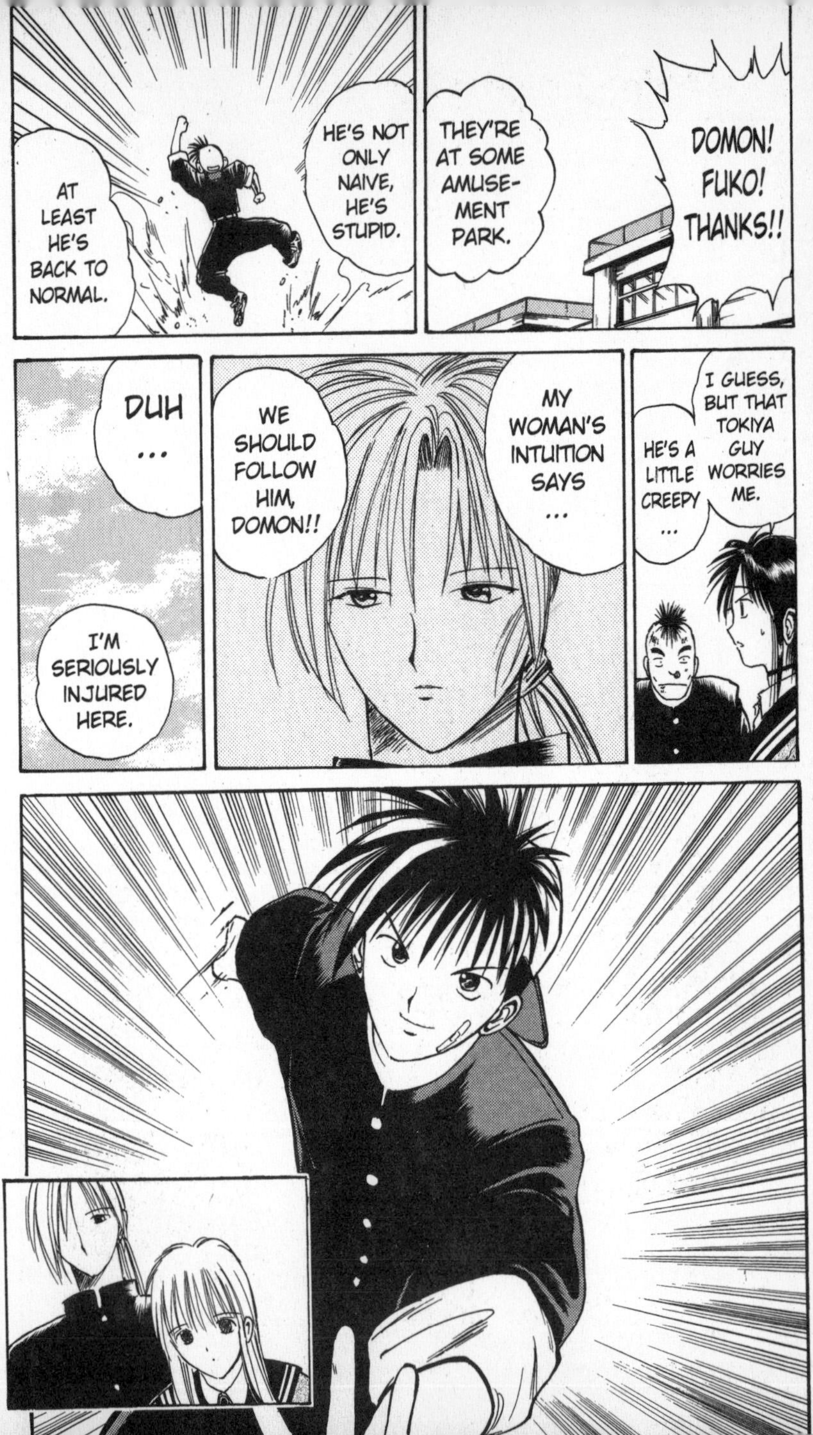
DOMON! FUKO! THANKS!!
THEY'RE AT SOME AMUSE-MENT PARK.
HE'S NOT ONLY NAIVE, HE'S STUPID.
AT LEAST HE'S BACK TO NORMAL.
I GUESS, BUT THAT TOKIYA GUY WORRIES ME.
HE'S A LITTLE CREEPY ...
MY WOMAN'S INTUITION SAYS ...
WE SHOULD FOLLOW HIM, DOMON!!
DUH ...
I'M SERIOUSLY INJURED HERE.

Part Fourteen: The Water Swordsman (4) (Mikagami's Past)

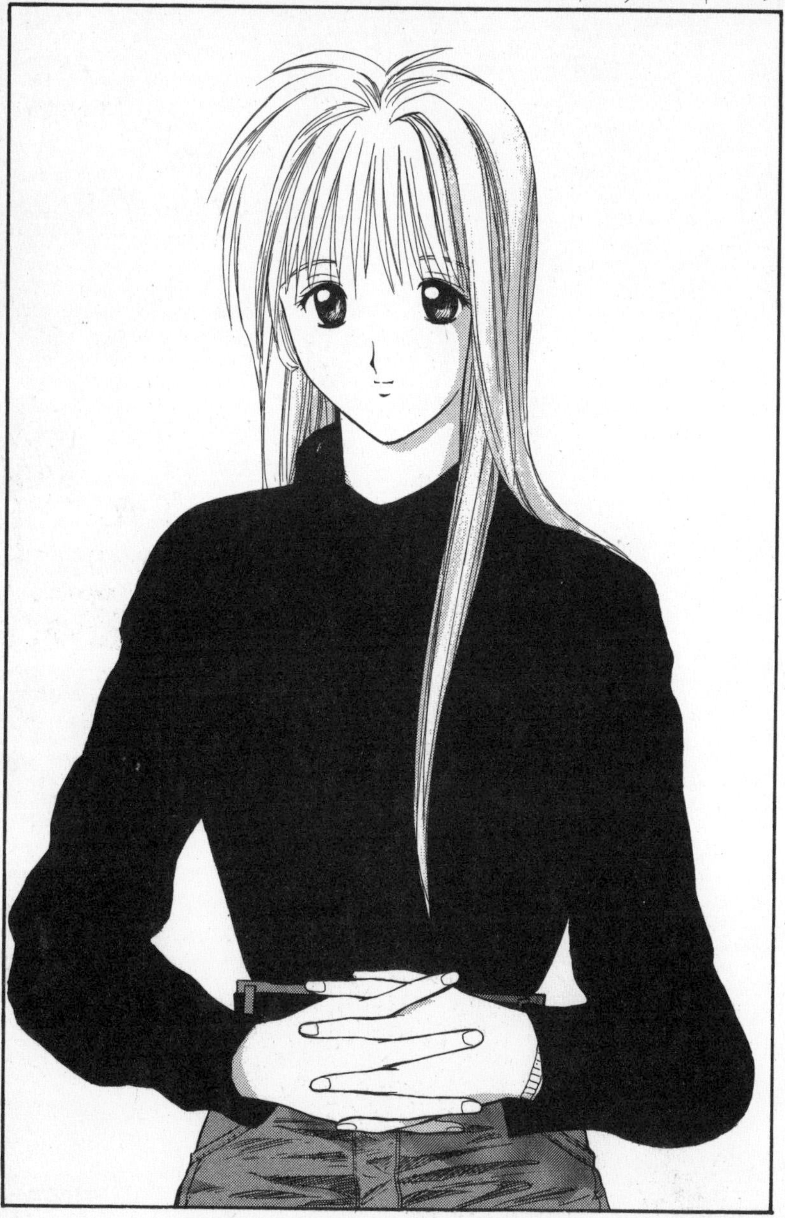

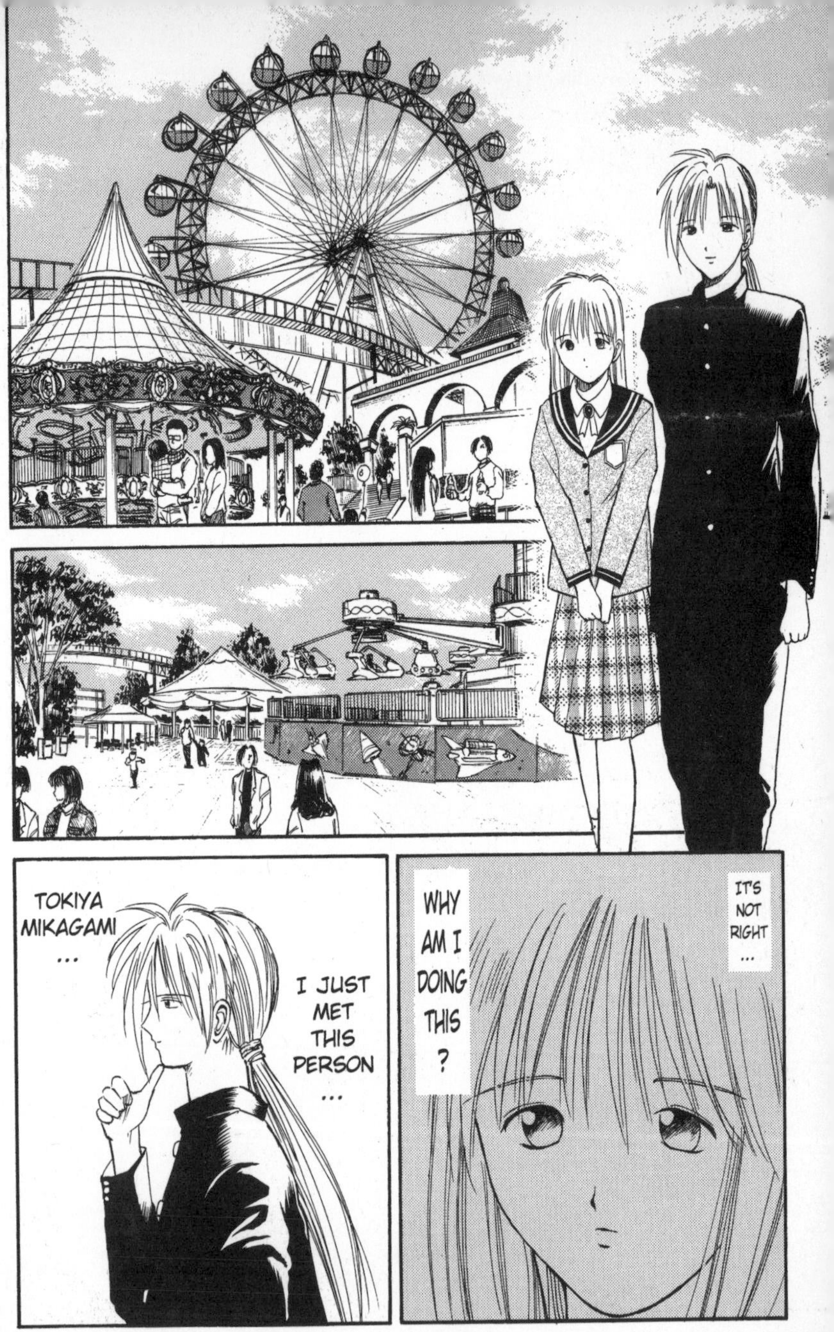
IT'S NOT RIGHT ...
WHY AM I DOING THIS ?
TOKIYA MIKAGAMI ...
I JUST MET THIS PERSON ...

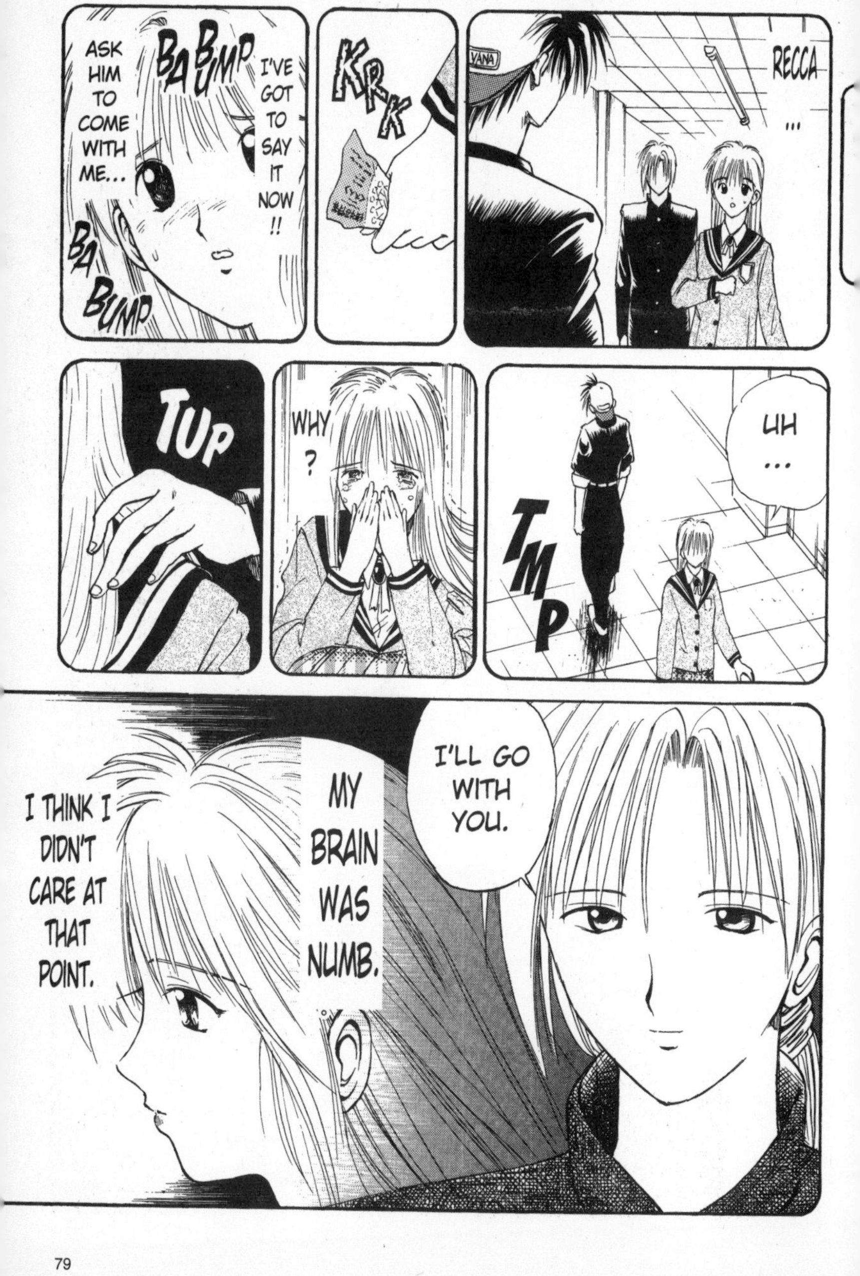
RECCA ...
KRK
I'VE GOT TO SAY IT NOW!!
BA BUMP
ASK HIM TO COME WITH ME...
BA BUMP
UH ...
TMP
WHY?
TUP
I'LL GO WITH YOU.
MY BRAIN WAS NUMB.
I THINK I DIDN'T CARE AT THAT POINT.

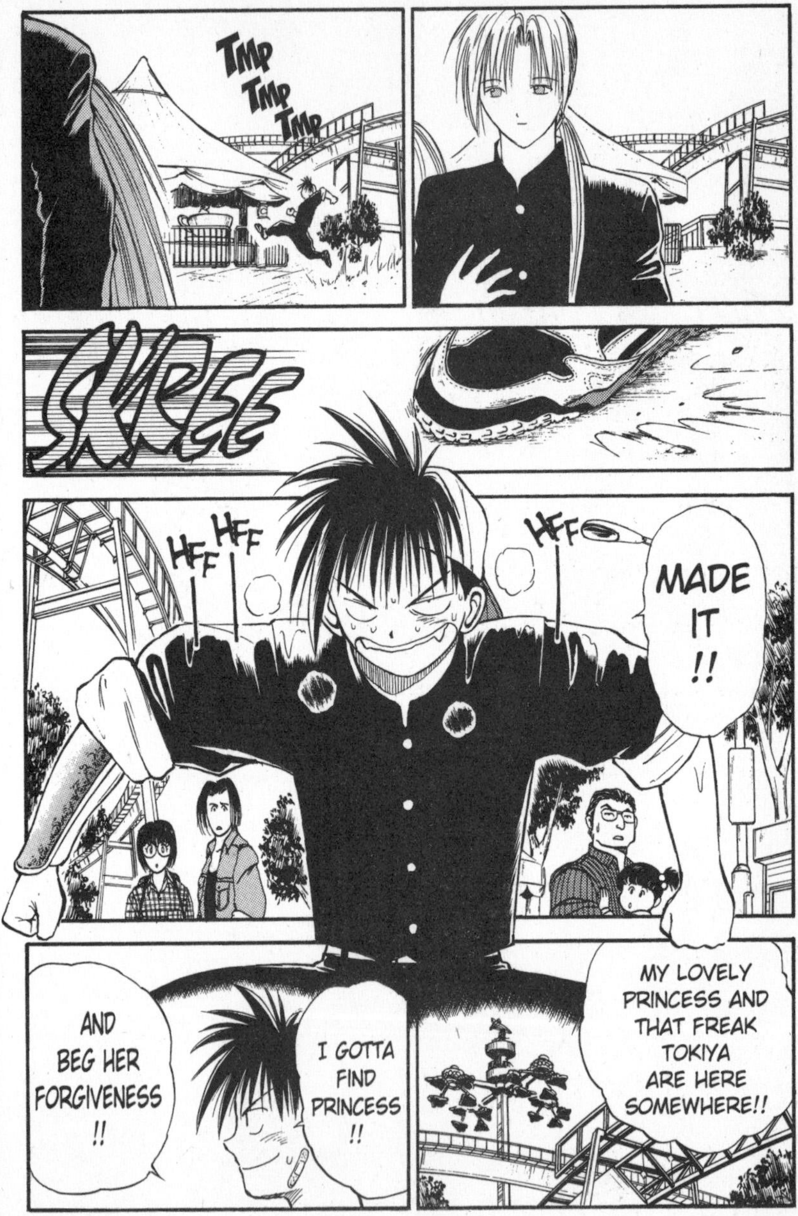
TMP TMP TMP
SKREE
HFF HFF
HFF
MADE IT !!
MY LOVELY PRINCESS AND THAT FREAK TOKIYA ARE HERE SOMEWHERE!!
I GOTTA FIND PRINCESS !!
AND BEG HER FORGIVENESS !!

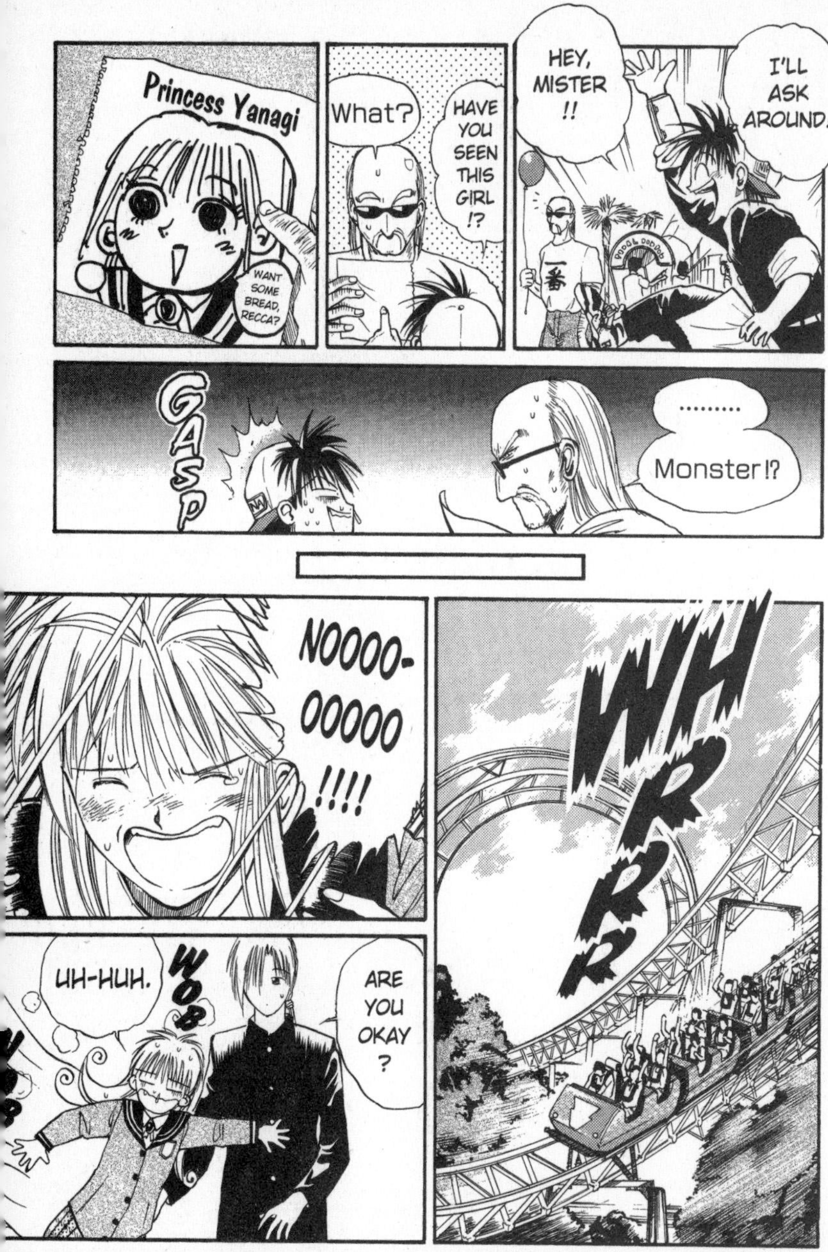

I'LL ASK AROUND!
HEY, MISTER !!
HAVE YOU SEEN THIS GIRL !?
What?
Princess Yanagi
WANT SOME BREAD, RECCA?
....
Monster !?
GASP
WHRRRR
NOOOO-OOOOO !!!!
ARE YOU OKAY ?
UH-HUH.
WOB

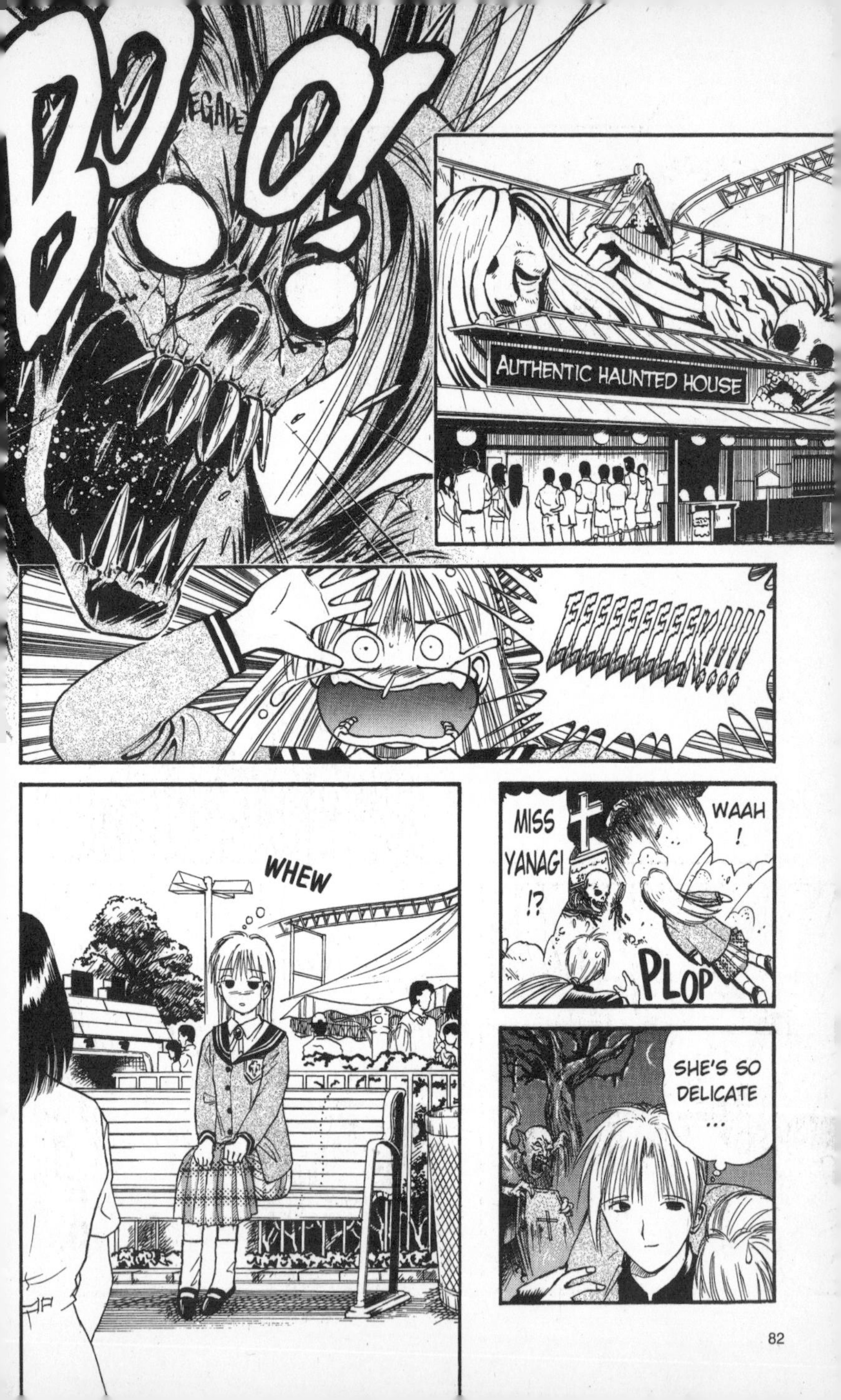
AUTHENTIC HAUNTED HOUSE
BOO!
EEEEEEEEEK!!!!
WAAH !
MISS YANAGI !?
PLOP
SHE'S SO DELICATE ...
WHEW

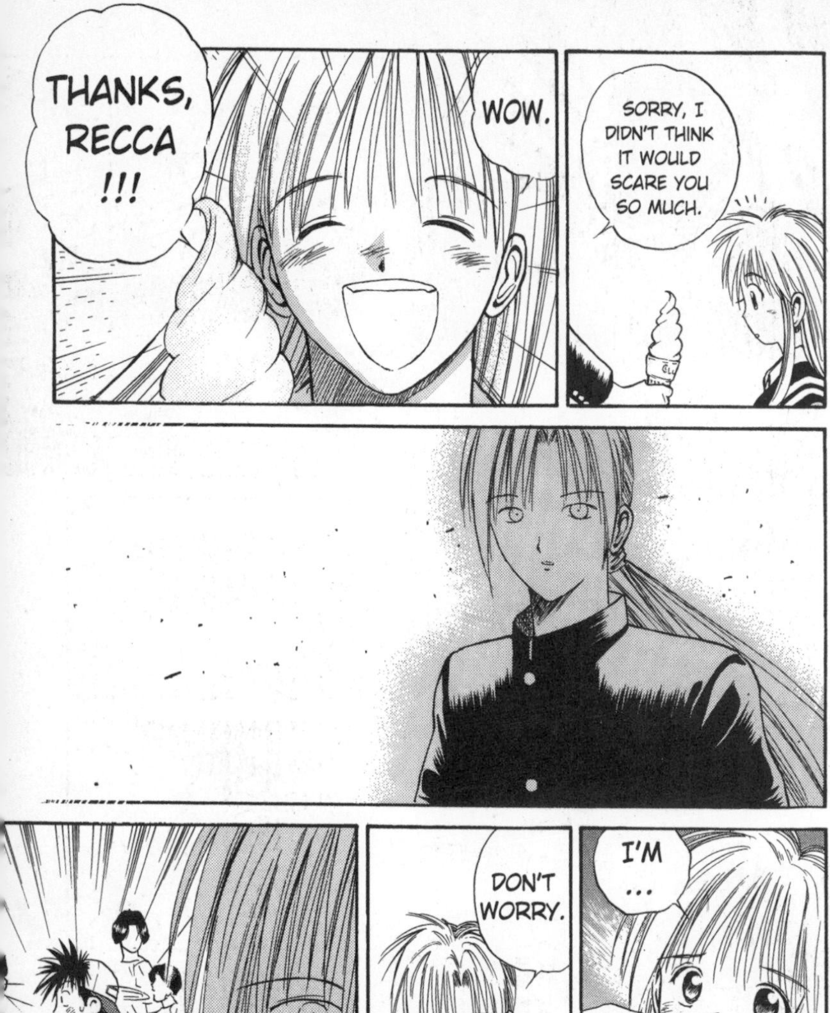
SORRY, I DIDN'T THINK IT WOULD SCARE YOU SO MUCH.
WOW.
THANKS, RECCA !!!
I'M ...
I'M SORRY ...
GASP
DON'T WORRY.
THAT WAS THE FIRST TIME YOU'VE SMILED ALL DAY.
I JUST WISH IT HAD BEEN FOR ME.
!!

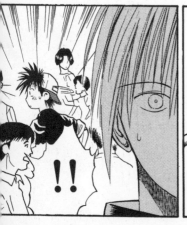

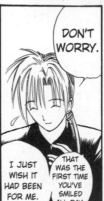

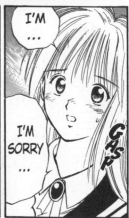

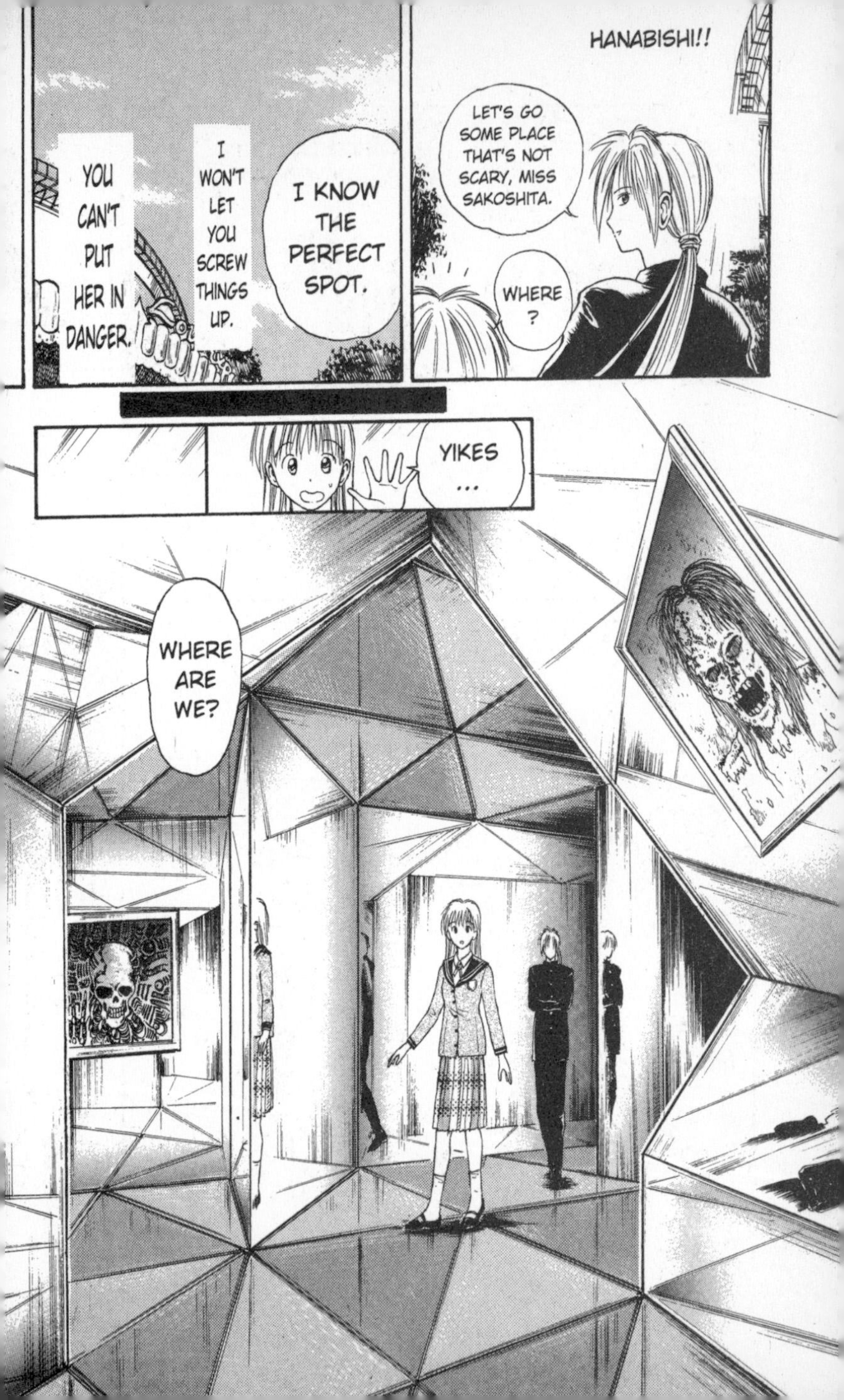
HANABISHI!!
LET'S GO SOME PLACE THAT'S NOT SCARY, MISS SAKOSHITA.
WHERE?
I KNOW THE PERFECT SPOT.
I WON'T LET YOU SCREW THINGS UP.
YOU CAN'T PUT HER IN DANGER.
YIKES ...
WHERE ARE WE?

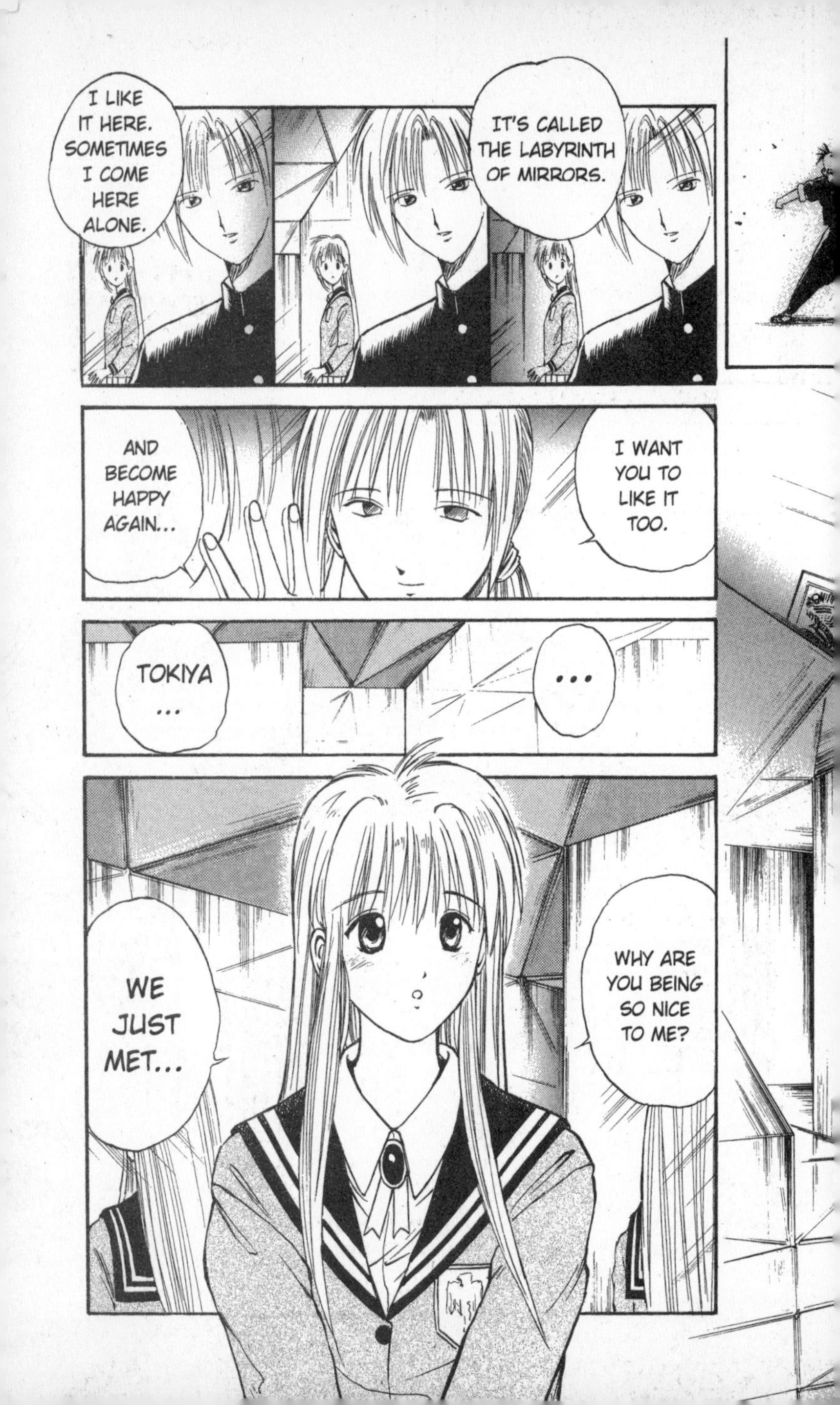
IT'S CALLED THE LABYRINTH OF MIRRORS.
I LIKE IT HERE. SOMETIMES I COME HERE ALONE.
I WANT YOU TO LIKE IT TOO.
AND BECOME HAPPY AGAIN...
...
TOKIYA ...
WHY ARE YOU BEING SO NICE TO ME?
WE JUST MET...

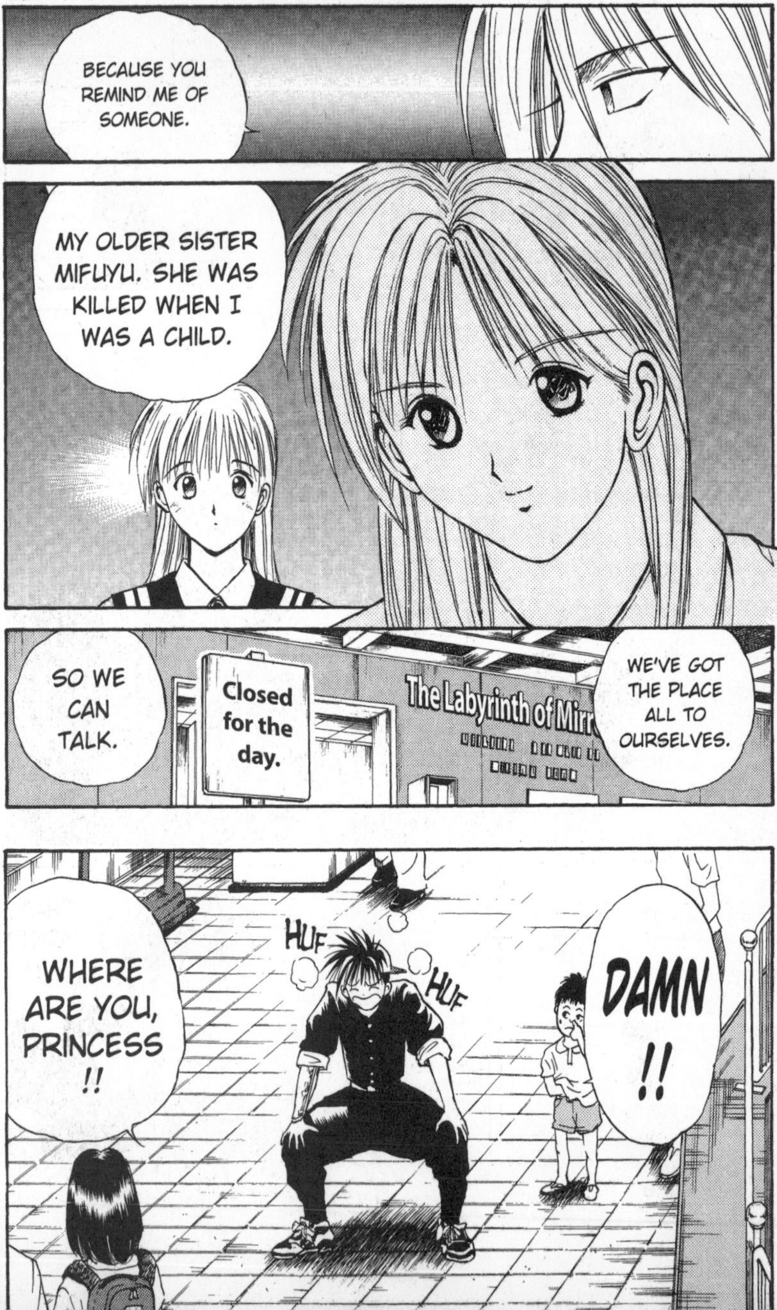
BECAUSE YOU REMIND ME OF SOMEONE.
MY OLDER SISTER MIFUYU. SHE WAS KILLED WHEN I WAS A CHILD.
WE'VE GOT THE PLACE ALL TO OURSELVES.
Closed for the day.
The Labyrinth of Mirr
SO WE CAN TALK.
DAMN !!
HUF
HUF
WHERE ARE YOU, PRINCESS !!

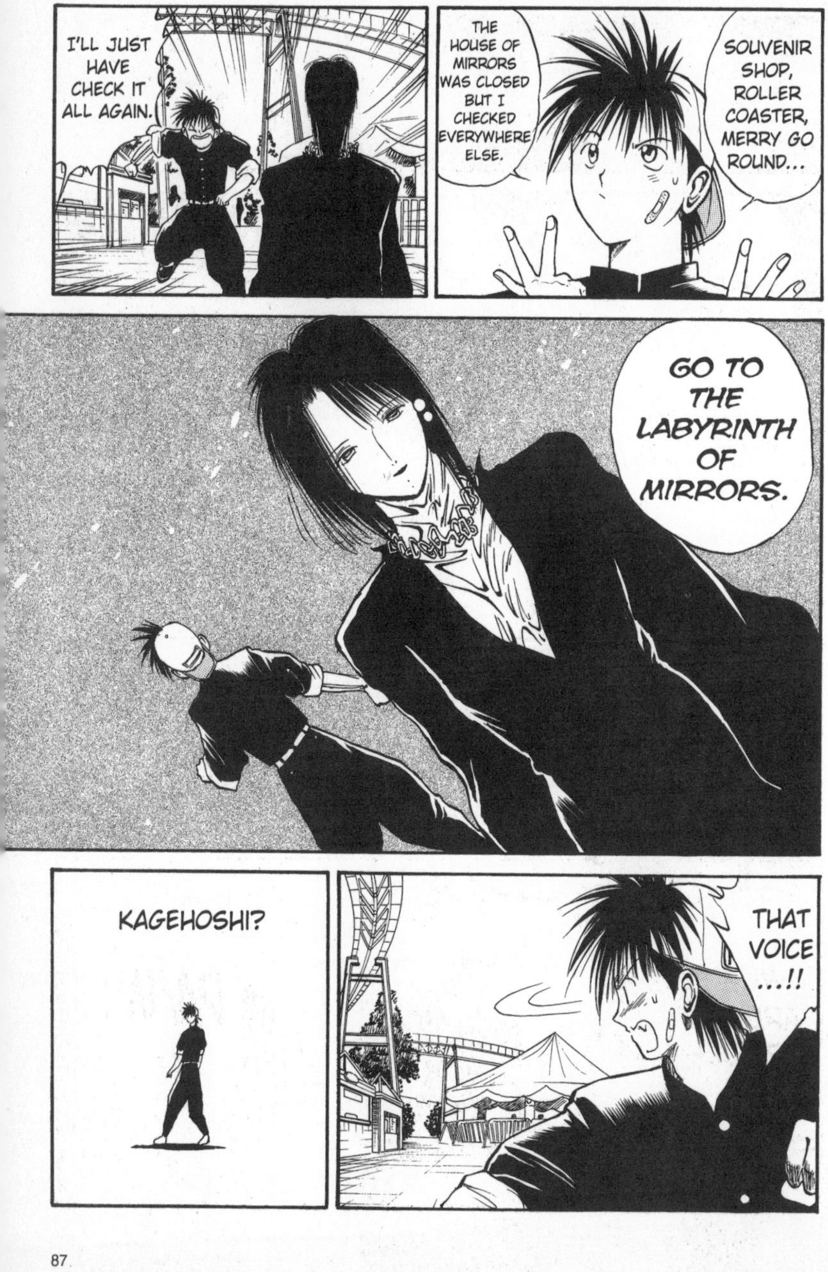
SOUVENIR SHOP, ROLLER COASTER, MERRY GO ROUND...
THE HOUSE OF MIRRORS WAS CLOSED BUT I CHECKED EVERYWHERE ELSE.
I'LL JUST HAVE CHECK IT ALL AGAIN.
GO TO THE LABYRINTH OF MIRRORS.
THAT VOICE ...!!
KAGEHOSHI?

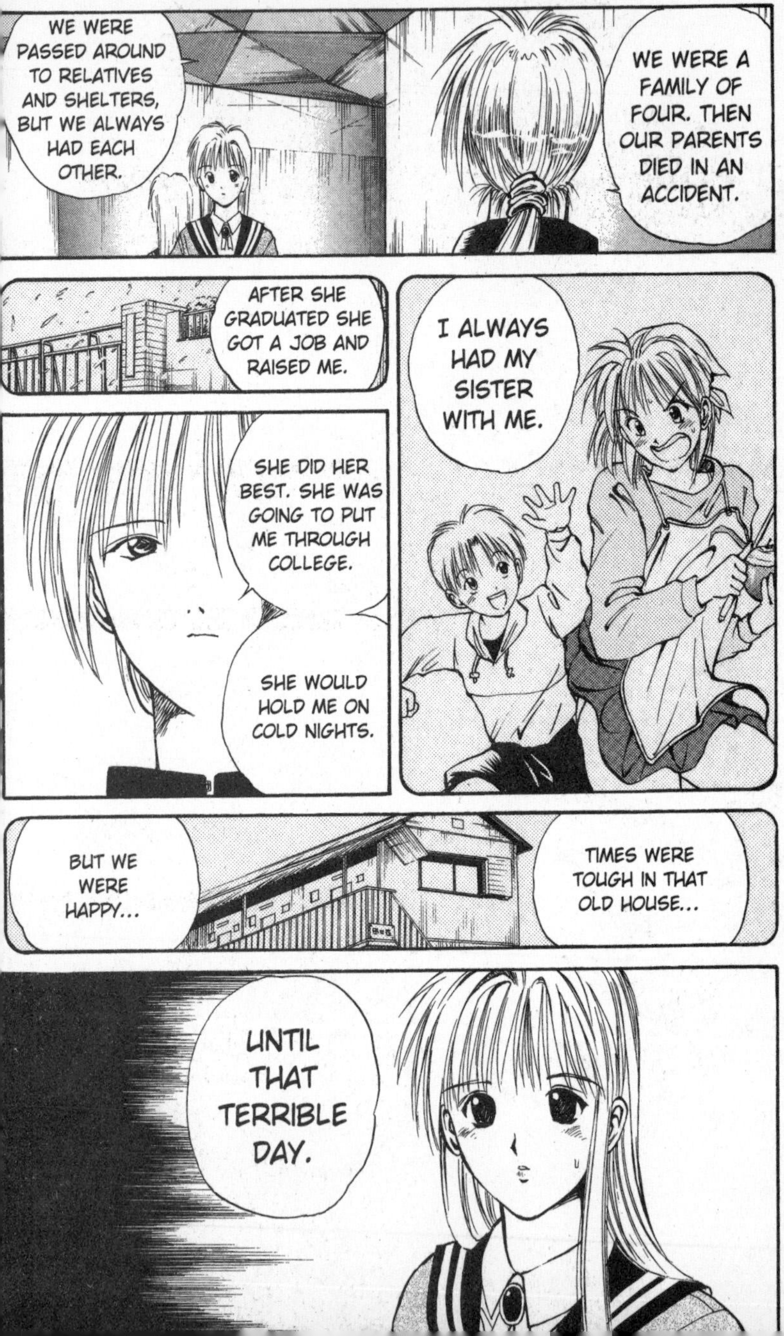
WE WERE A FAMILY OF FOUR. THEN OUR PARENTS DIED IN AN ACCIDENT.
WE WERE PASSED AROUND TO RELATIVES AND SHELTERS, BUT WE ALWAYS HAD EACH OTHER.
I ALWAYS HAD MY SISTER WITH ME.
AFTER SHE GRADUATED SHE GOT A JOB AND RAISED ME.
SHE DID HER BEST. SHE WAS GOING TO PUT ME THROUGH COLLEGE.
SHE WOULD HOLD ME ON COLD NIGHTS.
TIMES WERE TOUGH IN THAT OLD HOUSE...
BUT WE WERE HAPPY...
UNTIL THAT TERRIBLE DAY.

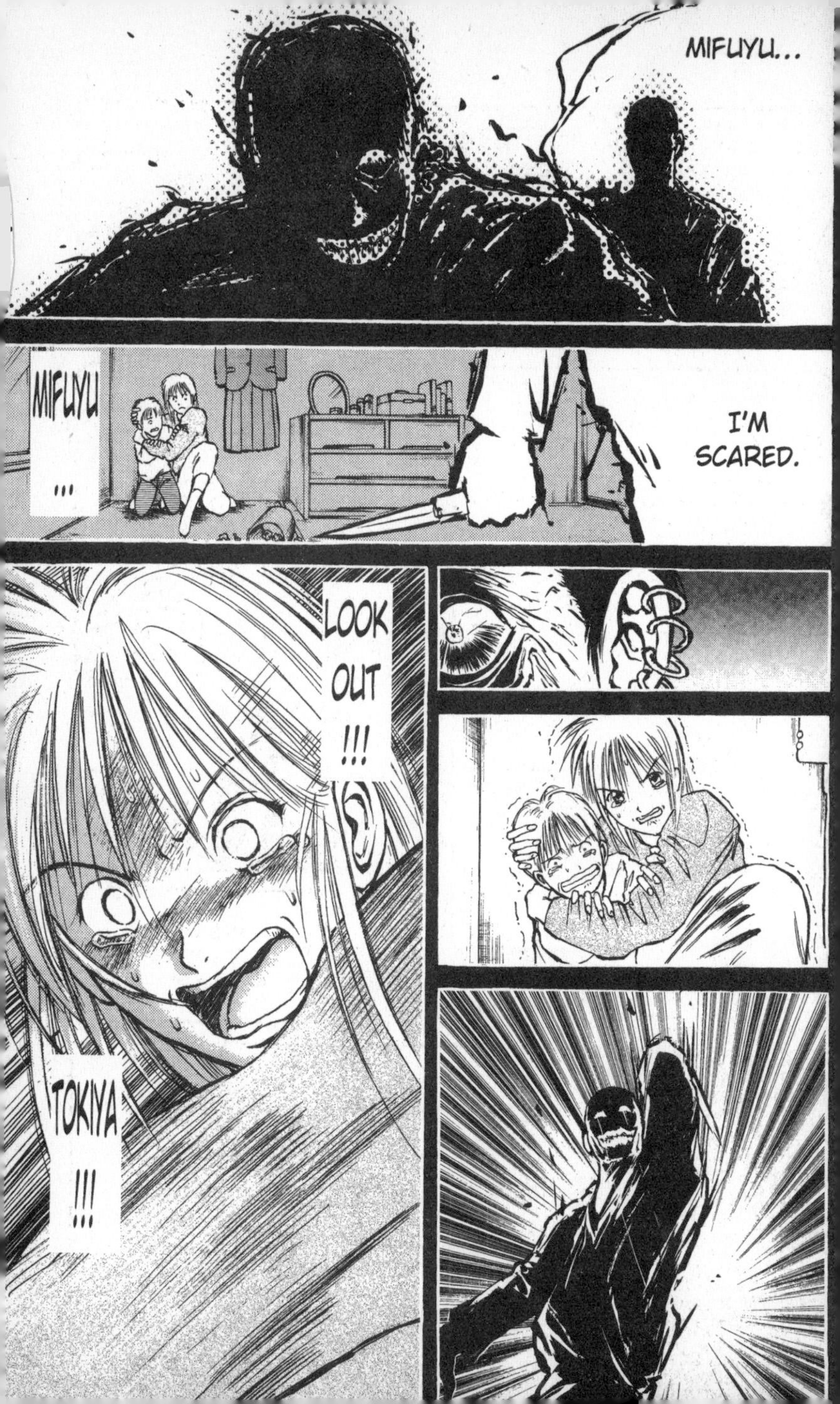

MIFUYU...
I'M SCARED.
MIFUYU ...
LOOK OUT !!!
TOKIYA !!!

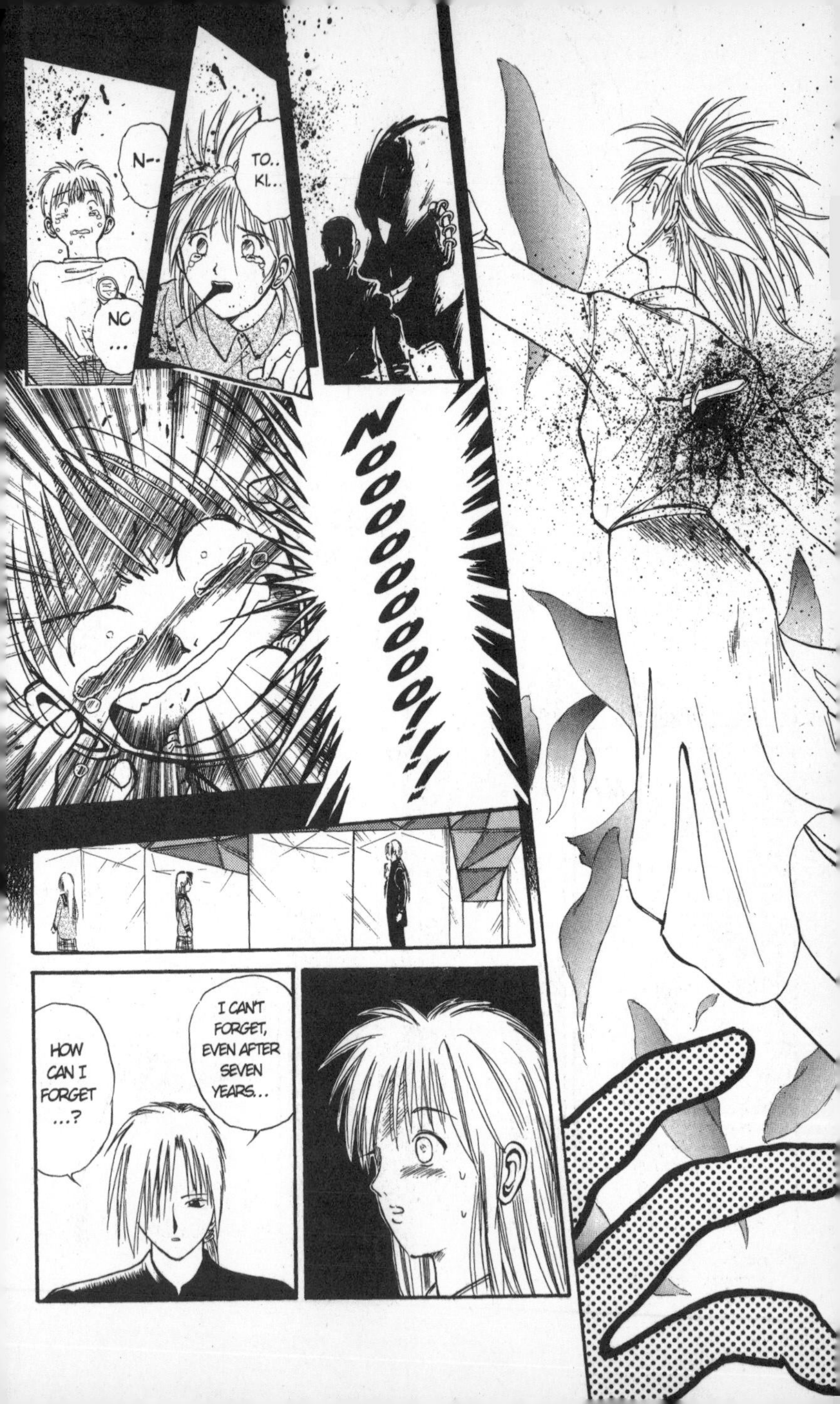
TO.. KI..
N--
NO ...
NOOOOOOOOOO!!!
I CAN'T FORGET, EVEN AFTER SEVEN YEARS...
HOW CAN I FORGET ...?

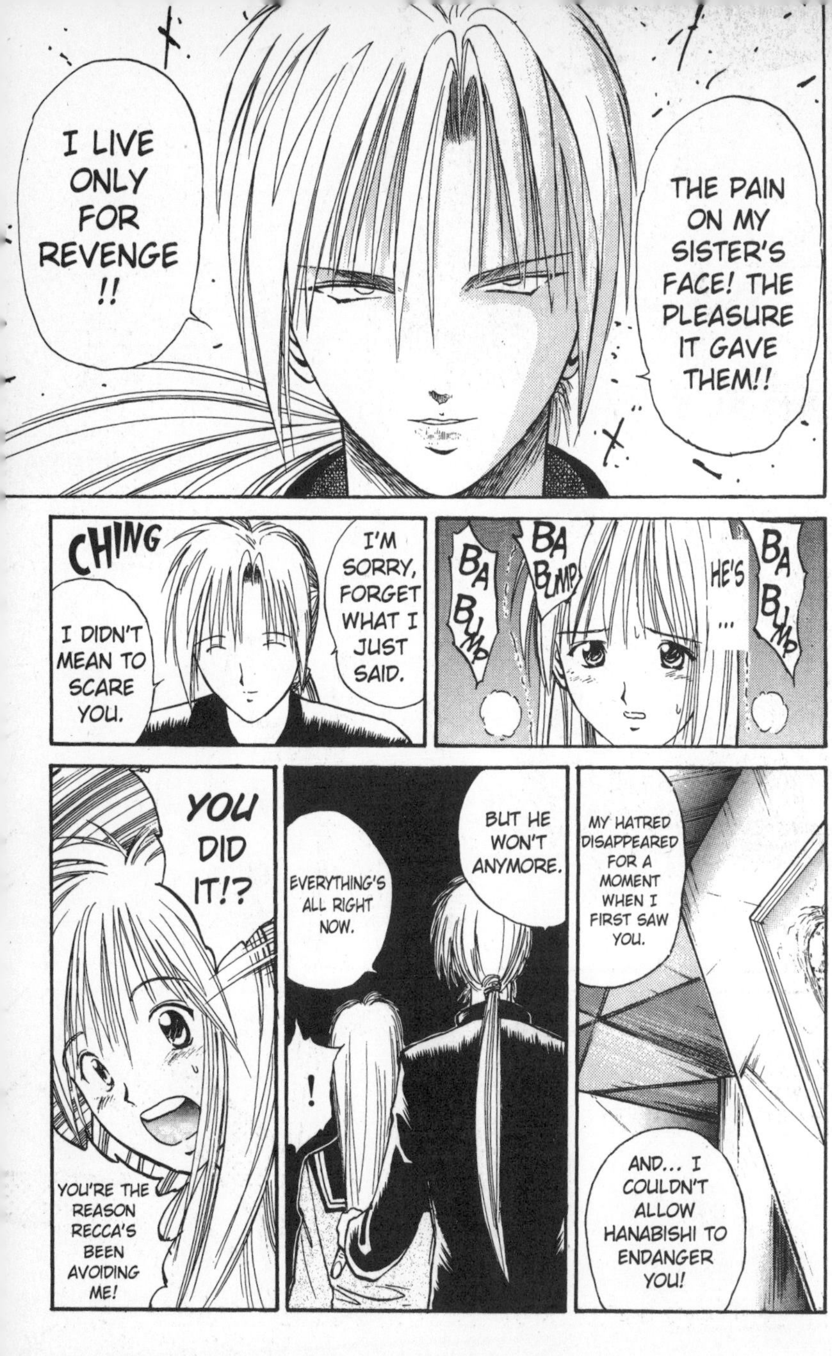
THE PAIN ON MY SISTER'S FACE! THE PLEASURE IT GAVE THEM!!
I LIVE ONLY FOR REVENGE!!
BA BUMP
BA BUMP
HE'S...
BA BUMP
CHING
I'M SORRY, FORGET WHAT I JUST SAID.
I DIDN'T MEAN TO SCARE YOU.
MY HATRED DISAPPEARED FOR A MOMENT WHEN I FIRST SAW YOU.
AND... I COULDN'T ALLOW HANABISHI TO ENDANGER YOU!
BUT HE WON'T ANYMORE.
EVERYTHING'S ALL RIGHT NOW.
!
YOU DID IT!?
YOU'RE THE REASON RECCA'S BEEN AVOIDING ME!

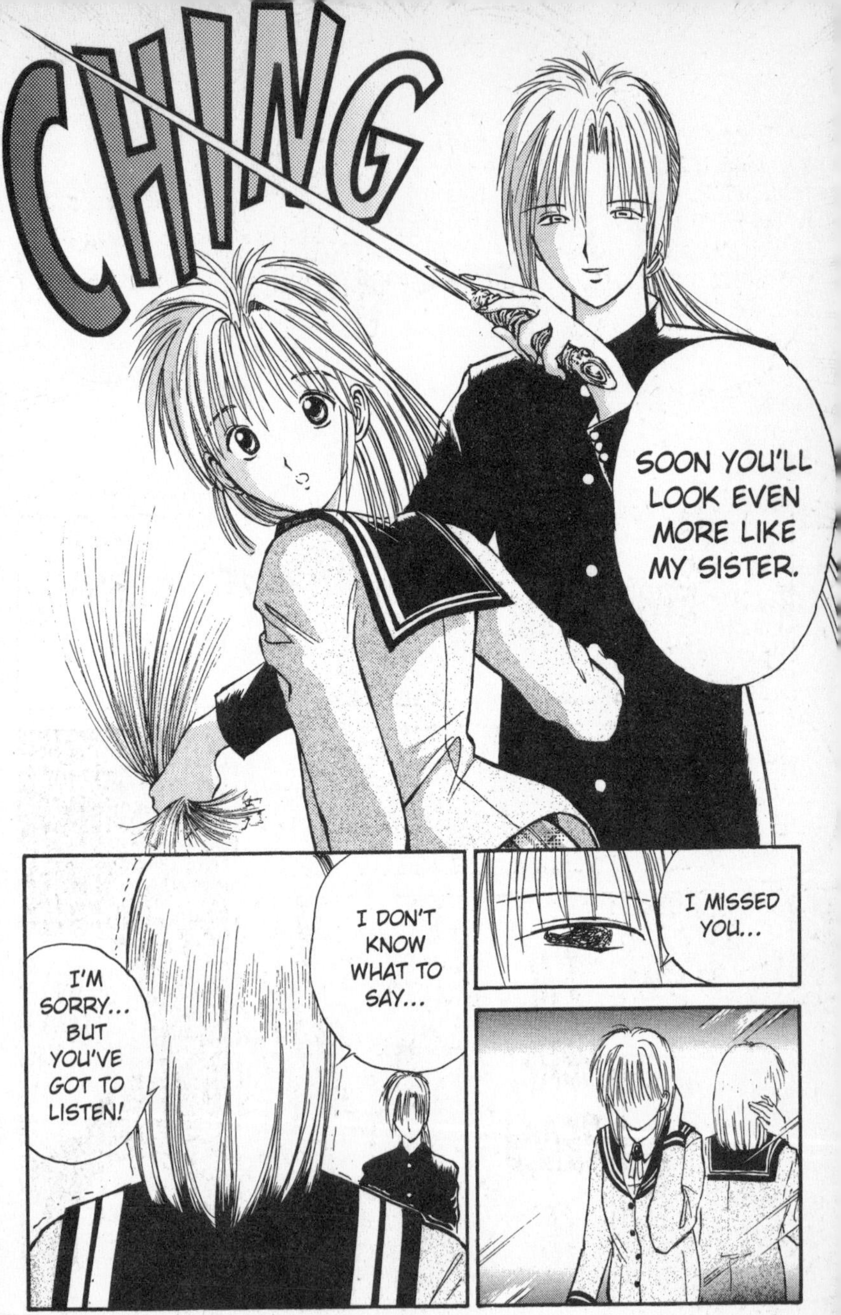
CHING
SOON YOU'LL LOOK EVEN MORE LIKE MY SISTER.
I MISSED YOU...
I DON'T KNOW WHAT TO SAY...
I'M SORRY... BUT YOU'VE GOT TO LISTEN!

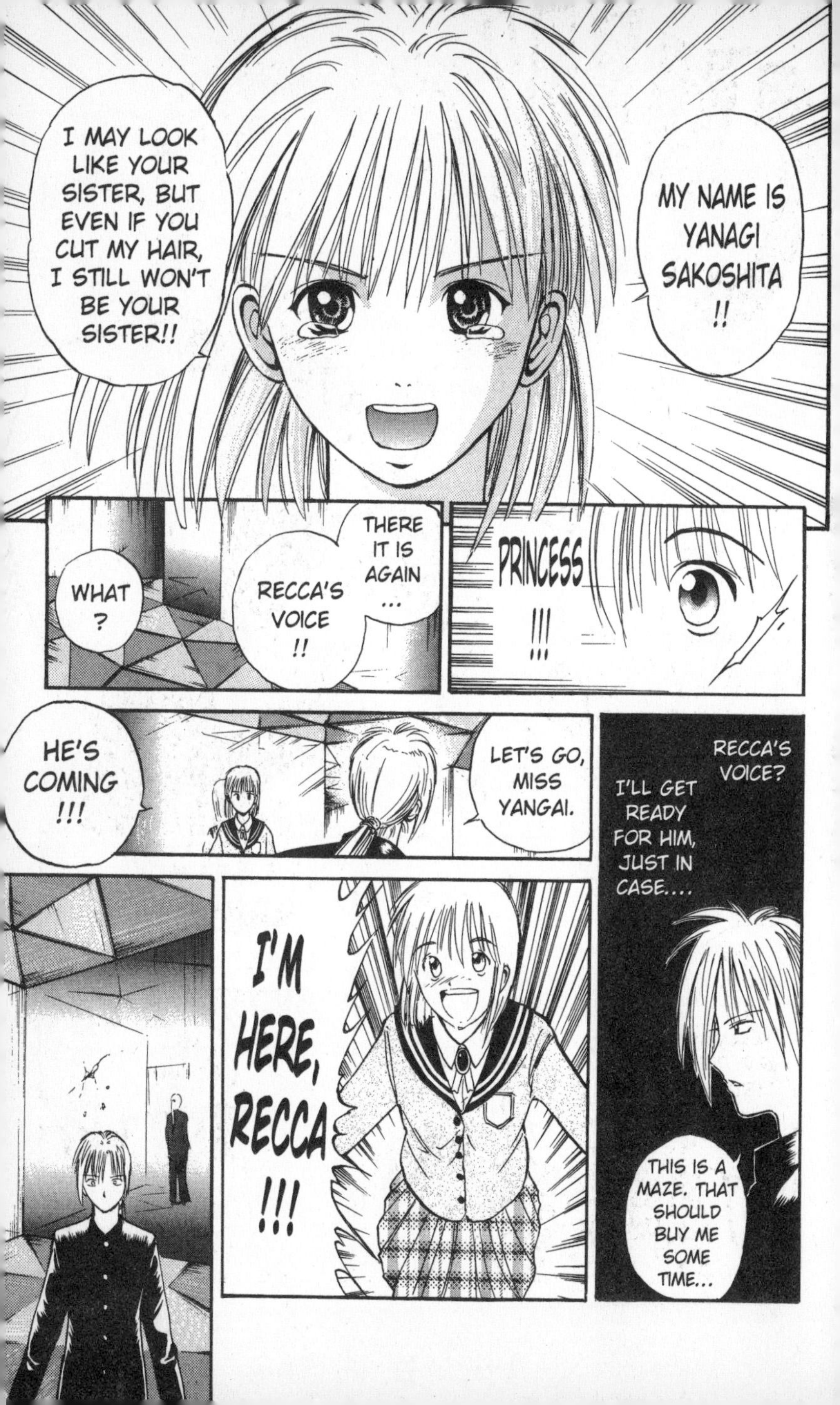
MY NAME IS YANAGI SAKOSHITA!!
I MAY LOOK LIKE YOUR SISTER, BUT EVEN IF YOU CUT MY HAIR, I STILL WON'T BE YOUR SISTER!!
PRINCESS!!!
THERE IT IS AGAIN...
RECCA'S VOICE!!
WHAT?
RECCA'S VOICE?
I'LL GET READY FOR HIM, JUST IN CASE....
THIS IS A MAZE. THAT SHOULD BUY ME SOME TIME...
LET'S GO, MISS YANGAI.
HE'S COMING!!!
I'M HERE, RECCA!!!

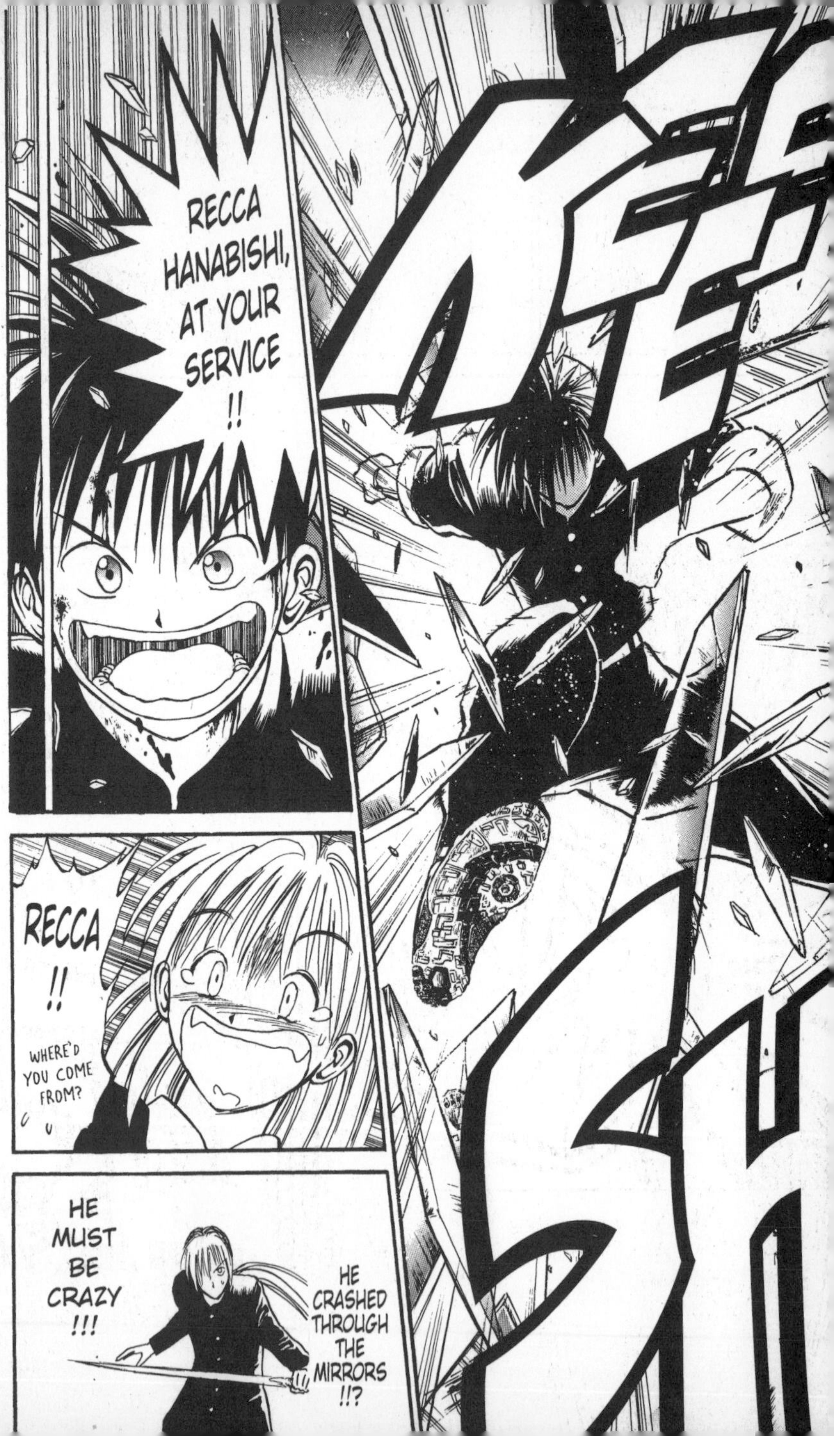

RECCA HANABISHI, AT YOUR SERVICE !!
RECCA !!
WHERE'D YOU COME FROM?
HE MUST BE CRAZY !!!
HE CRASHED THROUGH THE MIRRORS !!?

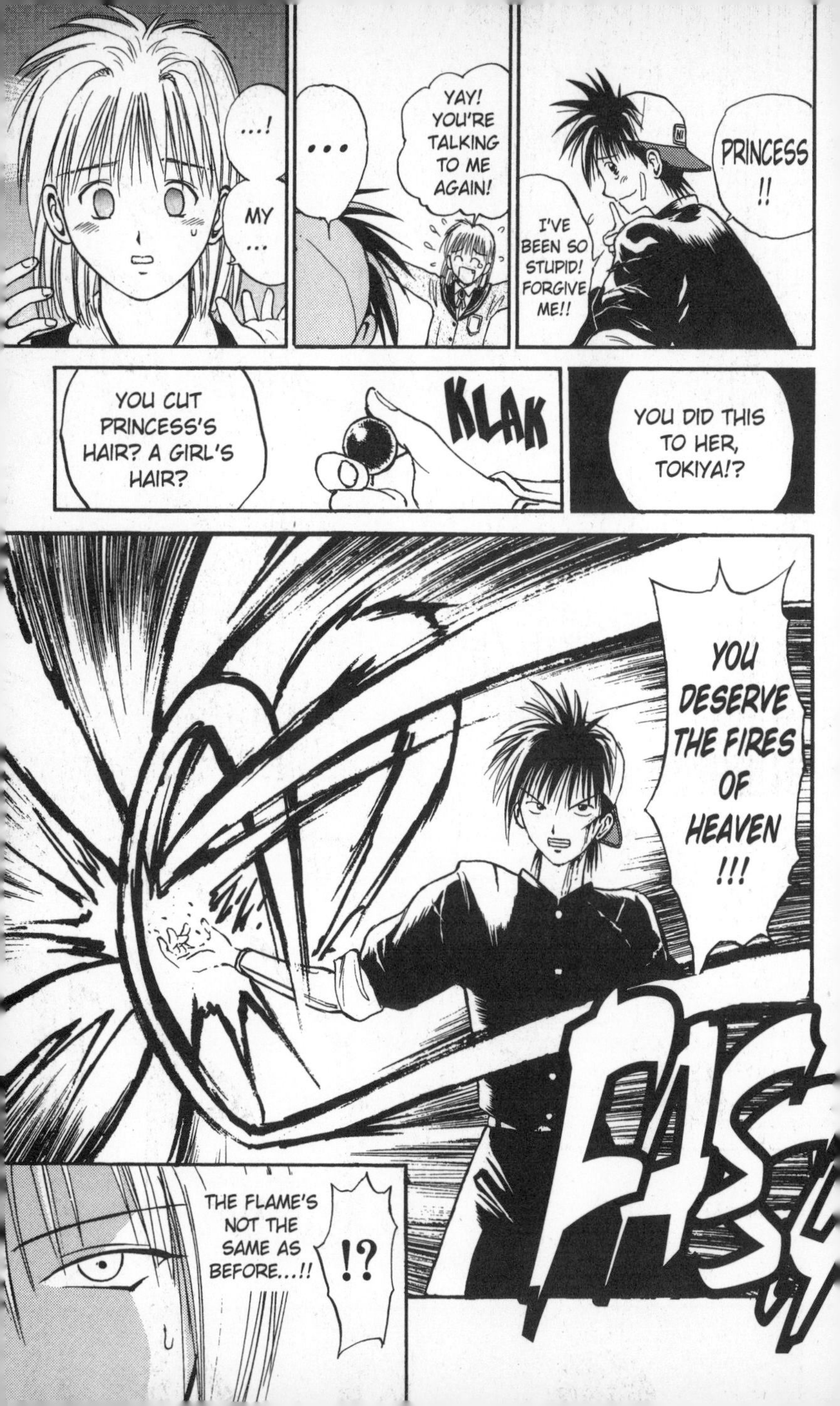
PRINCESS !!
I'VE BEEN SO STUPID! FORGIVE ME!!
YAY! YOU'RE TALKING TO ME AGAIN!
...
...!
MY ...
YOU DID THIS TO HER, TOKIYA!?
KLAK
YOU CUT PRINCESS'S HAIR? A GIRL'S HAIR?
YOU DESERVE THE FIRES OF HEAVEN !!!
!?
THE FLAME'S NOT THE SAME AS BEFORE...!!

烈火の炎
~FLAME OF RECCA~

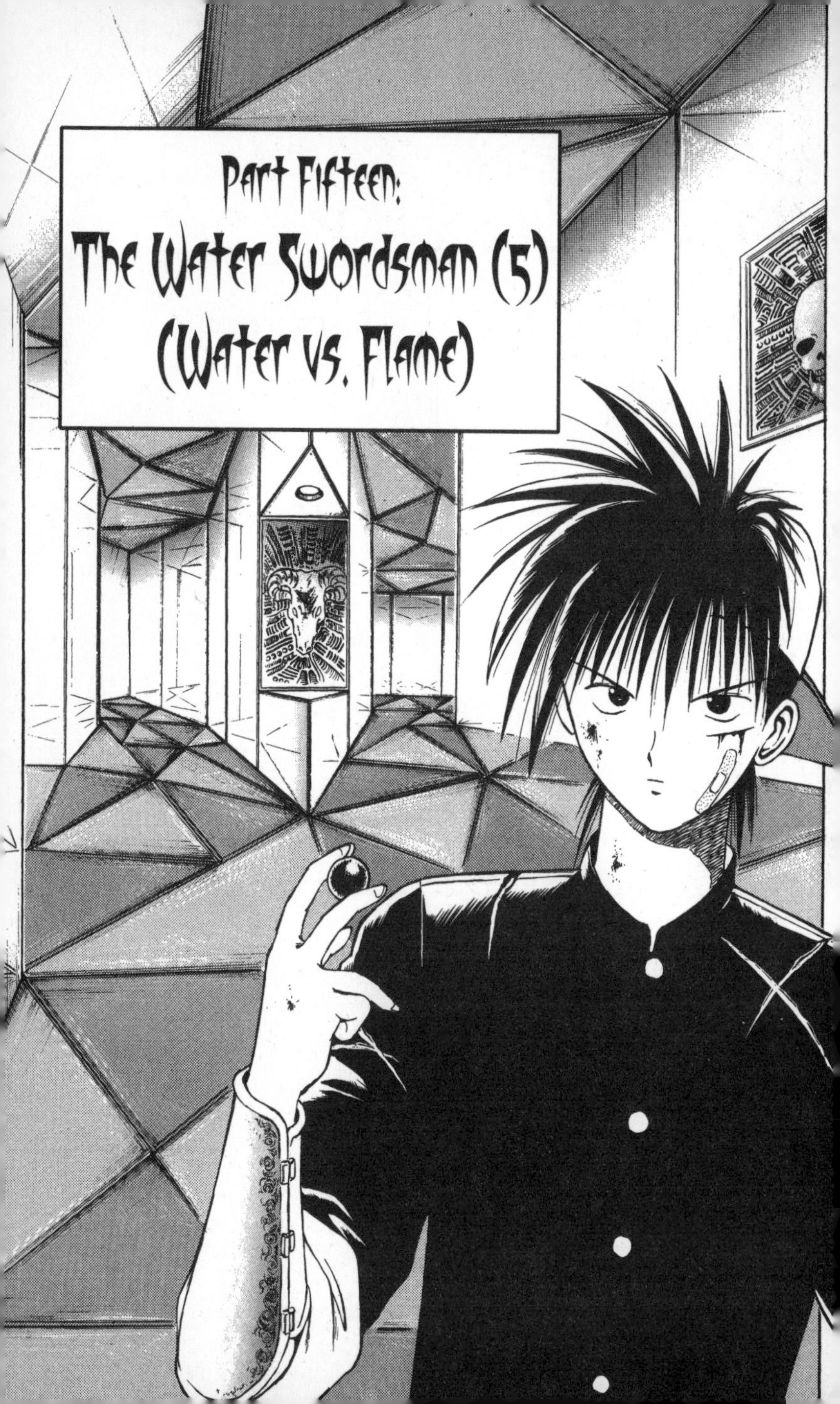
Part Fifteen:
The Water Swordsman (5)
(Water vs. Flame)

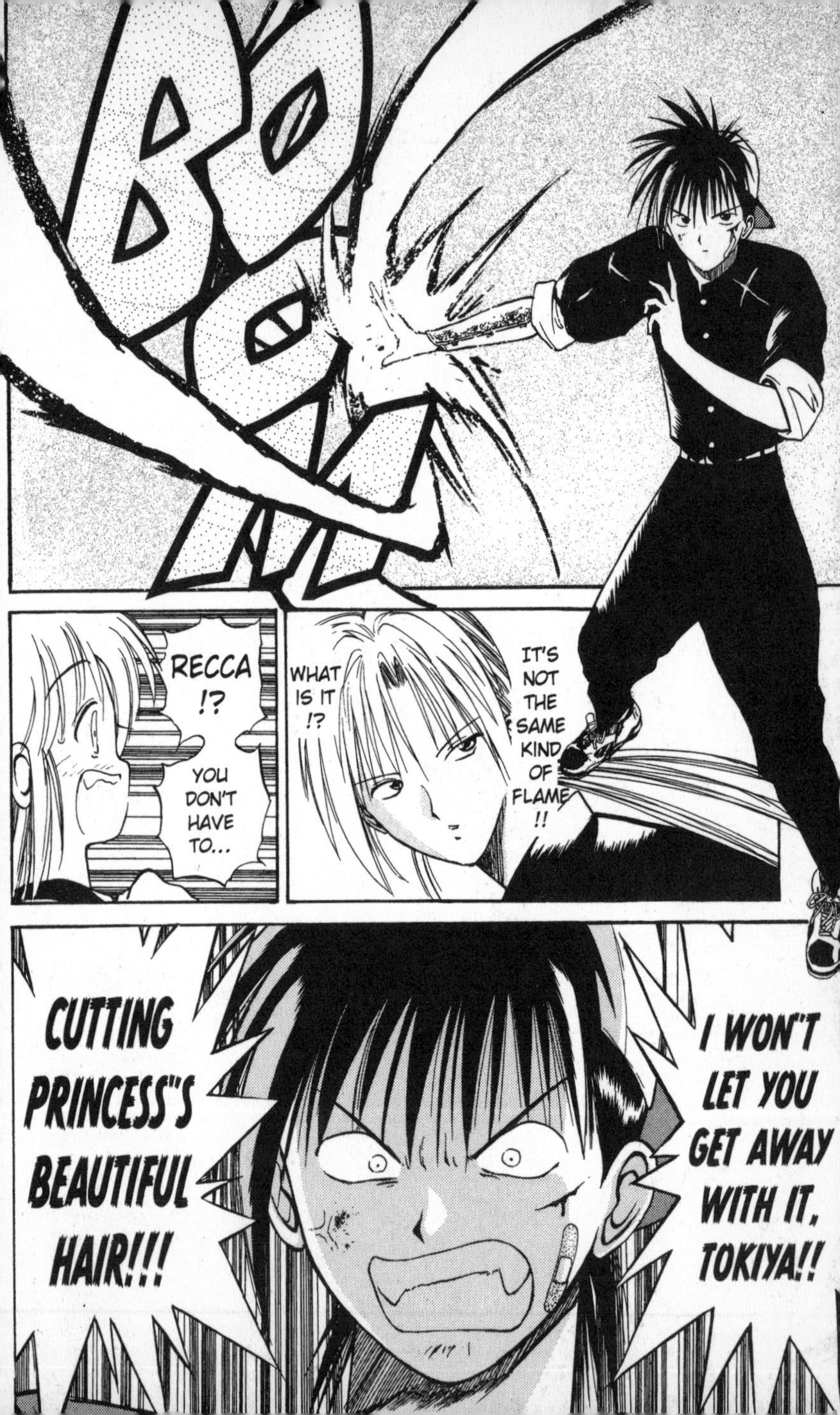
IT'S NOT THE SAME KIND OF FLAME !!
WHAT IS IT !?
RECCA !?
YOU DON'T HAVE TO...
I WON'T LET YOU GET AWAY WITH IT, TOKIYA!!
CUTTING PRINCESS"S BEAUTIFUL HAIR!!!

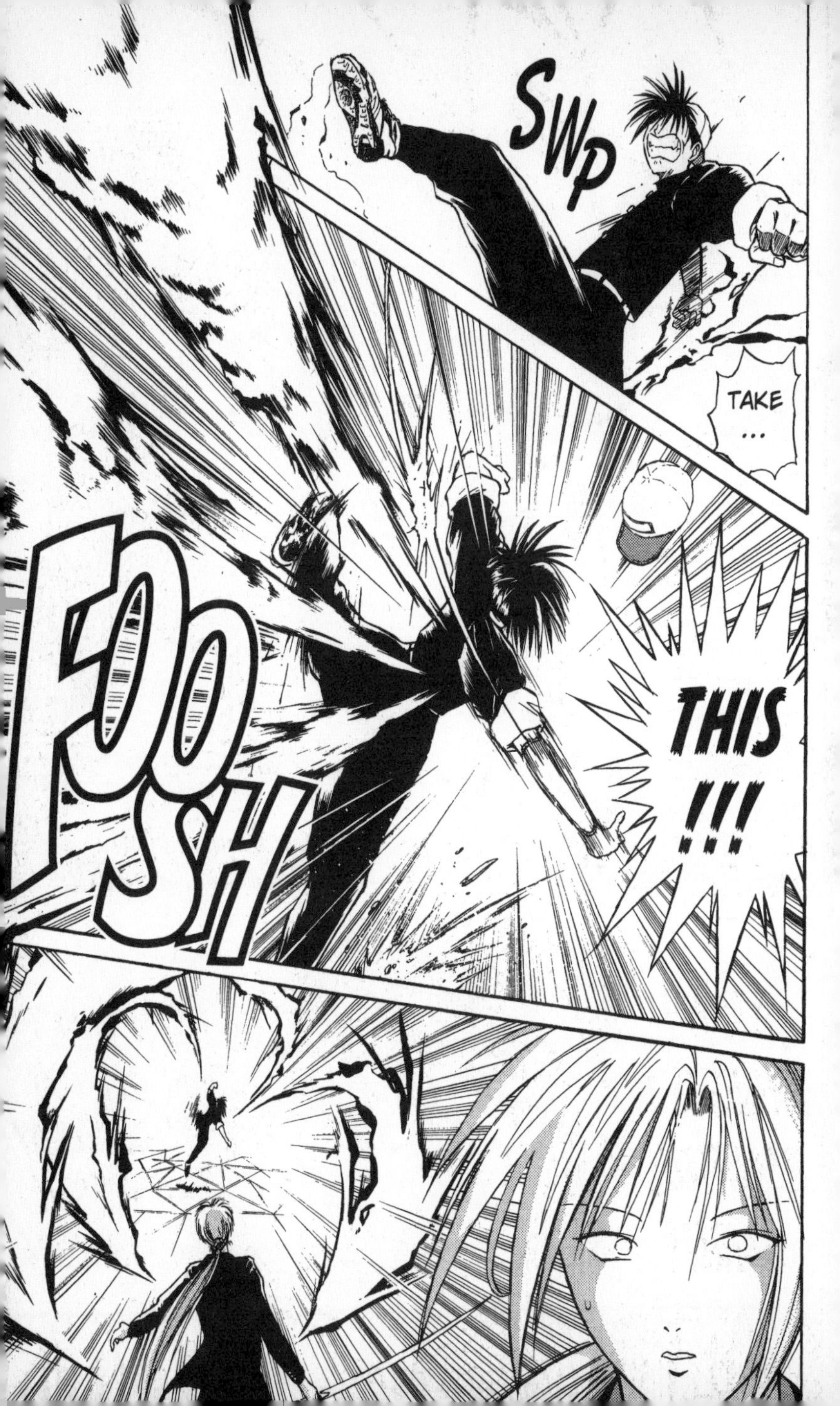
SWP
TAKE ...
THIS !!!
FOOSH

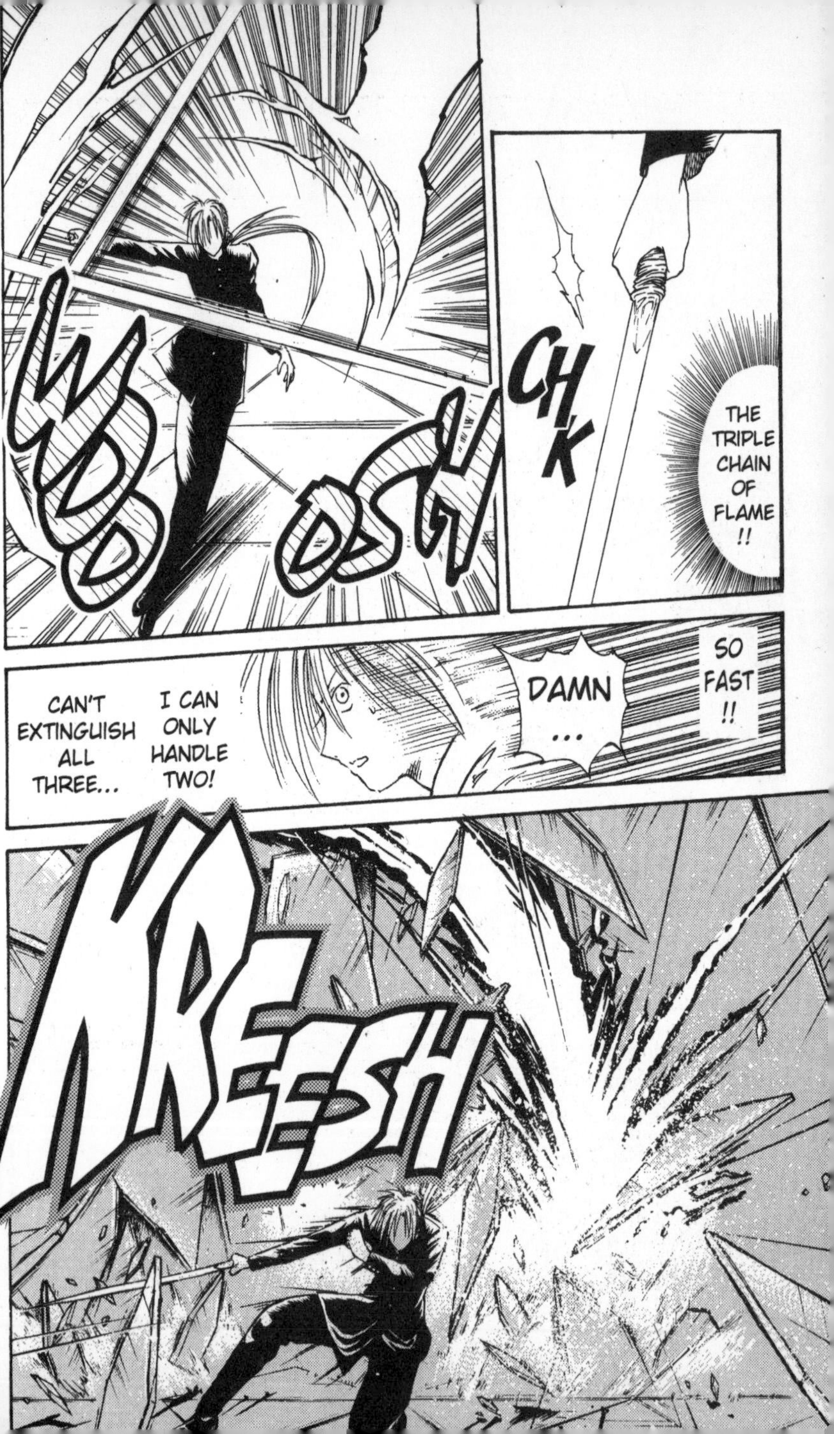
THE TRIPLE CHAIN OF FLAME !!
CH'K
WOOSH
SO FAST !!
DAMN ...
I CAN ONLY HANDLE TWO!
CAN'T EXTINGUISH ALL THREE...
KREESH

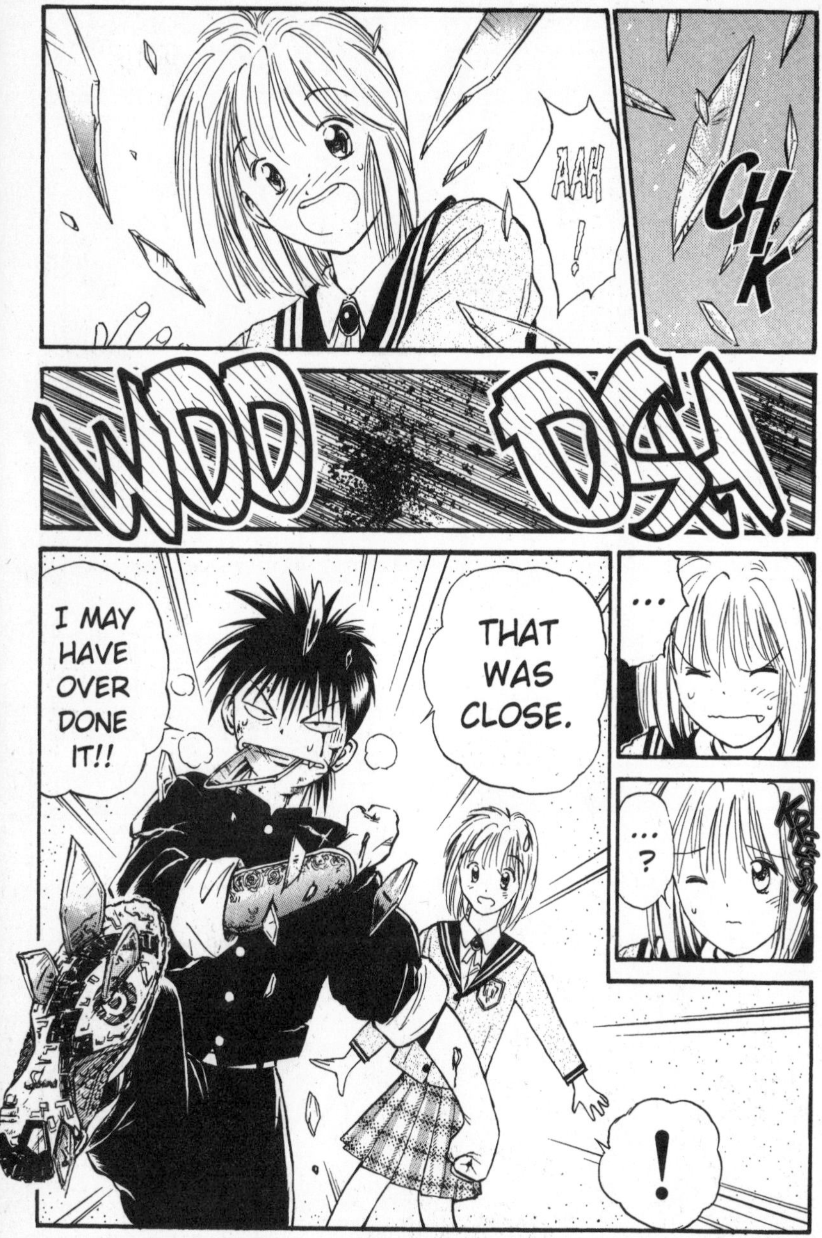
CHK
AAH!
...
...?
THAT WAS CLOSE.
I MAY HAVE OVER DONE IT!!
!

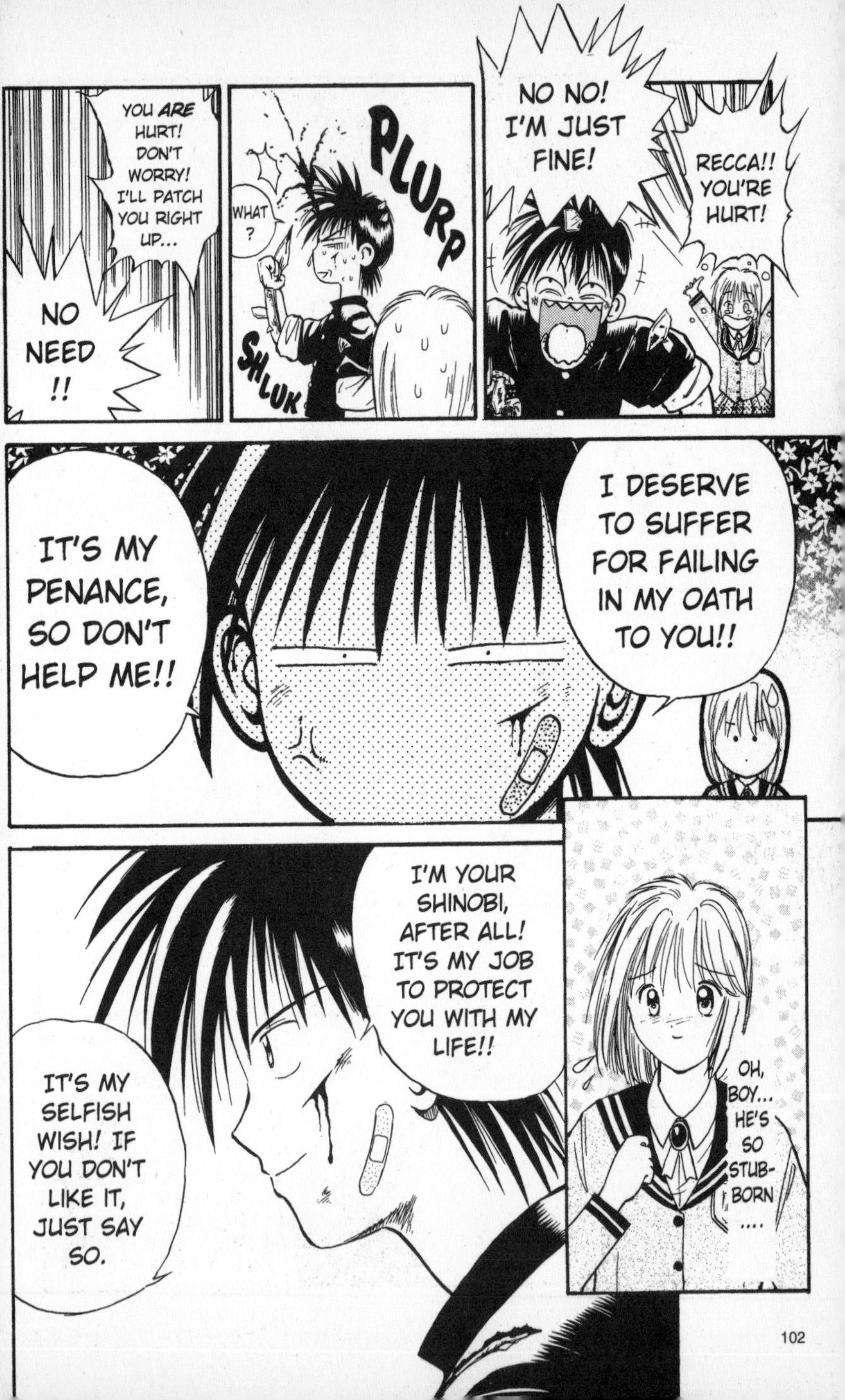
RECCA!! YOU'RE HURT!
NO NO! I'M JUST FINE!
PLURP
WHAT ?
SHLUK
YOU *ARE* HURT! DON'T WORRY! I'LL PATCH YOU RIGHT UP...
NO NEED !!
I DESERVE TO SUFFER FOR FAILING IN MY OATH TO YOU!!
IT'S MY PENANCE, SO DON'T HELP ME!!
I'M YOUR SHINOBI, AFTER ALL! IT'S MY JOB TO PROTECT YOU WITH MY LIFE!!
IT'S MY SELFISH WISH! IF YOU DON'T LIKE IT, JUST SAY SO.
OH, BOY... HE'S SO STUB-BORN ....

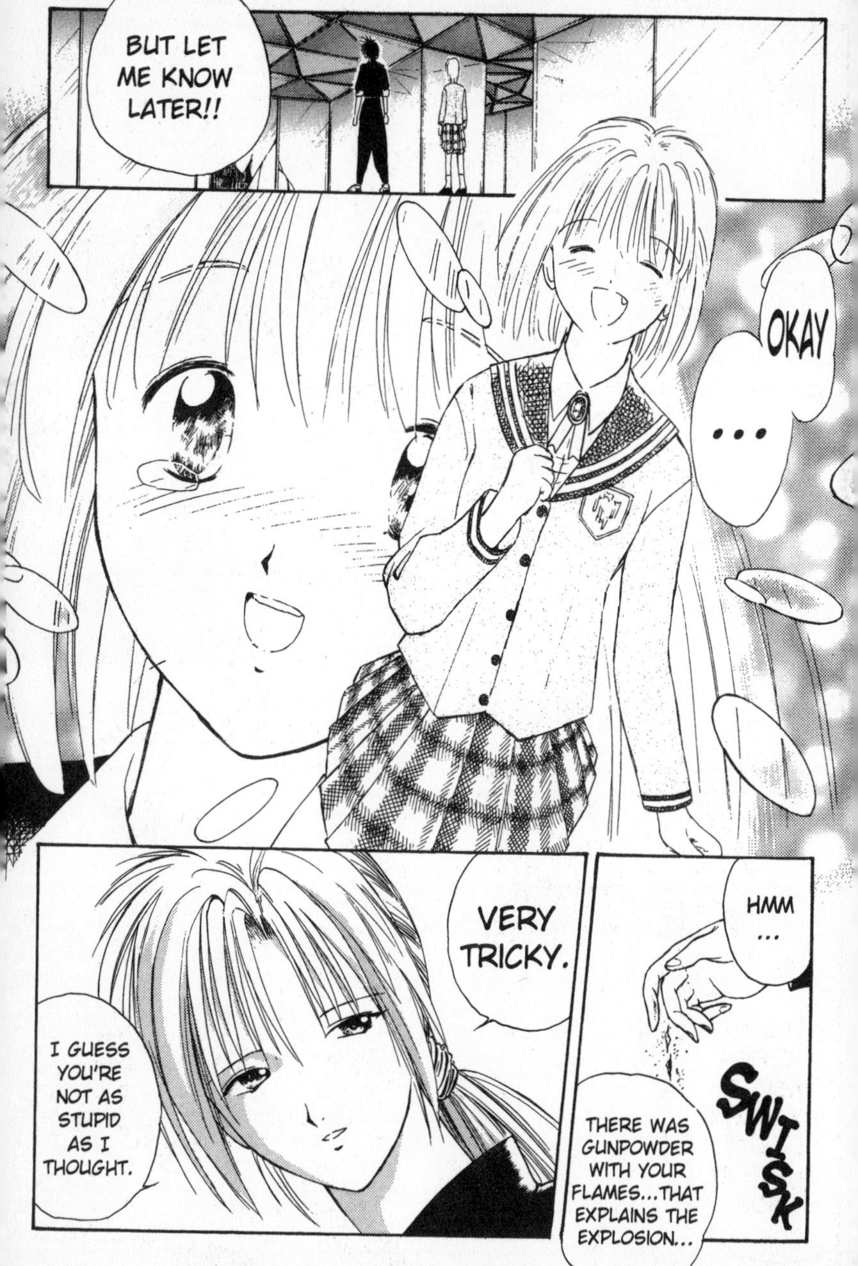
BUT LET ME KNOW LATER!!
OKAY
...
HMM ...
SWISK
THERE WAS GUNPOWDER WITH YOUR FLAMES...THAT EXPLAINS THE EXPLOSION...
VERY TRICKY.
I GUESS YOU'RE NOT AS STUPID AS I THOUGHT.

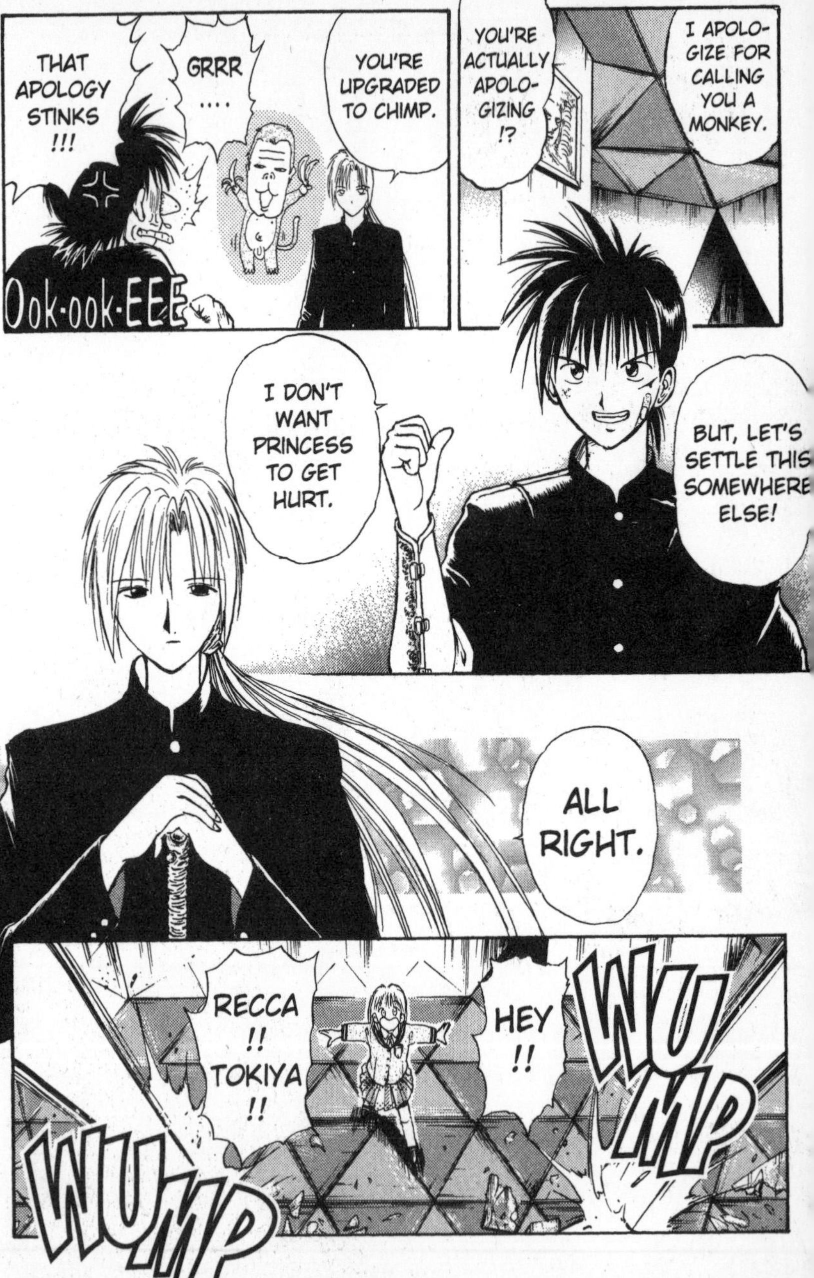
I APOLOGIZE FOR CALLING YOU A MONKEY.
YOU'RE ACTUALLY APOLOGIZING !?
YOU'RE UPGRADED TO CHIMP.
GRRR ....
THAT APOLOGY STINKS !!!
Ook-ook-EEE
BUT, LET'S SETTLE THIS SOMEWHERE ELSE!
I DON'T WANT PRINCESS TO GET HURT.
ALL RIGHT.
WUMP
HEY !!
RECCA !! TOKIYA !!
WUMP

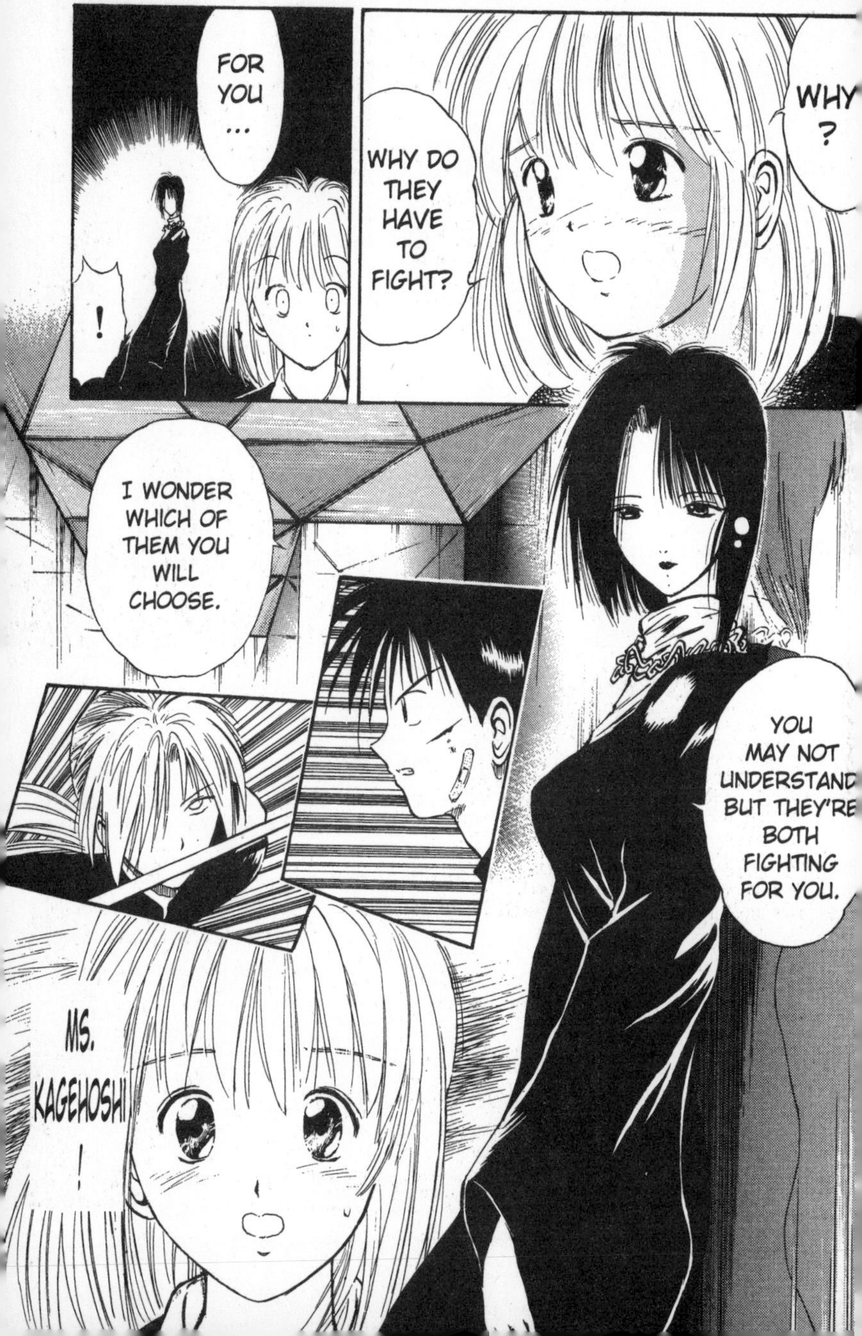
WHY?
WHY DO THEY HAVE TO FIGHT?
FOR YOU...
!
YOU MAY NOT UNDERSTAND BUT THEY'RE BOTH FIGHTING FOR YOU.
I WONDER WHICH OF THEM YOU WILL CHOOSE.
MS. KAGEHOSHI!

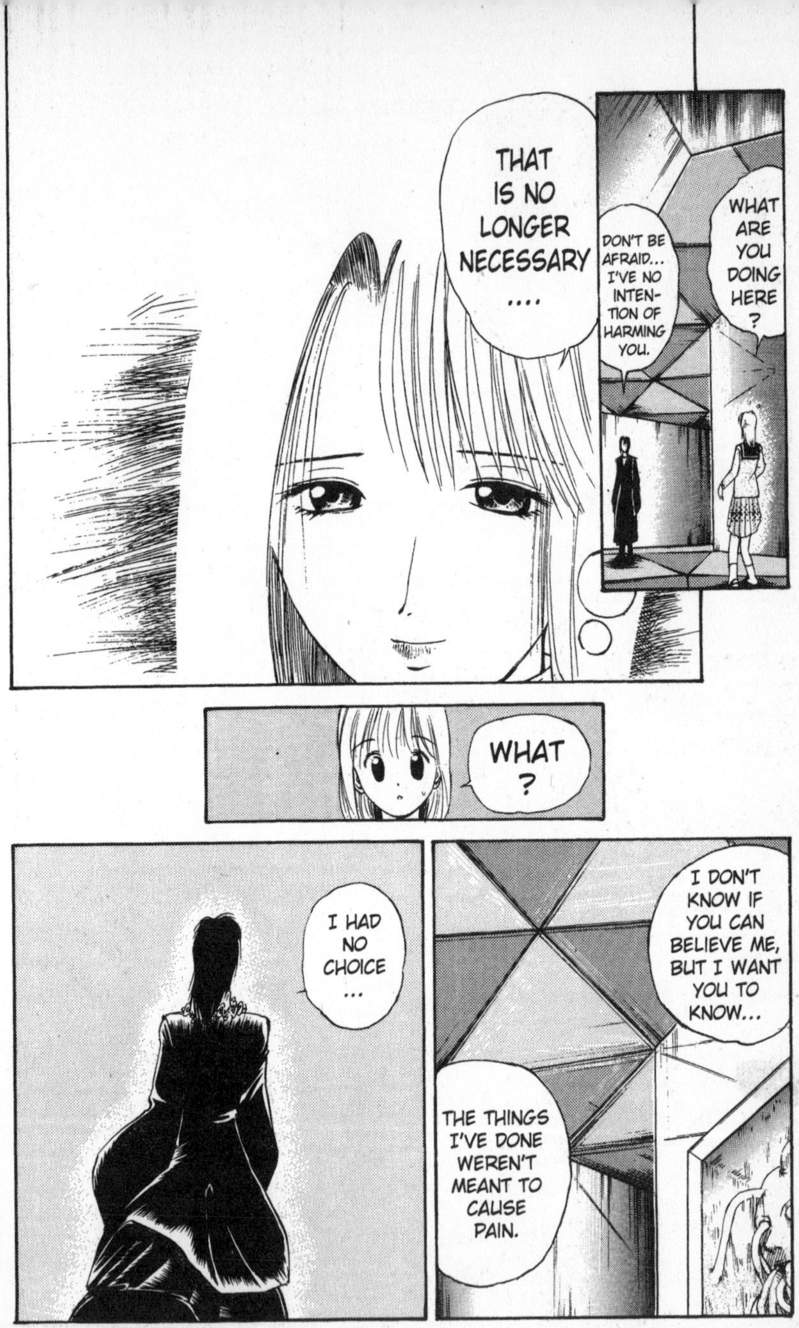
WHAT ARE YOU DOING HERE ?
DON'T BE AFRAID... I'VE NO INTEN- TION OF HARMING YOU.
THAT IS NO LONGER NECESSARY ....
WHAT ?
I DON'T KNOW IF YOU CAN BELIEVE ME, BUT I WANT YOU TO KNOW...
THE THINGS I'VE DONE WEREN'T MEANT TO CAUSE PAIN.
I HAD NO CHOICE ...

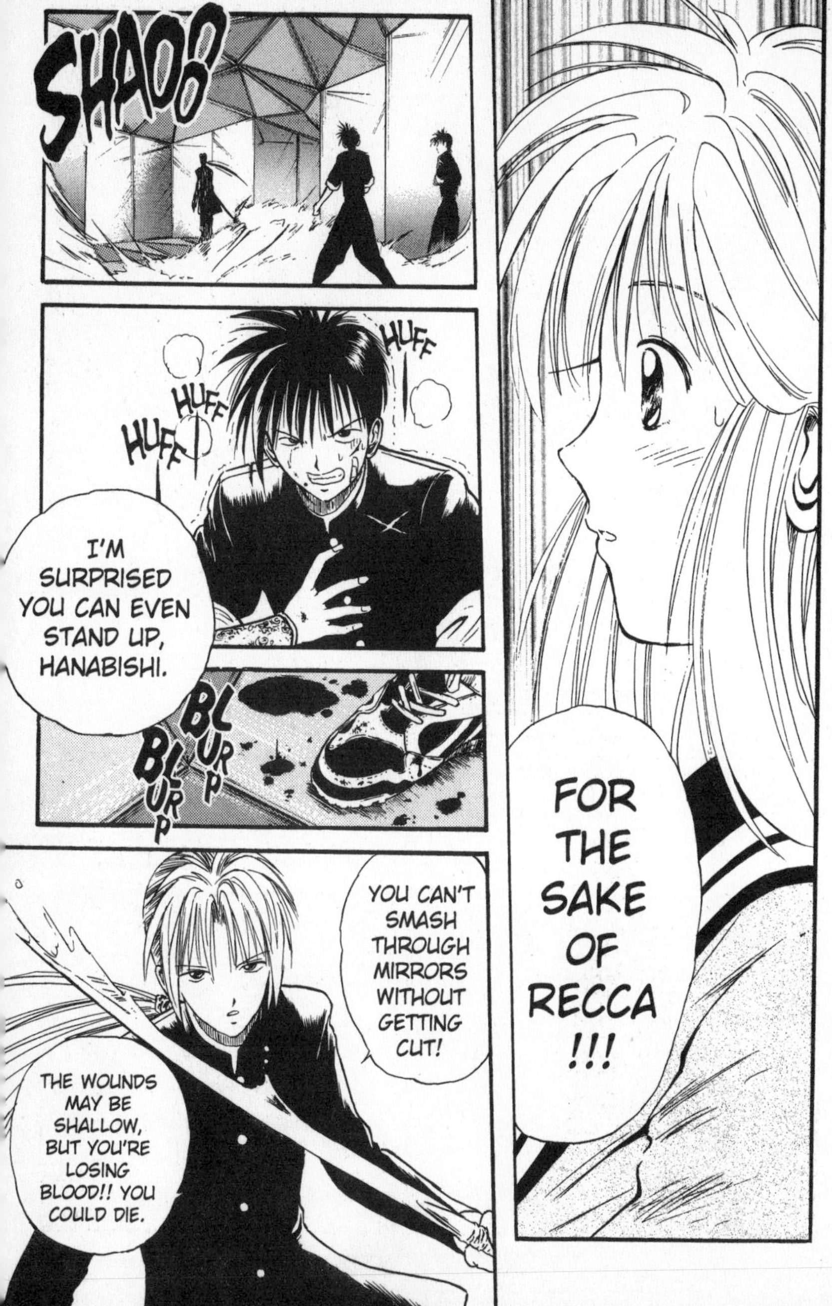
FOR THE SAKE OF RECCA!!!
SHAOO
HUFF
HUFF
HUFF
I'M SURPRISED YOU CAN EVEN STAND UP, HANABISHI.
BLURP
BLURP
YOU CAN'T SMASH THROUGH MIRRORS WITHOUT GETTING CUT!
THE WOUNDS MAY BE SHALLOW, BUT YOU'RE LOSING BLOOD!! YOU COULD DIE.

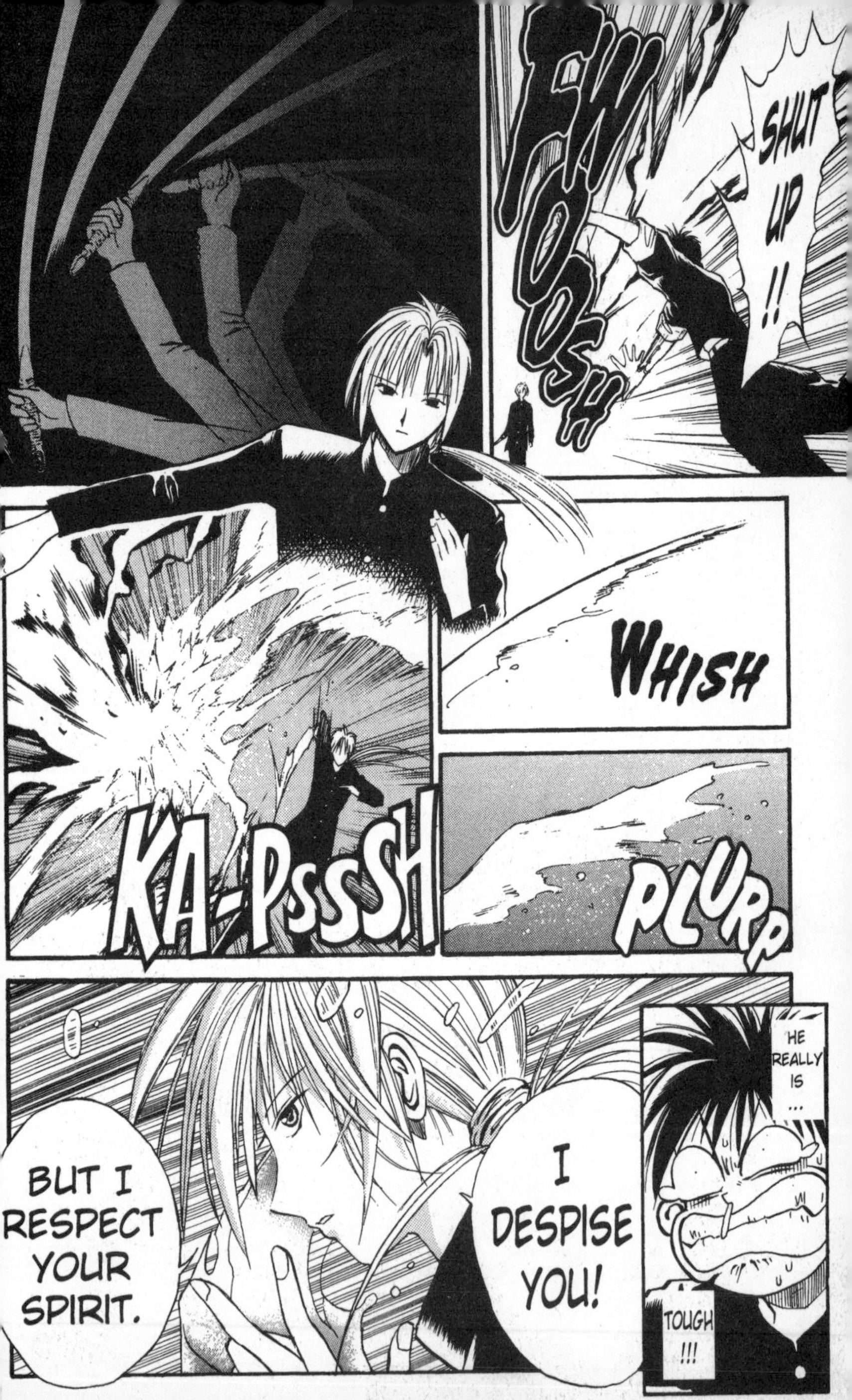
SHUT UP!!
FWOOSH
WHISH
KA-PSSSH
PLURP
HE REALLY IS ...
TOUGH!!!
I DESPISE YOU!
BUT I RESPECT YOUR SPIRIT.

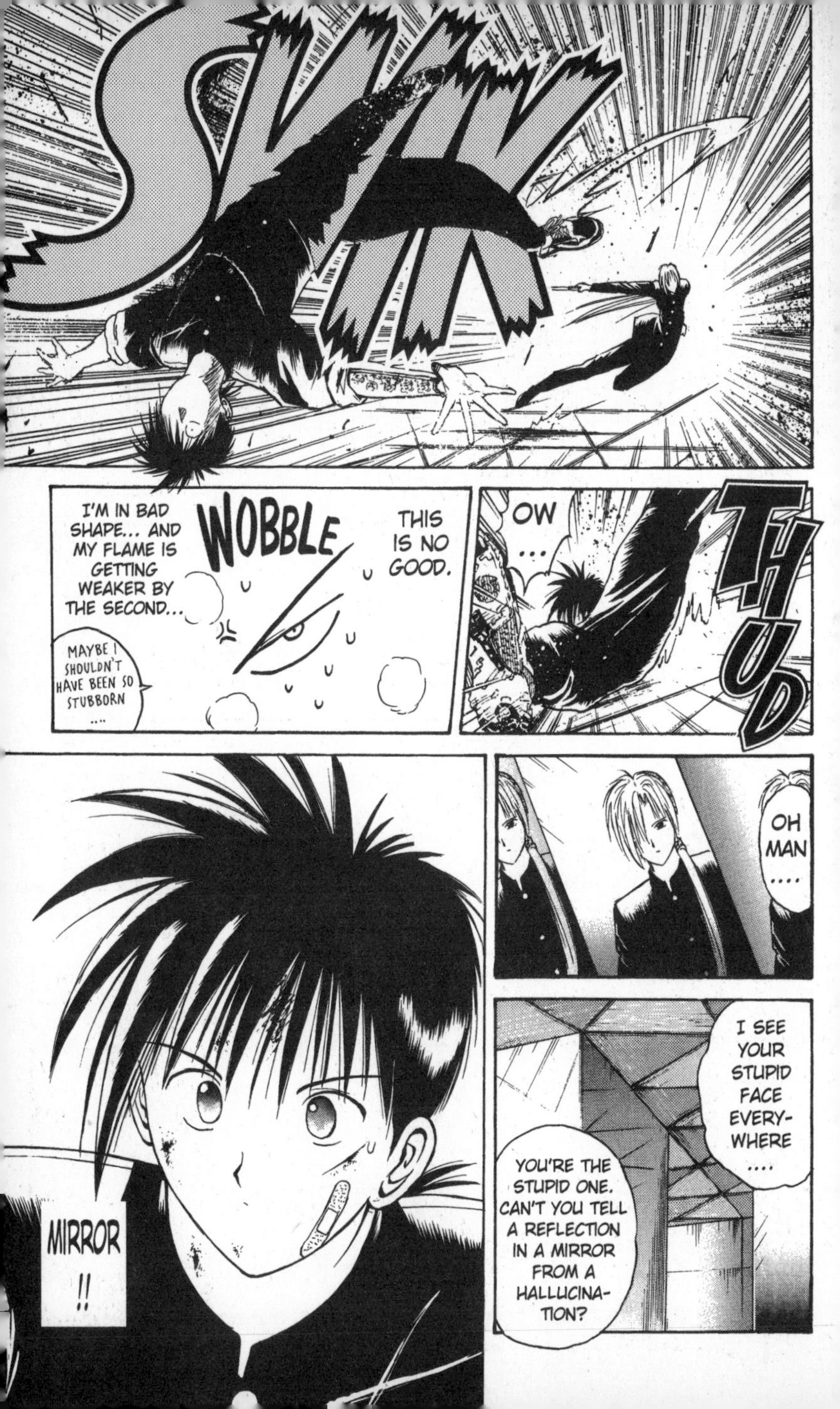
SWAN
THUD
OW ...
THIS IS NO GOOD.
WOBBLE
I'M IN BAD SHAPE... AND MY FLAME IS GETTING WEAKER BY THE SECOND...
MAYBE I SHOULDN'T HAVE BEEN SO STUBBORN ....
OH MAN ....
I SEE YOUR STUPID FACE EVERY-WHERE ....
YOU'RE THE STUPID ONE. CAN'T YOU TELL A REFLECTION IN A MIRROR FROM A HALLUCINA-TION?
MIRROR !!

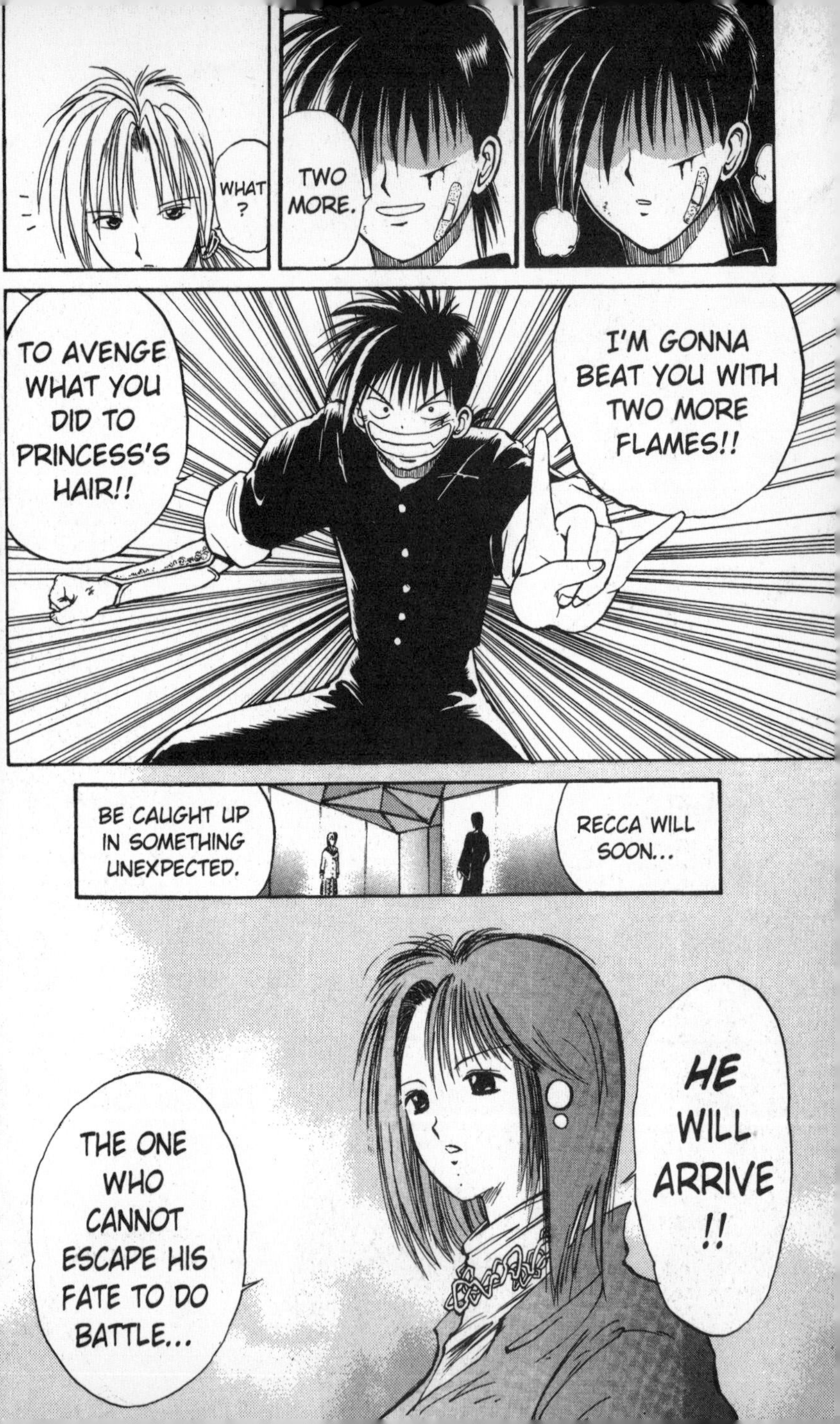
TWO MORE.
WHAT ?
I'M GONNA BEAT YOU WITH TWO MORE FLAMES!!
TO AVENGE WHAT YOU DID TO PRINCESS'S HAIR!!
RECCA WILL SOON...
BE CAUGHT UP IN SOMETHING UNEXPECTED.
HE WILL ARRIVE !!
THE ONE WHO CANNOT ESCAPE HIS FATE TO DO BATTLE...

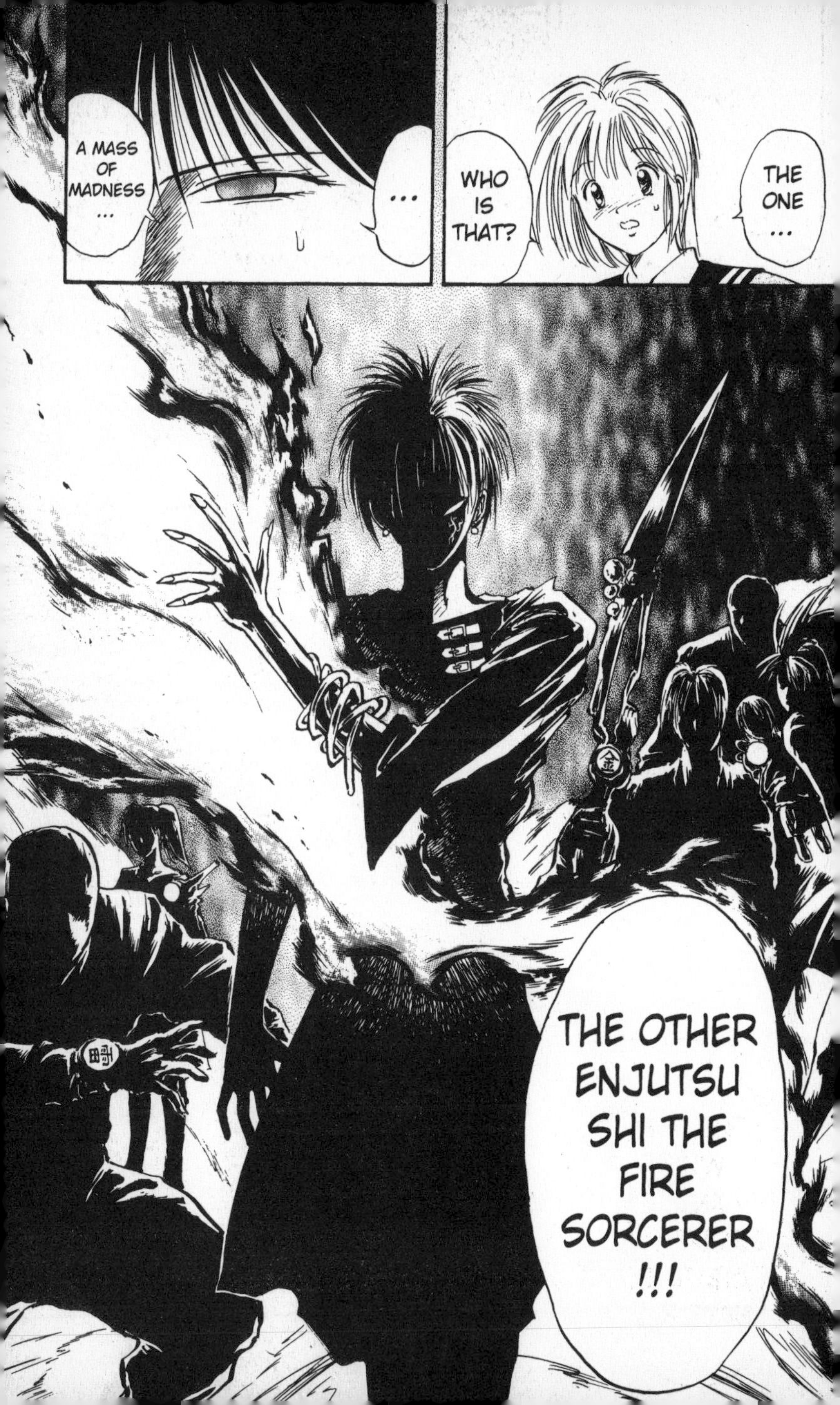
THE ONE ...
WHO IS THAT?
...
A MASS OF MADNESS ...
THE OTHER ENJUTSU SHI THE FIRE SORCERER !!!

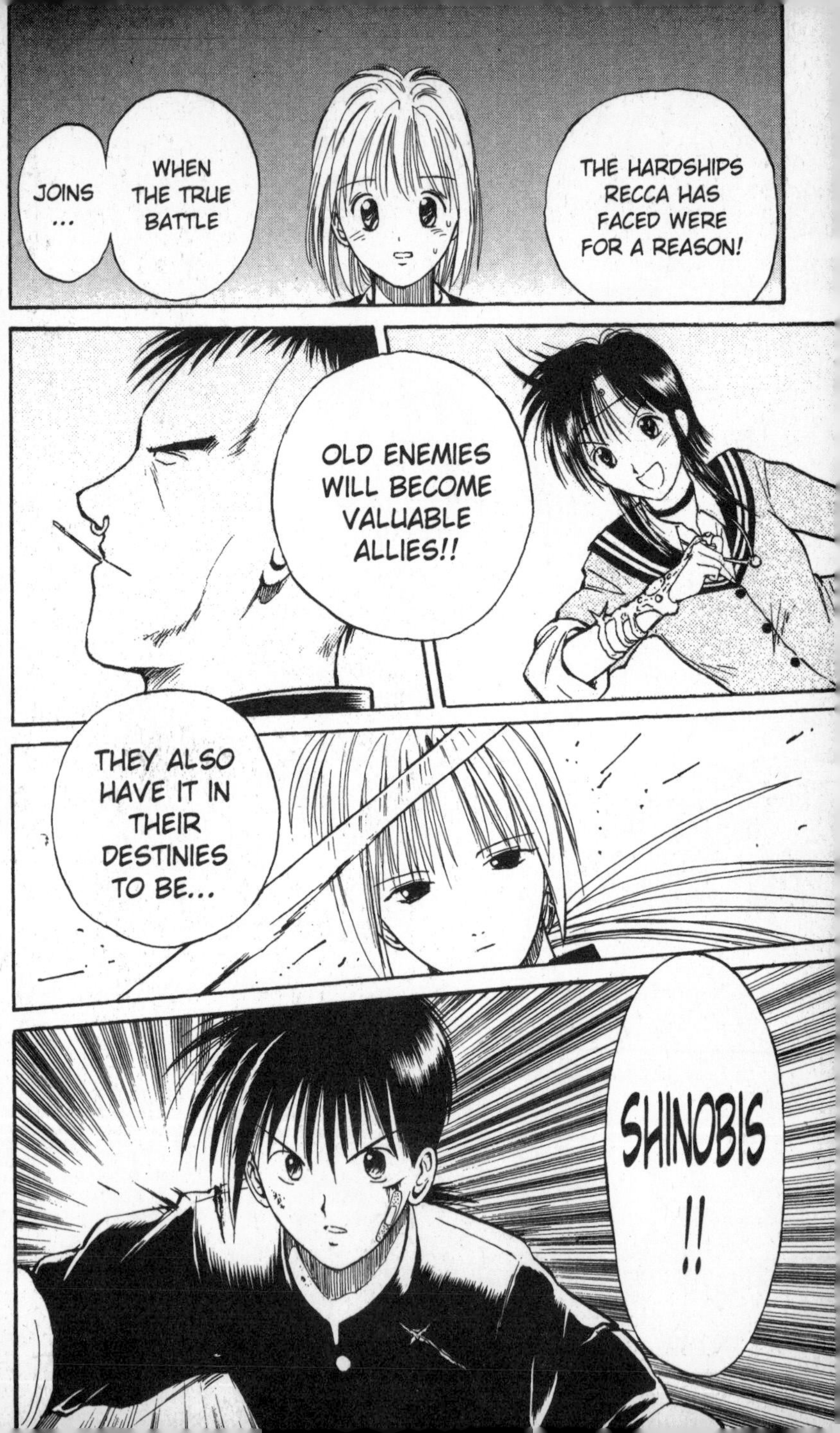
THE HARDSHIPS RECCA HAS FACED WERE FOR A REASON!
WHEN THE TRUE BATTLE
JOINS ...
OLD ENEMIES WILL BECOME VALUABLE ALLIES!!
THEY ALSO HAVE IT IN THEIR DESTINIES TO BE...
SHINOBIS !!

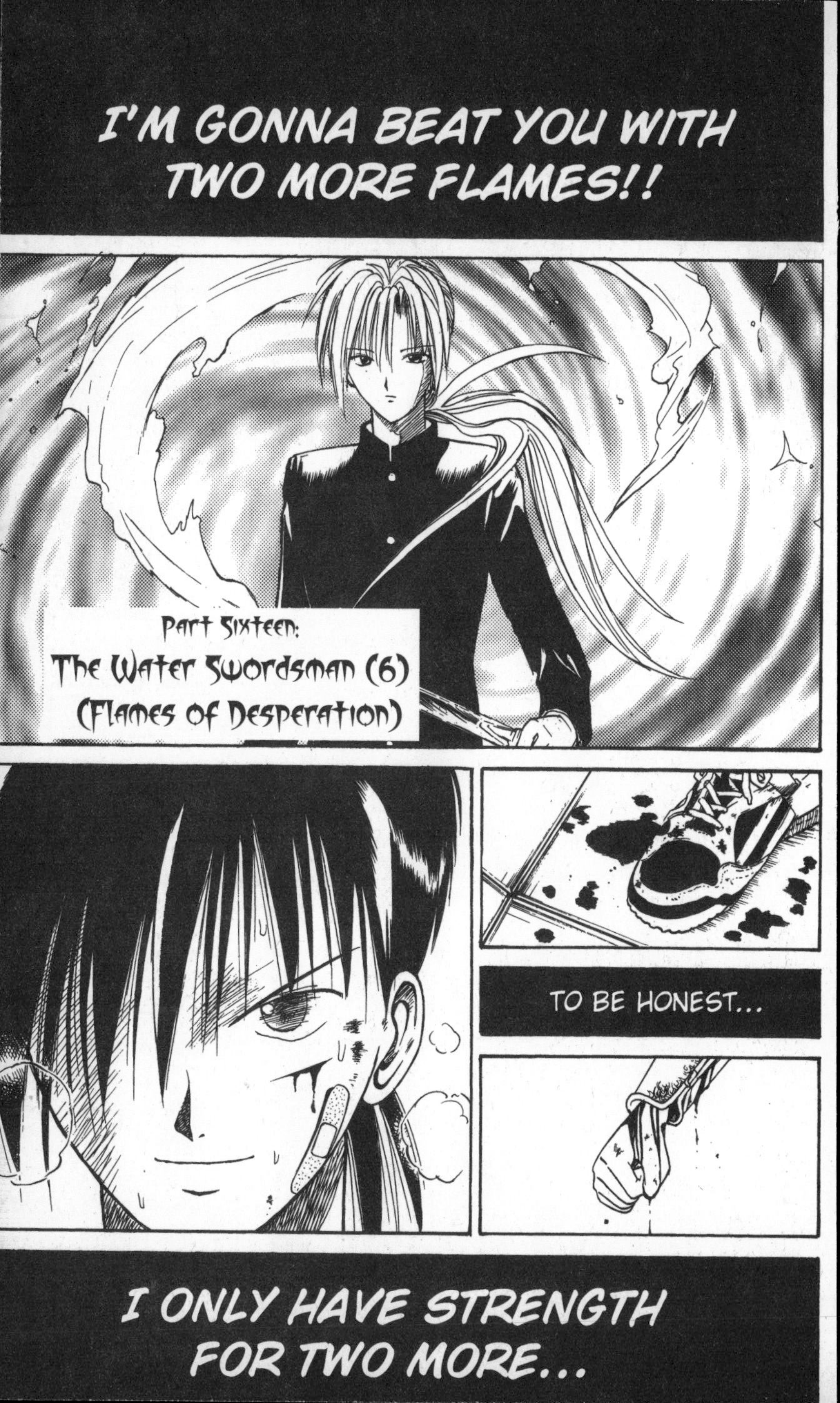
I'M GONNA BEAT YOU WITH TWO MORE FLAMES!!
Part Sixteen:
The Water Swordsman (6)
(Flames of Desperation)
TO BE HONEST...
I ONLY HAVE STRENGTH FOR TWO MORE...

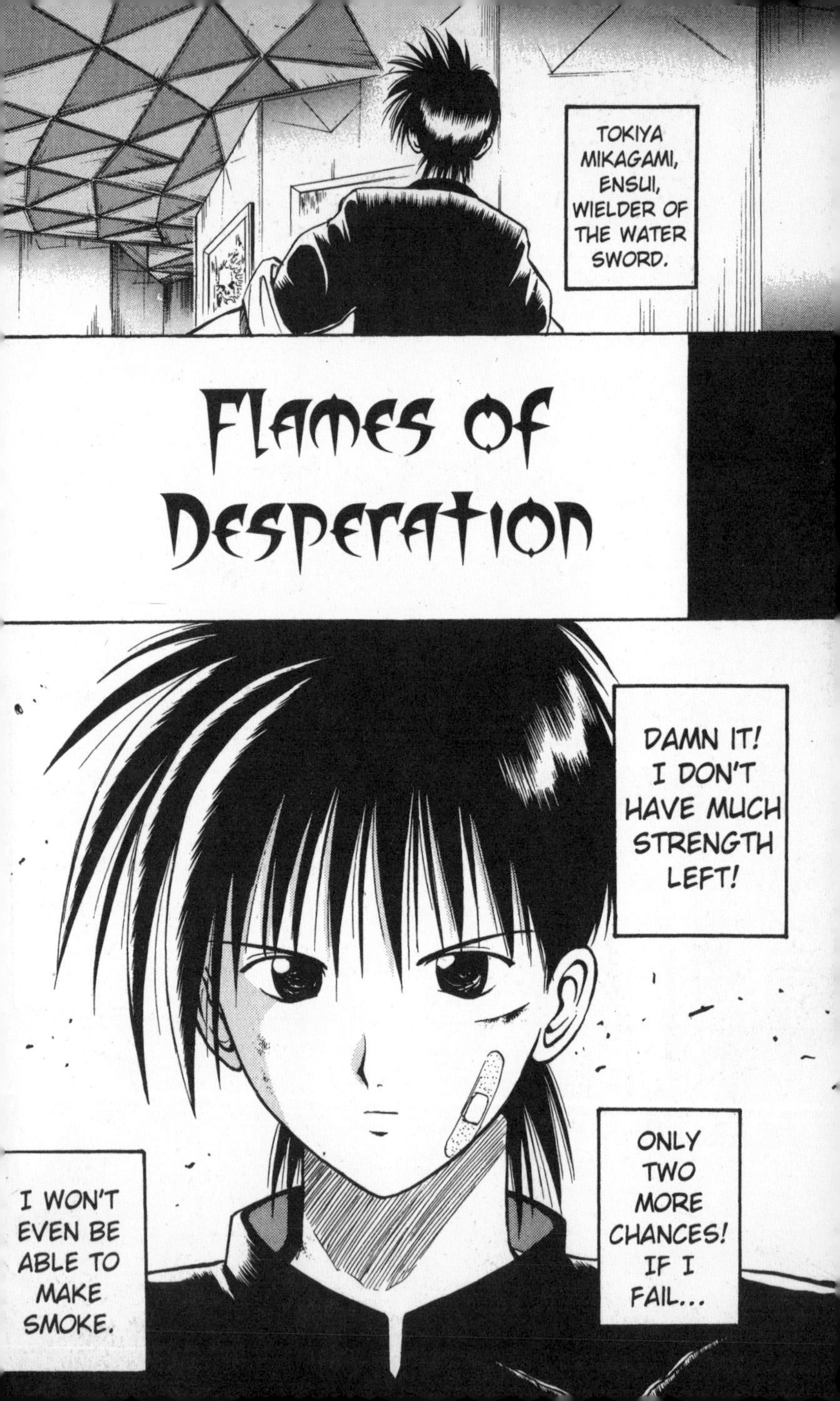
TOKIYA MIKAGAMI, ENSUI, WIELDER OF THE WATER SWORD.
Flames of Desperation
DAMN IT! I DON'T HAVE MUCH STRENGTH LEFT!
ONLY TWO MORE CHANCES! IF I FAIL...
I WON'T EVEN BE ABLE TO MAKE SMOKE.

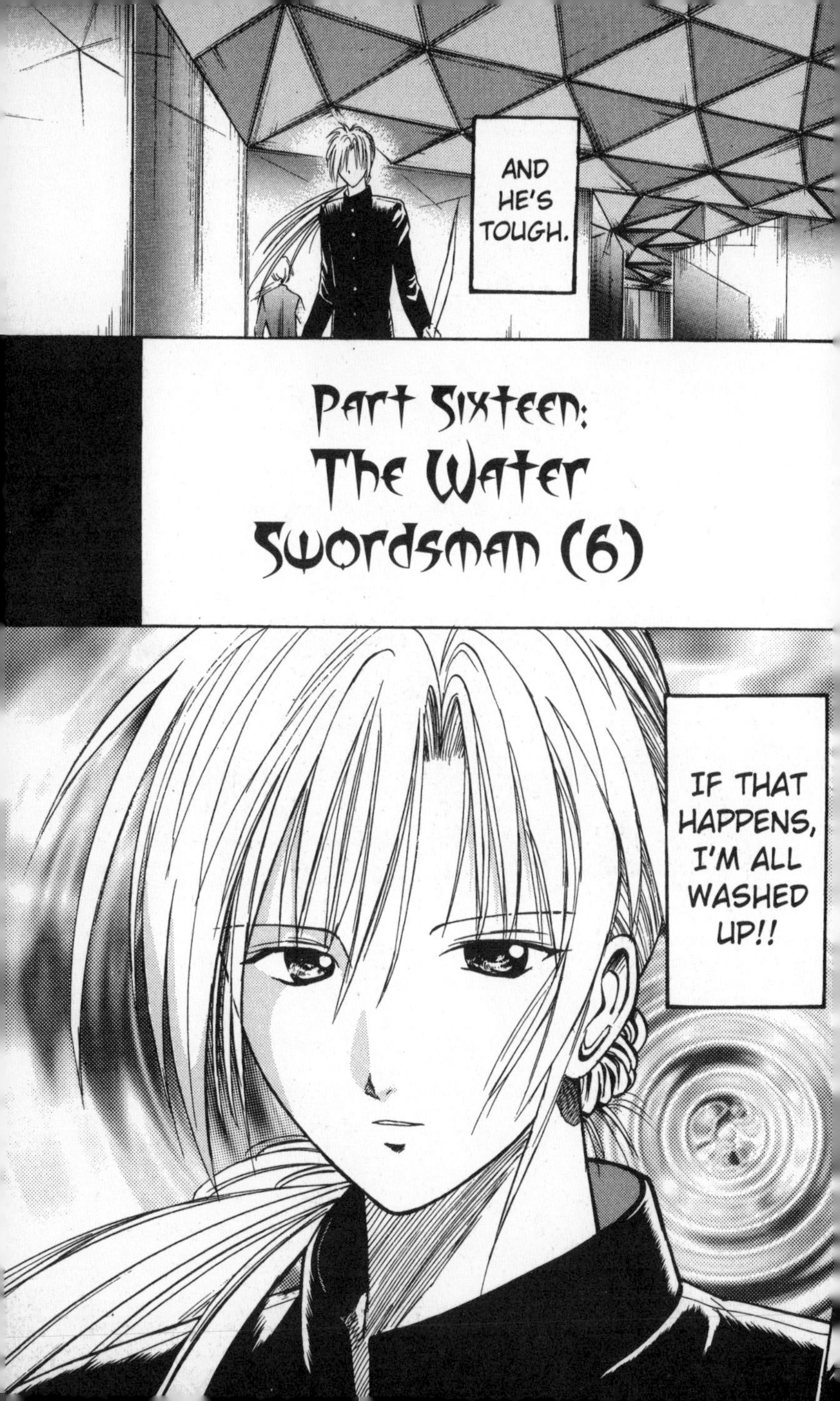
AND HE'S TOUGH.
Part Sixteen: The Water Swordsman (6)
IF THAT HAPPENS, I'M ALL WASHED UP!!

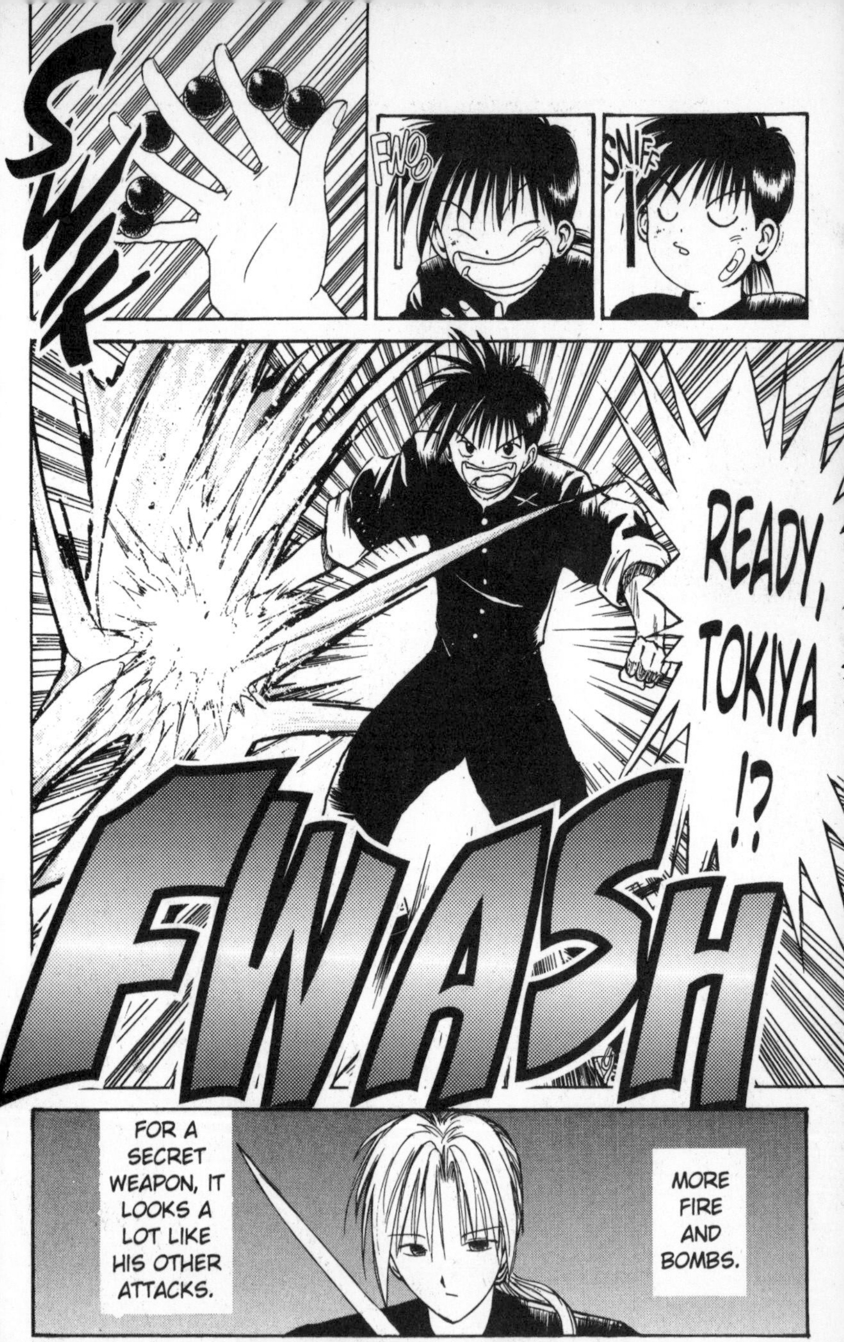
SWIK
FWOO
SNIFF
READY, TOKIYA!?
FWASH
FOR A SECRET WEAPON, IT LOOKS A LOT LIKE HIS OTHER ATTACKS.
MORE FIRE AND BOMBS.

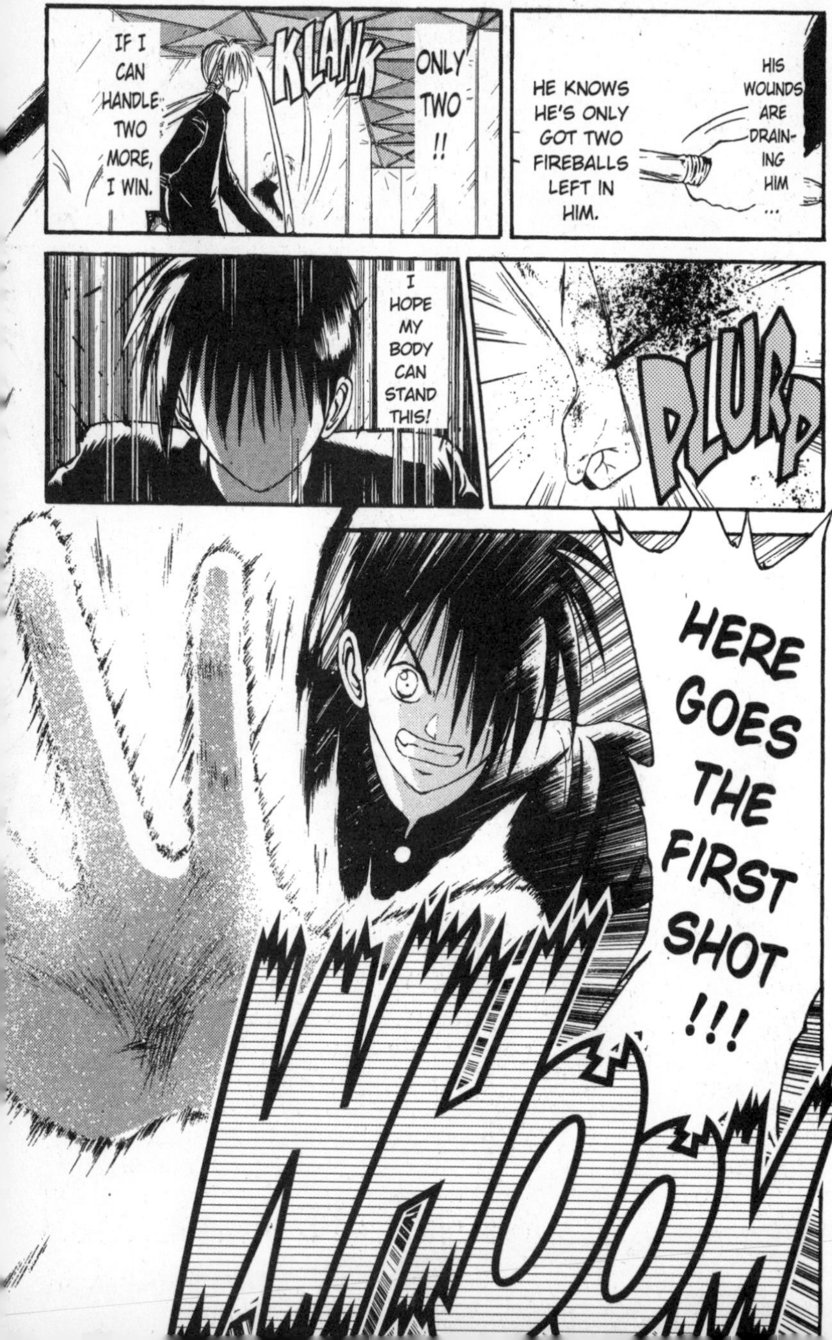

HIS WOUNDS ARE DRAIN-ING HIM ...
HE KNOWS HE'S ONLY GOT TWO FIREBALLS LEFT IN HIM.
ONLY TWO !!
KLANK
IF I CAN HANDLE TWO MORE, I WIN.
PLURP
I HOPE MY BODY CAN STAND THIS!
HERE GOES THE FIRST SHOT !!!
WHOOM

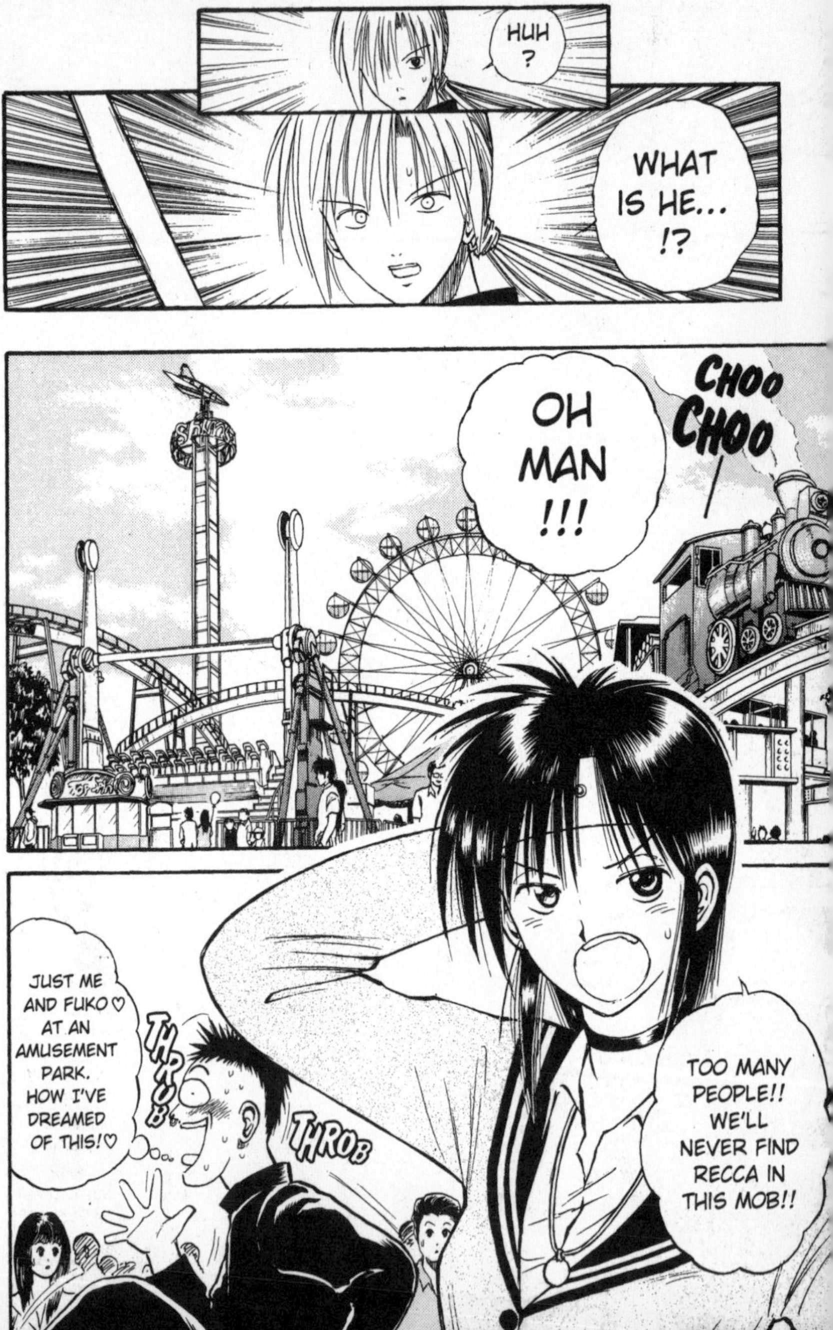
HUH?
WHAT IS HE...!?
CHOO CHOO
OH MAN!!!
TOO MANY PEOPLE!! WE'LL NEVER FIND RECCA IN THIS MOB!!
THROB
THROB
JUST ME AND FUKO♡ AT AN AMUSEMENT PARK. HOW I'VE DREAMED OF THIS!♡

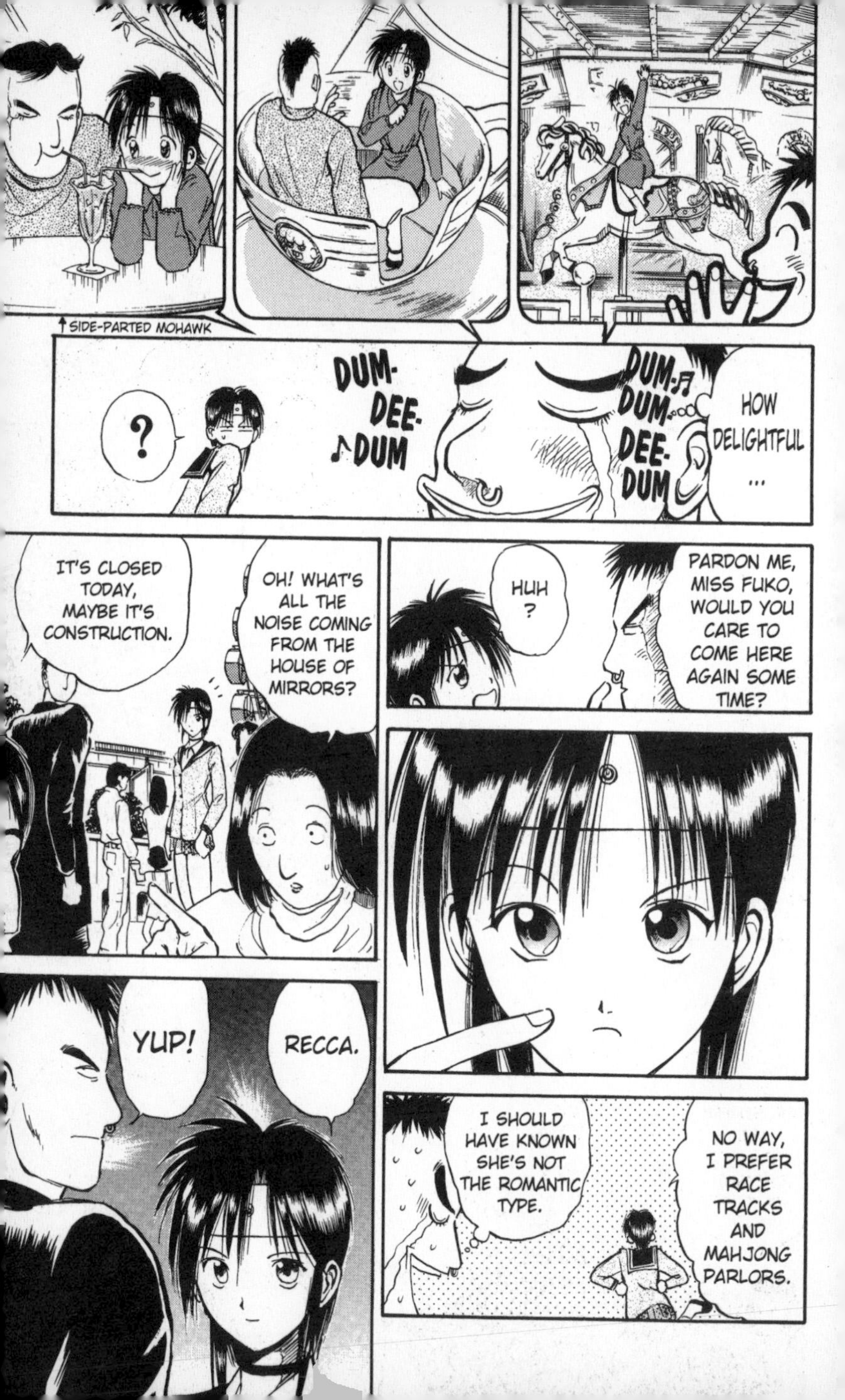

↑SIDE-PARTED MOHAWK
HOW DELIGHTFUL ...
DUM-DUM-DEE-DUM
DUM-DEE-DUM
?
PARDON ME, MISS FUKO, WOULD YOU CARE TO COME HERE AGAIN SOME TIME?
HUH?
NO WAY, I PREFER RACE TRACKS AND MAHJONG PARLORS.
I SHOULD HAVE KNOWN SHE'S NOT THE ROMANTIC TYPE.
OH! WHAT'S ALL THE NOISE COMING FROM THE HOUSE OF MIRRORS?
IT'S CLOSED TODAY, MAYBE IT'S CONSTRUCTION.
RECCA.
YUP!

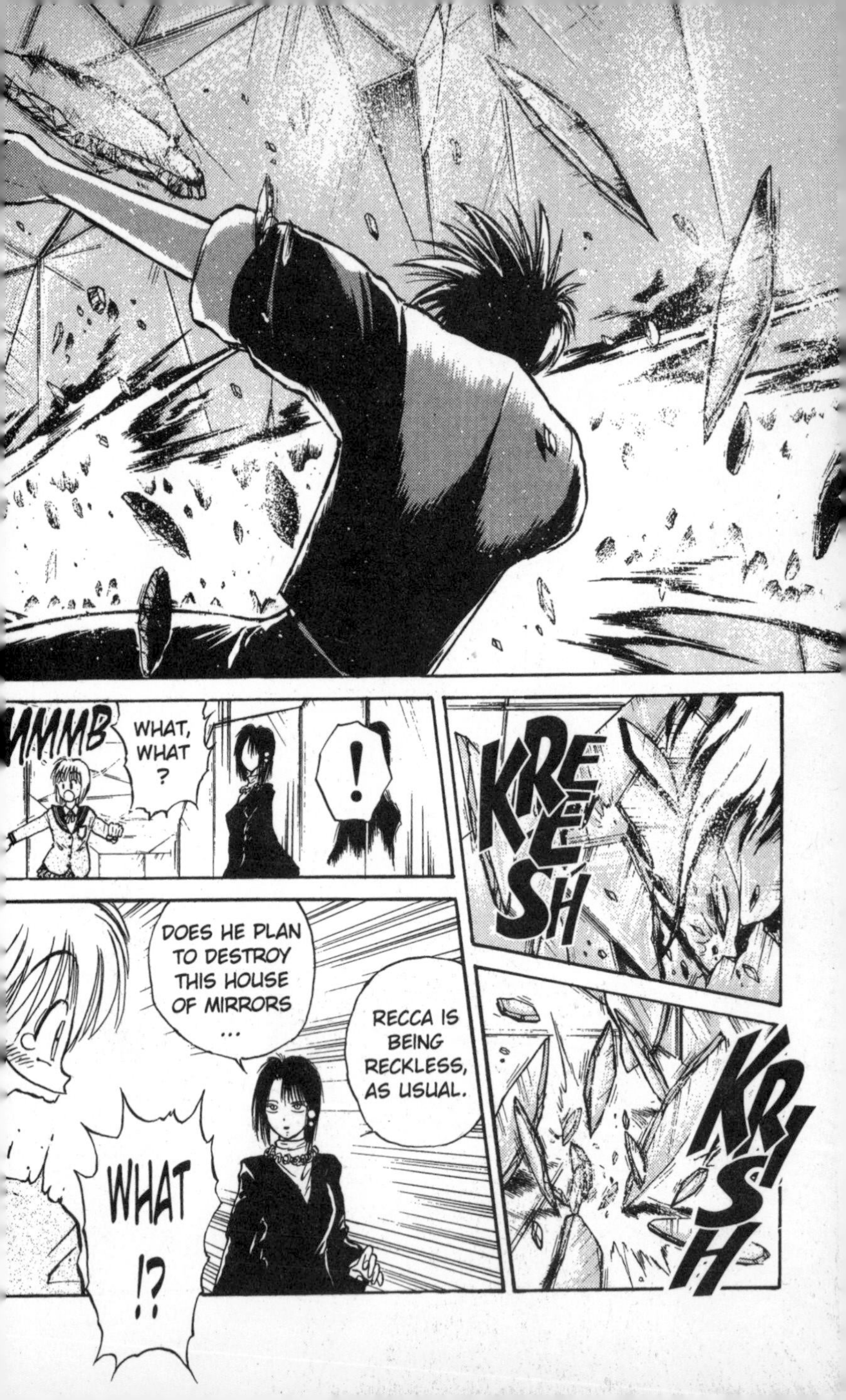
MMMB
WHAT, WHAT ?
!
KRESH
DOES HE PLAN TO DESTROY THIS HOUSE OF MIRRORS ...
RECCA IS BEING RECKLESS, AS USUAL.
WHAT !?
KRISH

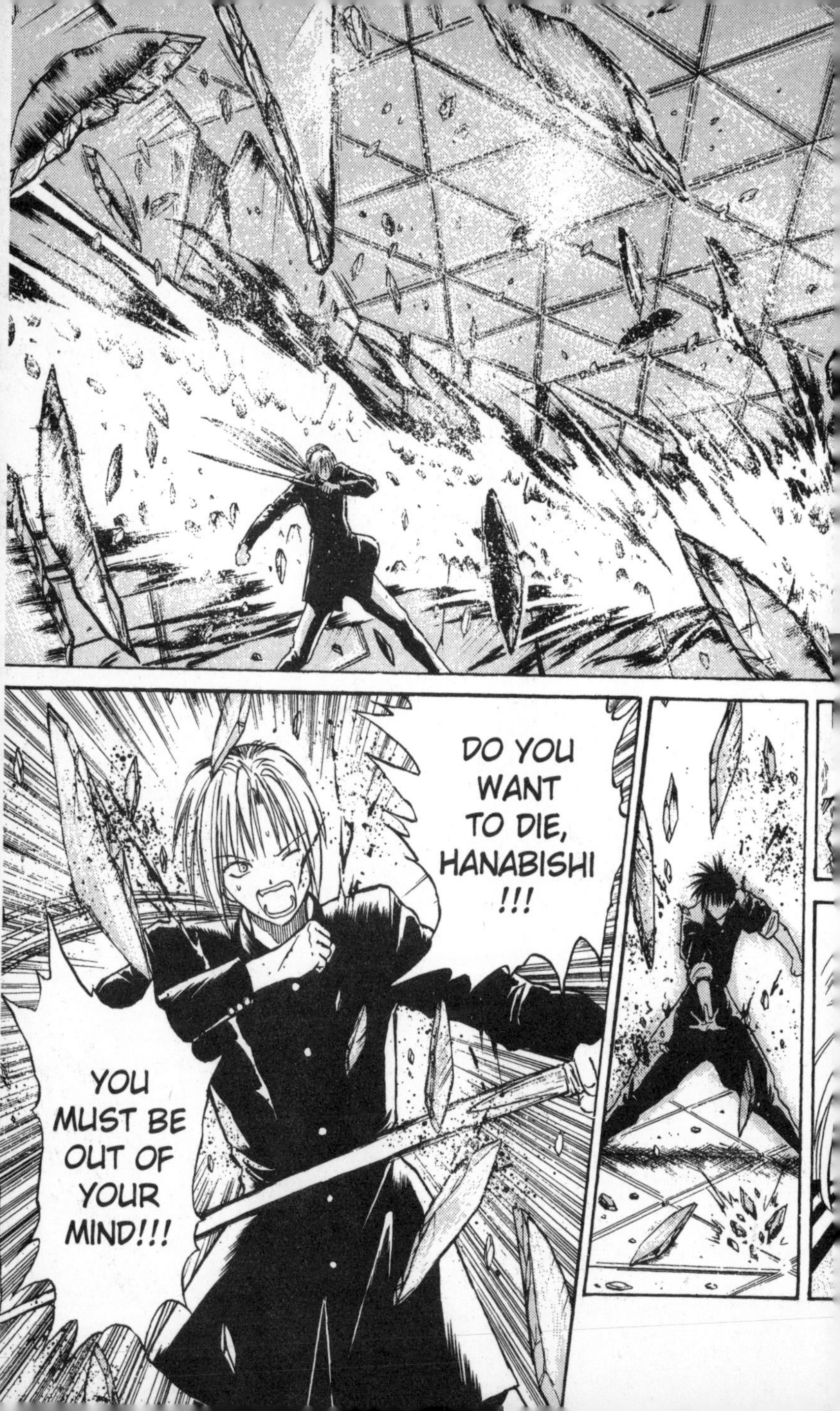

DO YOU WANT TO DIE, HANABISHI !!!
YOU MUST BE OUT OF YOUR MIND!!!

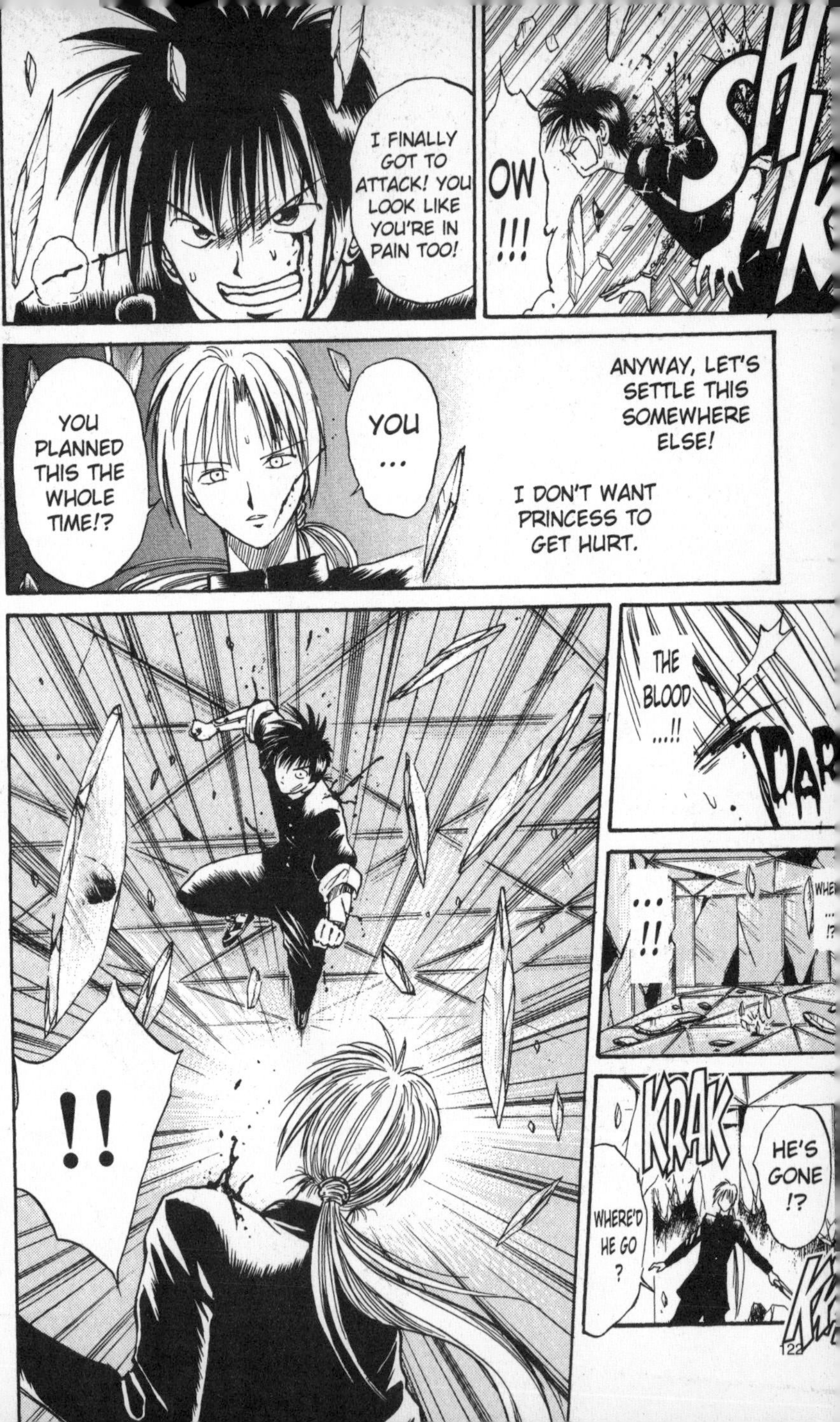
SHK
OW !!!
I FINALLY GOT TO ATTACK! YOU LOOK LIKE YOU'RE IN PAIN TOO!
ANYWAY, LET'S SETTLE THIS SOMEWHERE ELSE!
I DON'T WANT PRINCESS TO GET HURT.
YOU ...
YOU PLANNED THIS THE WHOLE TIME!?
THE BLOOD ...!!
DAR
...!!
KRAK
HE'S GONE !?
WHERE'D HE GO ?
!!

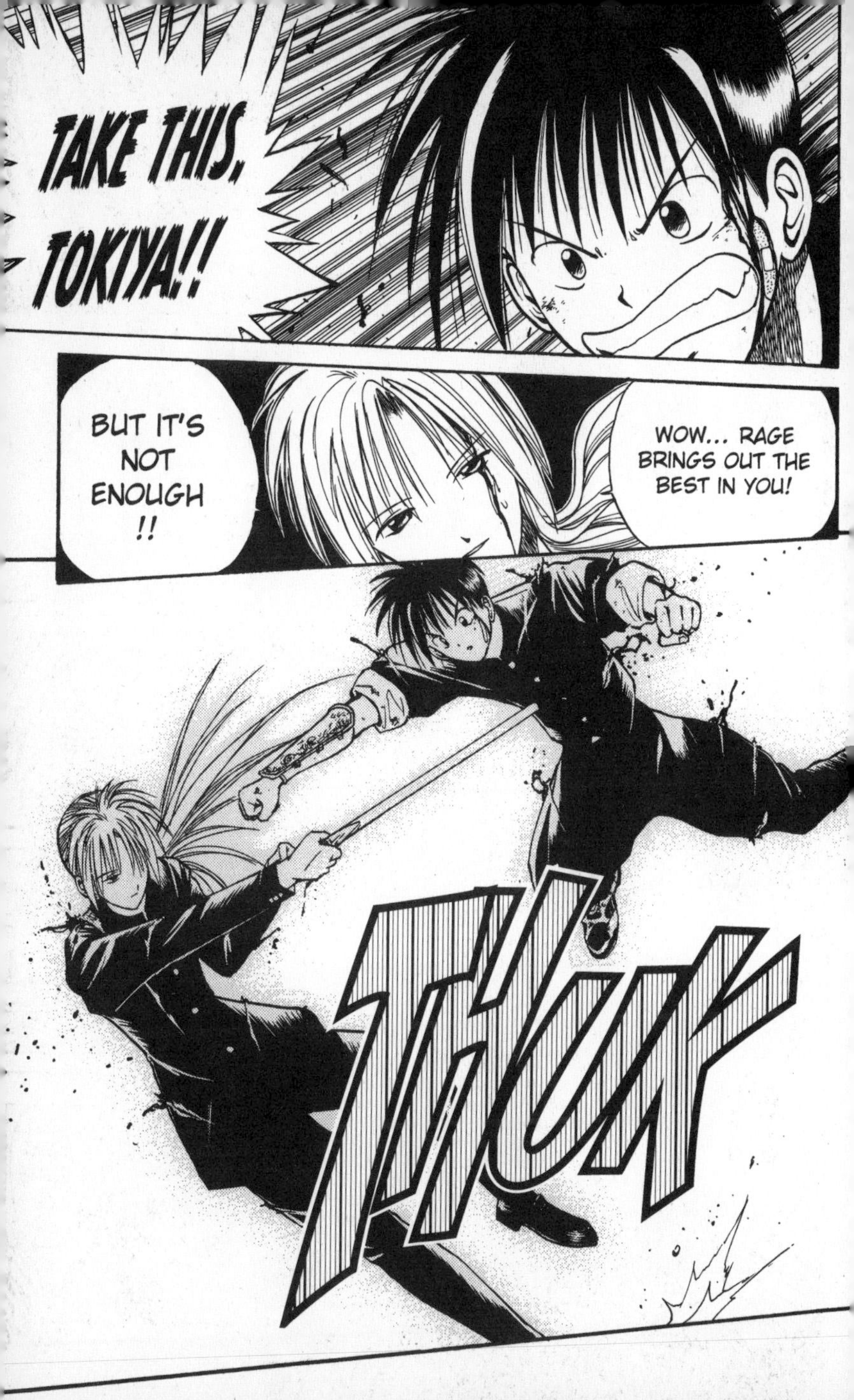
TAKE THIS, TOKIYA!!
WOW... RAGE BRINGS OUT THE BEST IN YOU!
BUT IT'S NOT ENOUGH !!
THUK

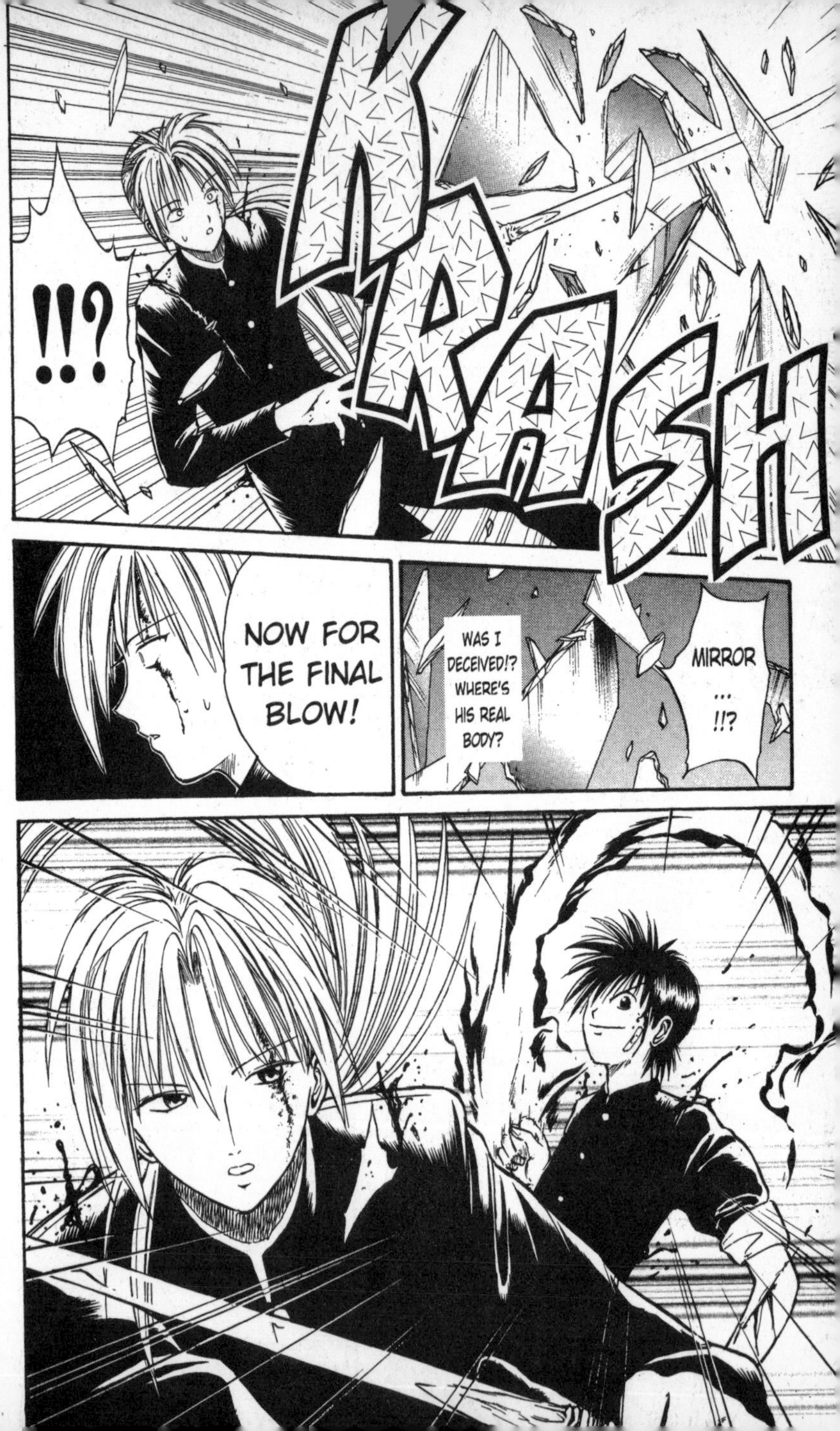
KRASH
!!?
MIRROR ... !!?
WAS I DECEIVED!? WHERE'S HIS REAL BODY?
NOW FOR THE FINAL BLOW!

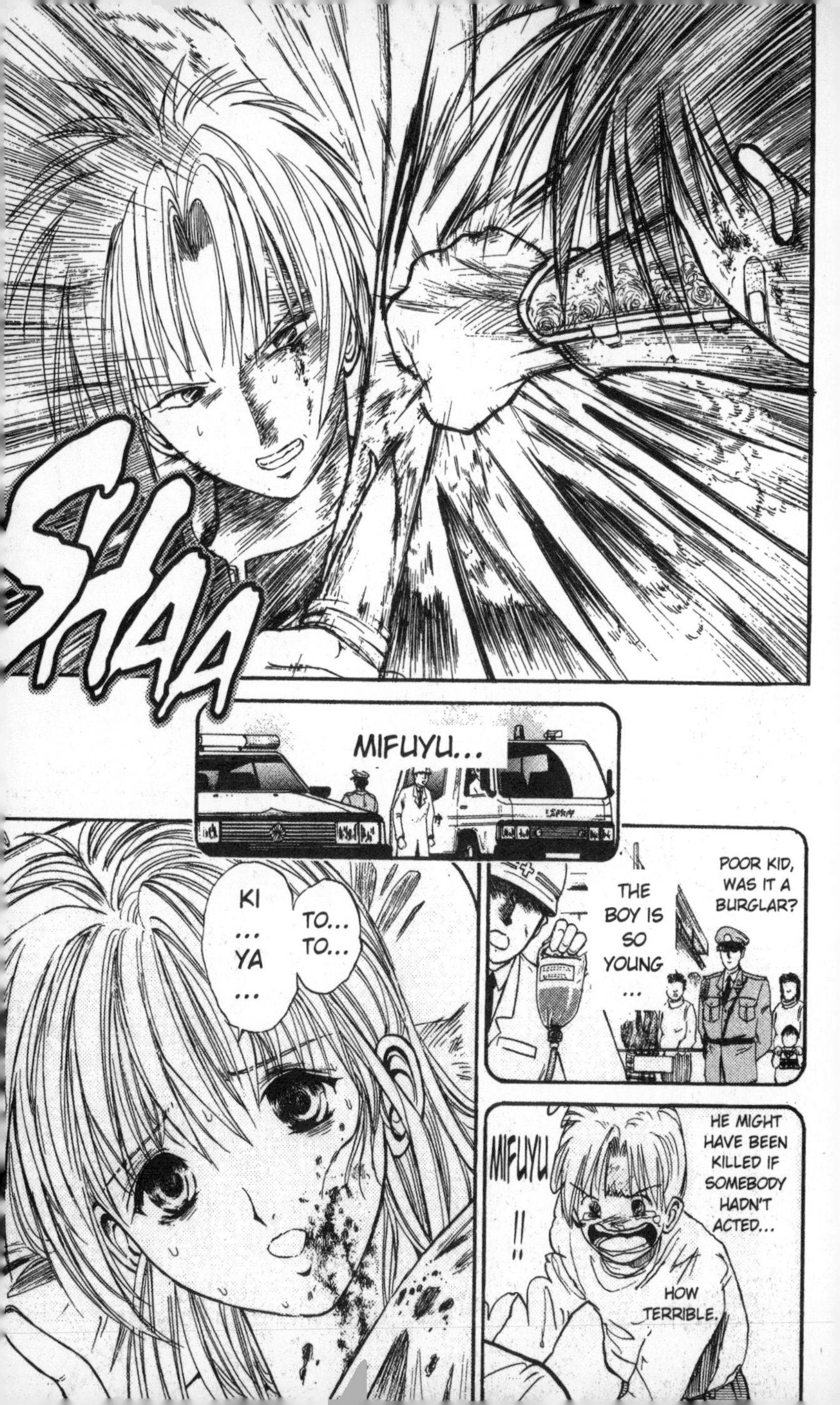
SHAA
MIFUYU...
POOR KID, WAS IT A BURGLAR?
THE BOY IS SO YOUNG ...
HE MIGHT HAVE BEEN KILLED IF SOMEBODY HADN'T ACTED...
MIFUYU !!
HOW TERRIBLE.
TO... TO...
KI ... YA ...

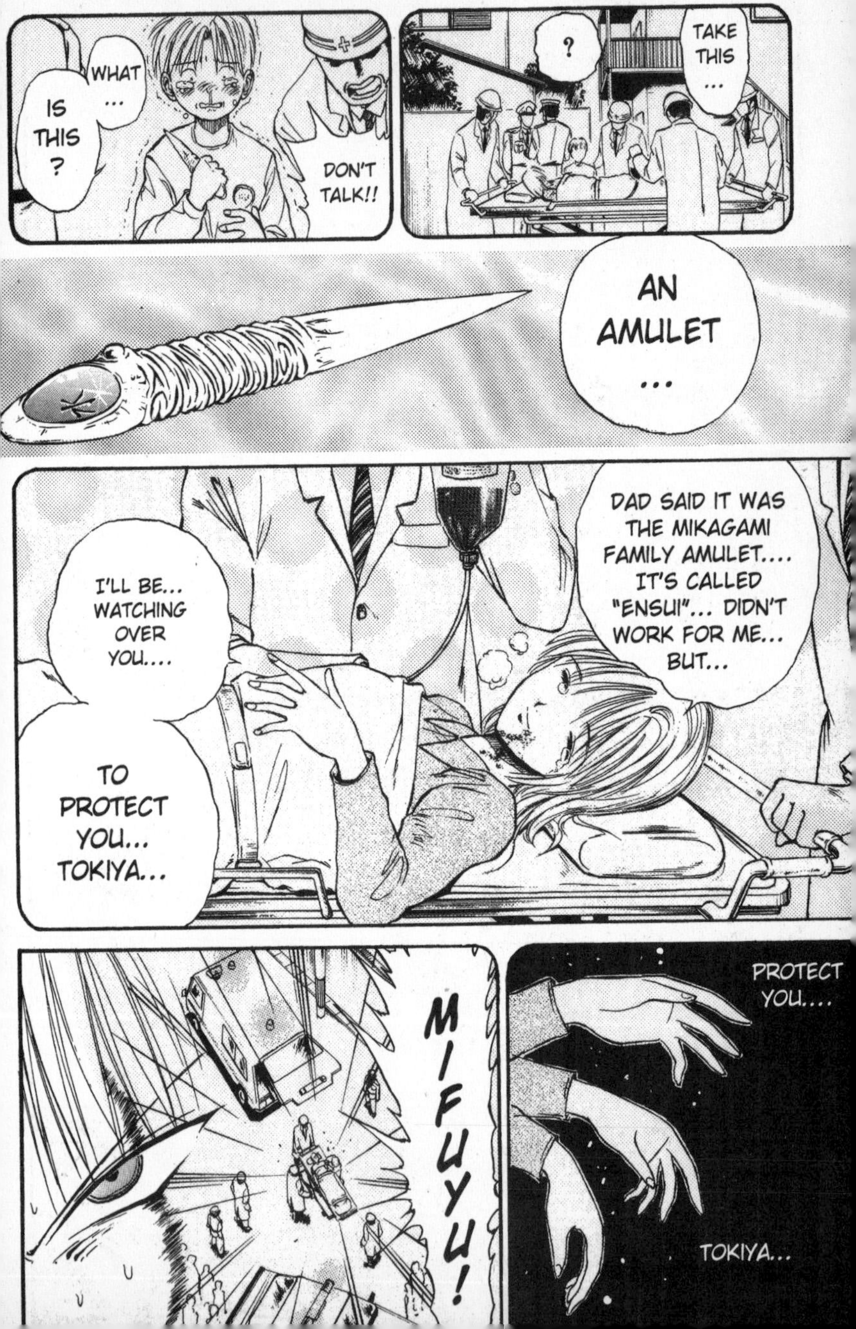
TAKE THIS ...
?
DON'T TALK!!
WHAT ...
IS THIS ?
AN AMULET ...
DAD SAID IT WAS THE MIKAGAMI FAMILY AMULET.... IT'S CALLED "ENSUI"... DIDN'T WORK FOR ME... BUT...
I'LL BE... WATCHING OVER YOU....
TO PROTECT YOU... TOKIYA...
PROTECT YOU....
TOKIYA...
MIFUYU!

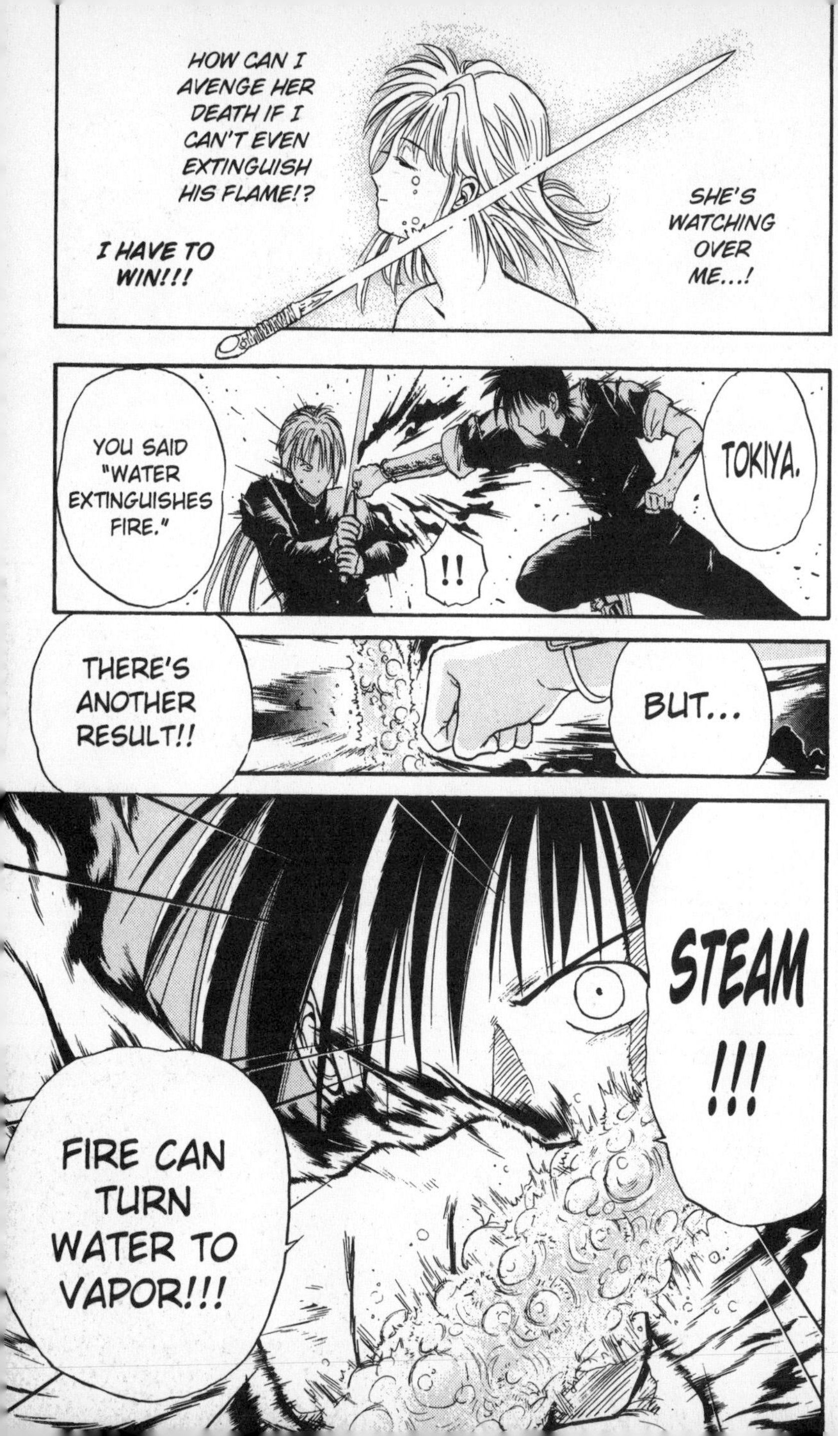
SHE'S WATCHING OVER ME...!
HOW CAN I AVENGE HER DEATH IF I CAN'T EVEN EXTINGUISH HIS FLAME!?
I HAVE TO WIN!!!
TOKIYA.
YOU SAID "WATER EXTINGUISHES FIRE."
!!
BUT...
THERE'S ANOTHER RESULT!!
STEAM !!!
FIRE CAN TURN WATER TO VAPOR!!!

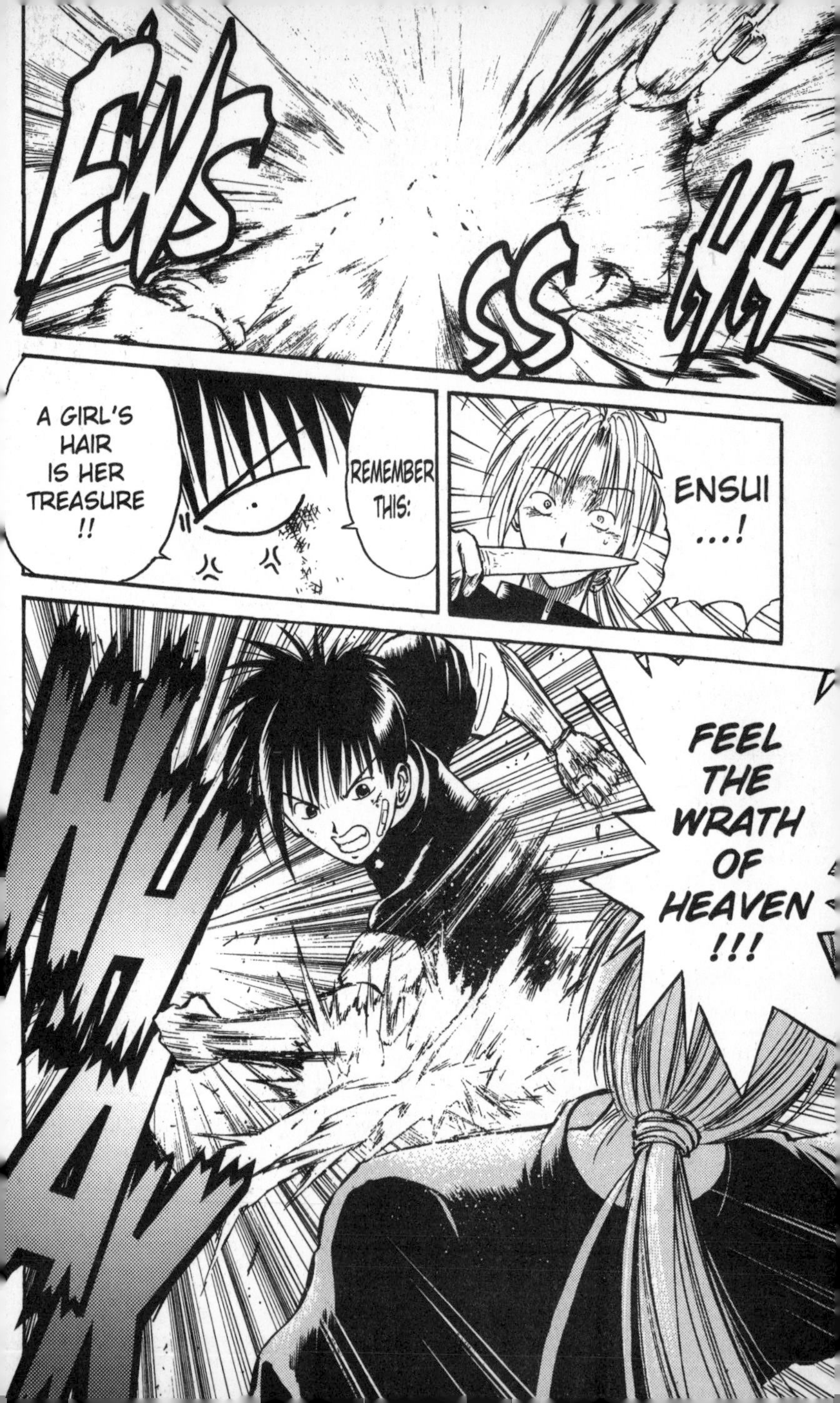

ENSUI ...!
REMEMBER THIS:
A GIRL'S HAIR IS HER TREASURE !!
FEEL THE WRATH OF HEAVEN !!!

Part Seventeen: Memories of a Dream

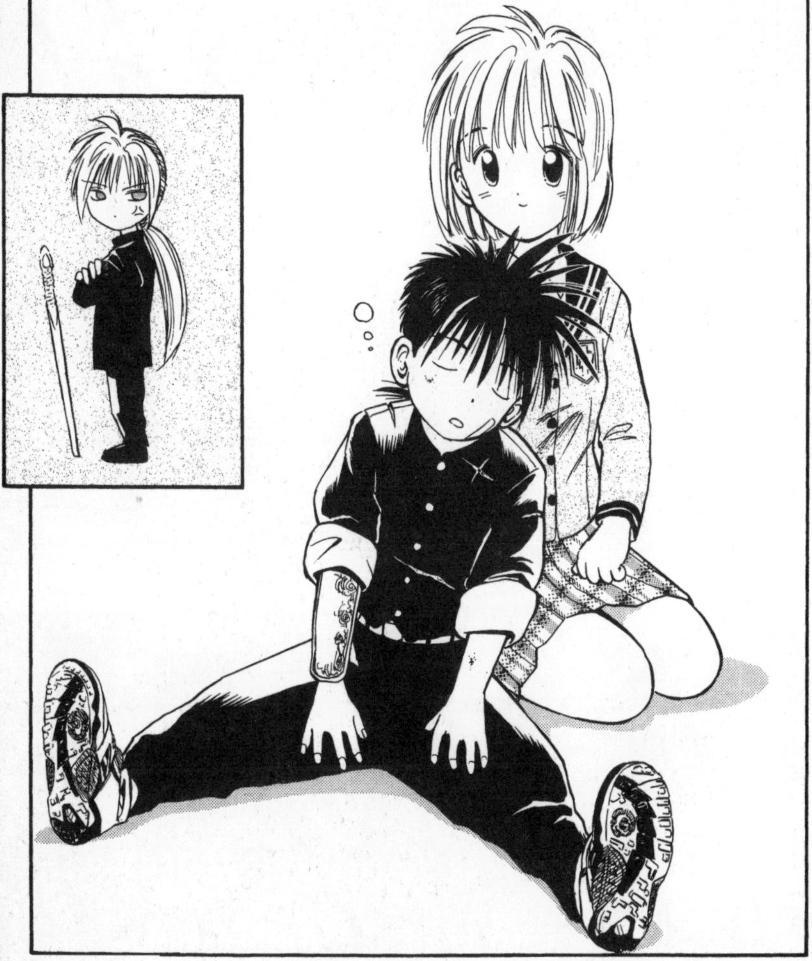

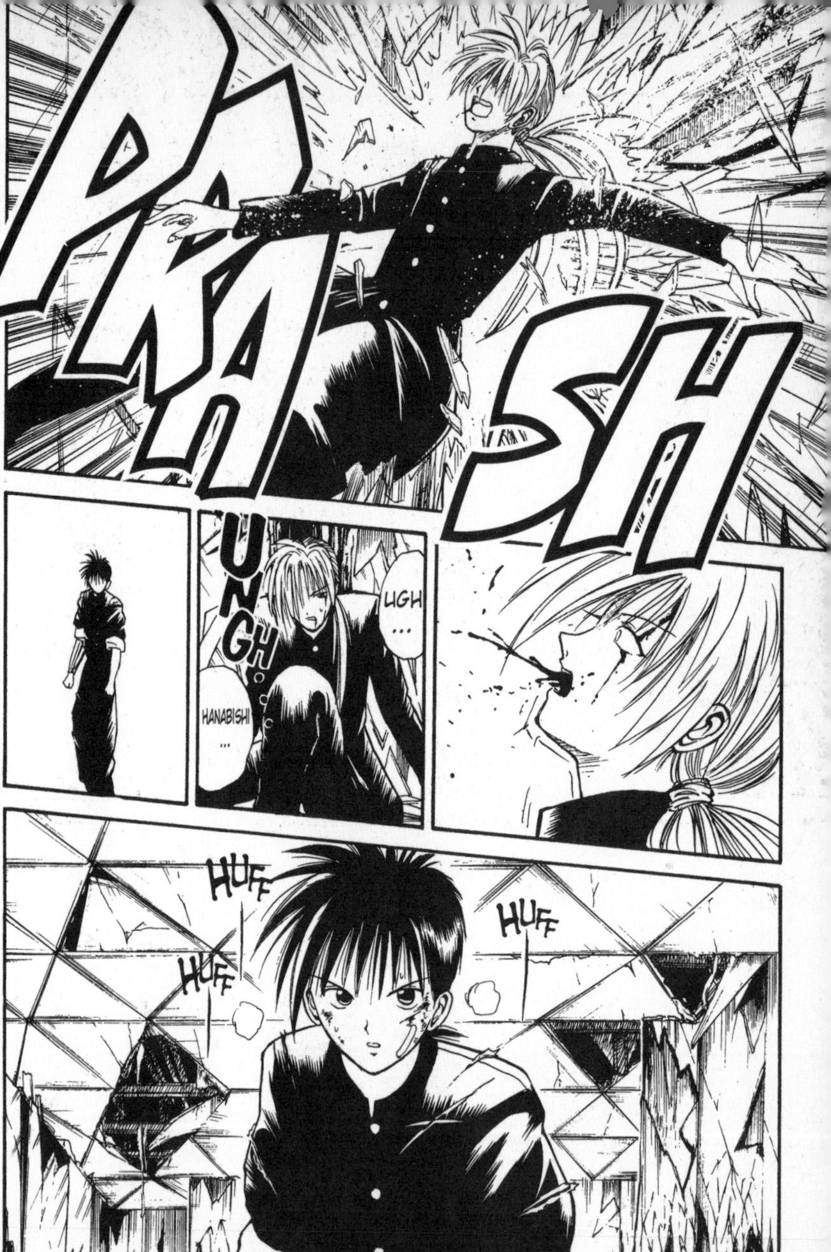

KRASH
UGH ...
UNGH
HANABISHI ...
HUFF
HUFF
HUFF

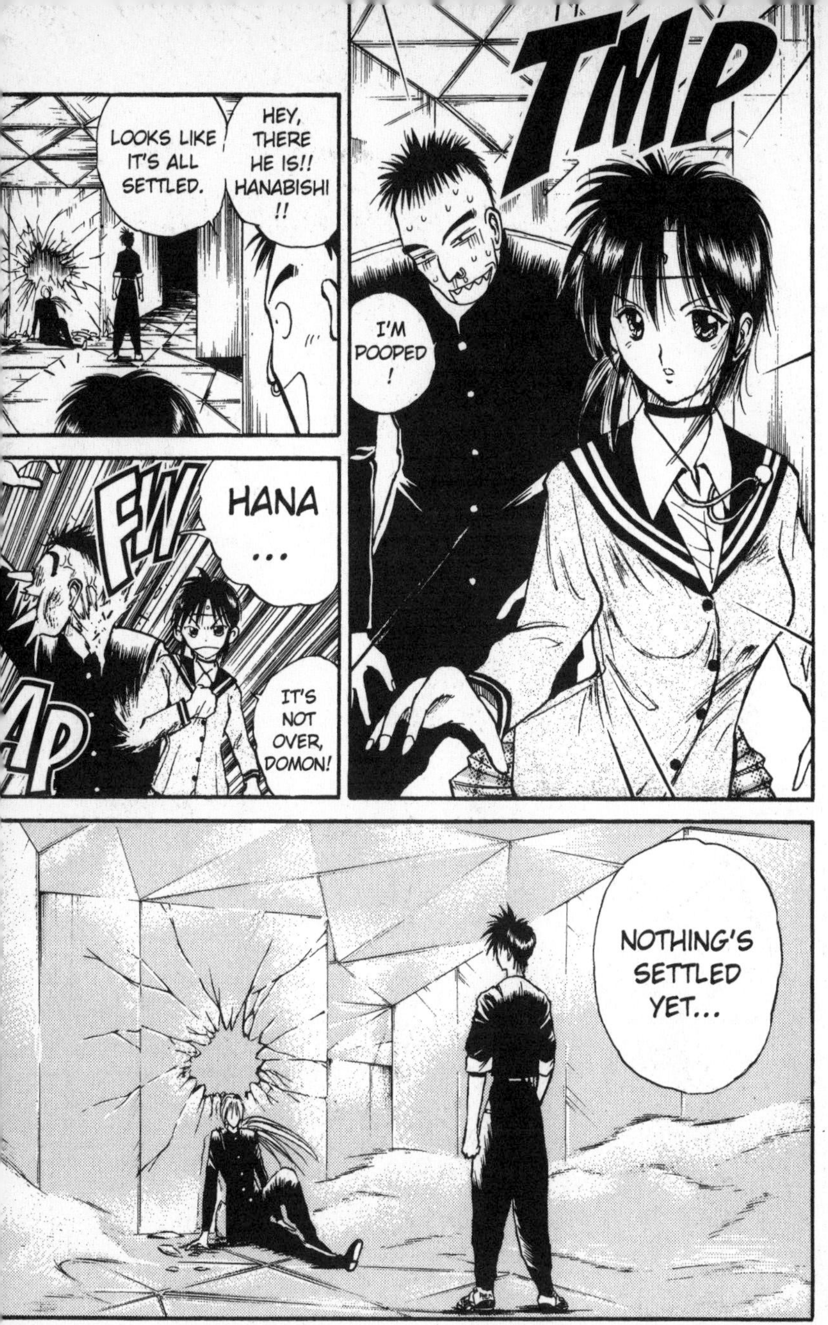
TMP
I'M POOPED!
HEY, THERE HE IS!! HANABISHI!!
LOOKS LIKE IT'S ALL SETTLED.
HANA...
FW
AP
IT'S NOT OVER, DOMON!
NOTHING'S SETTLED YET...

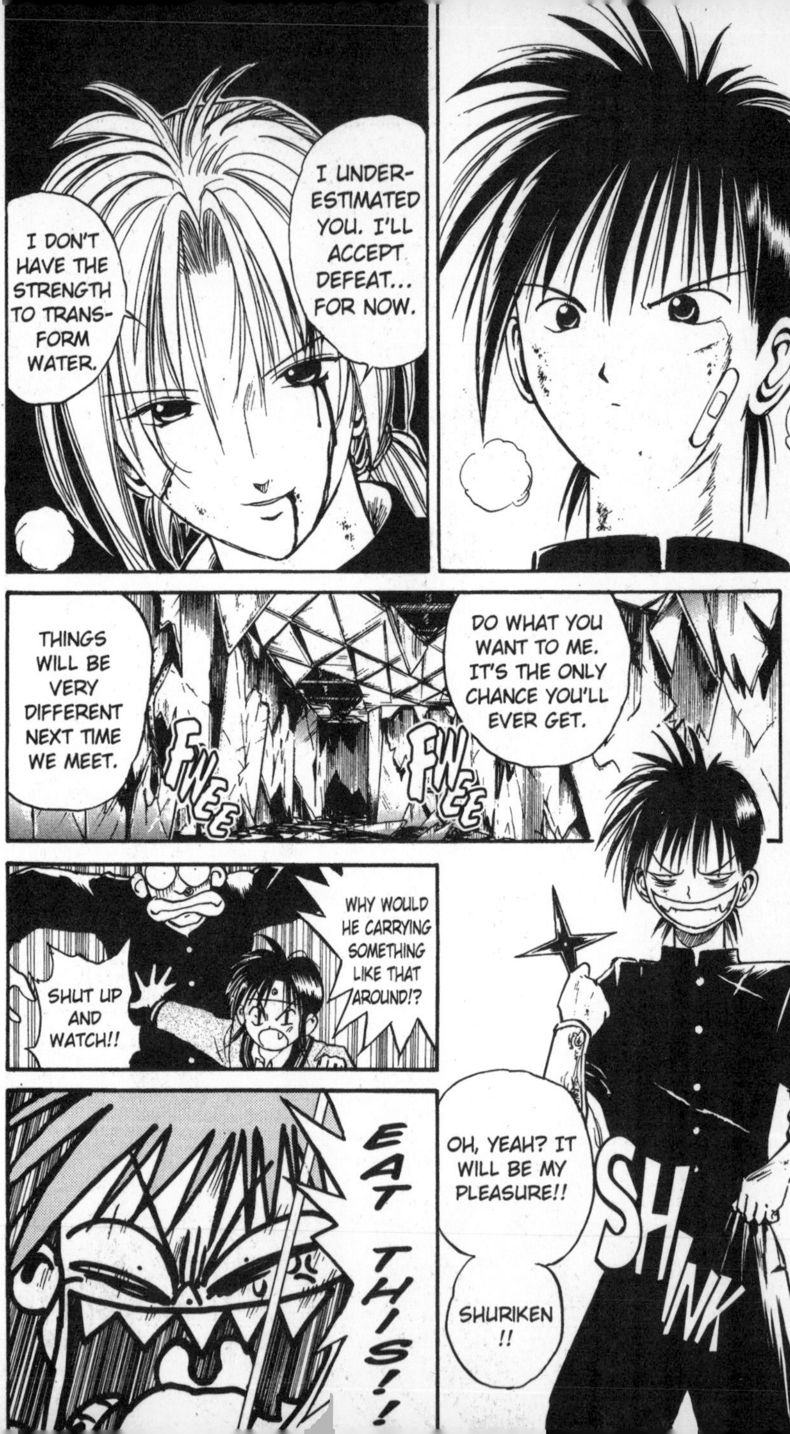
I UNDER-ESTIMATED YOU. I'LL ACCEPT DEFEAT... FOR NOW.
I DON'T HAVE THE STRENGTH TO TRANS-FORM WATER.
DO WHAT YOU WANT TO ME. IT'S THE ONLY CHANCE YOU'LL EVER GET.
THINGS WILL BE VERY DIFFERENT NEXT TIME WE MEET.
FWEE
FWEE
OH, YEAH? IT WILL BE MY PLEASURE!!
SHINK
WHY WOULD HE CARRYING SOMETHING LIKE THAT AROUND!?
SHUT UP AND WATCH!!
SHURIKEN !!
EAT THIS!!

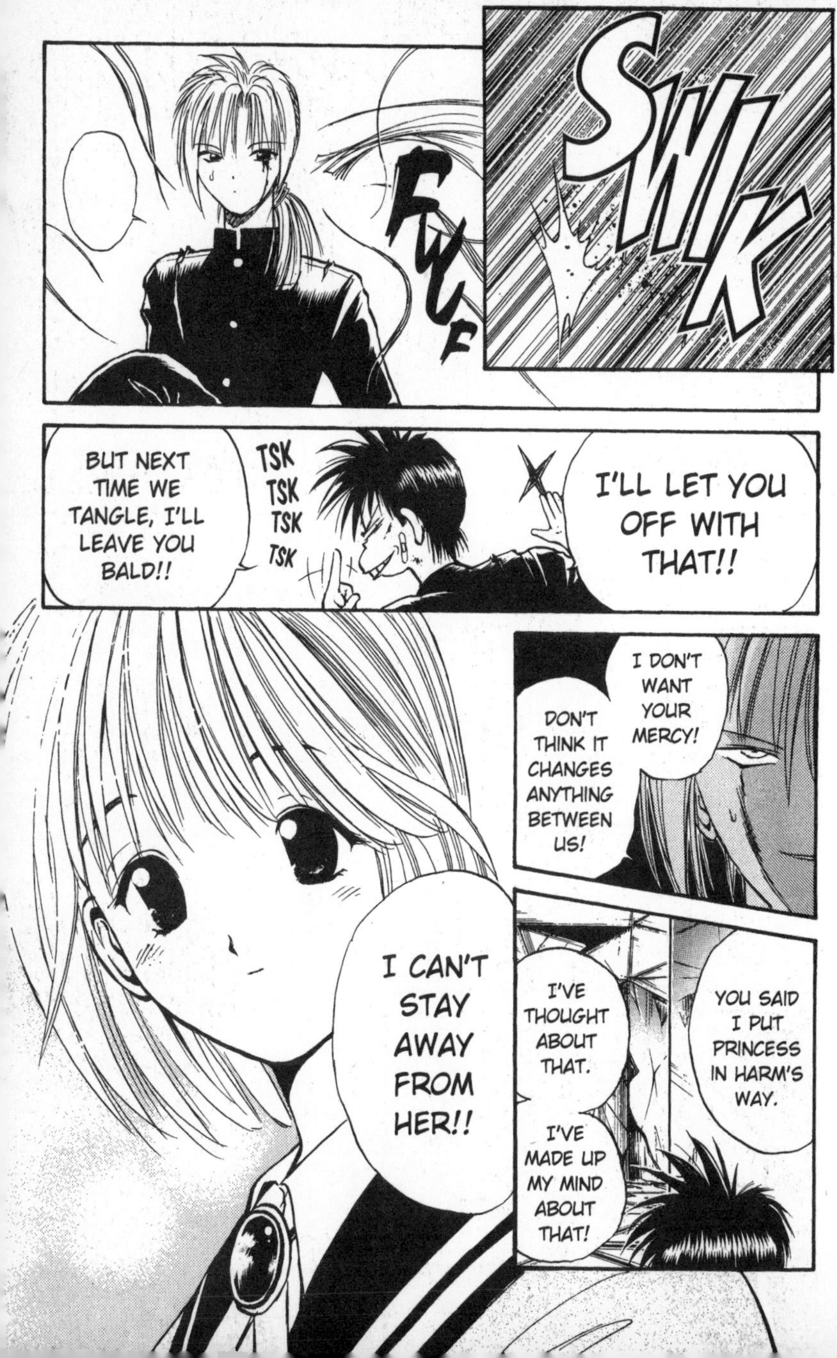
SHK
FWUF
I'LL LET YOU OFF WITH THAT!!
TSK TSK TSK TSK
BUT NEXT TIME WE TANGLE, I'LL LEAVE YOU BALD!!
I DON'T WANT YOUR MERCY!
DON'T THINK IT CHANGES ANYTHING BETWEEN US!
YOU SAID I PUT PRINCESS IN HARM'S WAY.
I'VE THOUGHT ABOUT THAT.
I'VE MADE UP MY MIND ABOUT THAT!
I CAN'T STAY AWAY FROM HER!!

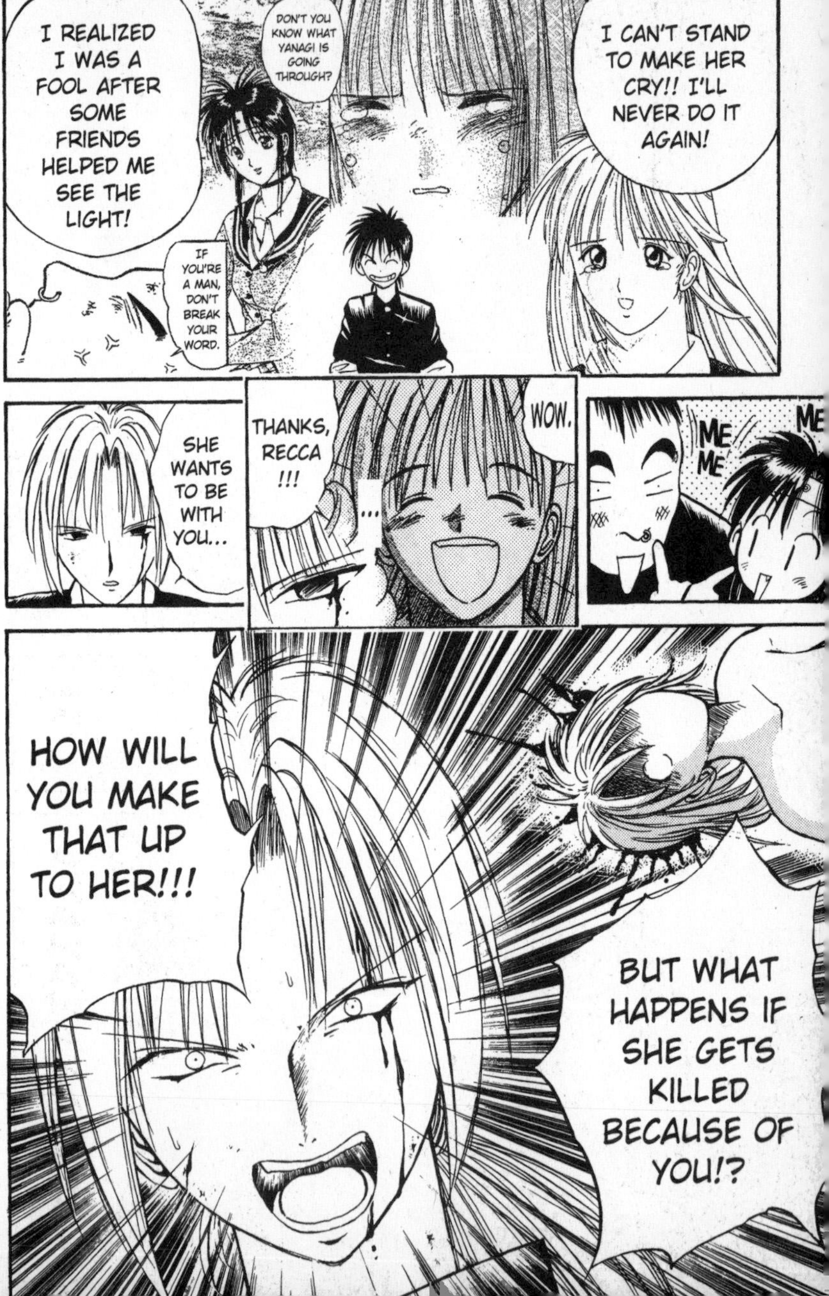
I CAN'T STAND TO MAKE HER CRY!! I'LL NEVER DO IT AGAIN!
DON'T YOU KNOW WHAT YANAGI IS GOING THROUGH?
I REALIZED I WAS A FOOL AFTER SOME FRIENDS HELPED ME SEE THE LIGHT!
IF YOU'RE A MAN, DON'T BREAK YOUR WORD.
ME
ME
ME
WOW.
THANKS, RECCA!!!
...
SHE WANTS TO BE WITH YOU...
BUT WHAT HAPPENS IF SHE GETS KILLED BECAUSE OF YOU!?
HOW WILL YOU MAKE THAT UP TO HER!!!

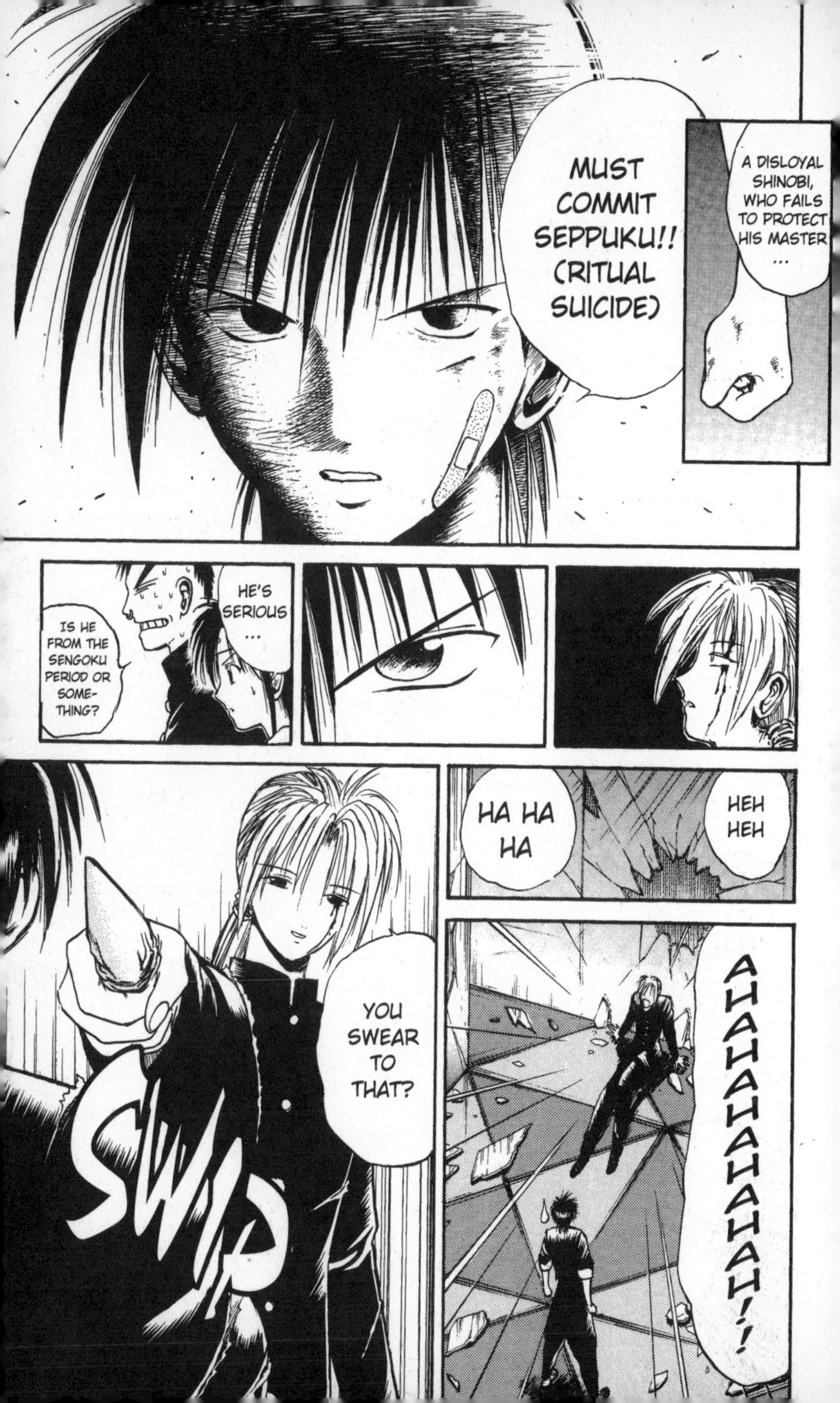
A DISLOYAL SHINOBI, WHO FAILS TO PROTECT HIS MASTER ...
MUST COMMIT SEPPUKU!! (RITUAL SUICIDE)
HE'S SERIOUS ...
IS HE FROM THE SENGOKU PERIOD OR SOME-THING?
HEH HEH
HA HA HA
AHAHAHAHAHAH!!
YOU SWEAR TO THAT?
SWIP

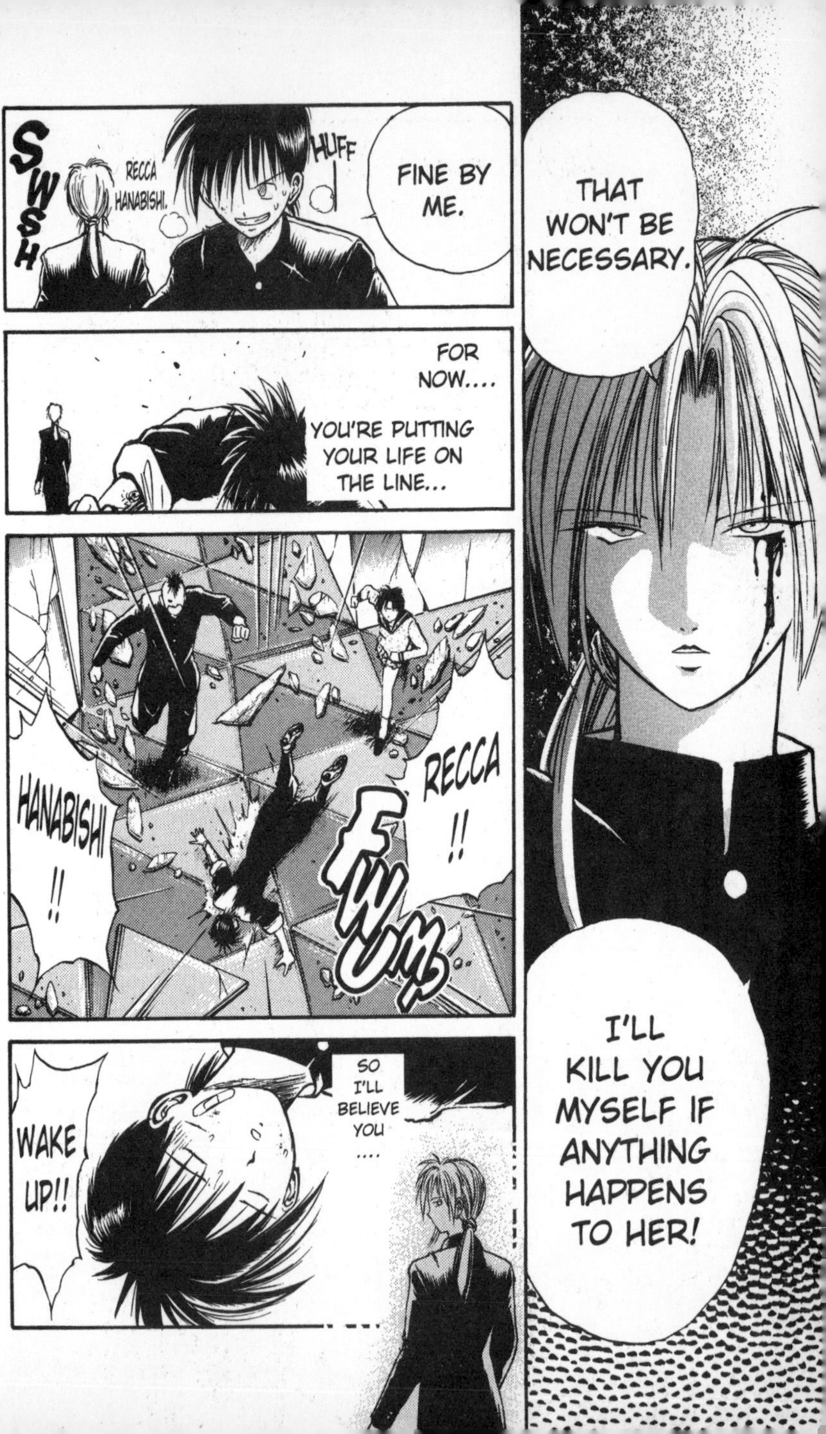
THAT WON'T BE NECESSARY.
I'LL KILL YOU MYSELF IF ANYTHING HAPPENS TO HER!
FINE BY ME.
HUFF
RECCA HANABISHI.
SWSH
FOR NOW....
YOU'RE PUTTING YOUR LIFE ON THE LINE...
RECCA !!
FWUMP
HANABISHI !!
SO I'LL BELIEVE YOU ....
WAKE UP!!

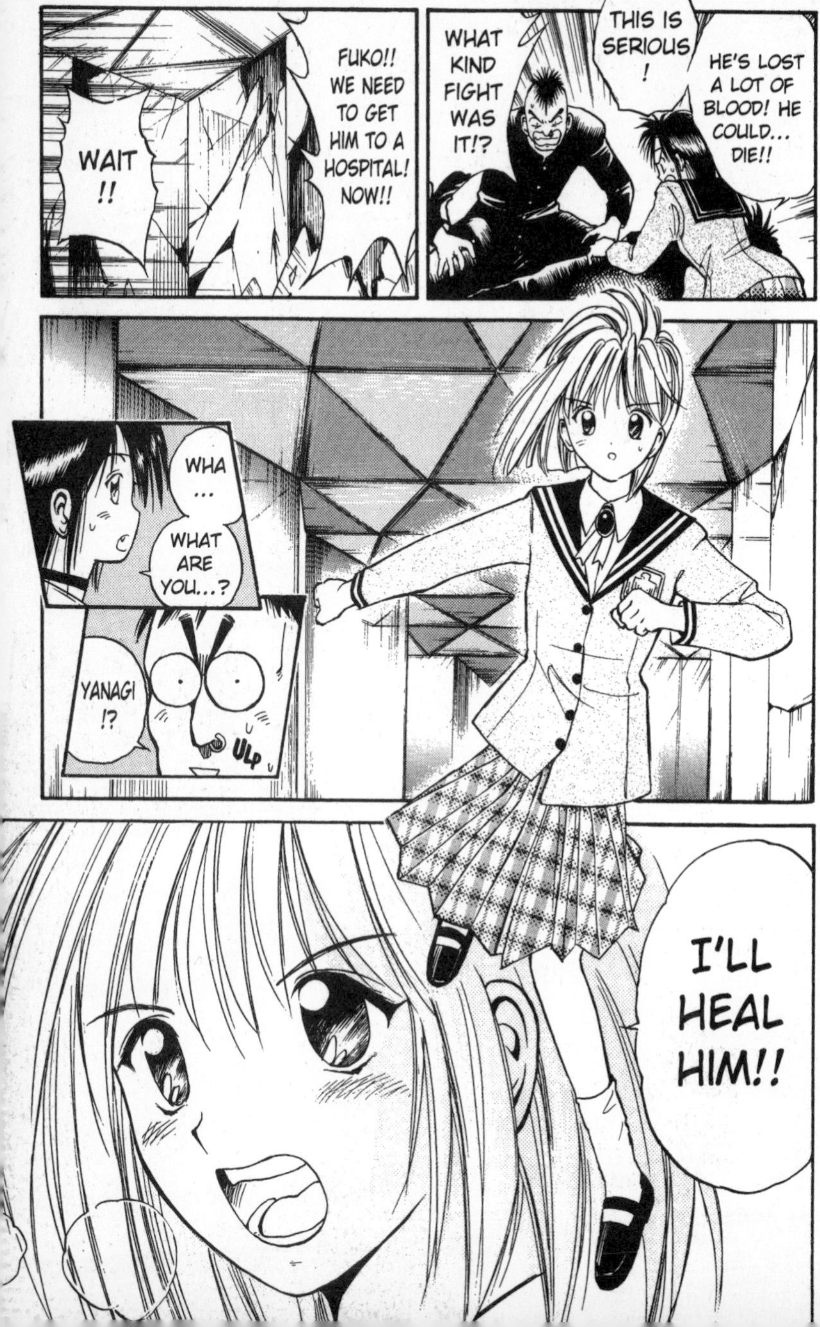
THIS IS SERIOUS!
HE'S LOST A LOT OF BLOOD! HE COULD... DIE!!
WHAT KIND FIGHT WAS IT!?
FUKO!! WE NEED TO GET HIM TO A HOSPITAL! NOW!!
WAIT!!
WHA...
WHAT ARE YOU...?
YANAGI!?
ULP
I'LL HEAL HIM!!

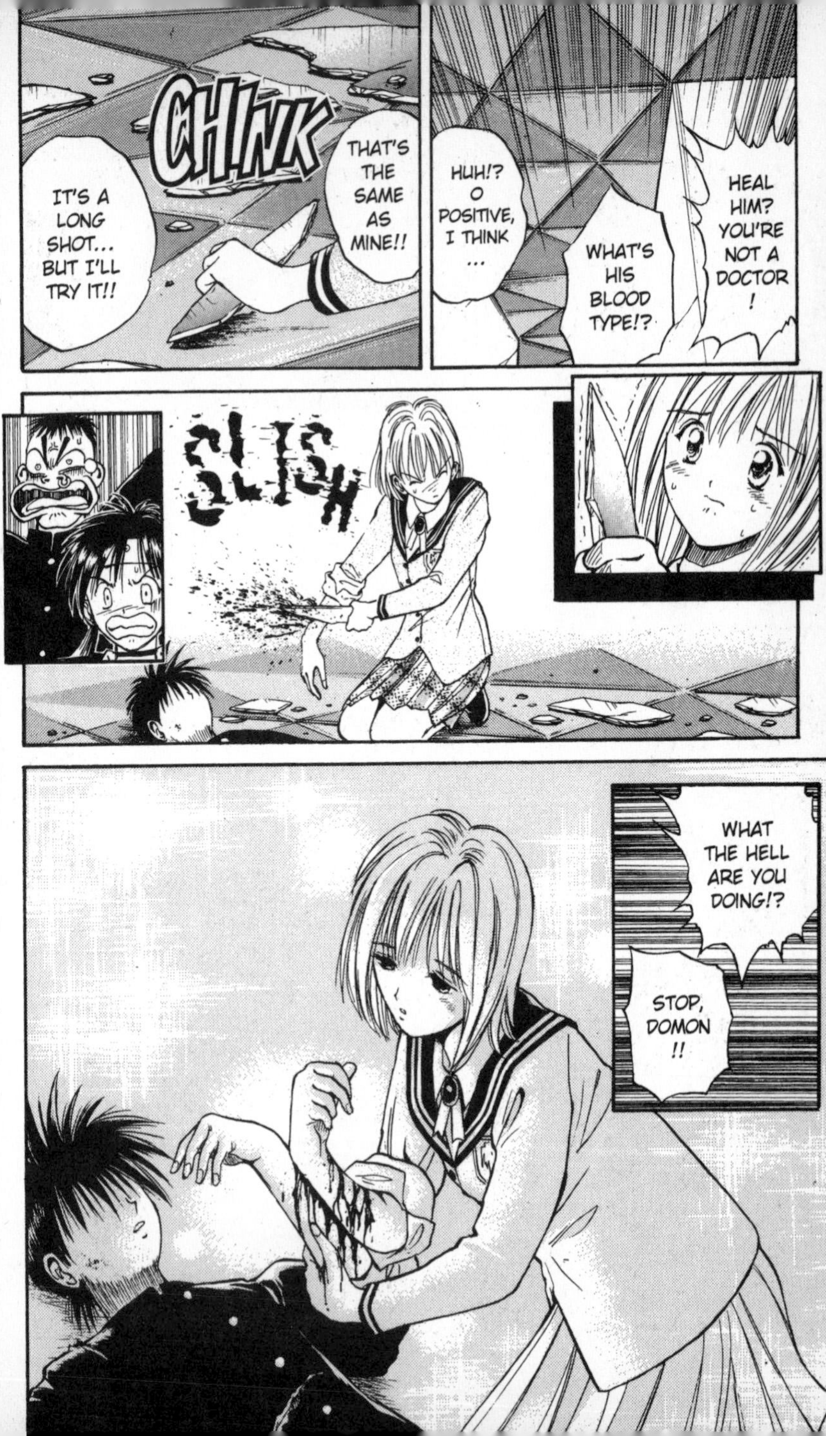
HEAL HIM? YOU'RE NOT A DOCTOR!
WHAT'S HIS BLOOD TYPE!?
HUH!? O POSITIVE, I THINK...
THAT'S THE SAME AS MINE!!
CHINK
IT'S A LONG SHOT... BUT I'LL TRY IT!!
SLISH
WHAT THE HELL ARE YOU DOING!?
STOP, DOMON!!

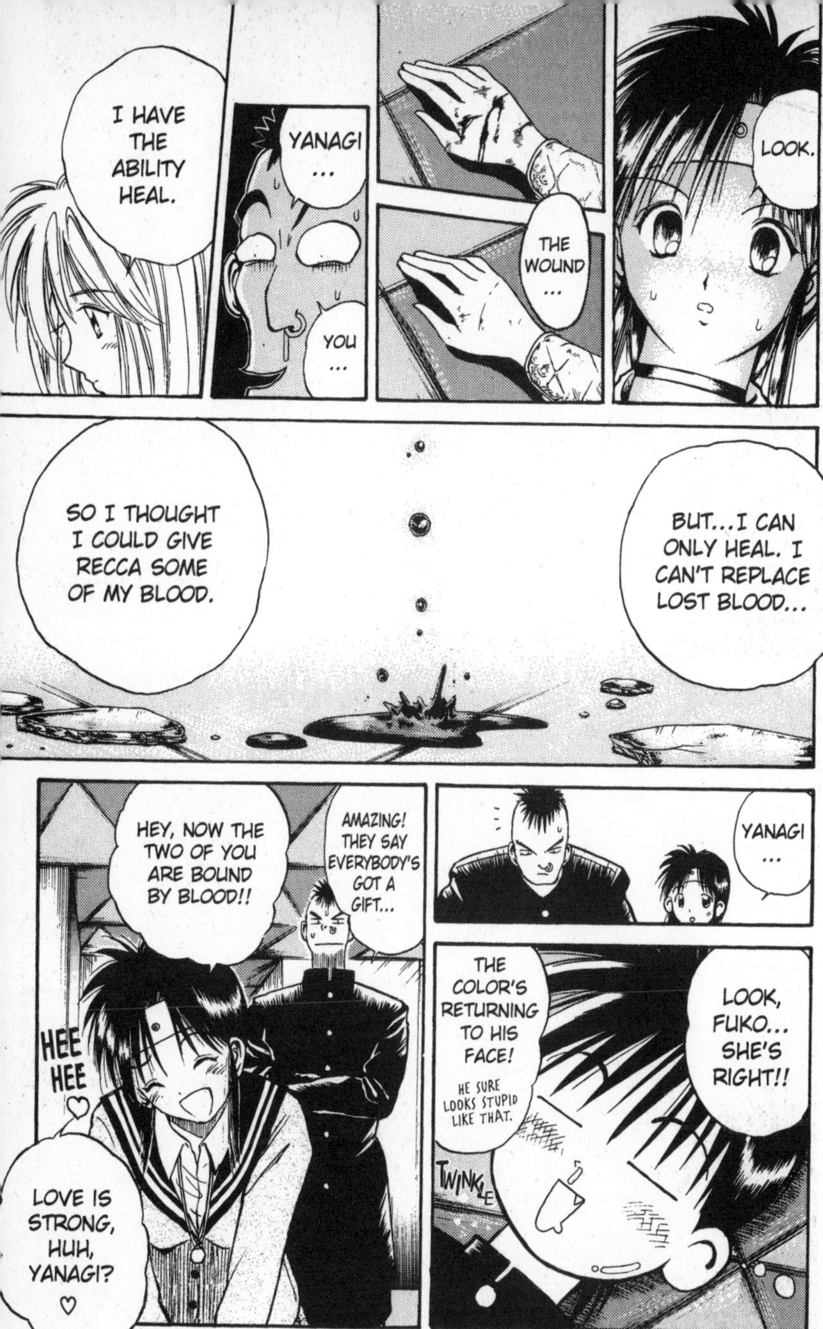

LOOK.
THE WOUND ...
YANAGI ...
YOU ...
I HAVE THE ABILITY HEAL.
BUT...I CAN ONLY HEAL. I CAN'T REPLACE LOST BLOOD...
SO I THOUGHT I COULD GIVE RECCA SOME OF MY BLOOD.
YANAGI ...
LOOK, FUKO... SHE'S RIGHT!!
THE COLOR'S RETURNING TO HIS FACE!
HE SURE LOOKS STUPID LIKE THAT.
TWINKLE
AMAZING! THEY SAY EVERYBODY'S GOT A GIFT...
HEY, NOW THE TWO OF YOU ARE BOUND BY BLOOD!!
HEE HEE ♡
LOVE IS STRONG, HUH, YANAGI? ♡
↑ RUDE.

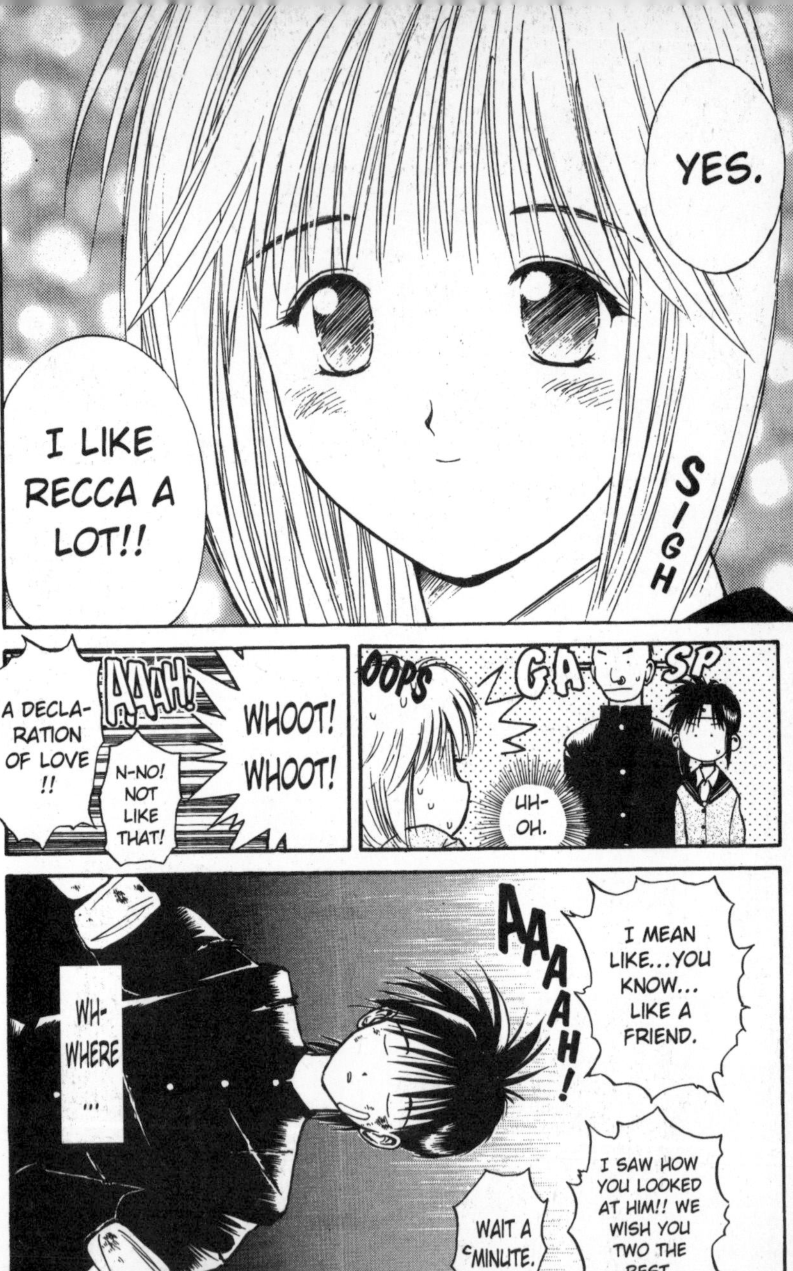

YES.
I LIKE RECCA A LOT!!
SIGH
GASP
OOPS
UH-OH.
WHOOT! WHOOT!
AAAH!
A DECLARATION OF LOVE!!
N-NO! NOT LIKE THAT!
I MEAN LIKE...YOU KNOW... LIKE A FRIEND.
AAAAAH!
WH-WHERE...
I SAW HOW YOU LOOKED AT HIM!! WE WISH YOU TWO THE BEST.
WAIT A MINUTE.

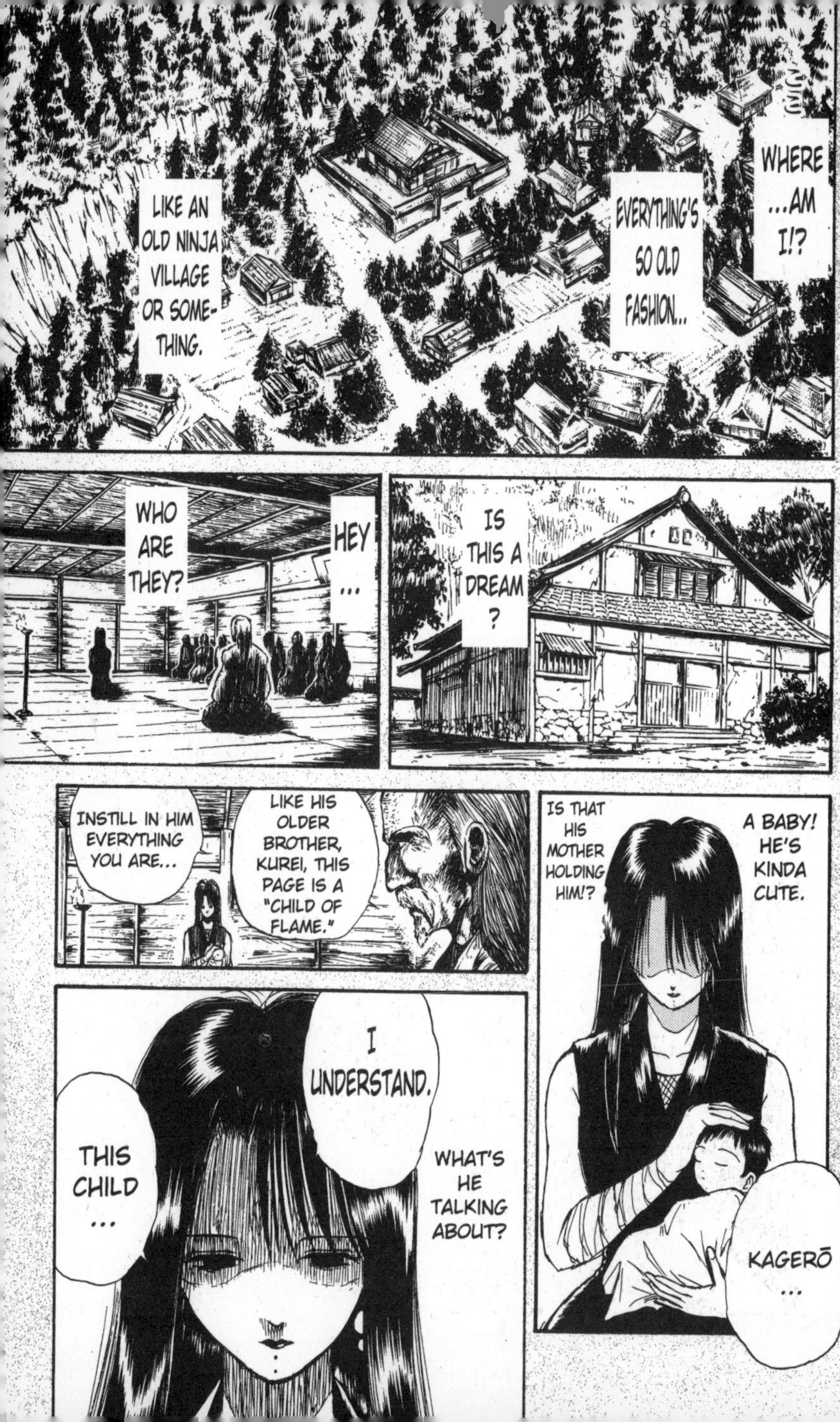
WHERE ...AM I!?
EVERYTHING'S SO OLD FASHION...
LIKE AN OLD NINJA VILLAGE OR SOME-THING.
IS THIS A DREAM ?
HEY ...
WHO ARE THEY?
A BABY! HE'S KINDA CUTE.
IS THAT HIS MOTHER HOLDING HIM!?
KAGERŌ ...
LIKE HIS OLDER BROTHER, KUREI, THIS PAGE IS A "CHILD OF FLAME."
INSTILL IN HIM EVERYTHING YOU ARE...
I UNDERSTAND.
WHAT'S HE TALKING ABOUT?
THIS CHILD ...

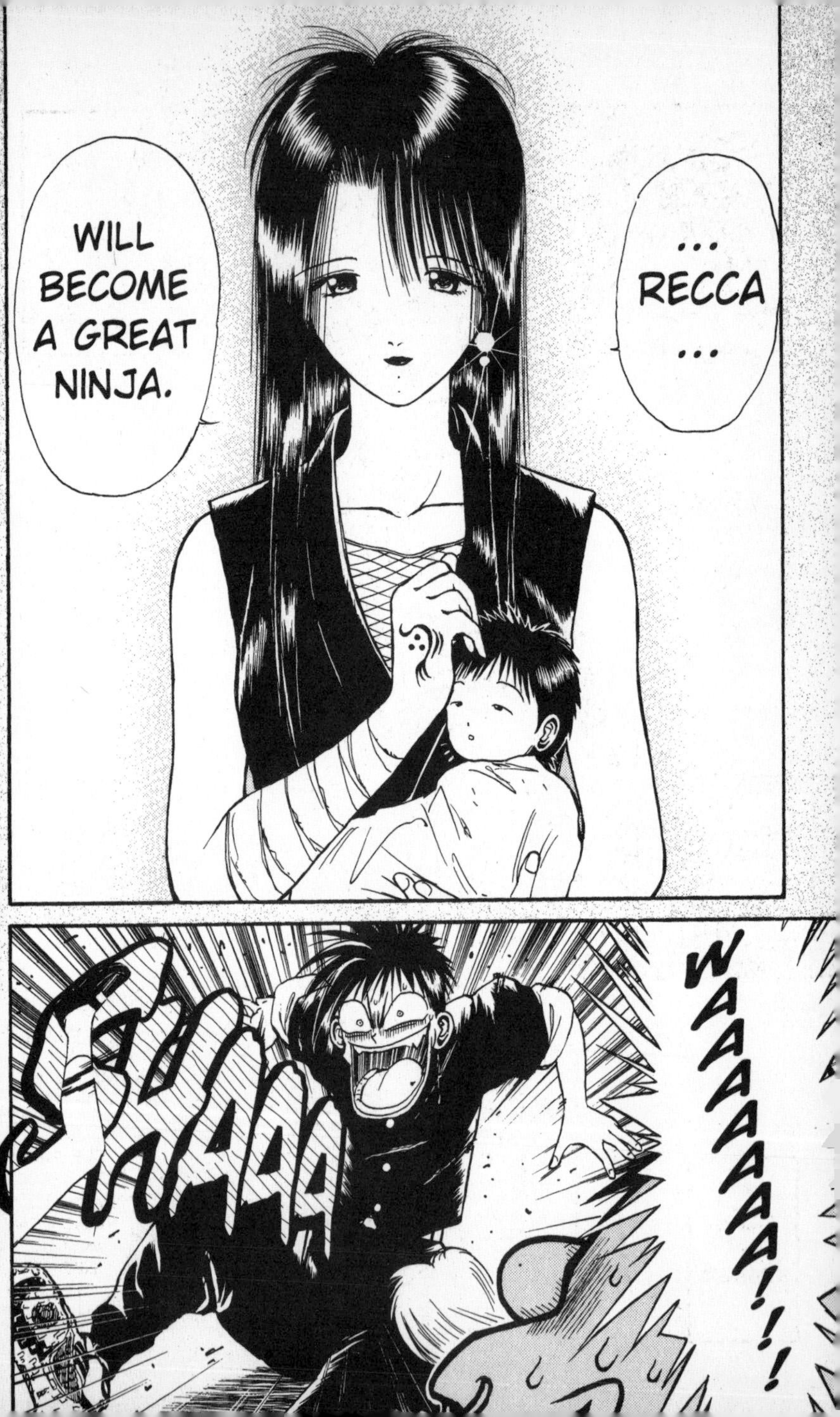
... RECCA ...
WILL BECOME A GREAT NINJA.
WAAAAAAAA!!!
WAAAA

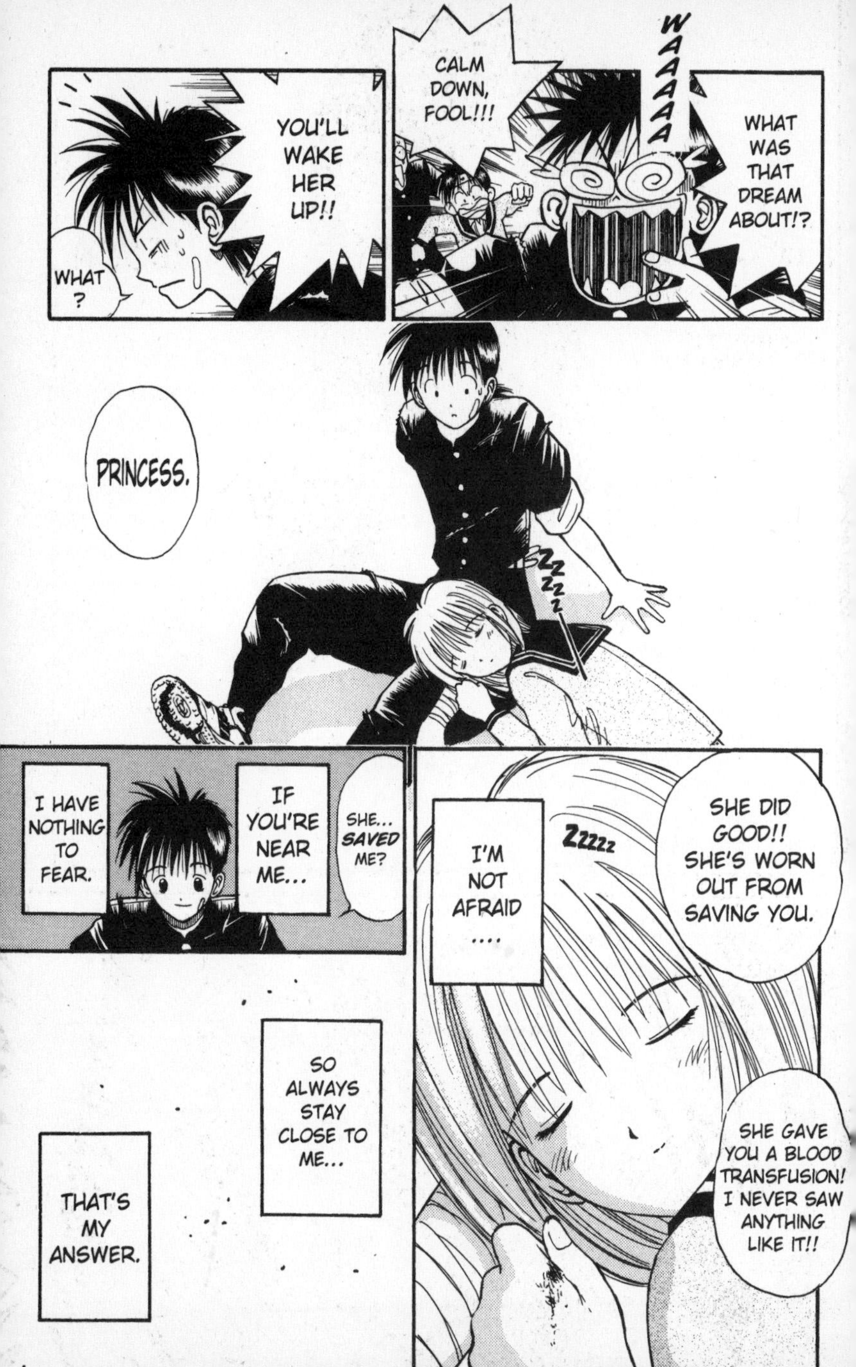
WAAAAAA
WHAT WAS THAT DREAM ABOUT!?
CALM DOWN, FOOL!!!
YOU'LL WAKE HER UP!!
WHAT ?
PRINCESS.
ZZZZZ
SHE DID GOOD!! SHE'S WORN OUT FROM SAVING YOU.
SHE GAVE YOU A BLOOD TRANSFUSION! I NEVER SAW ANYTHING LIKE IT!!
ZZZZZ
I'M NOT AFRAID ....
SHE... SAVED ME?
IF YOU'RE NEAR ME...
I HAVE NOTHING TO FEAR.
SO ALWAYS STAY CLOSE TO ME...
THAT'S MY ANSWER.

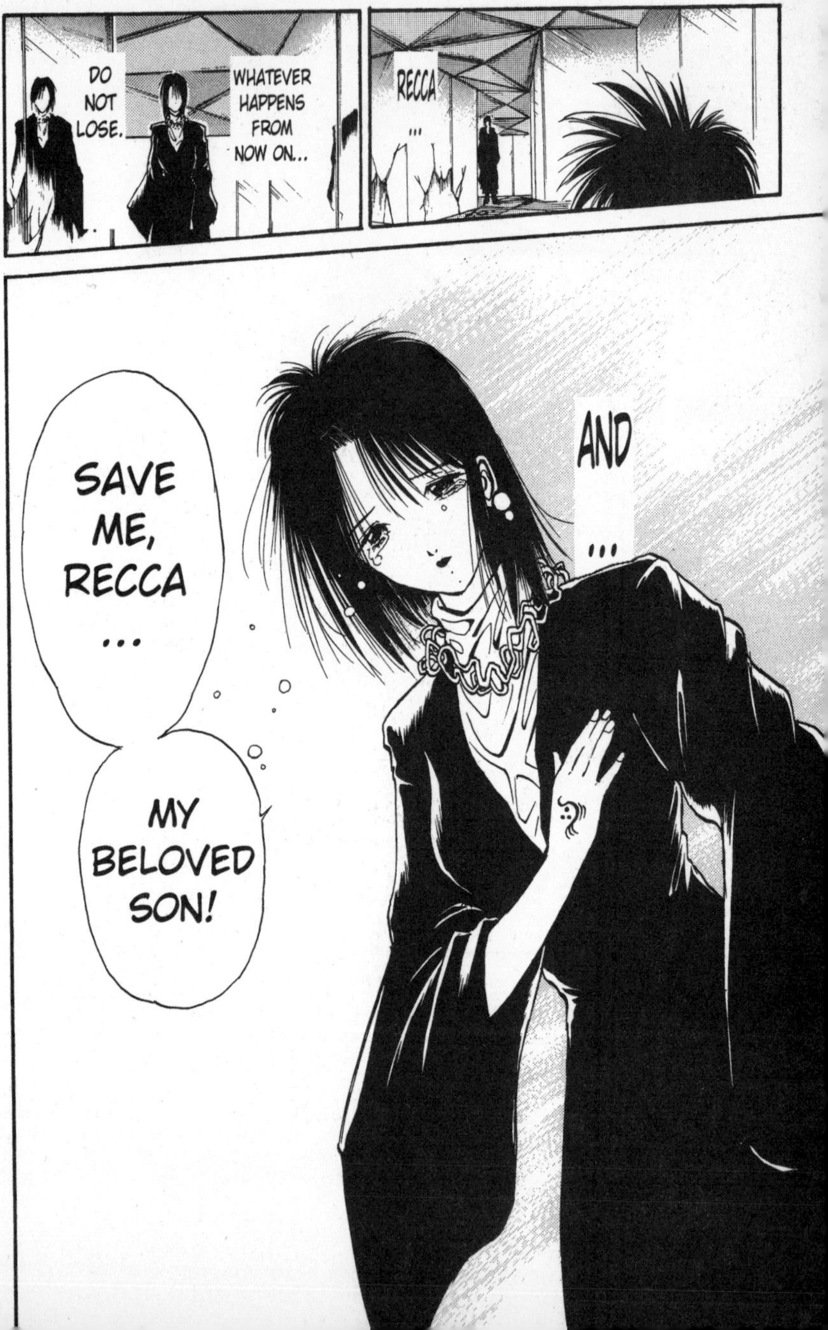
RECCA ...
WHATEVER HAPPENS FROM NOW ON...
DO NOT LOSE.
AND ...
SAVE ME, RECCA ...
MY BELOVED SON!

Part Eighteen:
A Glimmer of Light

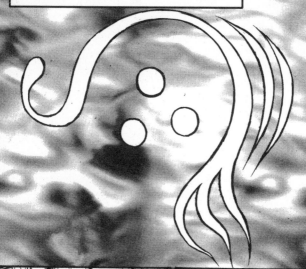

C-COM FOUNDATION DIRECTOR **KŌRAN MORI** WAS PRESENTED WITH AN AWARD.

FOR HIS DONATION TO CHILDREN'S SHELTERS ACROSS THE COUNTRY...

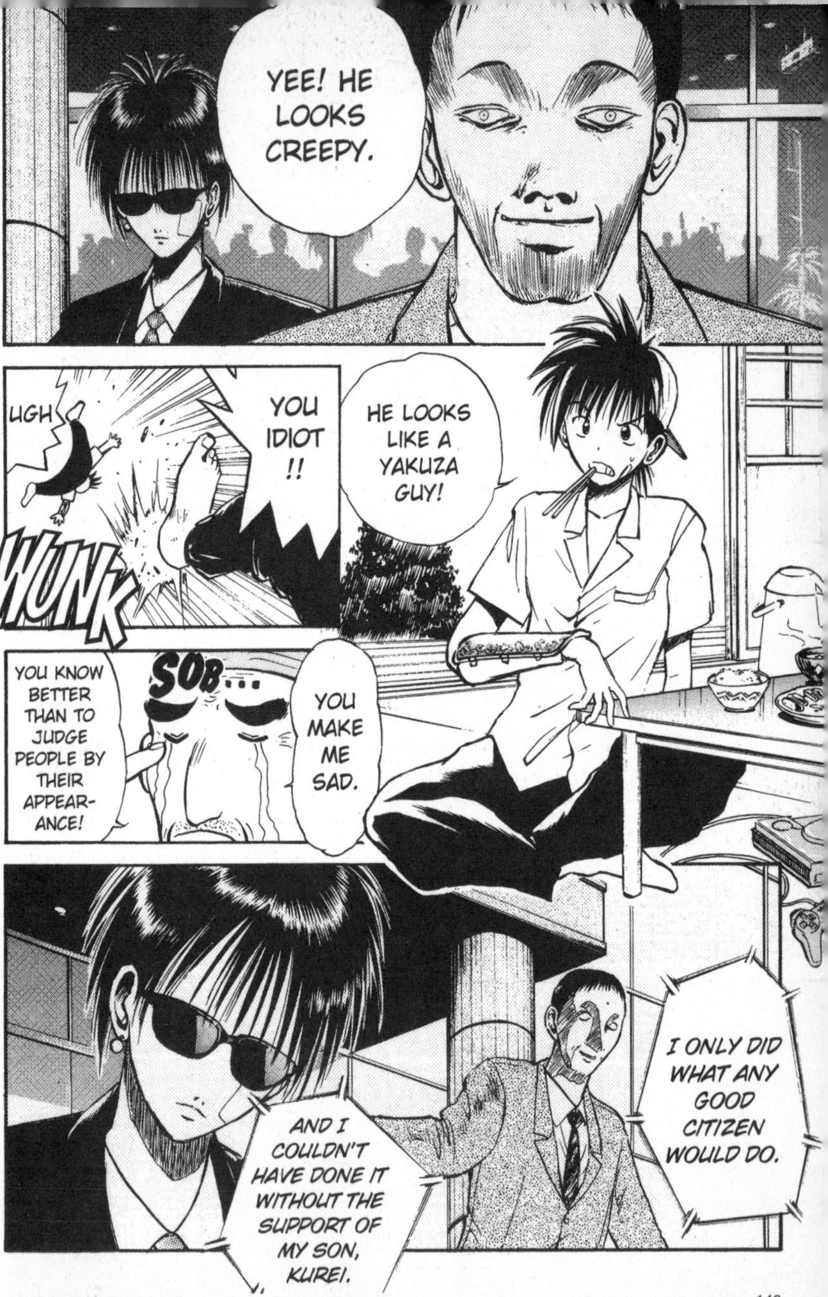
YEE! HE LOOKS CREEPY.
HE LOOKS LIKE A YAKUZA GUY!
YOU IDIOT !!
UGH
WUNK
YOU MAKE ME SAD.
SOB...
YOU KNOW BETTER THAN TO JUDGE PEOPLE BY THEIR APPEAR-ANCE!
I ONLY DID WHAT ANY GOOD CITIZEN WOULD DO.
AND I COULDN'T HAVE DONE IT WITHOUT THE SUPPORT OF MY SON, KUREI.

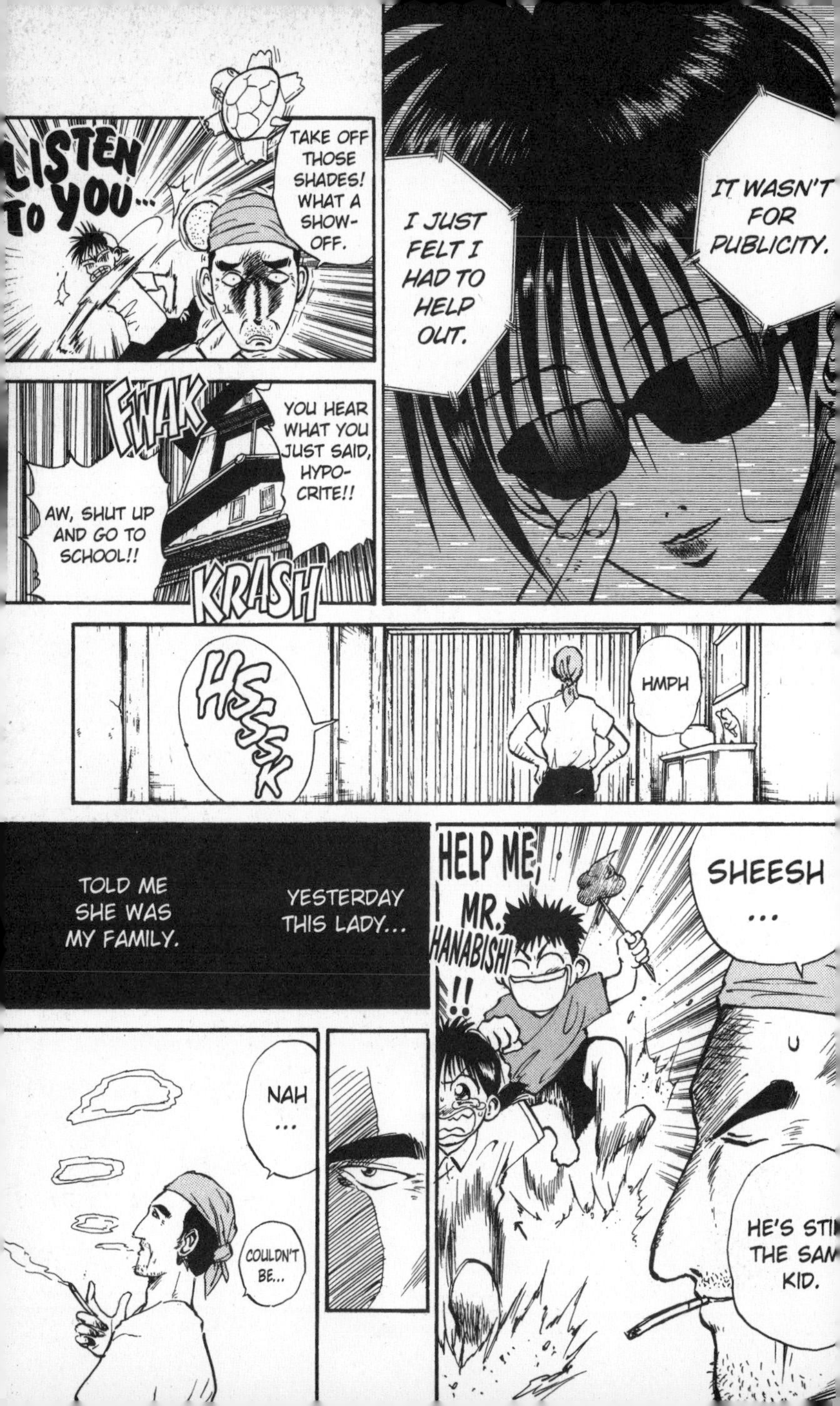
IT WASN'T FOR PUBLICITY.
I JUST FELT I HAD TO HELP OUT.
TAKE OFF THOSE SHADES! WHAT A SHOW-OFF.
LISTEN TO YOU...
YOU HEAR WHAT YOU JUST SAID, HYPOCRITE!!
FWAK
AW, SHUT UP AND GO TO SCHOOL!!
KRASH
HMPH
HSSSK
SHEESH ...
HELP ME, MR. HANABISHI!!
YESTERDAY THIS LADY...
TOLD ME SHE WAS MY FAMILY.
HE'S STI THE SAM KID.
NAH ...
COULDN'T BE...

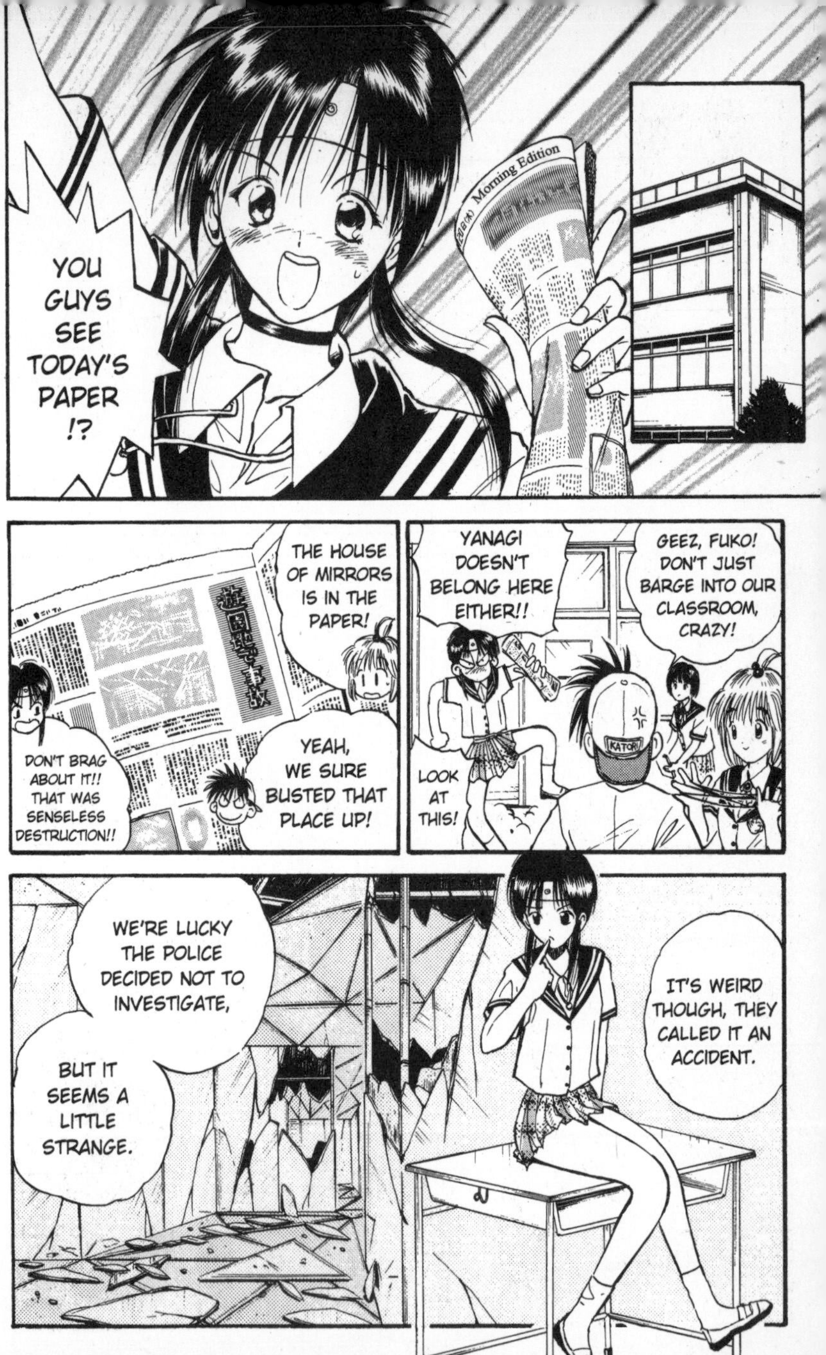

YOU GUYS SEE TODAY'S PAPER !?
Morning Edition
THE HOUSE OF MIRRORS IS IN THE PAPER!
YEAH, WE SURE BUSTED THAT PLACE UP!
DON'T BRAG ABOUT IT!! THAT WAS SENSELESS DESTRUCTION!!
LOOK AT THIS!
YANAGI DOESN'T BELONG HERE EITHER!!
GEEZ, FUKO! DON'T JUST BARGE INTO OUR CLASSROOM, CRAZY!
KATORI
WE'RE LUCKY THE POLICE DECIDED NOT TO INVESTIGATE,
BUT IT SEEMS A LITTLE STRANGE.
IT'S WEIRD THOUGH, THEY CALLED IT AN ACCIDENT.

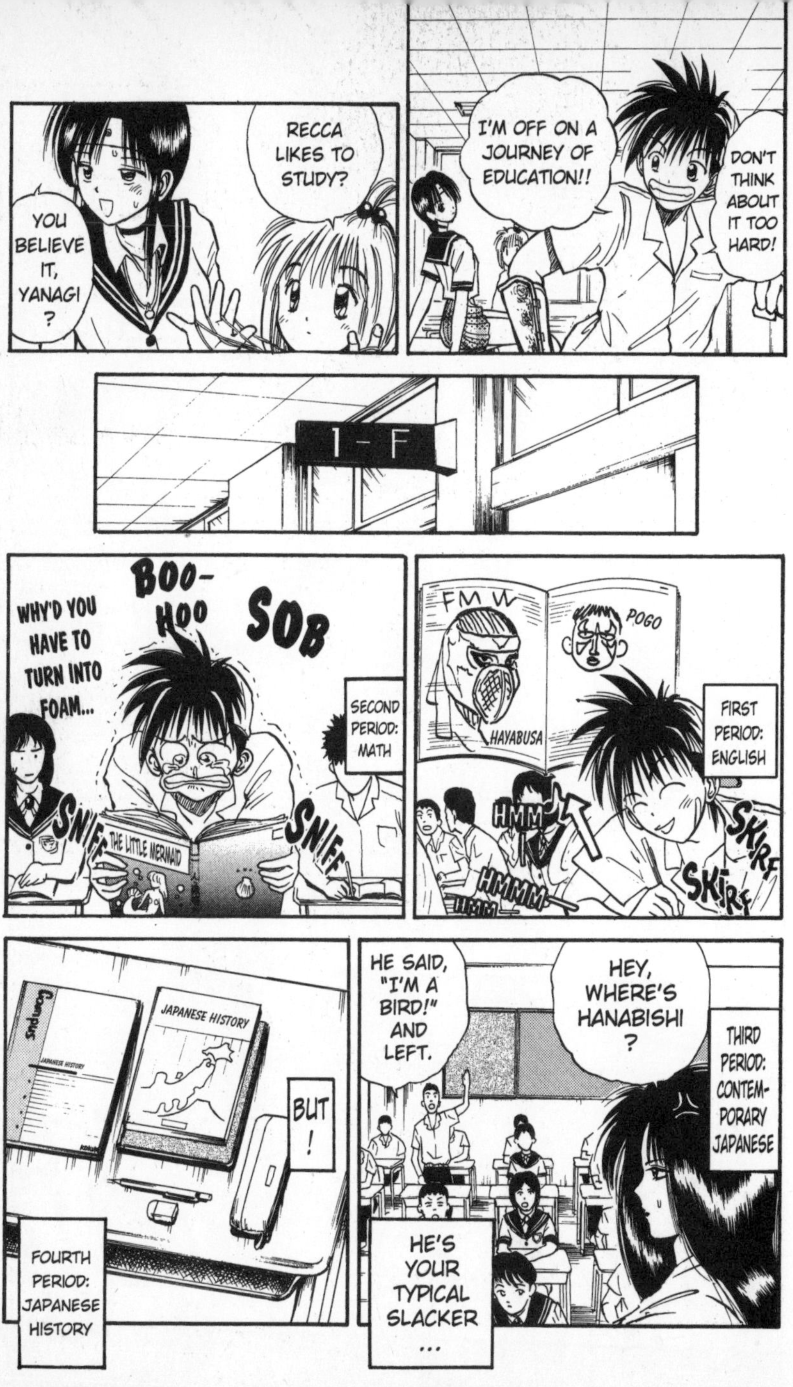

I'M OFF ON A JOURNEY OF EDUCATION!!
DON'T THINK ABOUT IT TOO HARD!
RECCA LIKES TO STUDY?
YOU BELIEVE IT, YANAGI?
1-F
FIRST PERIOD: ENGLISH
FMW
POGO
HAYABUSA
HMMM
HMMMM
SKIRF
SKIRF
SECOND PERIOD: MATH
BOO-HOO
SOB
WHY'D YOU HAVE TO TURN INTO FOAM...
THE LITTLE MERMAID
SNIFF
SNIFF
THIRD PERIOD: CONTEM-PORARY JAPANESE
HEY, WHERE'S HANABISHI?
HE SAID, "I'M A BIRD!" AND LEFT.
HE'S YOUR TYPICAL SLACKER...
BUT!
JAPANESE HISTORY
JAPANESE HISTORY
FOURTH PERIOD: JAPANESE HISTORY

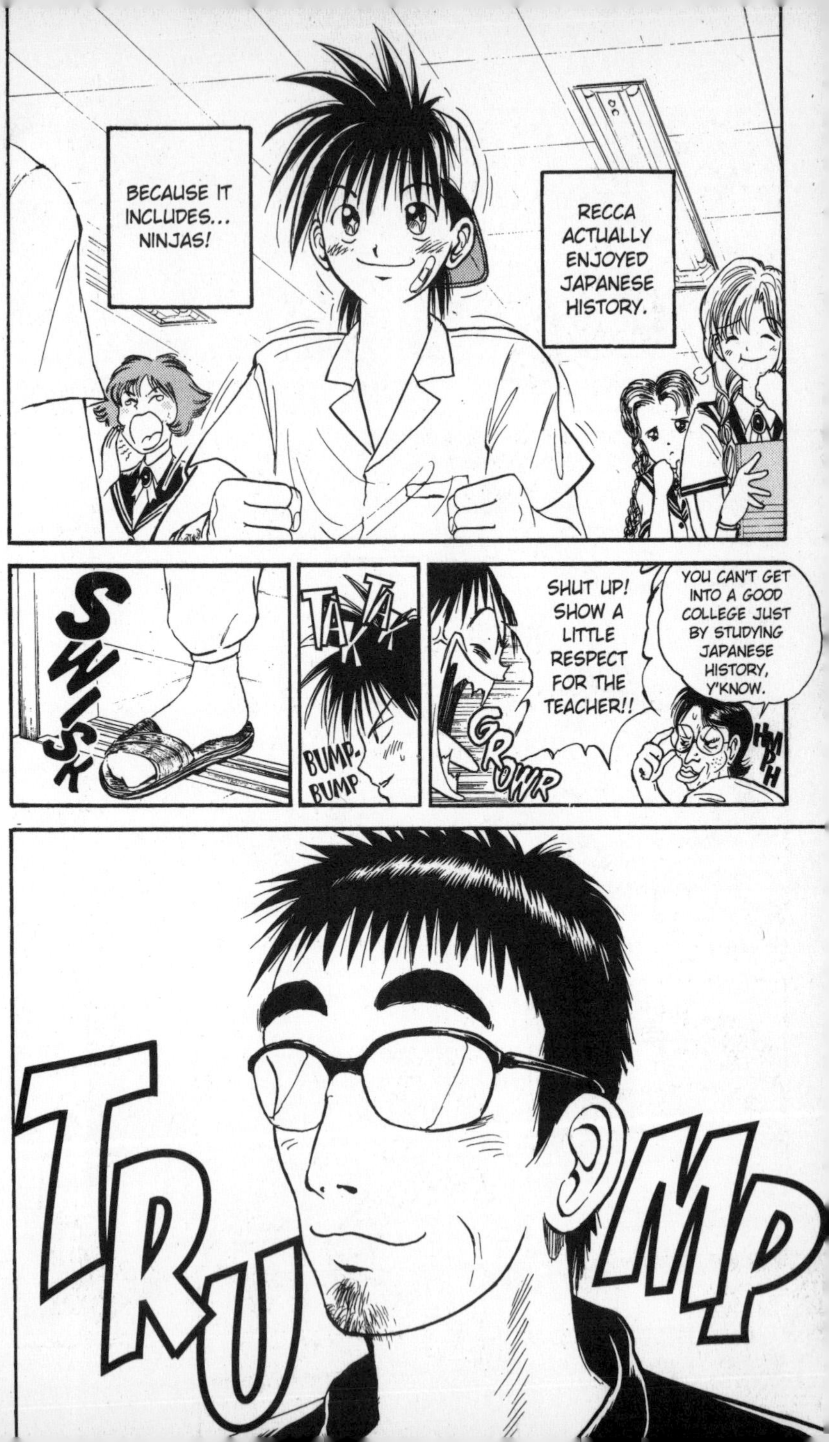
RECCA ACTUALLY ENJOYED JAPANESE HISTORY.
BECAUSE IT INCLUDES... NINJAS!
YOU CAN'T GET INTO A GOOD COLLEGE JUST BY STUDYING JAPANESE HISTORY, Y'KNOW.
HMPH
SHUT UP! SHOW A LITTLE RESPECT FOR THE TEACHER!!
GROWR
TAK TAK
BUMP-BUMP
SWISK
TRUMP

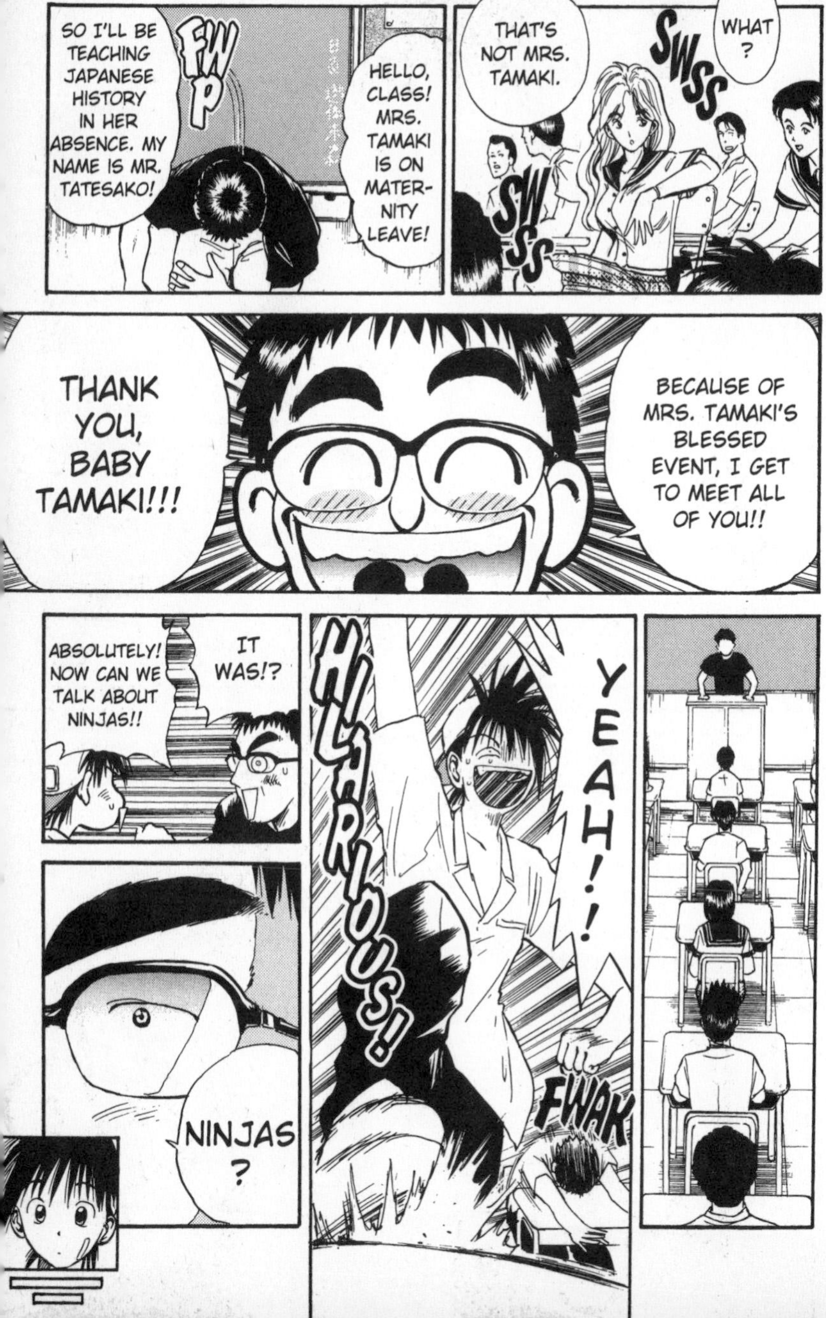
WHAT ?
SWSS
THAT'S NOT MRS. TAMAKI.
SWSS
HELLO, CLASS! MRS. TAMAKI IS ON MATERNITY LEAVE!
FWP
SO I'LL BE TEACHING JAPANESE HISTORY IN HER ABSENCE. MY NAME IS MR. TATESAKO!
BECAUSE OF MRS. TAMAKI'S BLESSED EVENT, I GET TO MEET ALL OF YOU!!
THANK YOU, BABY TAMAKI!!!
YEAH!!
HILARIOUS!
FWAK
IT WAS!?
ABSOLUTELY! NOW CAN WE TALK ABOUT NINJAS!!
NINJAS ?

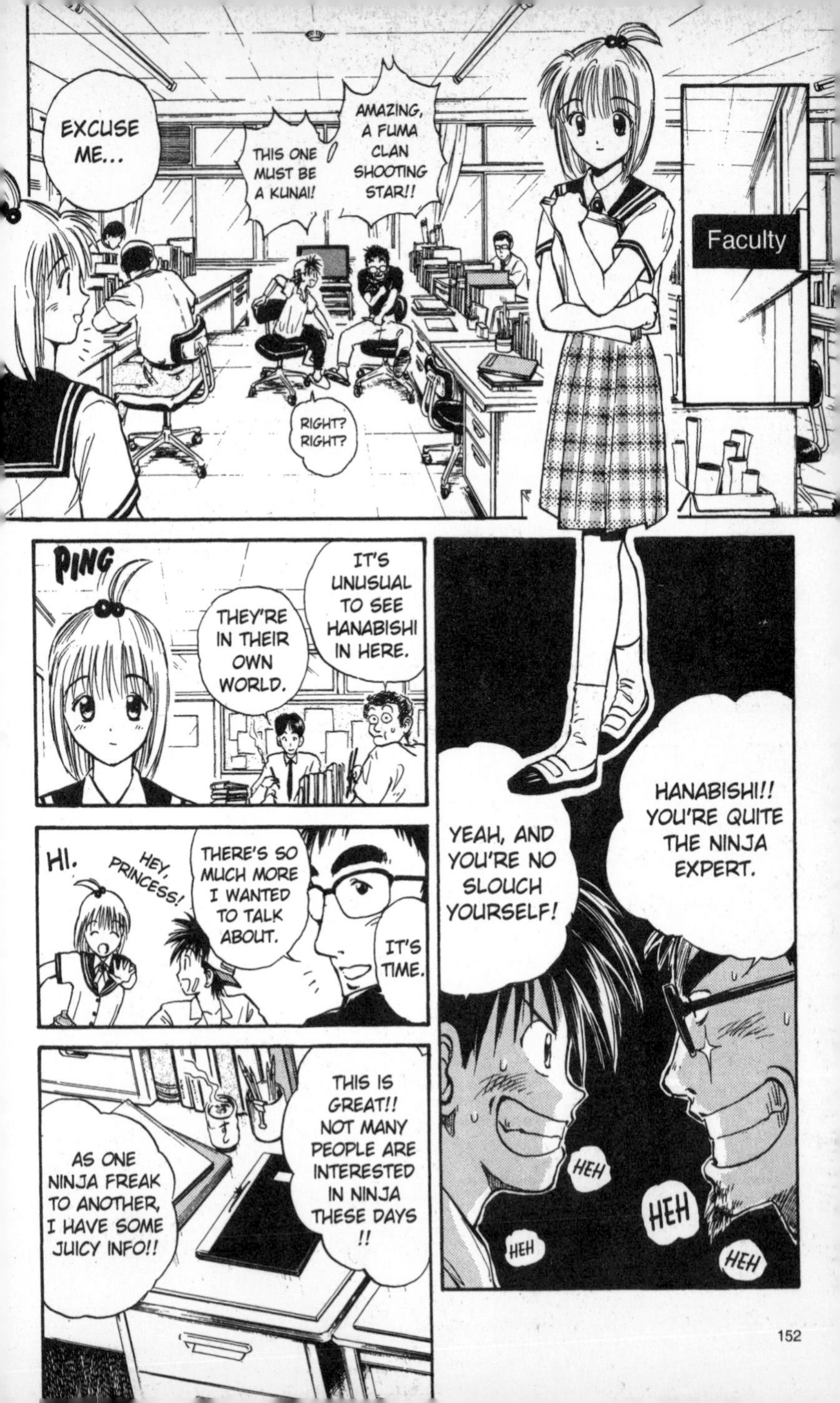
Faculty
AMAZING, A FUMA CLAN SHOOTING STAR!!
THIS ONE MUST BE A KUNAI!
RIGHT? RIGHT?
EXCUSE ME...
HANABISHI!! YOU'RE QUITE THE NINJA EXPERT.
YEAH, AND YOU'RE NO SLOUCH YOURSELF!
HEH
HEH
HEH
HEH
IT'S UNUSUAL TO SEE HANABISHI IN HERE.
THEY'RE IN THEIR OWN WORLD.
PING
IT'S TIME.
THERE'S SO MUCH MORE I WANTED TO TALK ABOUT.
HEY, PRINCESS!
HI.
THIS IS GREAT!! NOT MANY PEOPLE ARE INTERESTED IN NINJA THESE DAYS !!
AS ONE NINJA FREAK TO ANOTHER, I HAVE SOME JUICY INFO!!

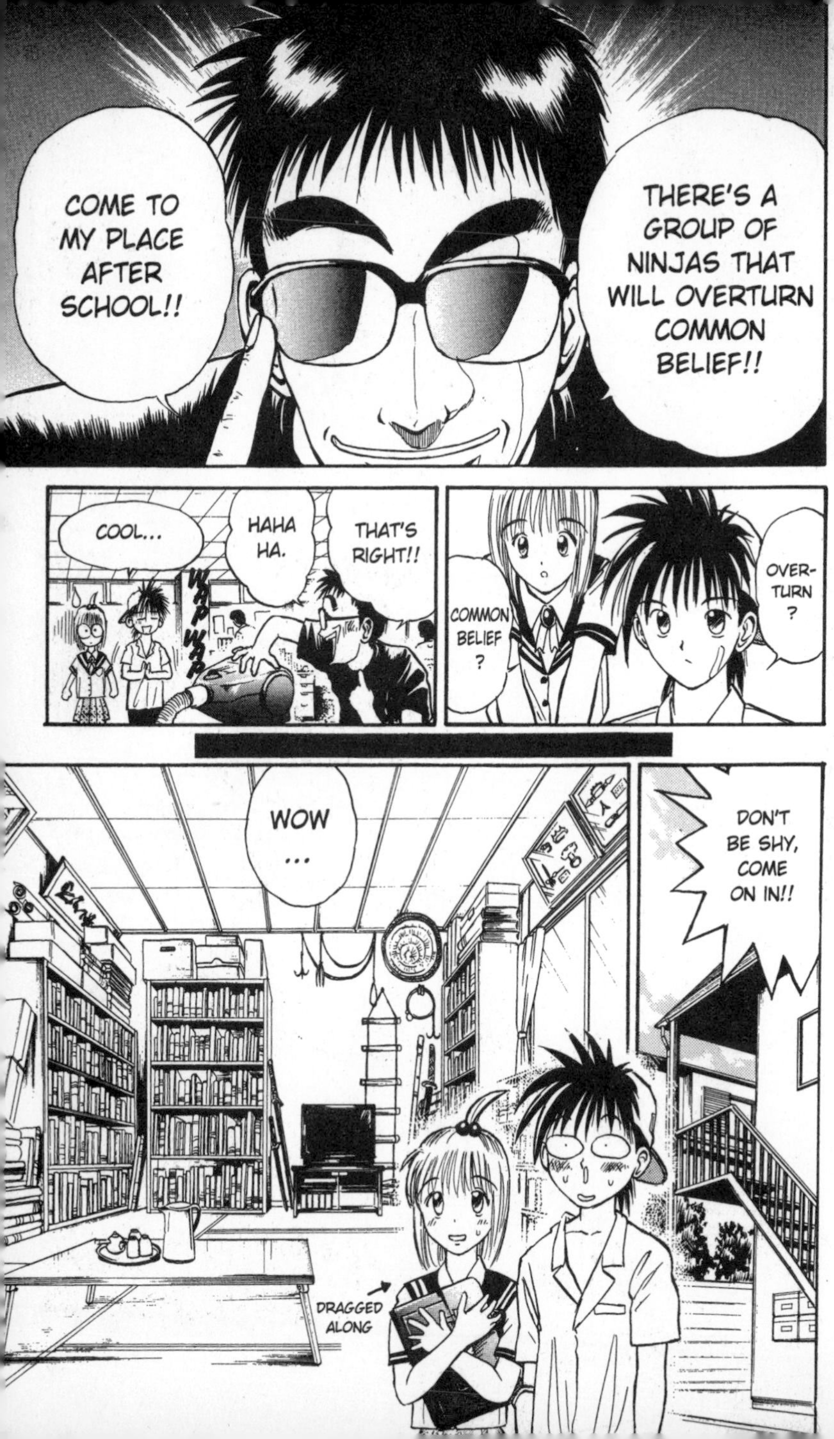
THERE'S A GROUP OF NINJAS THAT WILL OVERTURN COMMON BELIEF!!
COME TO MY PLACE AFTER SCHOOL!!
OVER-TURN ?
COMMON BELIEF ?
THAT'S RIGHT!!
HAHA HA.
COOL...
DON'T BE SHY, COME ON IN!!
WOW ...
DRAGGED ALONG

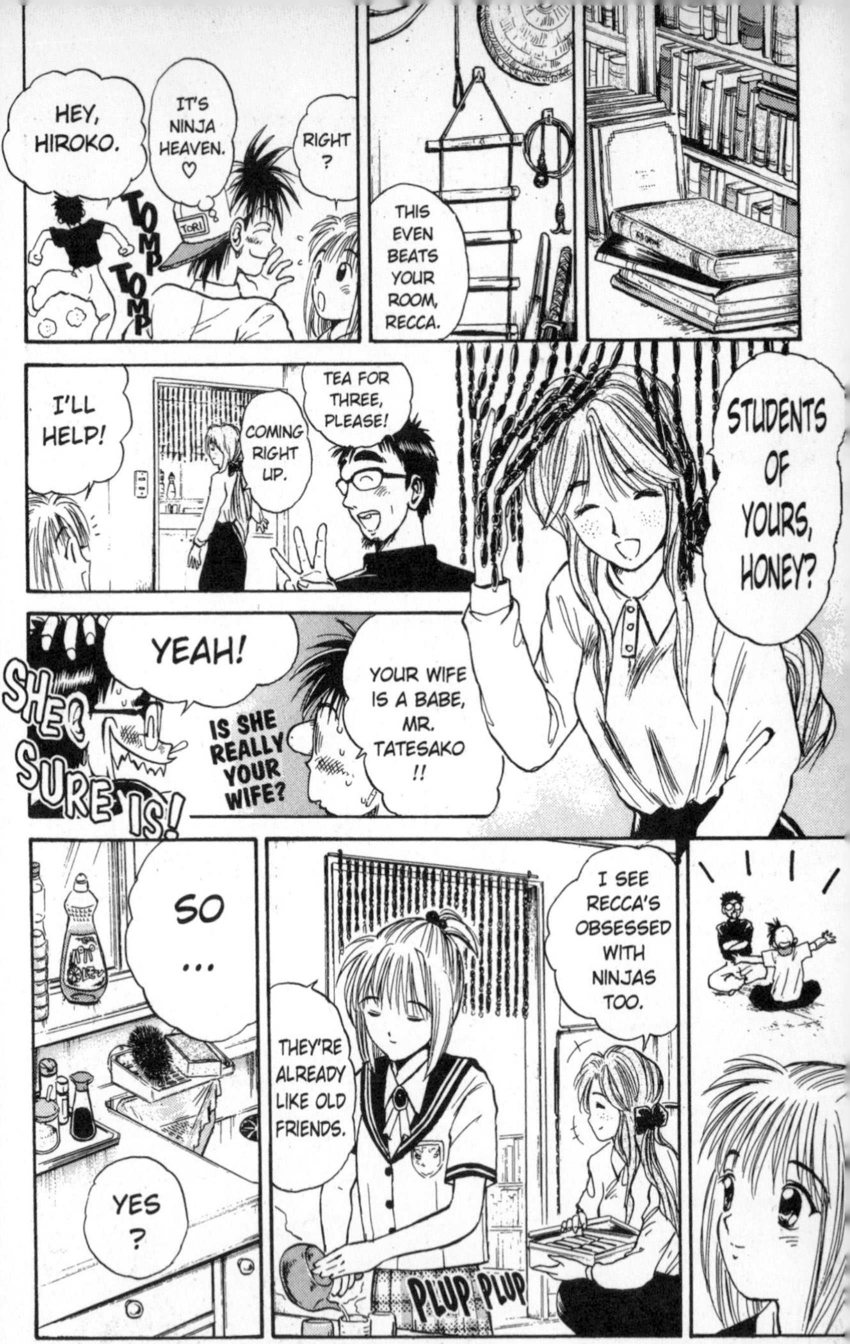

HEY, HIROKO.
IT'S NINJA HEAVEN. ♡
RIGHT?
TOMP TOMP
THIS EVEN BEATS YOUR ROOM, RECCA.
I'LL HELP!
COMING RIGHT UP.
TEA FOR THREE, PLEASE!
STUDENTS OF YOURS, HONEY?
YEAH!
SHE SURE IS!
IS SHE REALLY YOUR WIFE?
YOUR WIFE IS A BABE, MR. TATESAKO!!
SO...
YES?
THEY'RE ALREADY LIKE OLD FRIENDS.
I SEE RECCA'S OBSESSED WITH NINJAS TOO.
PLUP PLUP

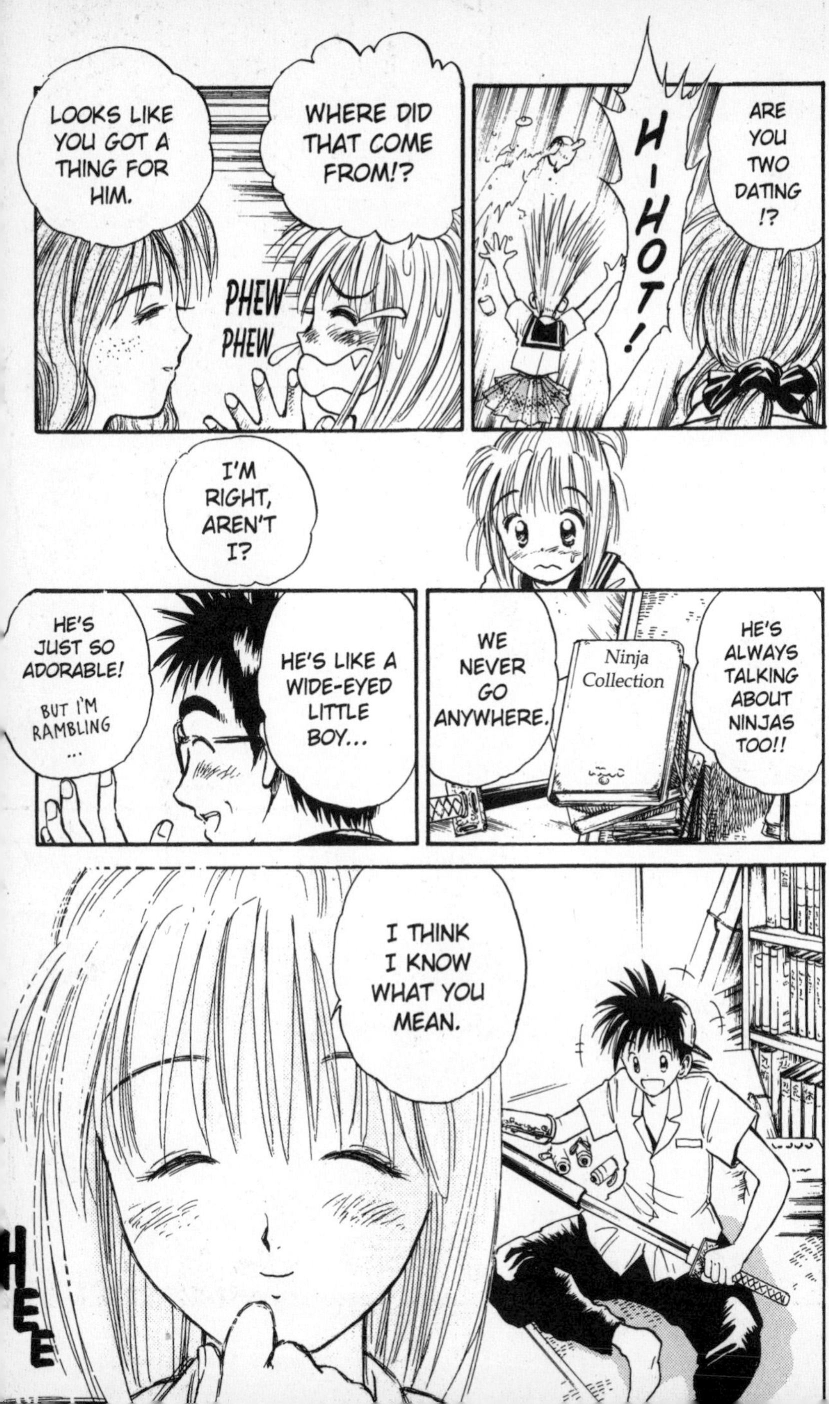
LOOKS LIKE YOU GOT A THING FOR HIM.
WHERE DID THAT COME FROM!?
PHEW PHEW
ARE YOU TWO DATING !?
HI-HOT!
I'M RIGHT, AREN'T I?
HE'S JUST SO ADORABLE!
BUT I'M RAMBLING ...
HE'S LIKE A WIDE-EYED LITTLE BOY...
WE NEVER GO ANYWHERE.
Ninja Collection
HE'S ALWAYS TALKING ABOUT NINJAS TOO!!
I THINK I KNOW WHAT YOU MEAN.
HEE

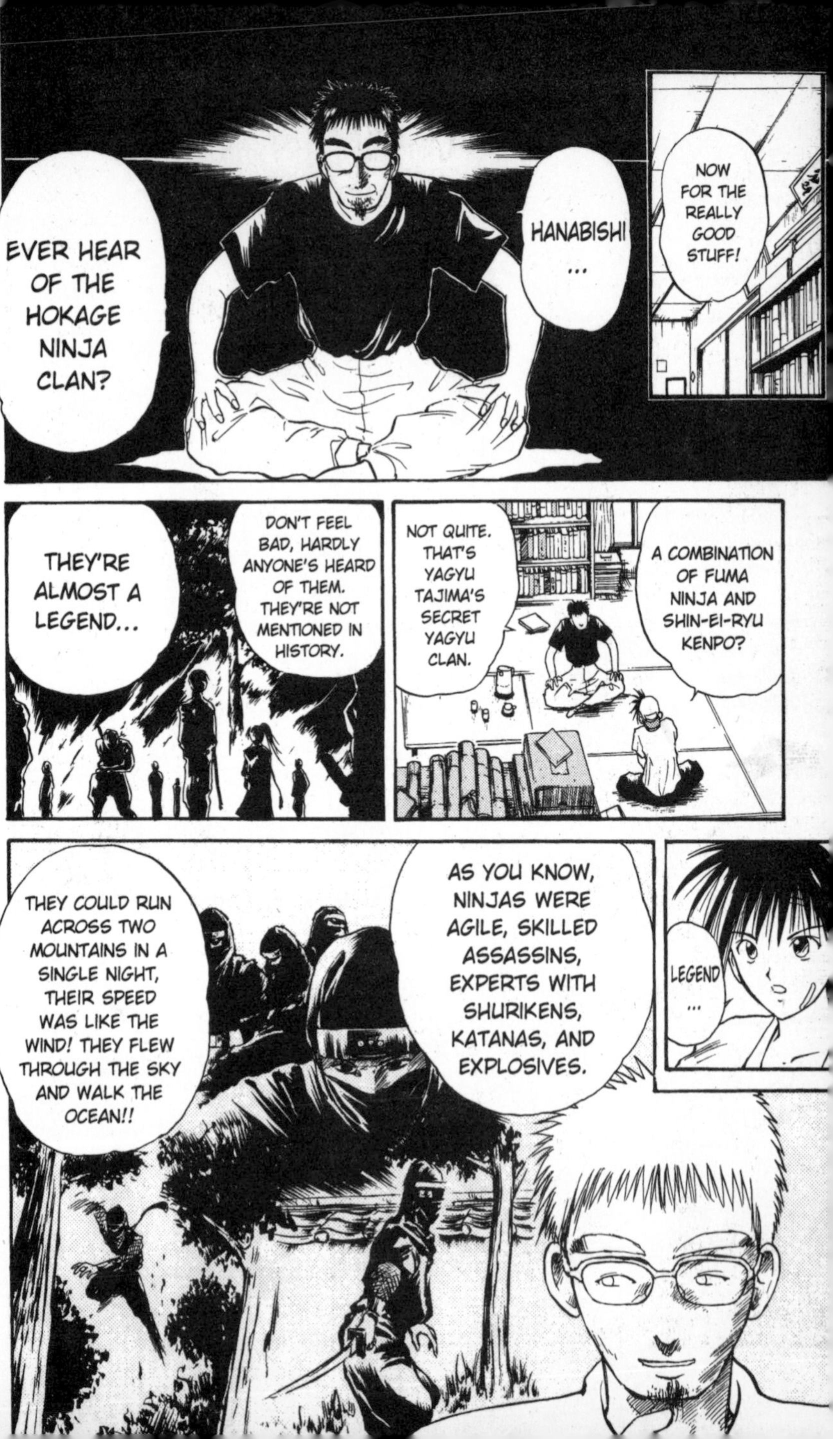
NOW FOR THE REALLY GOOD STUFF!
HANABISHI ...
EVER HEAR OF THE HOKAGE NINJA CLAN?
A COMBINATION OF FUMA NINJA AND SHIN-EI-RYU KENPO?
NOT QUITE. THAT'S YAGYU TAJIMA'S SECRET YAGYU CLAN.
DON'T FEEL BAD, HARDLY ANYONE'S HEARD OF THEM. THEY'RE NOT MENTIONED IN HISTORY.
THEY'RE ALMOST A LEGEND...
LEGEND ...
AS YOU KNOW, NINJAS WERE AGILE, SKILLED ASSASSINS, EXPERTS WITH SHURIKENS, KATANAS, AND EXPLOSIVES.
THEY COULD RUN ACROSS TWO MOUNTAINS IN A SINGLE NIGHT, THEIR SPEED WAS LIKE THE WIND! THEY FLEW THROUGH THE SKY AND WALK THE OCEAN!!

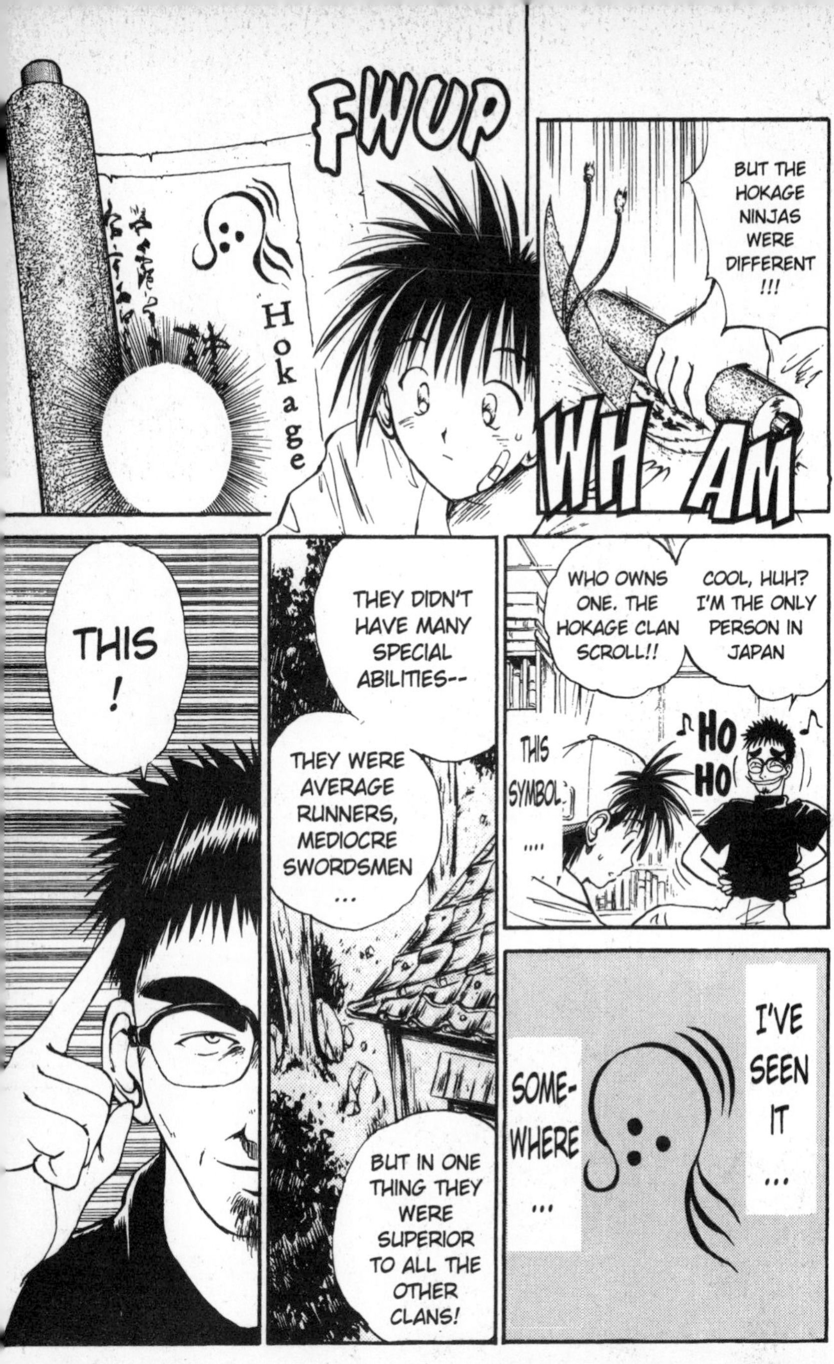
BUT THE HOKAGE NINJAS WERE DIFFERENT !!!
WH AM
FWUP
Hokage
COOL, HUH? I'M THE ONLY PERSON IN JAPAN
WHO OWNS ONE. THE HOKAGE CLAN SCROLL!!
HO HO
THIS SYMBOL ....
I'VE SEEN IT ...
SOME-WHERE ...
THEY DIDN'T HAVE MANY SPECIAL ABILITIES--
THEY WERE AVERAGE RUNNERS, MEDIOCRE SWORDSMEN ...
BUT IN ONE THING THEY WERE SUPERIOR TO ALL THE OTHER CLANS!
THIS !

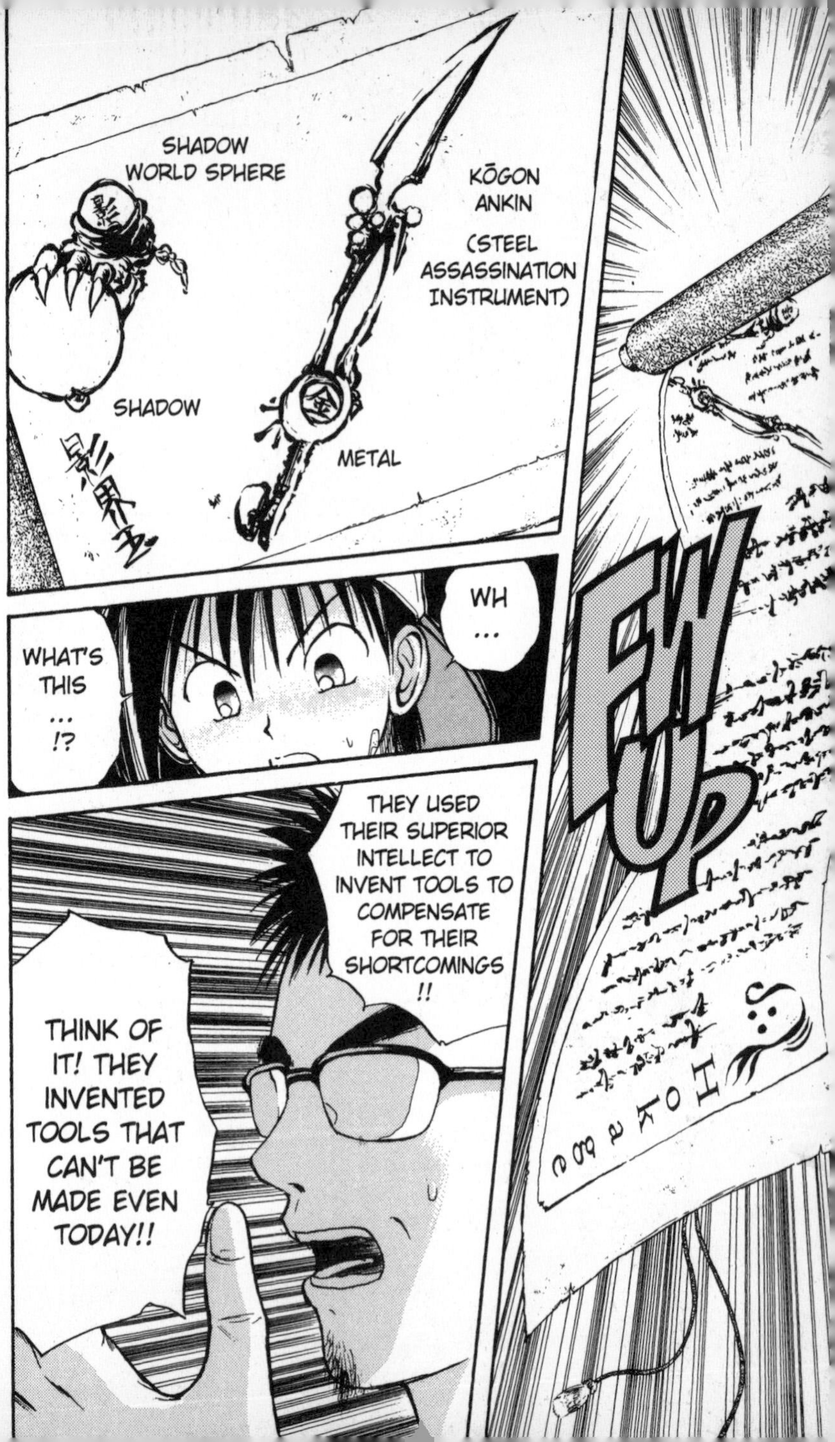

FWUP
SHADOW WORLD SPHERE
KŌGON ANKIN
(STEEL ASSASSINATION INSTRUMENT)
SHADOW
METAL
影界玉
WH …
WHAT'S THIS … !?
THEY USED THEIR SUPERIOR INTELLECT TO INVENT TOOLS TO COMPENSATE FOR THEIR SHORTCOMINGS !!
THINK OF IT! THEY INVENTED TOOLS THAT CAN'T BE MADE EVEN TODAY!!

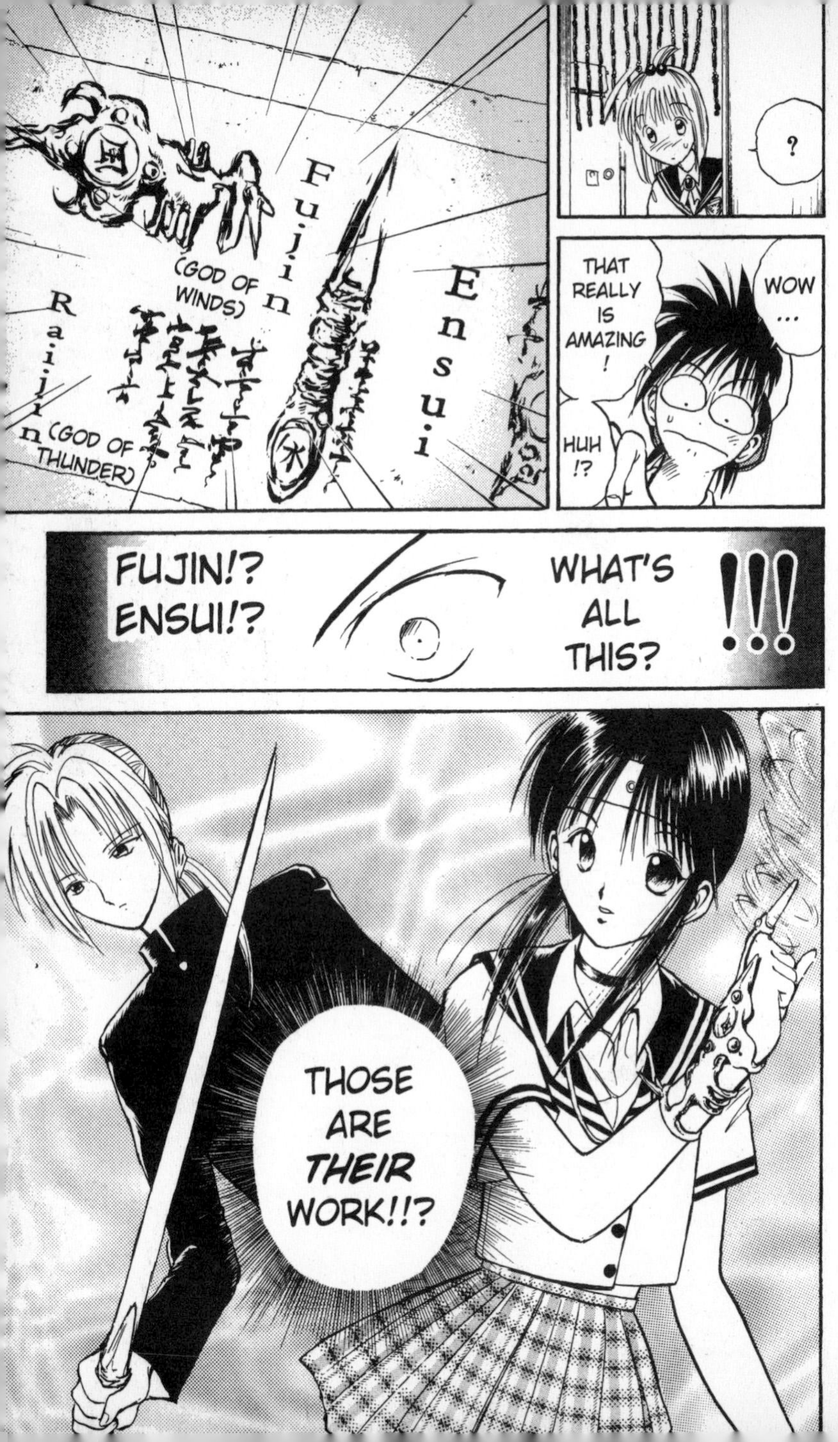
?
WOW ...
THAT REALLY IS AMAZING!
HUH!?
Fujin
(GOD OF WINDS)
Ensui
Raijin
(GOD OF THUNDER)
WHAT'S ALL THIS? !!!
FUJIN!? ENSUI!?
THOSE ARE THEIR WORK!!?

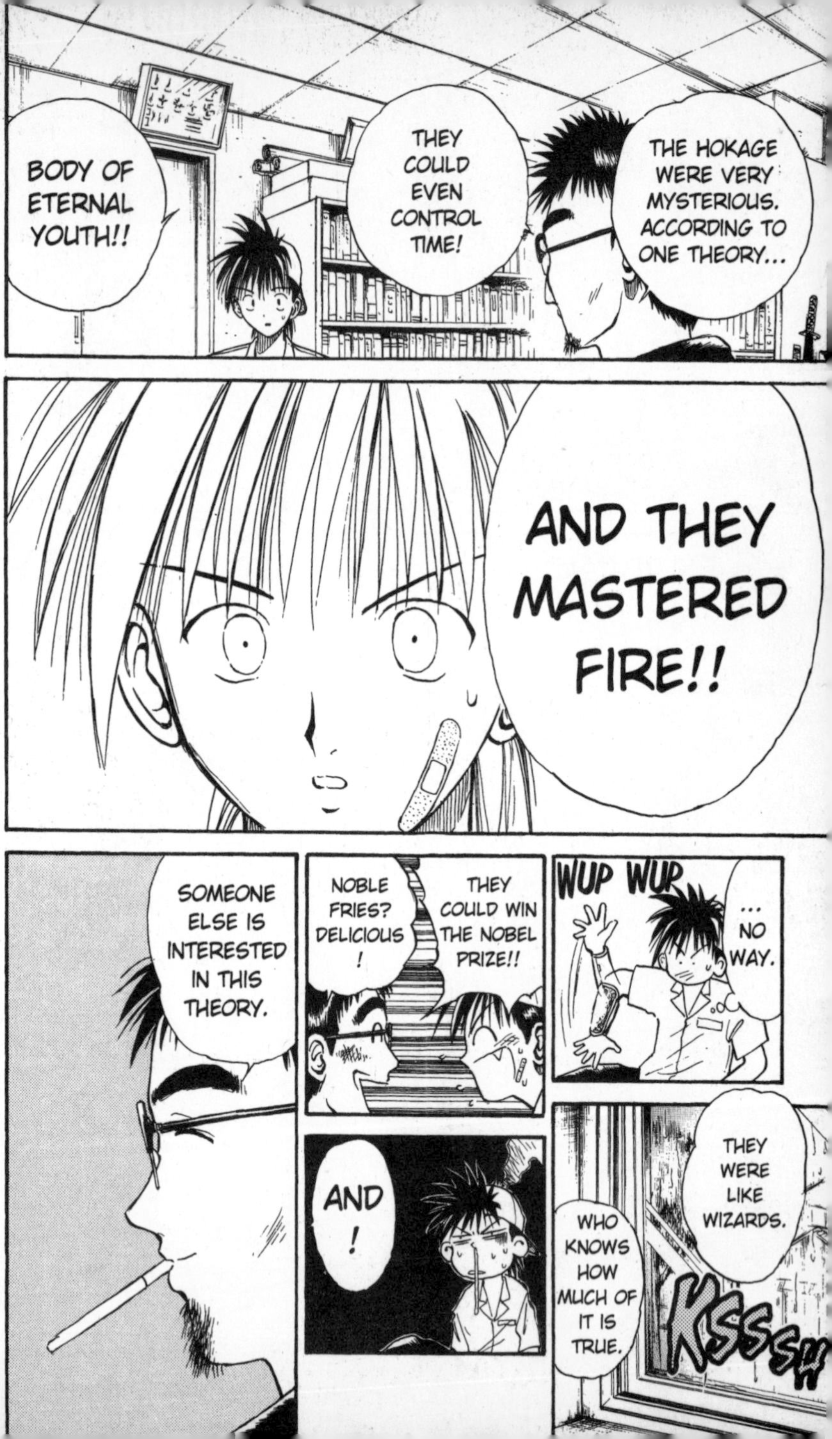
THE HOKAGE WERE VERY MYSTERIOUS. ACCORDING TO ONE THEORY...
THEY COULD EVEN CONTROL TIME!
BODY OF ETERNAL YOUTH!!
AND THEY MASTERED FIRE!!
WUP WUP
...NO WAY.
THEY COULD WIN THE NOBEL PRIZE!!
NOBLE FRIES? DELICIOUS!
THEY WERE LIKE WIZARDS.
WHO KNOWS HOW MUCH OF IT IS TRUE.
KSSSSH
AND!
SOMEONE ELSE IS INTERESTED IN THIS THEORY.

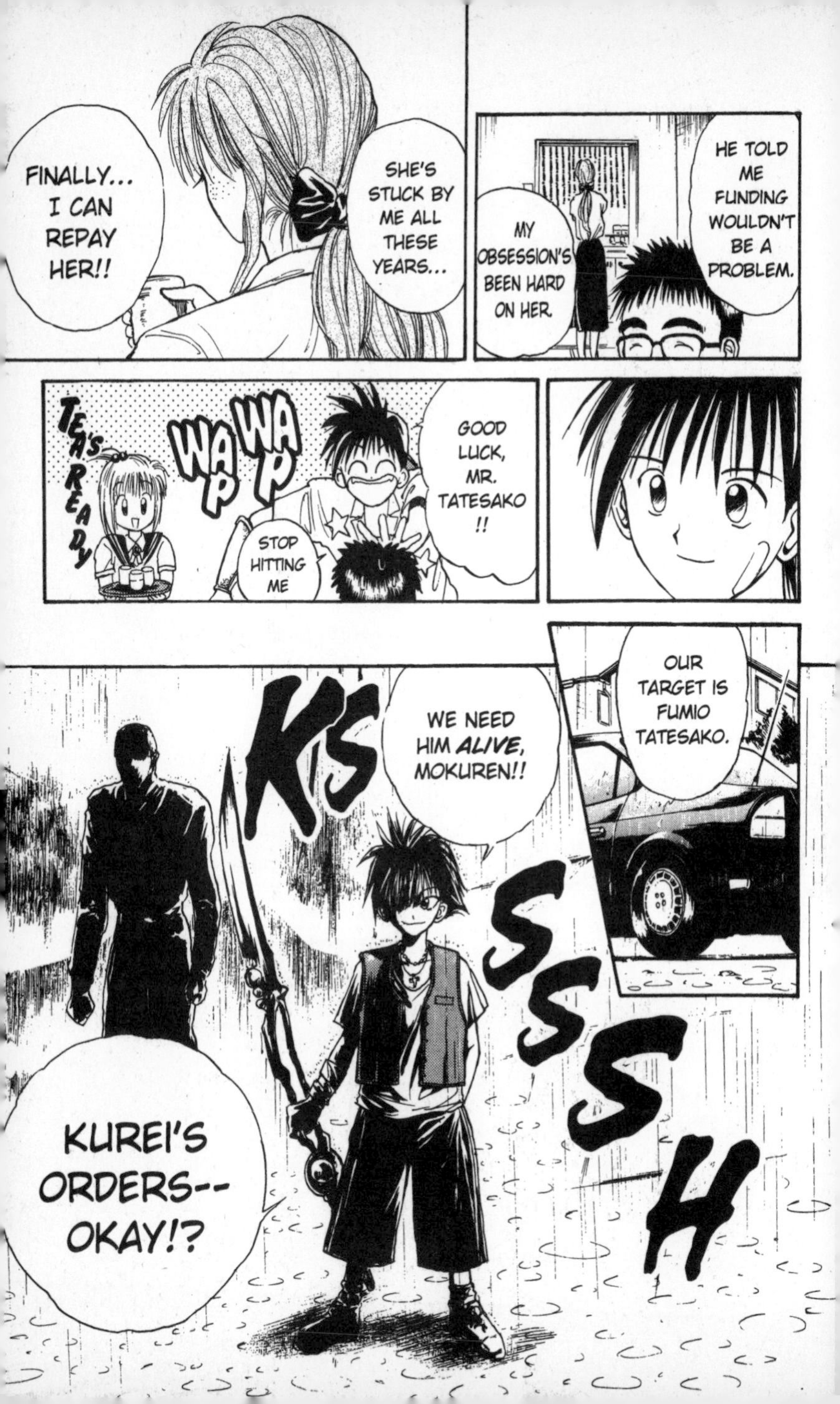
HE TOLD ME FUNDING WOULDN'T BE A PROBLEM.
MY OBSESSION'S BEEN HARD ON HER.
SHE'S STUCK BY ME ALL THESE YEARS...
FINALLY... I CAN REPAY HER!!
GOOD LUCK, MR. TATESAKO!!
STOP HITTING ME
WAP WAP
TEA'S READY
OUR TARGET IS FUMIO TATESAKO.
WE NEED HIM *ALIVE*, MOKUREN!!
KSSSSH
KUREI'S ORDERS--OKAY!?

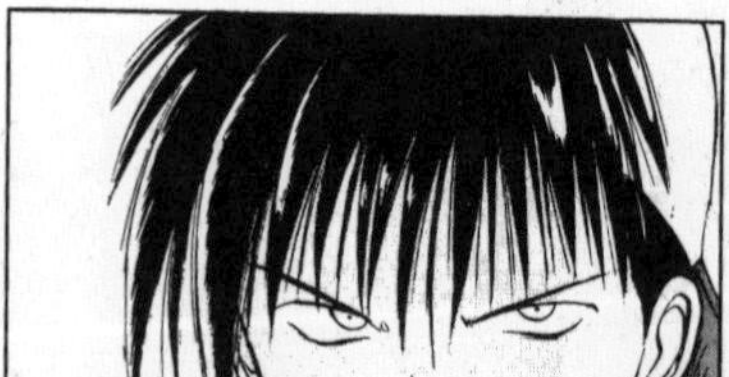

烈火の炎

~FLAME OF RECCA~

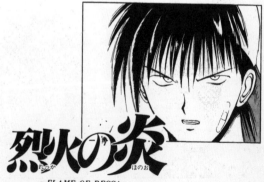

Part Nineteen: Boy of Gold - Man of Wood

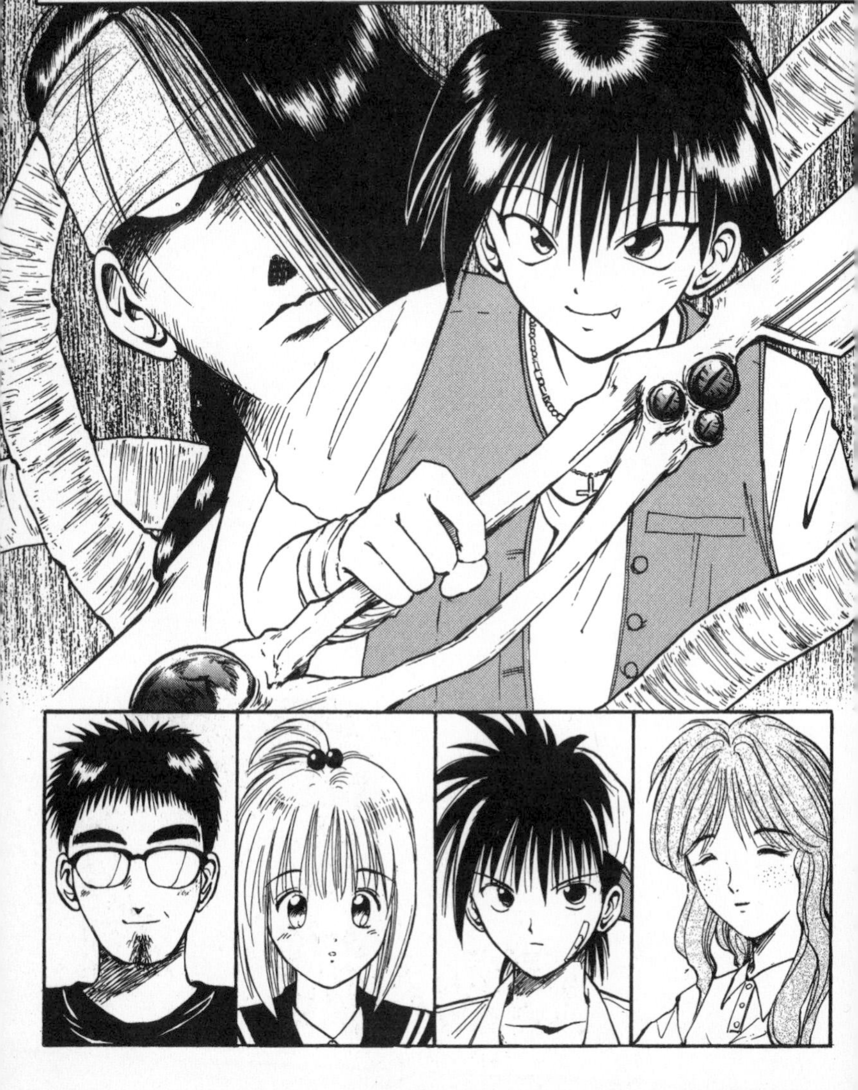

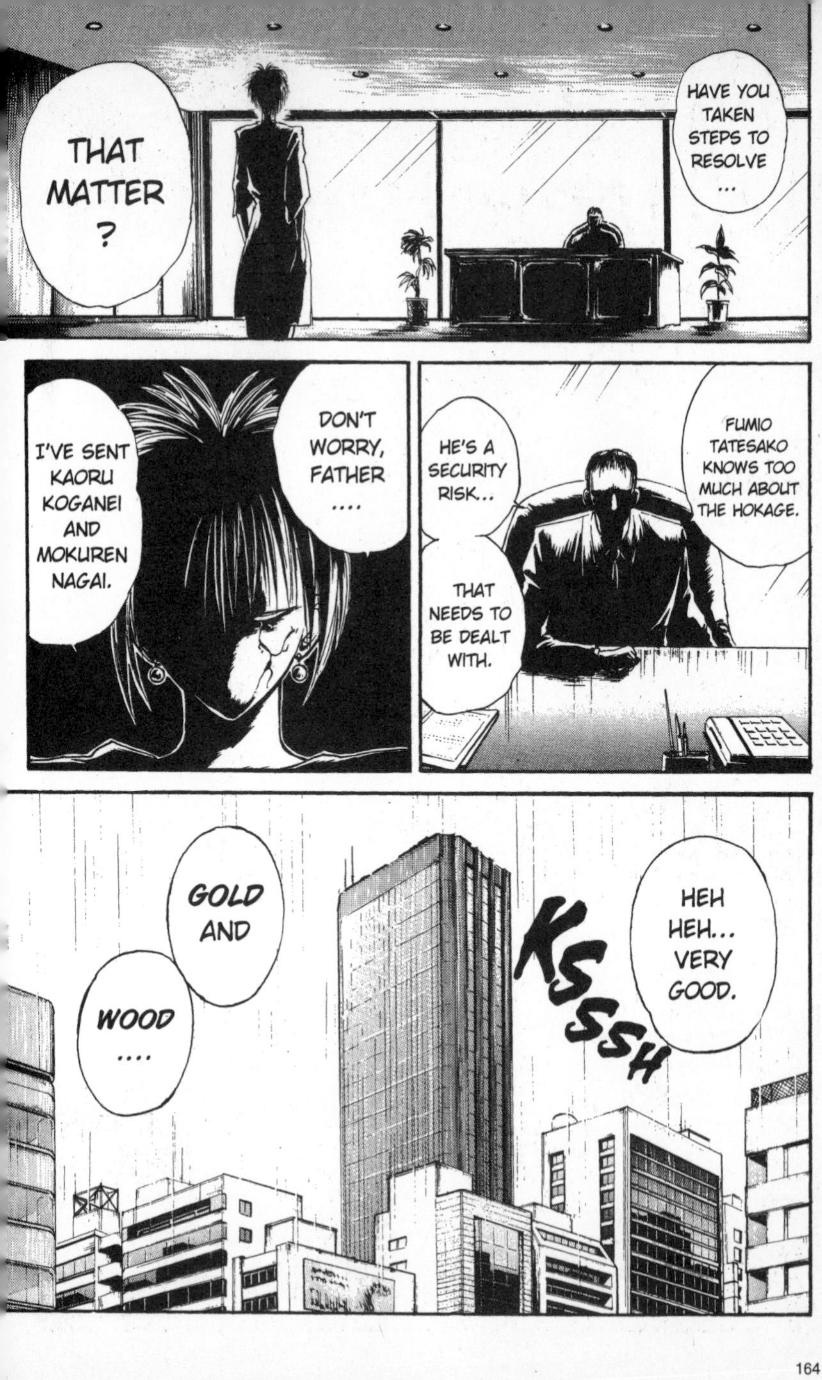
HAVE YOU TAKEN STEPS TO RESOLVE ...
THAT MATTER ?
FUMIO TATESAKO KNOWS TOO MUCH ABOUT THE HOKAGE.
HE'S A SECURITY RISK...
THAT NEEDS TO BE DEALT WITH.
DON'T WORRY, FATHER ....
I'VE SENT KAORU KOGANEI AND MOKUREN NAGAI.
HEH HEH... VERY GOOD.
KSSSH
GOLD AND
WOOD ....

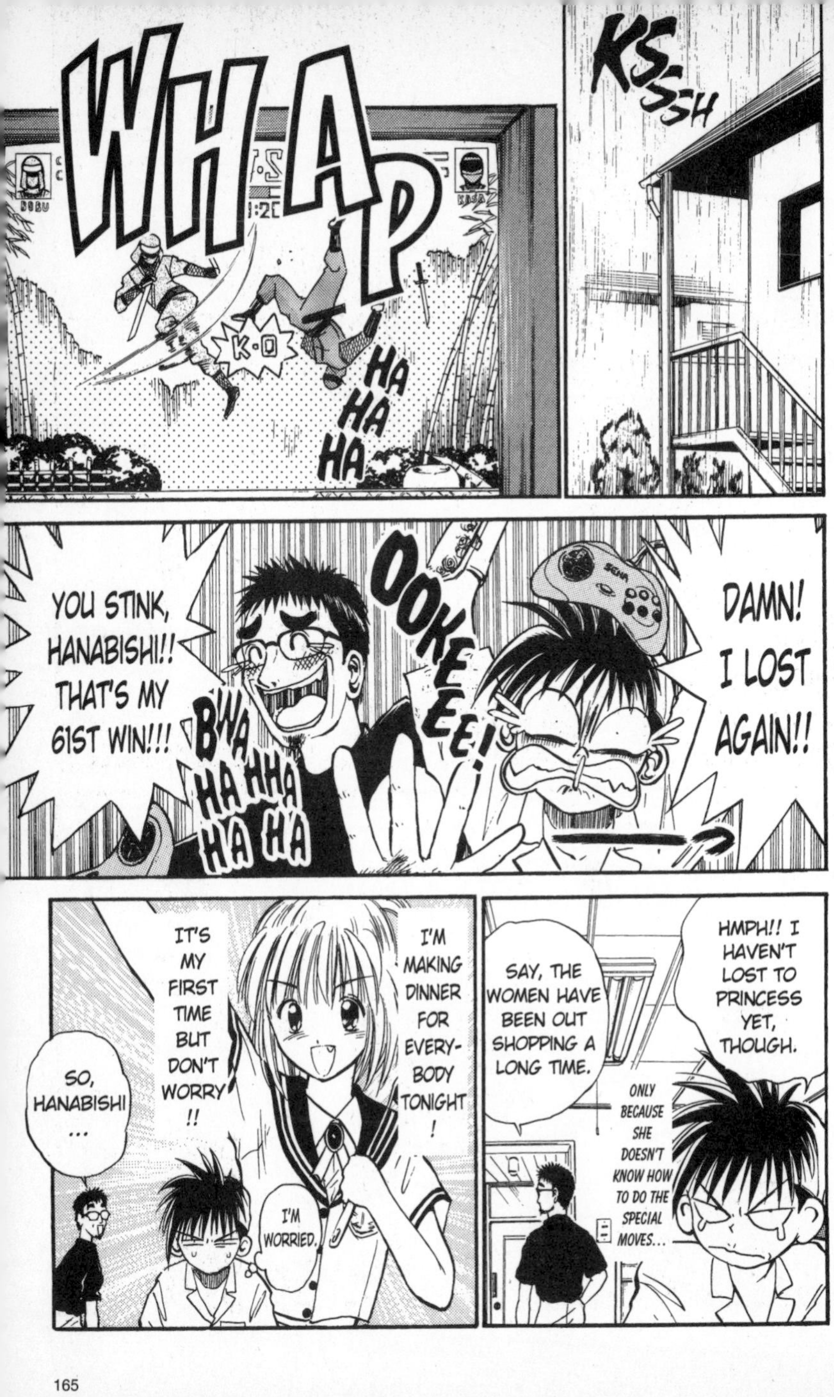
KS-S-SH
WHAP
K·O
HA HA HA HA
DAMN! I LOST AGAIN!!
OOKEEEE!
BWAHAHHAHAHA HA
YOU STINK, HANABISHI!! THAT'S MY 61ST WIN!!!
HMPH!! I HAVEN'T LOST TO PRINCESS YET, THOUGH.
ONLY BECAUSE SHE DOESN'T KNOW HOW TO DO THE SPECIAL MOVES...
SAY, THE WOMEN HAVE BEEN OUT SHOPPING A LONG TIME.
I'M MAKING DINNER FOR EVERYBODY TONIGHT!
IT'S MY FIRST TIME BUT DON'T WORRY!!
I'M WORRIED.
SO, HANABISHI...

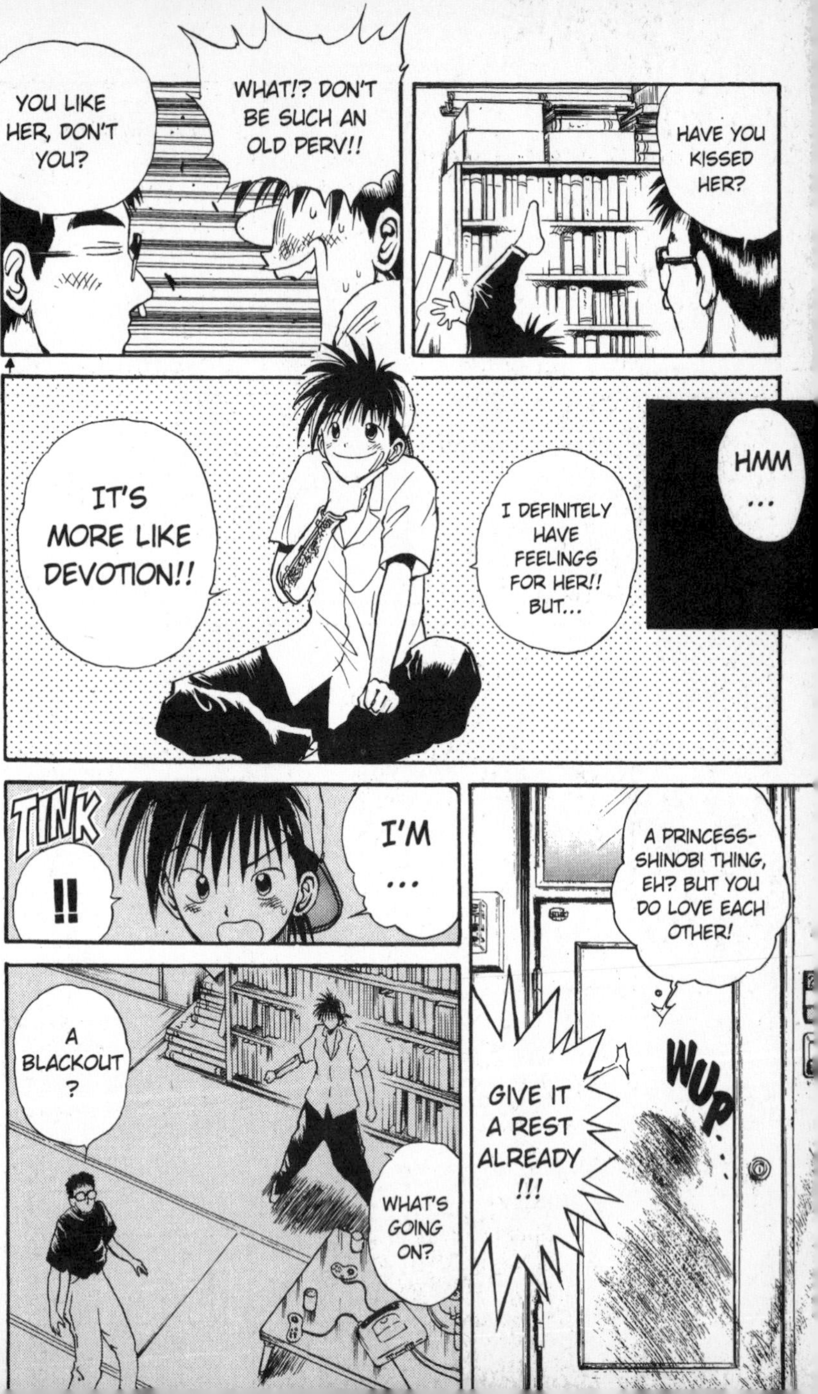
HAVE YOU KISSED HER?
WHAT!? DON'T BE SUCH AN OLD PERV!!
YOU LIKE HER, DON'T YOU?
HMM ...
I DEFINITELY HAVE FEELINGS FOR HER!! BUT...
IT'S MORE LIKE DEVOTION!!
A PRINCESS-SHINOBI THING, EH? BUT YOU DO LOVE EACH OTHER!
WUP
GIVE IT A REST ALREADY !!!
I'M ...
TINK
!!
WHAT'S GOING ON?
A BLACKOUT ?

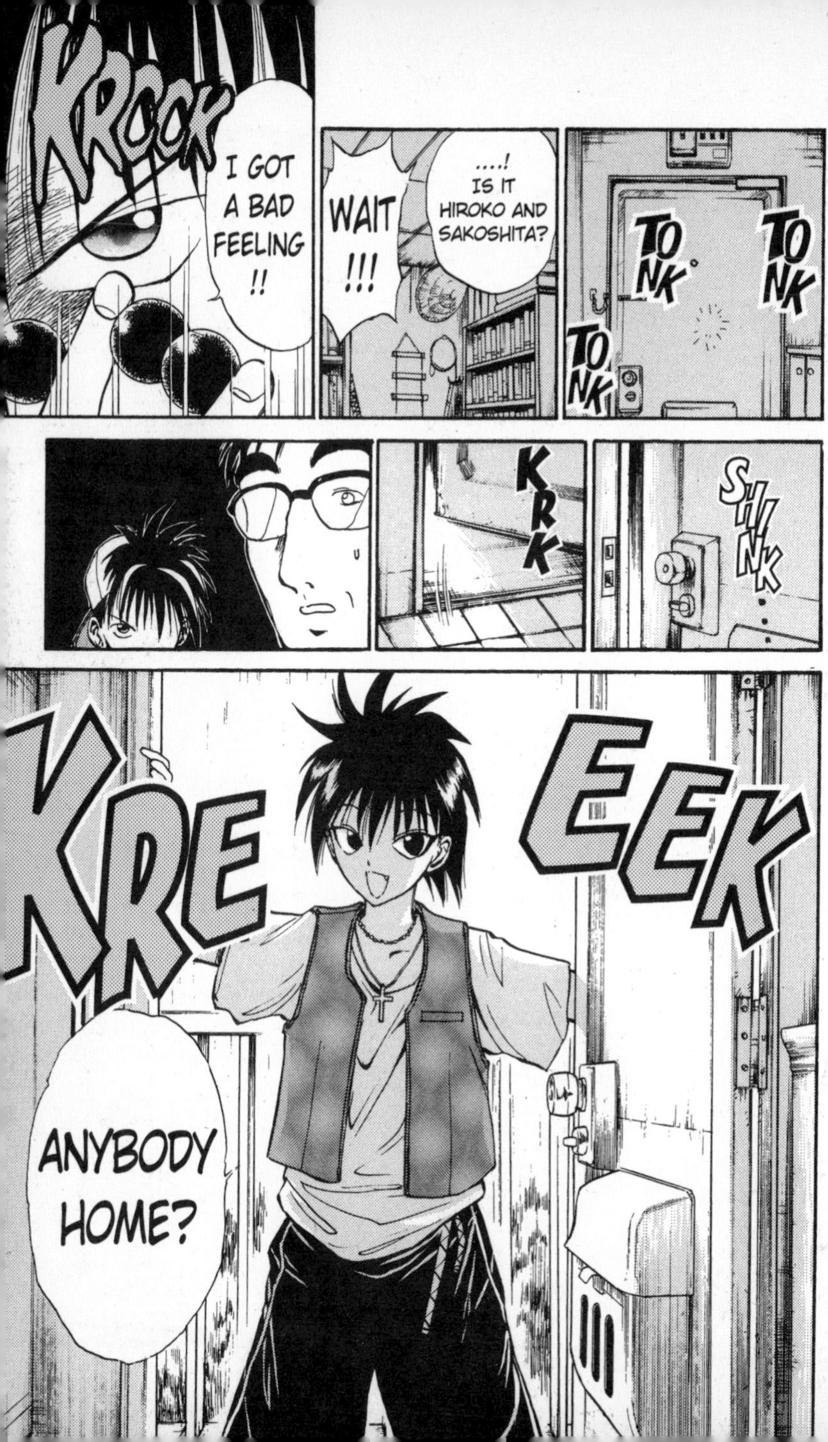

TONK
TONK
TONK
....! IS IT HIROKO AND SAKOSHITA?
WAIT !!!
KROOK
I GOT A BAD FEELING !!
SHINK
KRK
KREEEK
ANYBODY HOME?

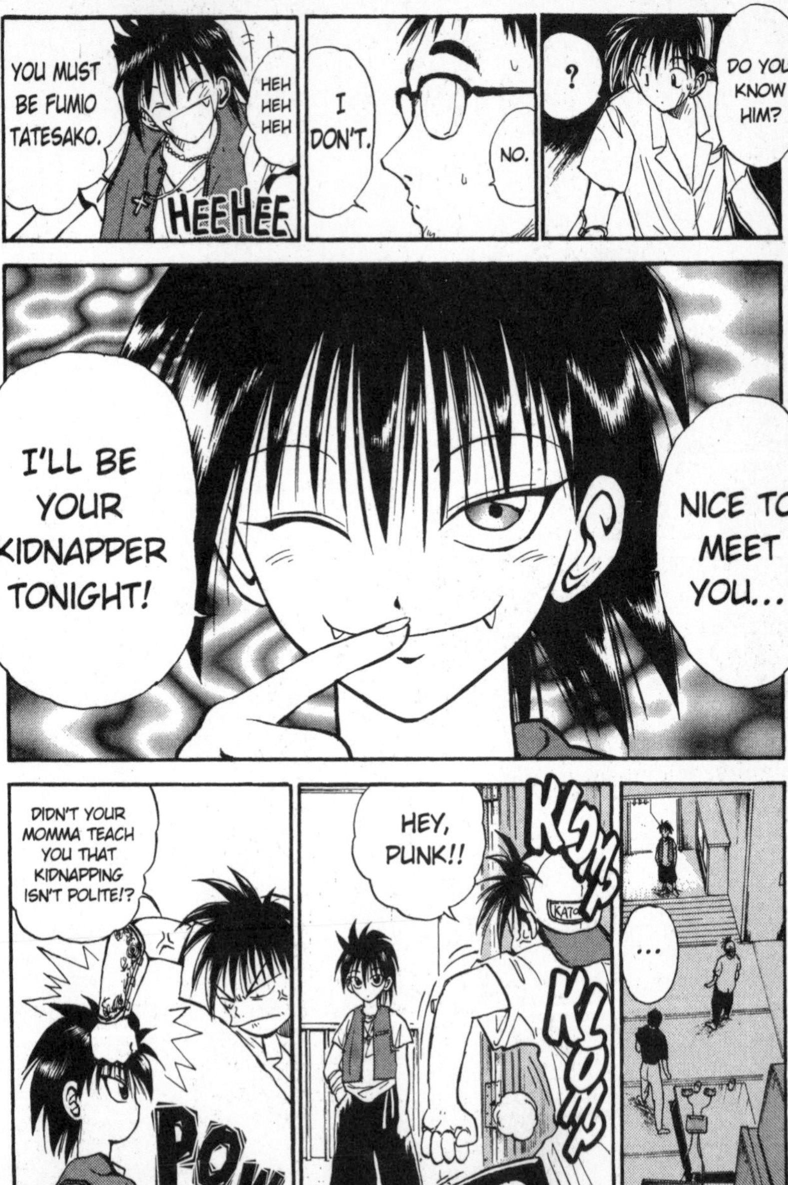
DO YOU KNOW HIM?
?
NO.
I DON'T.
HEH HEH HEH
YOU MUST BE FUMIO TATESAKO.
HEE HEE
NICE TO MEET YOU...
I'LL BE YOUR KIDNAPPER TONIGHT!
...
KLOMP
KLOMP
KATO
HEY, PUNK!!
POW
DIDN'T YOUR MOMMA TEACH YOU THAT KIDNAPPING ISN'T POLITE!?

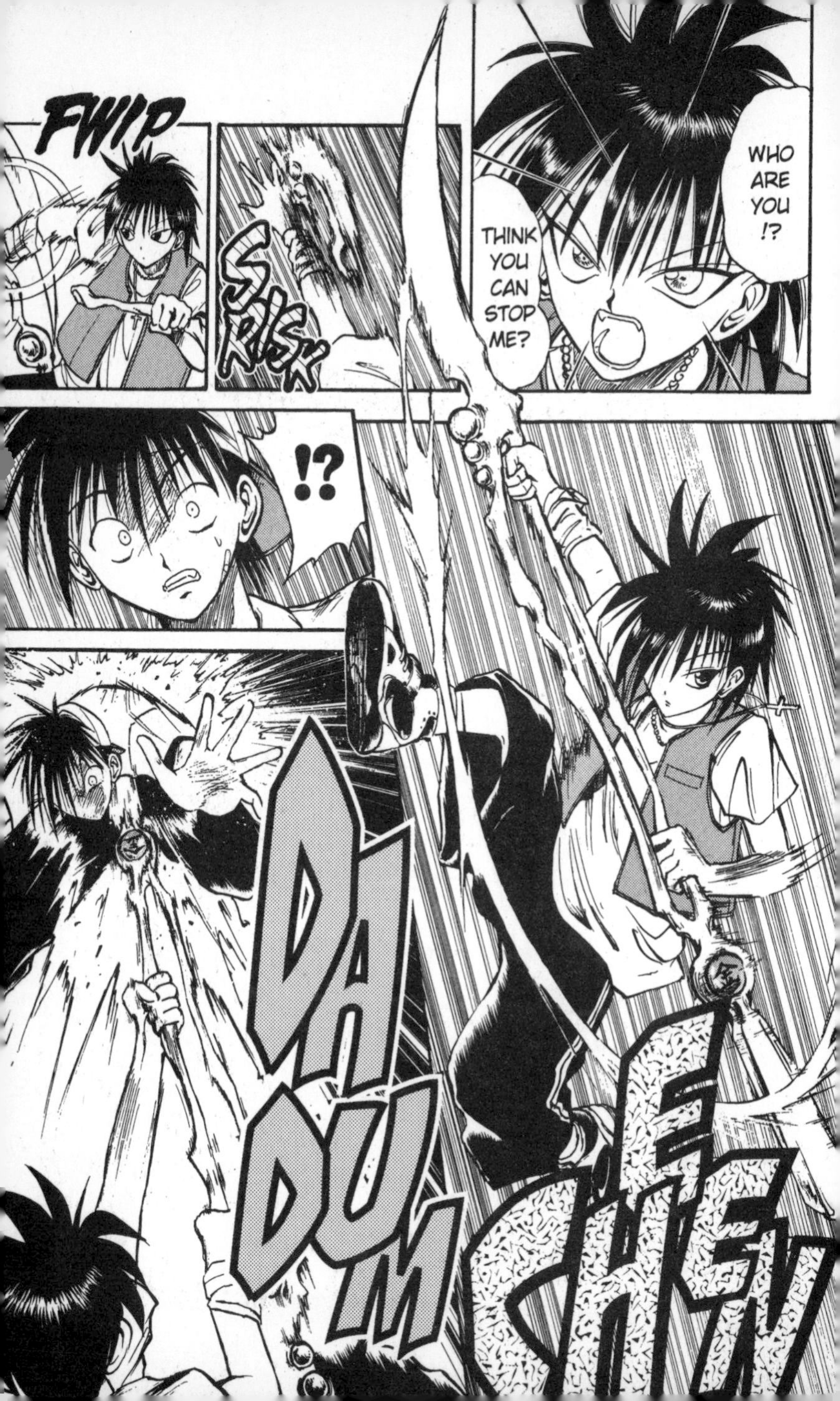
WHO ARE YOU !?
THINK YOU CAN STOP ME?
FWIP
!?

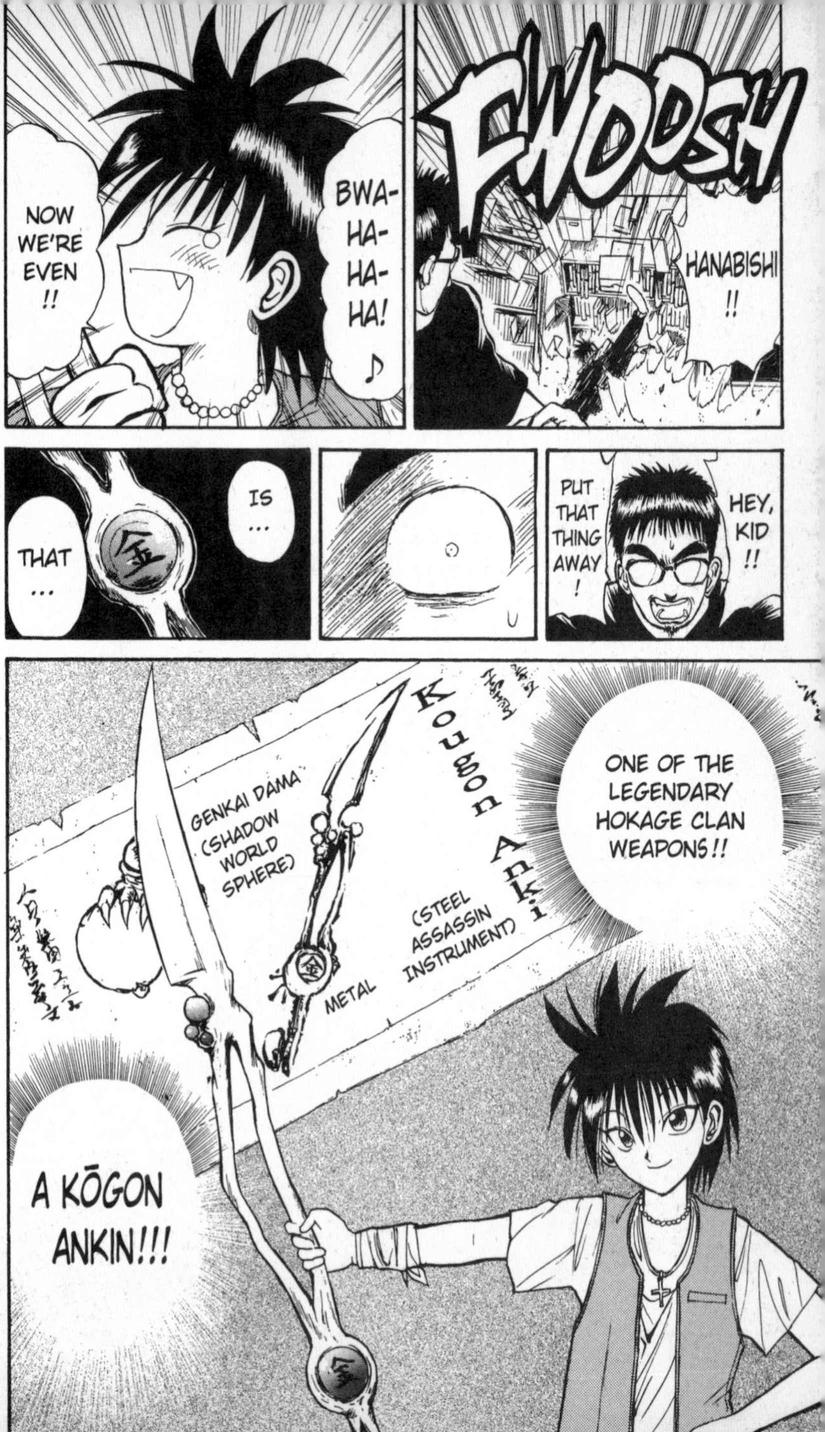
FWOOSH
HANABISHI !!
BWA-HA-HA-HA! ♪
NOW WE'RE EVEN !!
HEY, KID !!
PUT THAT THING AWAY !
THAT ...
IS ...
Kougon Anki
GENKAI DAMA (SHADOW WORLD SPHERE)
(STEEL ASSASSIN INSTRUMENT)
METAL
A KŌGON ANKIN!!!
ONE OF THE LEGENDARY HOKAGE CLAN WEAPONS!!

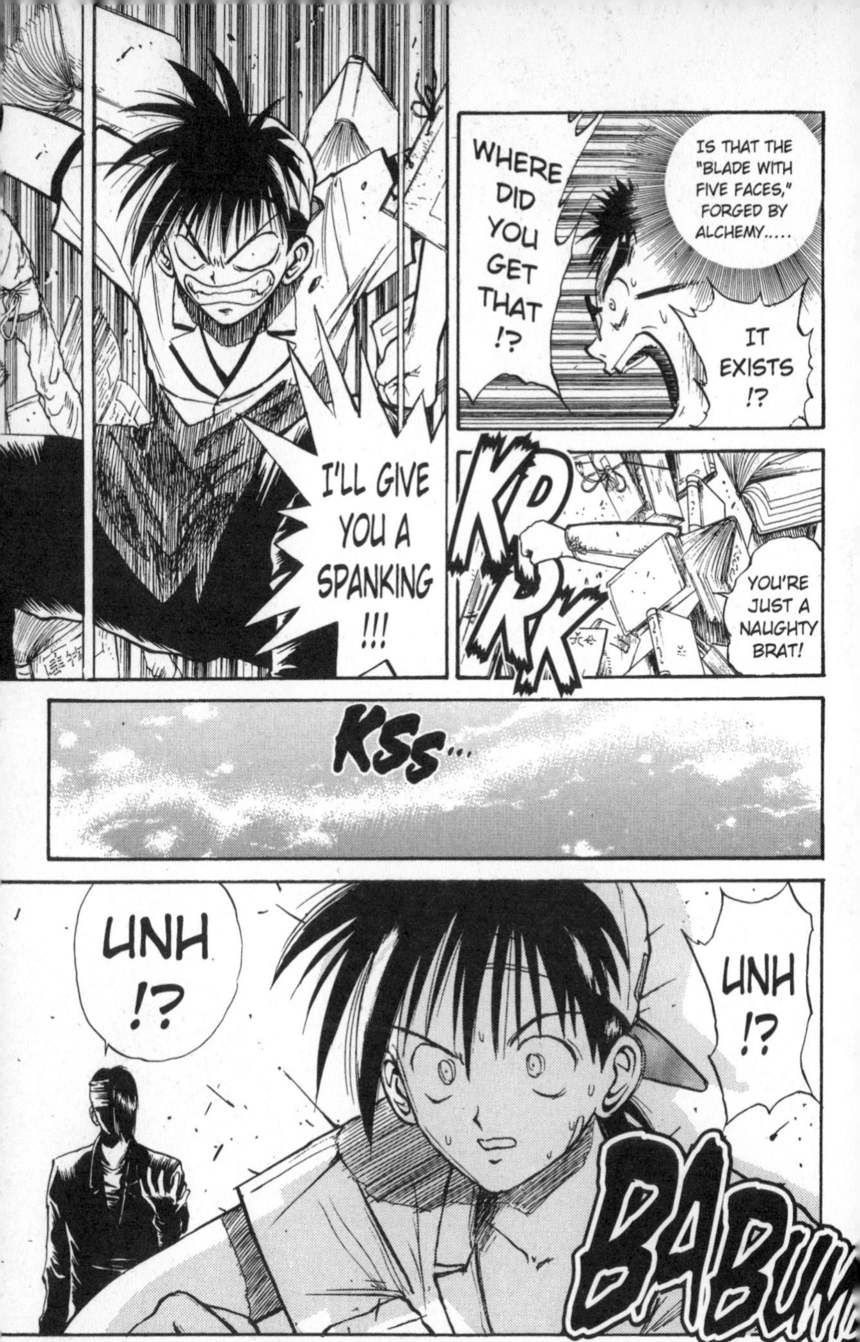
IS THAT THE "BLADE WITH FIVE FACES," FORGED BY ALCHEMY.....
IT EXISTS !?
WHERE DID YOU GET THAT !?
KRRK
YOU'RE JUST A NAUGHTY BRAT!
I'LL GIVE YOU A SPANKING !!!
KSS...
UNH !?
UNH !?
BABUM

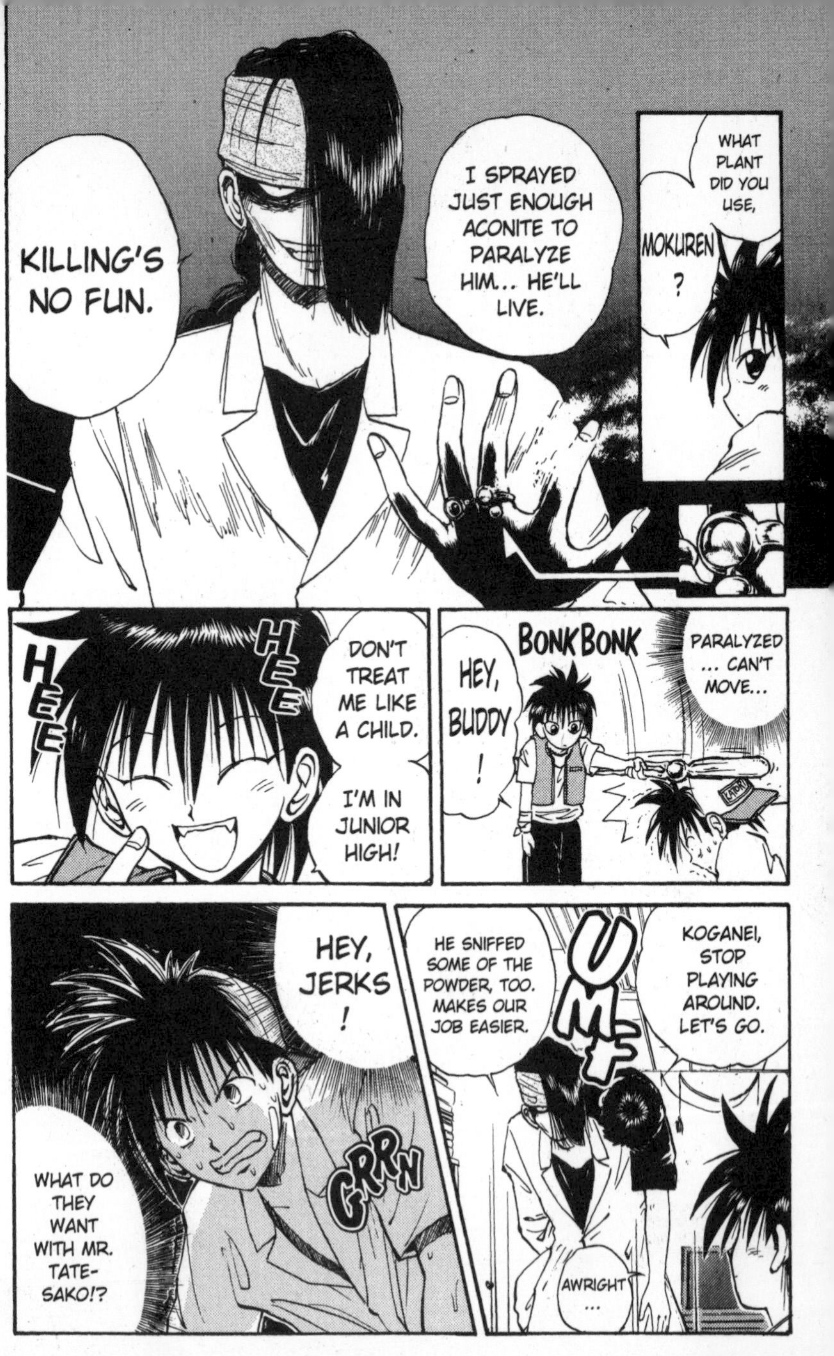
WHAT PLANT DID YOU USE, MOKUREN?
I SPRAYED JUST ENOUGH ACONITE TO PARALYZE HIM... HE'LL LIVE.
KILLING'S NO FUN.
PARALYZED... CAN'T MOVE...
BONK BONK
HEY, BUDDY!
HEE HEE
DON'T TREAT ME LIKE A CHILD.
I'M IN JUNIOR HIGH!
KOGANEI, STOP PLAYING AROUND. LET'S GO.
UMF
HE SNIFFED SOME OF THE POWDER, TOO. MAKES OUR JOB EASIER.
AWRIGHT...
HEY, JERKS!
GRRN
WHAT DO THEY WANT WITH MR. TATE-SAKO!?

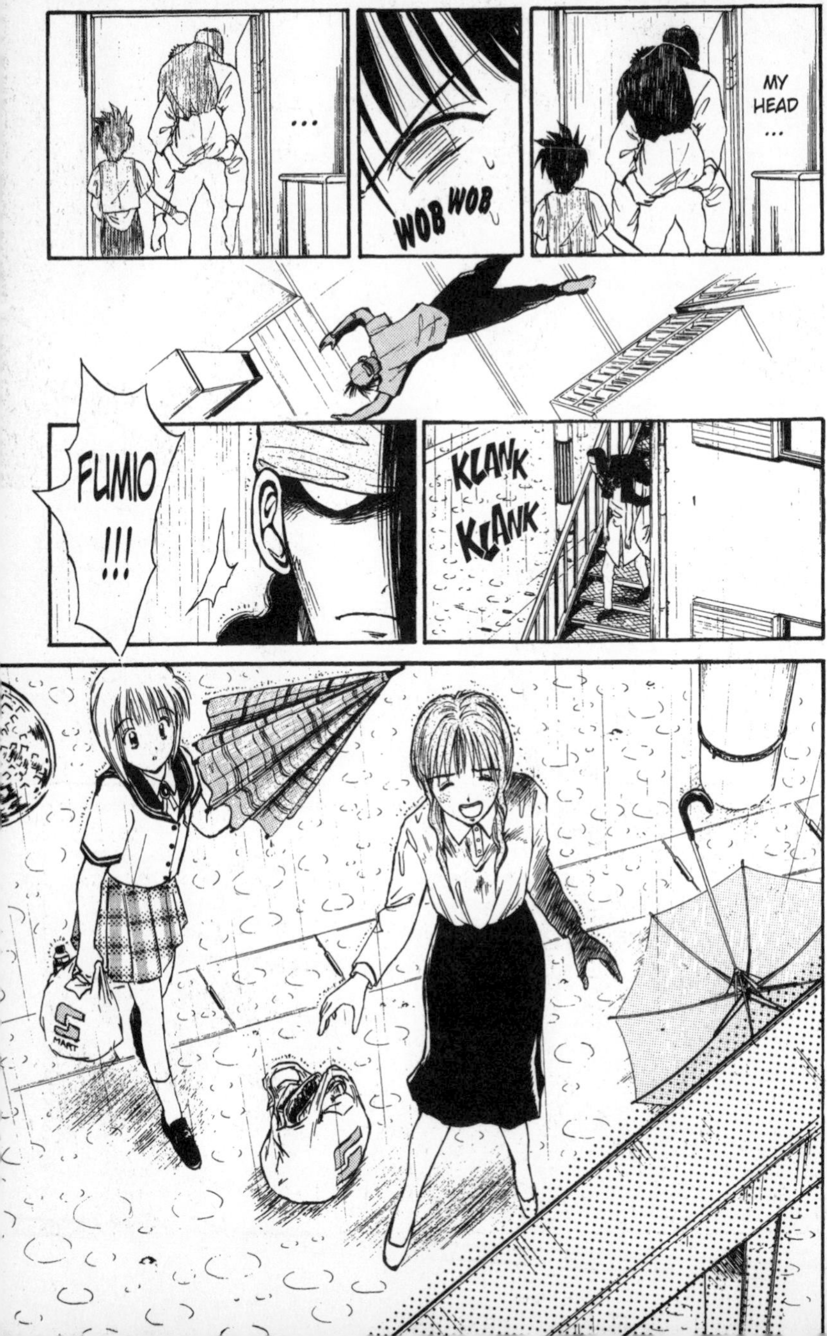

MY HEAD ...
WOB WOB
...
KLANK KLANK
FUMIO !!!

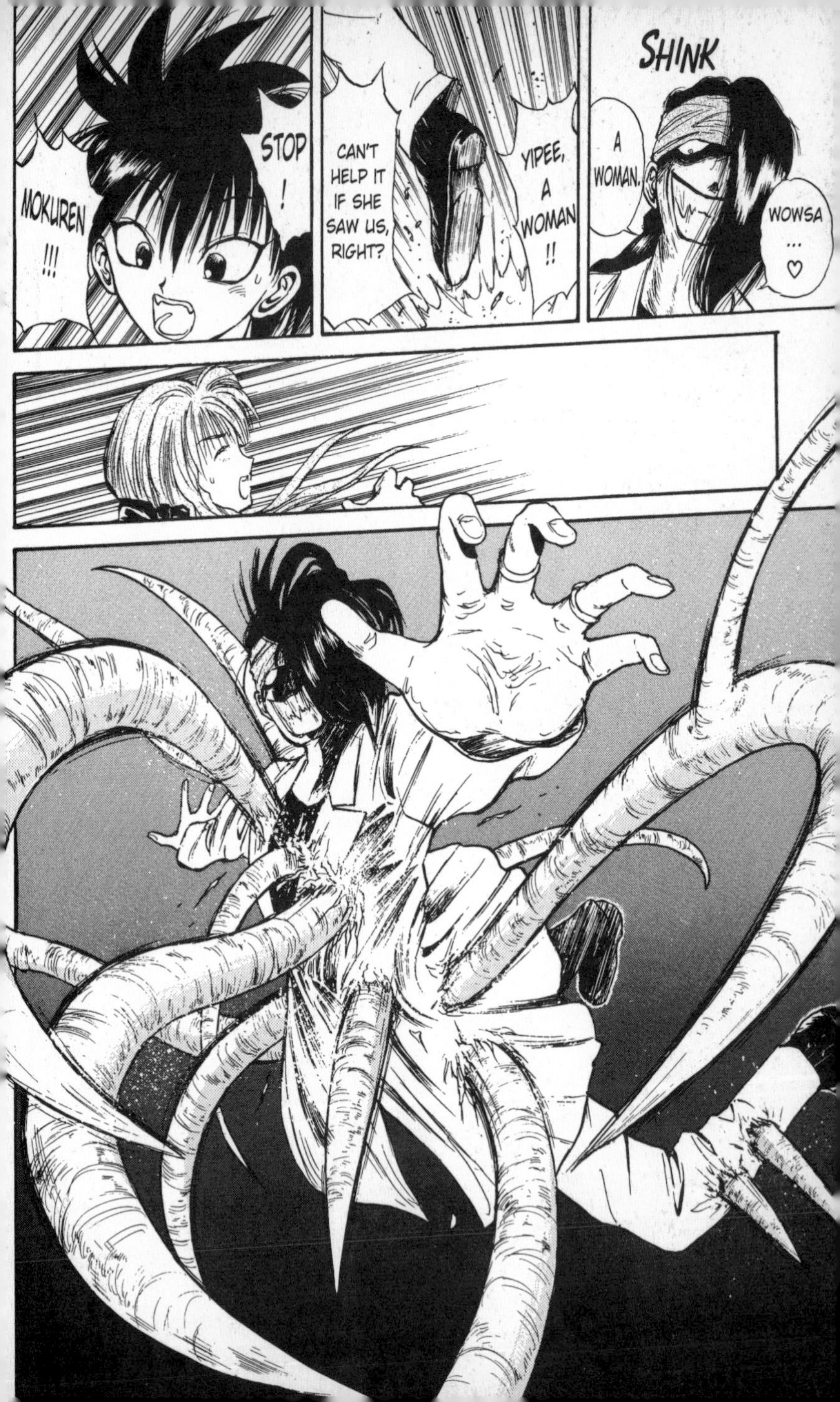

SHINK
A WOMAN.
WOWSA ... ♡
YIPEE, A WOMAN !!
CAN'T HELP IT IF SHE SAW US, RIGHT?
STOP !
MOKUREN !!!

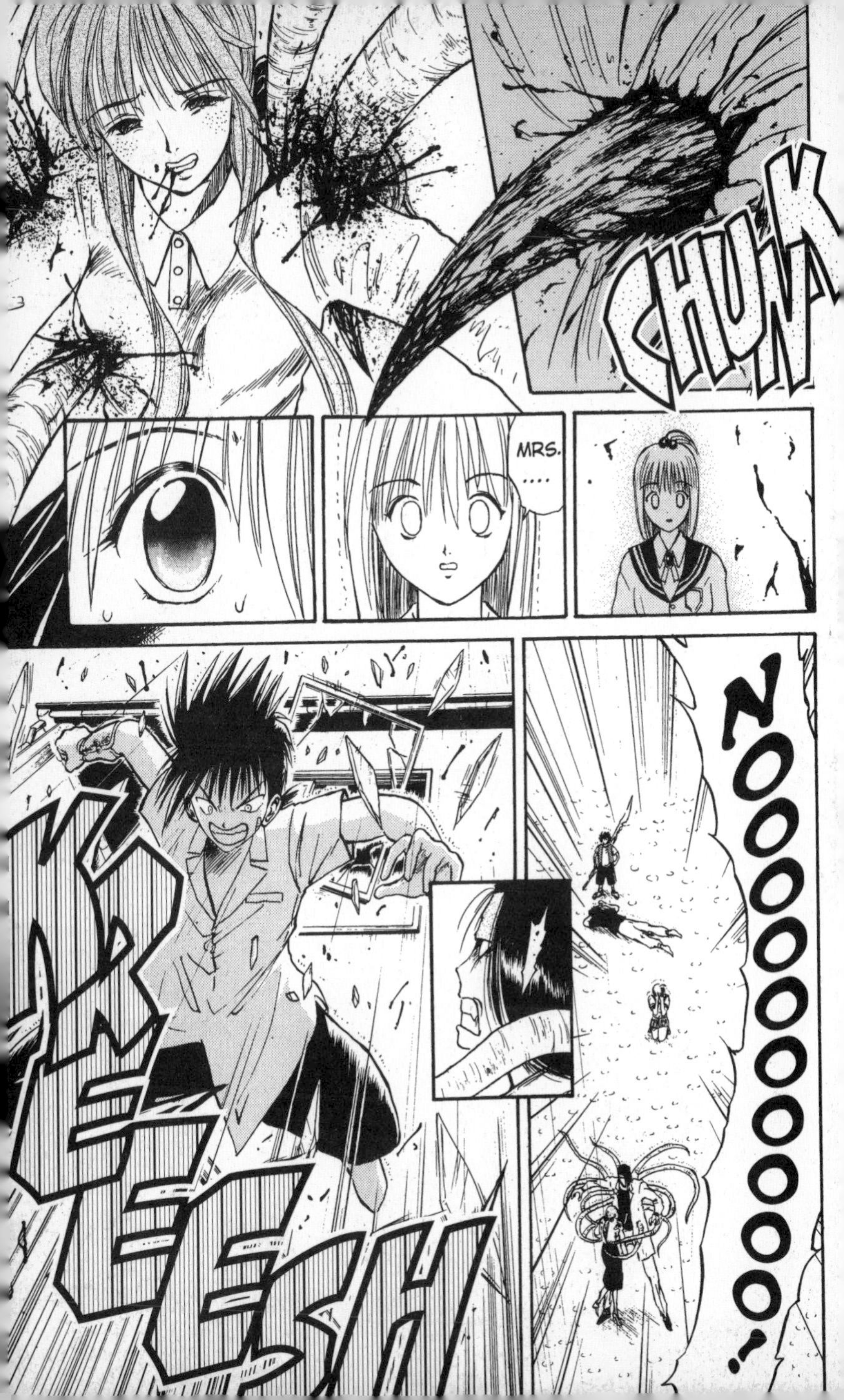
CHUNK
MRS.
....
NOOOOOOOOOOO...!
HYEEEEEEEH

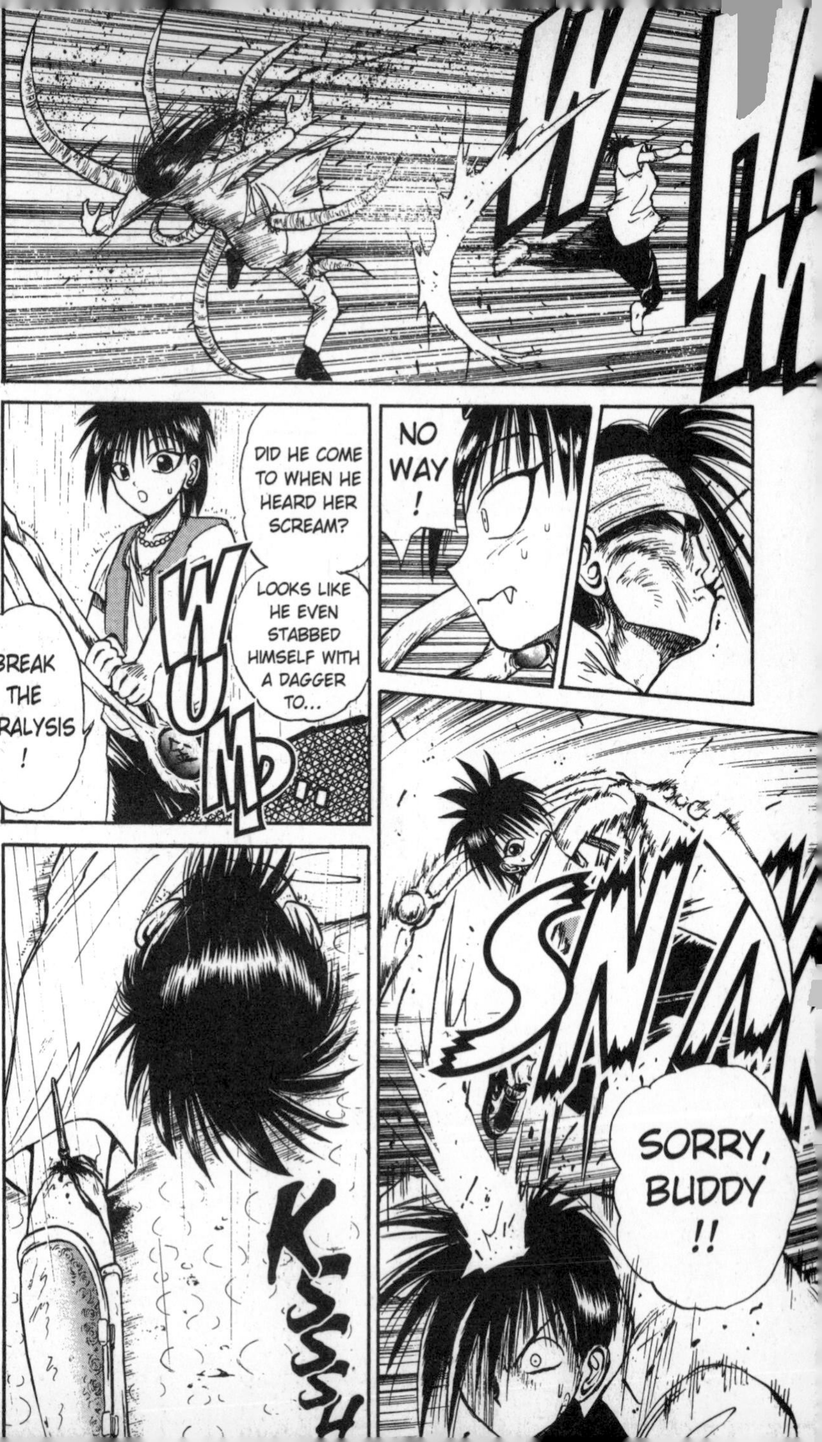

NO WAY!
DID HE COME TO WHEN HE HEARD HER SCREAM?
LOOKS LIKE HE EVEN STABBED HIMSELF WITH A DAGGER TO...
WUMP..
BREAK THE PARALYSIS!
SORRY, BUDDY!!

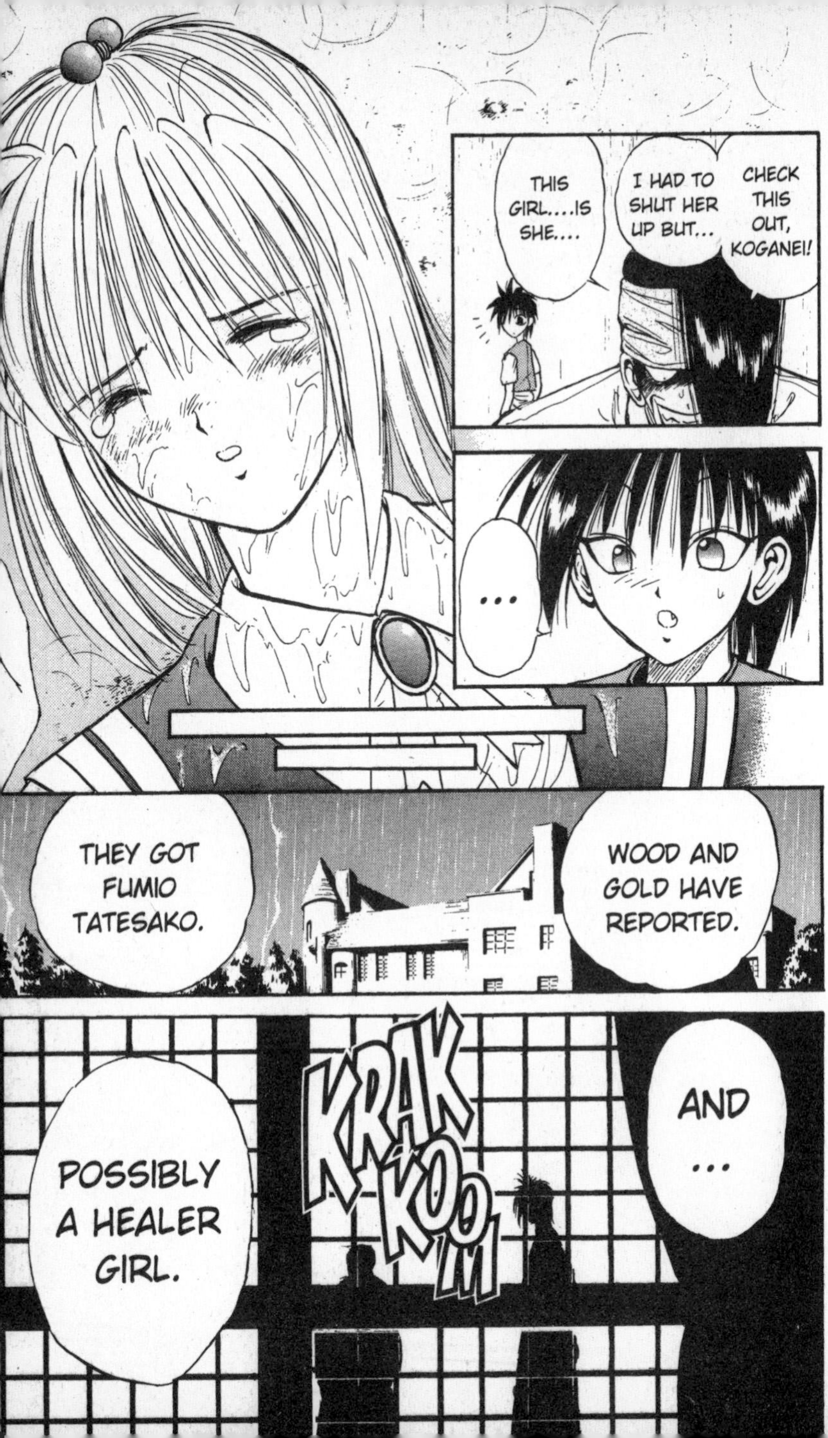
CHECK THIS OUT, KOGANEI!
I HAD TO SHUT HER UP BUT...
THIS GIRL....IS SHE....
...
WOOD AND GOLD HAVE REPORTED.
THEY GOT FUMIO TATESAKO.
AND ...
KRAK KOOM
POSSIBLY A HEALER GIRL.

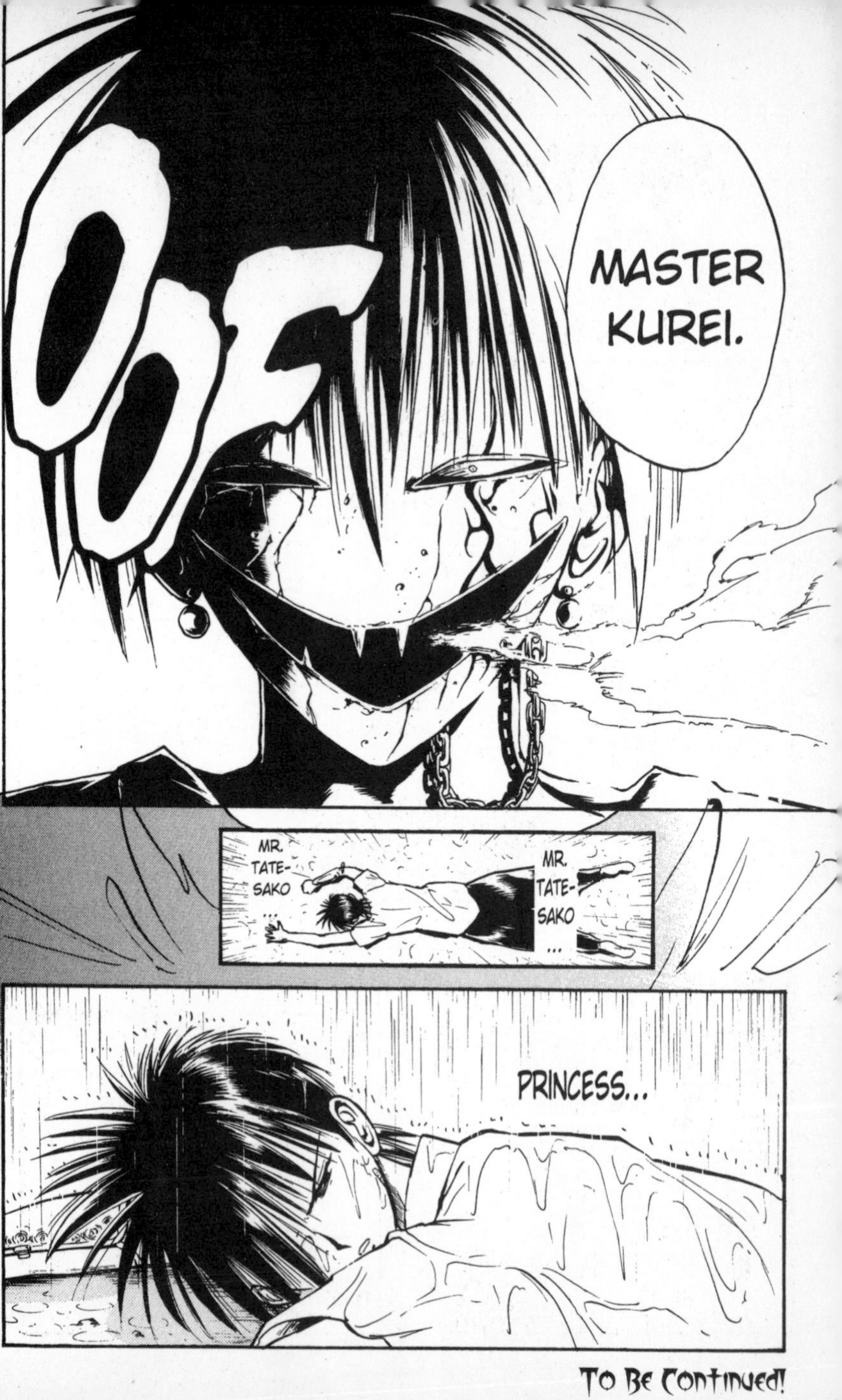
OOF
MASTER KUREI.
MR. TATE-SAKO ...
MR. TATE-SAKO ...
PRINCESS...

To Be Continued!

My Picture Diary

HEH-HEH HEH-HEH HEH-HEH **Exculsive Bonus Material--Ultimate Legend**

YOU'RE THE RECCA GROUP LEADER! SHAPE UP!!

I CAN'T SLEEP WITH YOU SNORING!

HUH!?

HEY, ANZAI!!

APPARENTLY MY SNORE IS UNBEARABLE.

HROONK

I'VE GOT TO DO SOMETHING ABOUT IT TO KEEP UP MY WARRIORS' MORALE...OR THEY MIGHT STAGE A COUP D'ETAT...

WHAT SHOULD I DO ....

← DEEP THOUGHT

NO ONE EVER TOLD ME I SNORED UNTIL I STARTED WORKING ON "RECCA."

HOW WOULD I KNOW IF I SNORE?

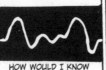

LOOK! HE'S DRINKING AGAIN!

HOW IRRE-SPONSI-BLE!

IT'S ONLY PLUM WINE....

YELL ALL YOU WANT, BUT I CAN'T HELP IT.

HICCUP!

KOTANI? MIKAKO?

IT'S DOMON! IT'S DOMON!

I DISLIKED IT VERY QUICKLY.

FOR THOSE SUFFER-ING FROM EXCESSIVE SNORING, THIS SUP-POSEDLY WORKS!

THIS IS GREAT!

TA DA!

SNORE STOPPER!!

JUST PLUG IT INTO YOUR NOSE.

¥2,884

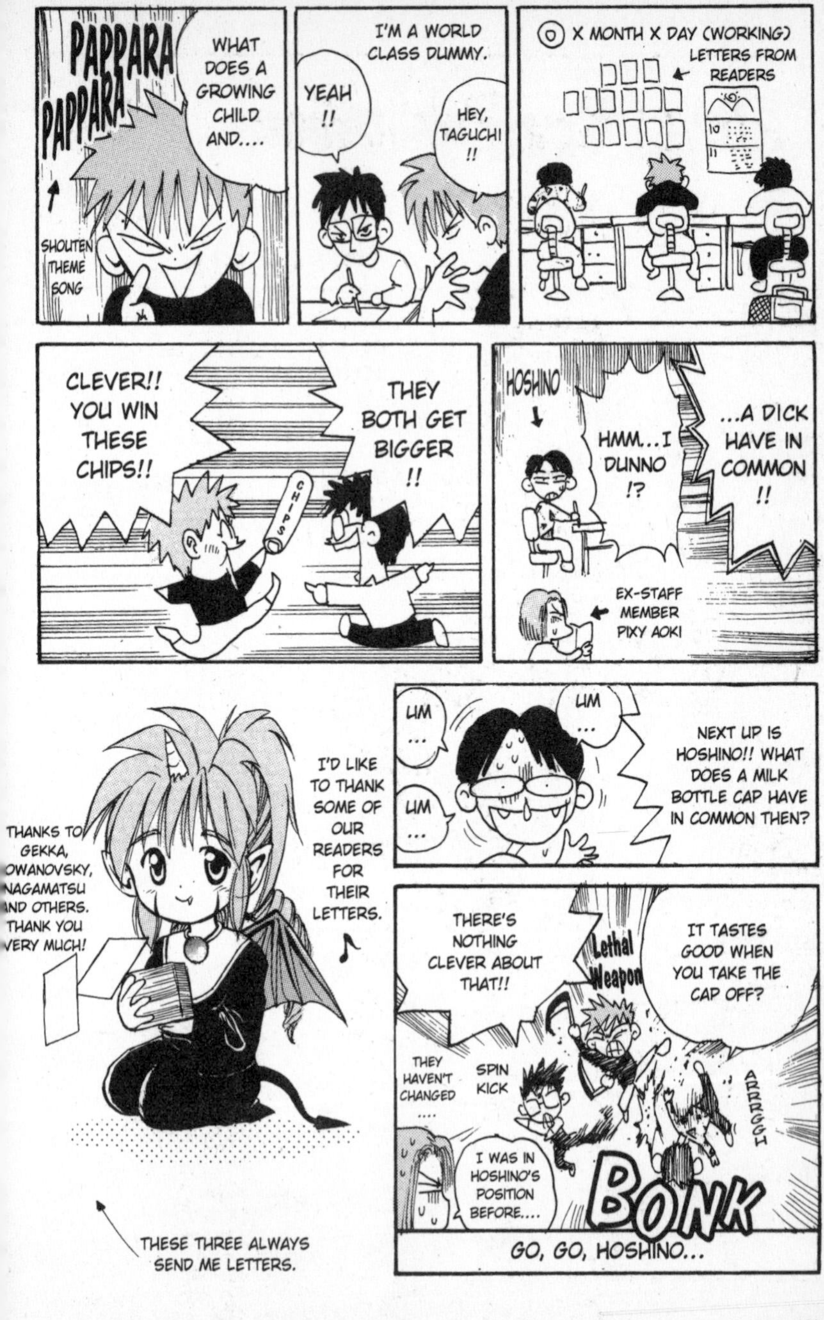

X MONTH X DAY (WORKING)
LETTERS FROM READERS
I'M A WORLD CLASS DUMMY.
HEY, TAGUCHI !!
YEAH !!
PAPPARA PAPPARA
WHAT DOES A GROWING CHILD AND....
SHOUTEN THEME SONG
HOSHINO
...A DICK HAVE IN COMMON !!
HMM...I DUNNO !?
EX-STAFF MEMBER PIXY AOKI
THEY BOTH GET BIGGER !!
CLEVER!! YOU WIN THESE CHIPS!!
CHIPS
NEXT UP IS HOSHINO!! WHAT DOES A MILK BOTTLE CAP HAVE IN COMMON THEN?
UM ...
UM ...
UM ...
IT TASTES GOOD WHEN YOU TAKE THE CAP OFF?
THERE'S NOTHING CLEVER ABOUT THAT!!
Lethal Weapon
ARRRGGH
SPIN KICK
THEY HAVEN'T CHANGED ....
I WAS IN HOSHINO'S POSITION BEFORE....
BONK
GO, GO, HOSHINO...
I'D LIKE TO THANK SOME OF OUR READERS FOR THEIR LETTERS.
THANKS TO GEKKA, OWANOVSKY, NAGAMATSU AND OTHERS. THANK YOU VERY MUCH!
THESE THREE ALWAYS SEND ME LETTERS.

Abrupt New Publication

Magical Girl: Run

◀Chapter 1▶

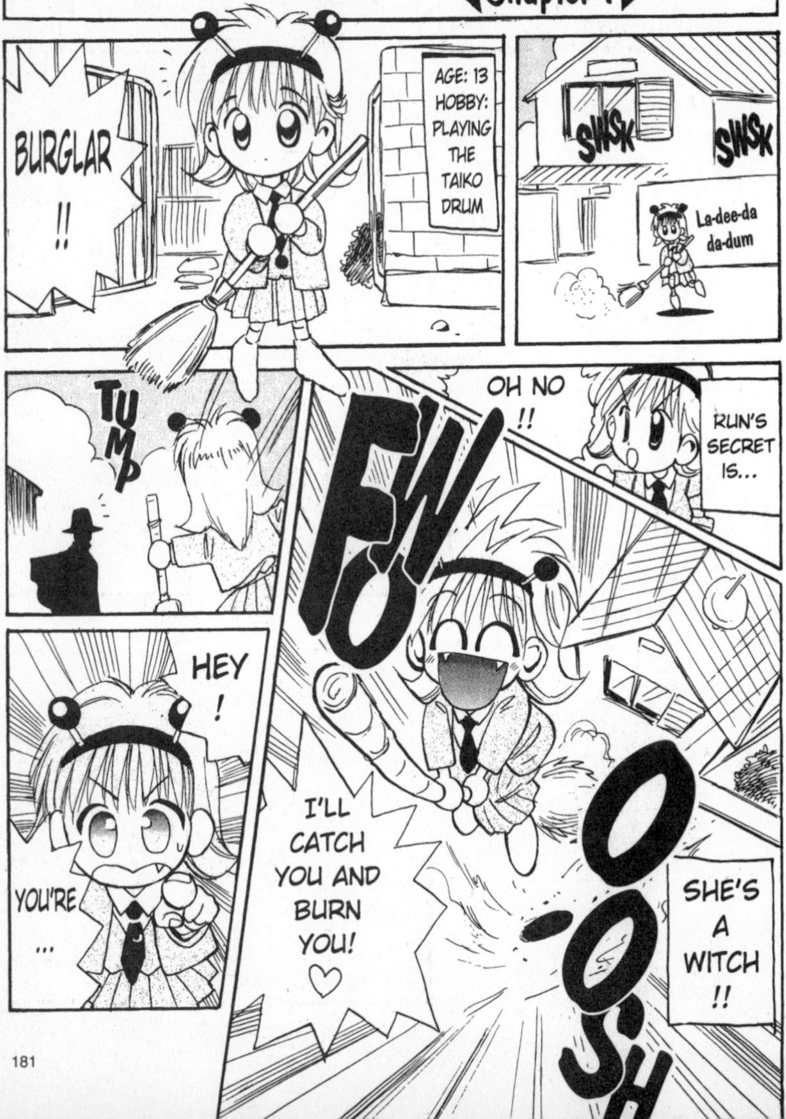

BURGLAR !!
AGE: 13 HOBBY: PLAYING THE TAIKO DRUM
SWSK
SWSK
La-dee-da da-dum
TUMP
OH NO !!
RUN'S SECRET IS...
HEY !
YOU'RE ...
FWOOSH
I'LL CATCH YOU AND BURN YOU! ♡
SHE'S A WITCH !!

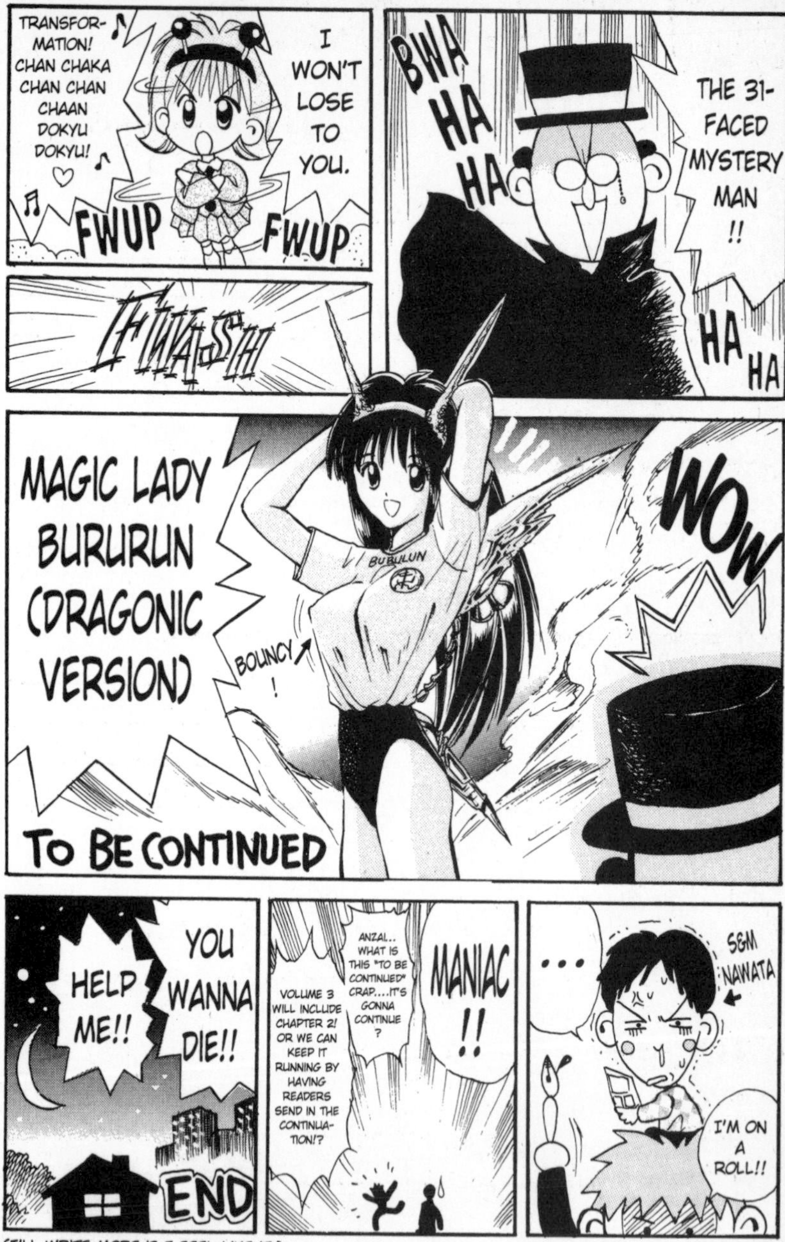
BWA HA HA
THE 31-FACED MYSTERY MAN!!
HA HA
I WON'T LOSE TO YOU.
TRANSFORMATION! CHAN CHAKA CHAN CHAN CHAAN DOKYU DOKYU! ♡
FWUP FWUP
FWASSH
WOW
BUBULUN
BOUNCY!
MAGIC LADY BURURUN (DRAGONIC VERSION)
TO BE CONTINUED
...
S&M NAWATA
I'M ON A ROLL!!
MANIAC!!
ANZAI... WHAT IS THIS "TO BE CONTINUED" CRAP....IT'S GONNA CONTINUE?
VOLUME 3 WILL INCLUDE CHAPTER 2! OR WE CAN KEEP IT RUNNING BY HAVING READERS SEND IN THE CONTINUATION!?
YOU WANNA DIE!!
HELP ME!!
END

(I'LL WRITE MORE IF I FEEL LIKE IT.)

COMPLETE OUR SURVEY AND LET US KNOW WHAT YOU THINK!

☐ Please check here if you DO NOT wish to receive information or future offers from VIZ

Name: _____

Address: _____

City: _____ State: _____ Zip: _____

E-mail: _____

☐ Male ☐ Female   Date of Birth (mm/dd/yyyy): ___ / ___ / _____   (Under 13? Parental consent required)

What race/ethnicity do you consider yourself? (please check one)

☐ Asian/Pacific Islander   ☐ Black/African American   ☐ Hispanic/Latino

☐ Native American/Alaskan Native   ☐ White/Caucasian   ☐ Other: _____

What VIZ product did you purchase? (check all that apply and indicate title purchased)

☐ DVD/VHS _____

☐ Graphic Novel _____

☐ Magazines _____

☐ Merchandise _____

Reason for purchase: (check all that apply)

☐ Special offer   ☐ Favorite title   ☐ Gift

☐ Recommendation   ☐ Other _____

Where did you make your purchase? (please check one)

☐ Comic store   ☐ Bookstore   ☐ Mass/Grocery Store

☐ Newsstand   ☐ Video/Video Game Store   ☐ Other: _____

☐ Online (site: _____)

What other VIZ properties have you purchased/own? _____

_____

How many anime and/or manga titles have you purchased in the last year? How many were VIZ titles? **(please check one from each column)**

ANIME	MANGA	VIZ
☐ None	☐ None	☐ None
☐ 1-4	☐ 1-4	☐ 1-4
☐ 5-10	☐ 5-10	☐ 5-10
☐ 11+	☐ 11+	☐ 11+

I find the pricing of VIZ products to be: **(please check one)**

☐ Cheap ☐ Reasonable ☐ Expensive

What genre of manga and anime would you like to see from VIZ? **(please check two)**

☐ Adventure ☐ Comic Strip ☐ Detective ☐ Fighting
☐ Horror ☐ Romance ☐ Sci-Fi/Fantasy ☐ Sports

What do you think of VIZ's new look?

☐ Love It ☐ It's OK ☐ Hate It ☐ Didn't Notice ☐ No Opinion

THANK YOU! Please send the completed form to:

NJW Research
42 Catharine St.
Poughkeepsie, NY 12601

All information provided will be used for internal purposes only. We promise not to sell or otherwise divulge your information.